SITTING WITH KOANS

SITTING WITH KOANS

ESSENTIAL WRITINGS ON ZEN KOAN INTROSPECTION

Edited by
John Daido Loori

foreword by
Thomas Yuho Kirchner

Wisdom Publications • Boston

Wisdom Publications
199 Elm Street
Somerville, MA 02144 USA
www.wisdompubs.org

© 2006 Dharma Communications Press
All rights reserved.

Library of Congress Cataloging-in-Publication Data
Sitting with koans : essential writings on Zen koan introspection / edited
   by John Daido Loori ; foreword by Thomas Yuho Kirchner.
      p. cm.
   Includes bibliographical references and index.
   ISBN 0-86171-369-9 (pbk. : alk. paper)
      1. Koan. 2. Meditation—Zen Buddhism.   I. Loori, John Daido.
   II. Title: Essential writings on Zen koan introspection.
   BQ9289.5.S59 2005
   294.3'443—dc22
                                        2005025144

First edition
09 08 07 06 06
5 4 3   2 1

Cover design by Gopa & Ted2, Inc., and Josh Bartok.
Interior by Gopa & Ted2, Inc.
Cover photo © John Daido Loori

Printed in Canada.

CONTENTS

Acknowledgments

I AM VERY GRATEFUL to all the masters, ancient and modern, whose teachings have been included in this volume. It was their wisdom, insight and skillful means that made this project possible. Special thanks to Vanessa Zuisei Goddard for her research and work in collecting the pieces included in this book. Her skillful editing and proofreading were indispensable, as was the editorial input of Konrad Ryushin Marchaj. Thanks to Josh Bartok of Wisdom Publications for recognizing the importance and need of a volume such as this for Western students, and for vigorously working toward its completion. Finally, a deep bow to the many students who provided assistance in the form of copy editing, graphic designing, indexing and the like. May the collective effort of the fine practitioners who contributed to the creation of this book nourish future generations on their spiritual journeys.

FOREWORD

Thomas Yuho Kirchner

FEW ASPECTS OF BUDDHIST PRACTICE have so captured the popular imagination as the Zen koan. On first encounter koans seem the ultimate riddles, challenging us to transcend ordinary logic and offering the promise of spiritual insight. They are undoubtedly one of the main reasons for Zen's association with intuitive creativity, and for the mystique that has inspired any number of book titles beginning with *Zen and the Art of*....

For most people the mystery of the koans begins with the enigmatic wording of the koans themselves. Why would the Chinese master Zhaozhou Congshen reply, "The juniper tree in the garden," when asked the meaning of Bodhidharma's coming from the west? When Baizhang Huaihai put a jug on the floor and said, "If you can't call this a jug, what do you call it?" why did his student Guishan Lingyou kick over the jug and walk away? And what does it signify that such enigmatic responses, properly understood, are equally meaningful for modern American Zen students as for Song-dynasty Chinese monks?

Questions of this type generally resolve themselves with serious zazen practice and deepening insight. Students find that koans have their own inner logic, a logic that reveals itself as practitioners come to know the mind out of which the koans emerged—a mind beyond thought and time, in which, as John Daido Loori Roshi says in his Introduction, "there are no paradoxes." Here Chinese monk and American Zen student stand on equal footing.

And yet with continued practice other, sometimes more perplexing, enigmas emerge. The effectiveness of the koans in Zen training has been demonstrated through the centuries, and many of the greatest masters, such as Dahui and Hakuin (both represented in the present volume), proclaim them incomparable as a way to precipitate awakening and clarify insight. Nevertheless, every long-time Zen practitioner knows certain intuitive individuals who are far advanced in koan work yet show little corresponding spiritual growth; this is as true among traditional Asian monastics as among Western lay practitioners. Conversely, other students, obviously mature in their practice, fail to ever connect with the koans, sometimes even after completing the entire system. Even Rinzai Zen masters often have misgivings about koan practice, warning against "collecting" koans at the risk of missing the true goal of Zen practice, which Dogen describes as, "to be enlightened by the ten thousand things, to eliminate the separation between self and other."

Why do some individuals seem to do so well with koans, and others seem to miss the mark? There may be as many answers to this question as there are people practicing Zen. In the end, there are no guarantees in the spiritual life; no method or technique, no matter how powerful, can by itself entirely overcome the subtle self-deceptions used by the ego to perpetuate its own existence. The koan is simply a tool, an aid to self-inquiry and realization that, as Daido Roshi points out, must be supported by the personal foundation one brings to the practice: great doubt, great faith, and great determination. Without, in particular, great doubt (the drive to resolve the question of life and death), the student can easily mistake koans as the goal of Zen practice, rather than as a means to that goal.

In his excellent contribution to this collection, Victor Sogen Hori stresses that koan work, like all Buddhist practices, is ultimately concerned with attaining the religious ideals of awakened wisdom and selfless compassion. If the essentially religious nature of the training is not understood, then the central reason for these training methods has been missed. In practical terms, the various aspects of a comprehensive spiritual practice have their respective strengths and weaknesses; zazen and koan work tend to be oriented chiefly towards deepening and clarifying the aspect of wisdom, and achieve their ultimate goals best when balanced by more explicitly compassion-oriented work in ethics and character development.

Nevertheless, to acknowledge that the koan is a tool, with a tool's limits, is not in any way to belittle it. Tools are as essential in cultivating the spiritual life as they are in cultivating the soil of a garden. For many Zen

practitioners the koan has proved an especially effective means of crys-
tallizing the problems that arise on the spiritual path and precipitating
the insights that help resolve those problems. The challenge is to employ
the koan-tool most effectively, and that, as with any tool, requires an
understanding of what it is and how it is used.

Sitting with Koans provides an excellent start toward such understanding, offering the reader—whether veteran meditator, inquiring
novice, or simply interested observer—a careful and well-organized
presentation of classic and modern source materials on many aspects of
traditional koan work. Chapters on the meaning, history, and dynamics
of koan practice are accompanied by a large selection of actual koans, with
commentaries by Chinese, Japanese, and American Zen masters. Solidly
oriented toward the religious dimension of Zen, the book's emphasis is
always on the koan as a spiritual practice.

Sitting with Koans joins Daido Roshi's many other books to form a
body of work dealing with virtually every aspect of practical Zen training, including *shikantaza (The Art of Just Sitting)*, ethics and morality
(The Heart of Being), the stages of practice *(Riding the Ox Home)*, and
art as spiritual training *(The Zen of Creativity)*. One of Daido Roshi's
central goals as a teacher has been the integration of traditional Buddhist
values into the cultural context of twenty-first century America, centered on the creation of a viable Buddhist monasticism that supports and
is in turn sustained by a solid lay practice. *Sitting with Koans* continues
this effort, clarifying the nature and history of koan training and demonstrating how it continues to evolve in the present-day Western world.
This is a book that will be of value to anyone interested in koan practice
and the transmission of this practice to the West.

INTRODUCTION
THE ANATOMY OF THE ZEN KOAN

John Daido Loori

ACCORDING TO THE LEGEND of Shakyamuni's birth, when the Buddha was born he took three steps forward, pointed to heaven with one hand and to the earth with the other and said, "Between heaven and earth I alone am the honored one." In Zen, we take this pivotal moment and study it as a koan—a fundamental question about the nature of reality that a student works with during periods of zazen, or Zen meditation.

These days, koans have become part of our everyday language. They appear in songs, movies, even beauty products. Some well-known koans are *What is the sound of one hand clapping?* or Zhaozhou's *Mu*. The common view of koans like these describes them as riddles or paradoxes, but the fact is there are no paradoxes. Paradox exists only in language, in the words and ideas that describe reality. In reality itself there are no paradoxes.

In order to see into a koan we must go beyond the words and ideas that describe reality and directly and intimately experience reality itself. The answer to a koan is not a fixed piece of information. It is one's own intimate and direct experience of the universe and its infinite facets. It is a state of consciousness.

A practitioner working on Shakyamuni's statement needs to sit with the questions: *Who* is that honored one? What does it mean to stand alone between heaven and earth? Although the Buddha lived over 2,500 years ago, these are not abstract questions. To ask *Who is the honored one?* is no different from asking *What is reality? What is life? What is death? What is God? Who am I?* These are questions about the basic truths of our lives. In Zen, the investigation into these questions takes the form of koan introspection within the context of zazen and the teacher-student relationship.

In the beginning stages of practice, zazen allows the mind to become quiet and focused, bringing attention to the present moment. Little by little, we learn to still our internal dialogue so we can put our attention on the breath, and eventually, on the koan. By working with our thoughts—acknowledging them, letting them go, coming back again and again to the breath—we begin to develop *joriki,* or self-power. Joriki prepares us to work on koans because it enables us to put our mind where we want it, when we want it, for as long as we want it there.

The further we go into zazen, the more confidence we develop in our ability to let go. As our confidence grows, our ability to process suppressed thoughts broadens. Little by little we work our way through the accumulated baggage of a lifetime. Gradually the mind settles and quiets down. Our zazen becomes serene and spacious.

Eventually, joriki turns into *samadhi,* or single-pointedness of mind. When samadhi has developed sufficiently, we begin to work with the first koan. Up until that point, the teacher has been supportive and nourishing in *dokusan,* or face-to-face teaching. But when the first koan is introduced, the teacher turns into an adversary, demanding clear responses. "What is it? Go deeper. Not good enough. Work harder." Suddenly the student is on her own: *What is it? What is it? What is it?* keeps resonating in her whole being. She knows there's an answer, and she knows other people have seen it, so she perseveres. She keeps trying, and she keeps getting rejected. She keeps getting thrown back on herself.

This is usually the most difficult period of practice. Sometimes it takes years to see the first koan. During this time the student will go to the teacher hundreds of times and present an understanding, and the teacher will reject it. If the student has not built up some self-esteem and some stability in zazen, she suddenly finds herself in a quandary because the teacher's support evaporates. The only place she can turn to is very deep inside herself. This personal foundation of self-study is often referred to as "the three pillars of Zen": great doubt, great faith, and great determination.

Great doubt is the question of life and death. Koans are a distilled essence of this question—the fuel behind the spiritual quest. Great doubt is described by the Chinese master Wumen as a red-hot fiery ball that's stuck in your throat. You can't swallow it and you can't spit it out.

Great faith is the sincere trust in the process. This trust is not only in Buddhism and Zen, but in koan introspection, and most importantly in oneself and one's own ability to break through the koan. To break through, you need to have total trust in yourself and your ability to do it. If you don't believe you can, you won't. It's not something that's going to happen by accident, but rather something you're going to do with your own body and mind.

Great faith and great doubt are in dynamic equilibrium. They create a spiritual tension that must be balanced with a third quality: great determination. Great determination is vital in koan study, particularly in respect to the shifting teacher-student relationship. This relationship is in a constant state of evolution, from the first meeting to the last. Our upbringing and educational system place immense value on approval, which can often lead to feeling dependent on the teacher or to a lack of trust in one's own self-sufficiency. Great determination is the kind of determination that Bodhidharma spoke of: "Seven times knocked down, eight times get up." There's nothing that can stop you. It may take time, it may take endless effort, it may take the rest of your life, but you're going to do it. You keep practicing until the intellect is completely exhausted and you make the quantum leap necessary to see the koan.

That initial insight is usually the first glimpse into the absolute basis of reality, the *dharmakaya.* Clarifying and thoroughly understanding the dharmakaya is a process that continues throughout the entirety of a student's training. Following the first koan and the initial breakthrough is a sequence of koans whose role is to clarify that original insight. In the training at Zen Mountain Monastery, there are one hundred miscellaneous koans that act as a prelude to the classic collections. The curriculum of koans that my teacher Maezumi Roshi used in training students include two-hundred miscellaneous koans, forty-eight koans of *The Gateless Gate*, one hundred koans of *The Blue Cliff Record*, one hundred koans of the *Book of Equanimity,* fifty-three koans of *The Record of Transmitting the Light*, the koans on the Five Ranks of Master Dongshan, and a hundred and twenty precept koans. Towards the end of training there are also the *kirigami* documents and oral teachings with koans embedded in them. Altogether this represents roughly seven hundred cases that students work with day by day, week by week, year by year, slowly and painstakingly transforming themselves and their lives.

Progression through the koan system varies from person to person, but most often it is irregular, with periods of smooth sailing interrupted by moments of self-doubt and confusion. A student may be moving along, passing koans, when all of a sudden he runs into an impassable wall—a killing-sword koan. The teacher will use these koans to "kill" the student's ego. Just when things are beginning to make sense, the teacher pulls out the rug. Nothing makes sense anymore, and the student is once again thrown into turmoil.

This pattern repeats itself throughout training. From one perspective, this dance is the basis of the teacher-student relationship. When the student gets comfortable, the teacher pulls out the rug and the student falls. The teacher rushes over and helps the student to his feet again; once the student is brushed off and standing firmly, the teacher pulls out the rug again and down he goes. This happens again and again until the teacher can pull the rug without the student falling. They bow to each other and the process is completed: the dharma is transmitted to the next generation.

To understand this dance, it is helpful to also understand how the mind-to-mind transmission works in Zen. When Shakyamuni Buddha realized himself under the bodhi tree, he realized that all sentient beings are—and always have been—perfect and complete, lacking nothing. But given this truth, teaching becomes a very difficult task. If we already have what we're looking for, what is there to teach? Knowing this, the Buddha developed myriad *upaya*, skillful means, in order to help us realize that which has always been present.

It is that realization that was transmitted on Mount Gridhrakuta years later, from Shakyamuni to Mahakashyapa. Two thousand students had gathered on Vulture Peak to hear the Buddha give a discourse. When the Buddha appeared, he held up a flower and without saying a word twirled it in his fingers. Of all the students listening, only Mahakashyapa smiled and blinked his eyes. The Buddha said, "I have the all-pervading true dharma, incomparable nirvana, the exquisite teaching of formless form. It does not rely on letters and is transmitted outside the scriptures. I now hand it to Mahakashyapa." As with the Buddha's birth, Zen takes up this event as a koan; the full case appears in *The Gateless Gate* with commentary and verse by Master Wumen.

Some time after the Buddha's death, the dharma was again transmitted to the next generation. Ananda, the Buddha's attendant and cousin, had been present at the assembly on Vulture Peak when Mahakashyapa received the transmission. It is said that Ananda had an incredible memory; all the sutras are purported to have come from his recitation of the Buddha's words. But despite Ananda's unparalleled knowledge, it was Mahakashyapa who received the Buddha's acknowledgment. Why? Why didn't Ananda get it? Because the mind-to-mind transmission is not based on knowledge or information.

After the Buddha died, Ananda became Mahakashyapa's attendant. One day Ananda was reflecting on the incident on Mount Gridhrakuta and he asked Mahakashyapa, "When the Buddha gave you the robe and bowl [the symbols of transmission] on Vulture Peak, what else did he give you?" He was full of doubt and asking, What do you have that I don't have? Mahakashyapa answered, "Ananda!" Ananda responded, "Yes Master!" Mahakashyapa said, "Take down the flagpole." Hearing these words, Ananda was greatly enlightened. "Take down the flagpole" is another way of saying "the lecture is over." In those days, whenever a discourse was given by a teacher, a banner would fly on the flagpole. To take down the flagpole meant that the talk had ended. This incident, according to the Zen tradition, marked the transmission from the second to the third generation.

The very same thread continued on for generation after generation for 2,500 years—not through lectures, sutras, philosophical treatises, or belief systems but mind-to-mind. A direct insight into the teaching was said to be carried for twenty-eight generations in India. Then it was brought to China by Bodhidharma. It flowered there during the Tang Dynasty and continued for fifty-one more generations in China and Japan, eventually coming to this continent at the turn of the twentieth century. It was always transmitted directly, intimately, from generation to generation, teacher to student.

Because of the nature of Zen training and its emphasis on direct experience, a book about koan practice is, in a way, a contradiction in terms.

Whole volumes on koans could not adequately explain how they work or what they're about. However, a text on the history and study of koans can act as *upaya*. One of the factors motivating modern practitioners these days is their intellect. So in order to do good "Zen fishing" and guide students into serious practice—one of the vows of a Zen teacher—it is sometimes useful to bait the hook with beautiful, juicy intellectual worms. *Sitting with Koans* is one of these worms.

The hundreds of dialogues, encounters, commentaries, and verses recorded in the koan collections provide a beautiful context for understanding the evolution of the dharma through the centuries. Ours is not a Buddhist culture, so it is important for practitioners to get a sense of the socio-historical background in which koan introspection developed and the effect it had on shaping Zen practice. The first section of this book provides just such an overview.

The second section lays the groundwork for a deeper understanding of the Japanese koan system, with special emphasis on works by great masters like Hakuin Ekaku and Eihei Dogen—pivotal figures in the revitalization of koan introspection, as well as avid and original commentators on koans.

The third section includes *teisho* (dharma discourses) by some of the Japanese masters who came to America at the turn of the twentieth century in order to establish Zen on these shores. These discourses are followed by talks by some of their successors, the American Zen masters who laid the groundwork for an authentic, yet distinctly Western, style of Zen. In selecting teachers for inclusion in this volume, I have chosen from among only those teachers who have received *inka* (formal Rinzai transmission, Rinzai Zen being the tradition most closely associated with koan practice).

Sitting with Koans is not meant to be taken as an academic text. Nor is it a how-to book meant to provide answers to life's questions. If anything, it will hopefully leave you with more questions. The only way to truly learn about koans is by doing them. Master Dogen said the koan is like a sharp lancet. You turn it toward yourself in order to pierce through the bag of skin—the idea of a separate self. Each koan, experienced with the whole body and mind, is an initiation into a new way of being. Each koan presents us with the possibility of experiencing true freedom.

We all have the potential to live a fully deluded or fully awakened life. It is up to us to choose. This boundless dharma is always present, whether we realize it or not. We should strive with all our might to keep it alive and vibrant. It is the most important thing that we will ever do with our lives.

EDITOR'S NOTE

IN ORDER to stay true to the original sources, we have kept masters' names the way they appear in each piece contained in this book, instead of changing them to the commonly used Pinyin Romanization style of Chinese names. Pinyin *is* used, when applicable, in the table of contents and titles. We have also retained each piece's capitalization and spelling of words like "Buddhas" and "Buddha-nature," as well as gender-specific pronouns when referring to monastics or Buddhist practitioners.

HISTORICAL PERSPECTIVE

The Definition of a Koan

Chung-feng Ming-pen

Translated by Ruth Fuller Sasaki

THE KOANS *[kungans]* may be compared to the case records of the public law court. Whether or not the ruler succeeds in bringing order to his realm depends in essence upon the existence of law. *Kung (ko)*, or "public," is the single track followed by all sages and worthy men alike, the highest principle which serves as a road for the whole world. *An (an)*, or "records," are the orthodox writings that record what the sages and worthy people regard as principles. There have never been rulers who did not have public law courts, and there have never been public law courts that did not have case records that are to be used as precedents of laws in order to stamp out injustice in the world. When these public case records (koans) are used, then principles and laws will come into effect; when these come into effect, the world will become upright; when the world is upright, the Kingly Way will be well ordered.

Now, when we use the word "koan" to refer to the teachings of the buddhas and ancestors, we mean the same thing. The koans do not represent the private opinion of a single person, but rather the hundreds and thousands of bodhisattvas of the three realms and the ten directions. This principle accords with the spiritual source, tallies with the mysterious meaning, destroys birth-and-death, and transcends the passions. It cannot be understood by logic; it cannot be transmitted in words; it cannot be explained in writing; it cannot be measured by reason. It is like the poisoned drum that kills all who hear it, or like a great fire that consumes all who come near it. What is called the "special transmission of the Vulture Peak" was the transmission of this; what is called the "direct pointing of Bodhidharma at Shao-lin-ssu" was pointing at this.

From the time long ago when the lotus flower was held up on Vulture

Peak until today, how can there have been only seventeen hundred koans? Yet the koans are something that can be used only by people with enlightened minds who wish to prove their understanding. They are certainly not intended to be used merely to increase one's lore and provide topics for idle discussion.

The so-called venerable masters of Zen are the chief officials of the public law courts of the monastic community, as it were, and their words on the transmission of Zen and their collections of sayings are the case records of points that have been vigorously advocated. Occasionally men of former times, in the intervals when they were not teaching, in spare moments when their doors were closed, would take up these case records and arrange them, give their judgment on them, compose verses of praise on them, and write their own answers to them. Surely they did not do this just to show off their erudition and contradict the worthy men of old. Rather, they did it because they could not bear to think that the Great Dharma might become corrupt. Therefore they stooped to using expedients in order to open up the Wisdom Eye of the people of later generations, hoping thereby to make it possible for them to attain the understanding of the Great Dharma for themselves in the same way. That is all.

The word *kung (ko)*, or "public," means that the koans put a stop to private understanding; the word *an (an)*, or "case records," means that they are guaranteed to accord with the buddhas and ancestors. When these koans are understood and accepted, then there will be an end to feeling and discrimination; when there is an end to feeling and discrimination, birth-and-death will become empty; when birth-and-death becomes empty, the Buddha-way will be ordered.

What do I mean by according with the buddhas and ancestors? The buddhas and ancestors have been greatly sorrowed to see that sentient beings bind themselves to the realm of birth-and-death and sensual delusion, so that, through the countless kalpas of the past down to the present, none have been able to free themselves. Therefore they displayed words in the midst of wordlessness and handed down forms in the midst of formlessness. But once the bonds of delusion have been loosed, how can there be any words and forms left to discuss?

If an ordinary man has some matter that he is not able to settle by himself, he will go to the public law court to seek a decision, and there the officials will look up the case records and, on the basis of them, settle the matter for him. In the same way, if a student has that in his understanding of enlightenment that he cannot settle for himself, he will ask his teacher about it, and the teacher, on the basis of the koans, will settle it for him.

The koan is a torch of wisdom that lights up the darkness of feeling and discrimination, a golden scraper that cuts away the film clouding the eye, a sharp ax that severs the root of birth-and-death, a divine mirror that reflects the original face of both the sacred and the secular. Through it, the intention of the patriarchs is made abundantly clear, the Buddha-mind is laid open and revealed. For the essentials of complete transcendence, final emancipation, total penetration, and identical attainment, nothing can surpass the koan.

THE SONG PERIOD: A TIME OF MATURATION

Heinrich Dumoulin

KOAN PRACTICE AND KOAN COLLECTIONS

ALTHOUGH THE PRACTICE of using koan took clear shape during the Song period, its origins lie further back in Zen history. The "paradoxical words and strange deeds" of the Zen masters of the T'ang period, which were assembled in the Zen chronicles and collected sayings of the Song period, provide the basic materials for all the classic koan cases. The historical sources for the koan are late and rather unreliable; with great literary freedom their authors took up the disconcerting answers and antics of Zen adepts and transformed these words and stories into what we have today—koan cases and specific aids on the way to enlightenment.

Literally, the word *koan* (Chin., *kung-an*) is a combination of graphs that signifies "public notice" or "public announcement." A koan, therefore, presents a challenge and an invitation to take seriously what has been announced, to ponder it and respond to it. But the special character of this "announcement" confronts the listener or reader with a perplexing puzzle. One becomes confused, and the more one tries to come up with an answer and search for a solution, the more confused one gets. The essence of the koan is to be rationally unresolvable and thus point to what is "arational." The koan urges us to abandon our rational thought structures and step beyond our usual state of consciousness in order to press into new and unknown dimensions. This is the common purpose of all koan, no matter how much they may differ in content or literary form.

We may begin our résumé of the history of koan practice with the Rinzai master Nan-yüan Hui-yung (d. 930), who was in fact the first to use koan, confronting his disciples with the words of the early masters in order to bring them to sudden enlightenment. Around this time, or perhaps somewhat later, Zen followers began to gather together the many stories about those early inventive and highly esteemed masters who could bring their students to enlightenment with a word or blow or bizarre gesture. These stories were then arranged in order, provided with clarifying commentaries, and adorned with verse.

The earliest koan collection is found in the writings of Fen-yang Shan-chao, who did much to revive the spirit of Lin-chi, the founder of his school. The chronicles describe him as an imposing, expansive personality. Among the many students who entrusted themselves to his guidance was Shih-shuang (Tz'u-ming) Ch'u-yüan who was put through a hard program of training before being named Fen-yang's Dharma heir. Fen-yang's writings were edited by Shih-shuang in a three-volume work entitled *Fun'yoroku* (Chin., *Fen-yang lu*). The work details his devoted discipleship as a follower of his great model, Lin-chi.

Fen-yang's writings are replete with paradoxical and dialectical statements and many other motifs from the *Rinzairoku*. The first book is composed of lectures and practical admonitions, and the third of religious poems and verse. In the second book we find three groups of one hundred koan each, the most important of which is the first series, which offers one hundred koan cases from the ancients (Jpn., *juko*), complete with commentaries and verses by Fen-yang. In these stories we hear from Bodhidharma, from the Sixth Patriarch, and from many well-known Zen masters of the T'ang period. The second series is made up of one hundred koan—questions called *kitsumon* (Chin., *chie-wen*), which were formulated by Fen-yang himself and clearly show his creative gifts. In the last hundred examples Fen-yang offers his own particular answers (Jpn., *betsugo*) to riddles of earlier times. We should not be surprised to find such a large number of cases at the very beginning of the development of koan practice. It is estimated that there are in all some 1,700 koan within the Zen tradition. Nor is it unusual to hear that Master Fen-yang composed so many of them himself. Even today, Zen masters continue to come up with new koan based on their own experience and dealings with their disciples.

Under Fen-yang's successor, Shih-shuang, the Rinzai school grew in popular esteem and the master himself was highly respected at the imperial court. The *Tensho kotoroku*, a work compiled by the nobleman Li Tsun-hsü that laid the foundations for the golden age of Rinzai in the Song empire, appeared during his lifetime (1036). It is counted among the five authoritative Zen chronicles of the Song period and contains much koan material. Shih-shuang's disciples Yang-ch'i and Huang-lung carried on the transmission of the spirit and teachings of Lin-chi faithfully.

Huang-lung Hui-nan, who gathered a dense "forest" of disciples about him, was distinguished by his ingenious use of paradox, as his well-known "three barriers" (Jpn., *sankan*) show. The following play of question and answer was later passed on as a koan:

> Question: "All people have their own native place owing to the causal nexus. Where is your native place?"
> Answer: "Early in the morning I ate white rice gruel; now I feel hungry again."
> Question: "In what way do my hands resemble the Buddha's hands?"
> Answer: "Playing the lute in the moonlight."
> Question: "In what way do my feet resemble the feet of a donkey?"
> Answer: "When the heron stands in the snow, its color is not the same."

Although important masters such as Hui-t'ang Tsu-hsin (1025–1100) and Tou-shuai Ts'ung-yüeh (1044–1092) number among the followers of Huang-lung, this branch of Zen disappeared in China before the end of the Song period. It was brought to Japan by the Japanese Buddhist monk Eisai (1141–1215).

It was in Yang-ch'i's line of the Rinzai school that Zen experienced its greatest development in China. A mild-mannered man who attracted many disciples, Yang-ch'i Fang-hui is the subject of many traditional stories. His second-generation disciple, Wu-tsu Fa-yen (1024–1104) holds a place of prominence. Under him and his immediate successors, the use of the koan during the Song period reached its high point.

The first part of Fa-yen's name, Wu-tsu (which has often led to his being confused with another master of the same name), literally means "fifth patriarch." It was given him because he had lived for over thirty years on the famous East Mountain in the region of the Yellow Plum—

which also came to be called the "Mountain of the Fifth Patriarch" after the death of the Fifth Patriarch, Hung-jen. Here he carried out his teaching in authentic Zen style. The four koan in the *Mumonkan* [Gateless Gate] that deal with him all have a distinctive flavor. In one, he places the student in a typical koan situation in which there is no exit:

> If you meet a man of Tao on the way, greet him neither with words nor with silence. Now tell me, how will you greet him? (Case 36)

Or:

> Shakyamuni and Maitreya are but his servants. Now tell me, who is *he*? (Case 45)

The answer could be: "the true human of no rank." He also gives his students this precious case to grapple with:

> To give an example, it is like a buffalo passing through a window. Its head, horns, and four legs have all passed through. Why is it that its tail cannot? (Case 38)

A question based on a folk legend invites the student to metaphysical reflection:

> Ch'ien-nü and her soul are separated: which is the true one? (Case 35)

With Wu-tsu Fa-yen we are truly in the middle of the world of the koan. Fa-yen's main disciple, Yüan-wu K'o-ch'in (1063–1135), was a central figure in the koan Zen of the Song period. Raised in a Confucian family, from early youth Yüan-wu displayed a strong intellectual curiosity and a phenomenal memory. After studying the Buddhist scriptures in a local Buddhist temple he decided to become a monk and set out on a long pilgrimage that ended at the feet of Master Wu-tsu Fa-yen. But he was only able to entrust himself fully to the master after an initial failure in which a serious sickness, foretold by the master, had broken his proud self-confidence. Under Wu-tsu's guidance he achieved an extraordinarily powerful and enduring experience of enlightenment.

After a short period of temple service, Yüan-wu returned to his home in Szechwan to care for his aged and ailing mother. We later meet him in the monastery of Reisen-in (Chin., *Ling-ch'üan-yüan*), where he was delivering lectures on sayings and stories from the ancients; the examples he used were to become the core of the famous *Hekiganroku* collection. He attracted many disciples and won the favor of the Northern Song emperor Hui-tsung (r. 1101–1125), a lover of art but politically weak. The emperor gave him the purple robe and the title "Zen Master of the Buddha Fruit" (Jpn., *Bukka zenji;* Chin., *Fo-kuo ch'an-shih*). When the northern kingdom fell, he escaped to the South where he lived for a time with his disciple and Dharma heir Ta-hui Tsung-kao (1089–1163) in the monastery of Shinnyo-in (Chin., *Chen-ju-yüan*). There the young Hung-chih Cheng-chüeh (1091–1157) of the Soto school visited him to pay his respects and receive instruction. On this occasion, the young guest may have also met Ta-hui, with whom he was later to have a formidable confrontation.

Yüan-wu was also highly regarded by Emperor Kao-tsung (r. 1127–1162) of the Southern Song, who honored him with the title "Zen Master of Full Enlightenment" (Jpn., *Engo zenji;* Chin., *Yüan-wu ch'an-shih*), the title by which he is known in Zen history. He passed his final years surrounded by his disciples in a local monastery in Szechwan. When he was preparing for death he wrote the following lines at the request of his disciples:

> My work slipped off into the night,
> For you no pretty song took flight.
> The hour is here; I must away.
> Fare ye well! Take care aright!

Yüan-wu K'o-ch'in never matched the creative originality of the great Zen masters of the T'ang period, but his own special gifts found a fitting outlet in the koan collection that he co-authored and brought to completion, the *Hekiganroku,* or *Blue Cliff Record.* He recognized the high quality of the cases and verses that Hsüeh-tou of the friendly House of

Yün-men had gathered and used them as the foundation for his own collection. From the thorough and intensive way in which he assembled and interpreted these cases, the most significant collection of koan in all of Zen took shape. The collection contains a hundred cases. The two basic texts—the cases (either episodes or accounts of experiences of enlightenment) and the verses—were drawn from Hsüeh-tou. To these Yüan-wu added notes and a commentary for each text. Thus a koan case from the *Hekiganroku* collection consists of seven parts: an introduction, case, notes, commentary on the case, verse, notes, and commentary on the verse.

In the verses, Hsüeh-tou shows himself to be a highly gifted poet. Yüan-wu's notes are pointed, often ironic, and always right on the mark; they stir one's interest and attention. The selection of one hundred cases is exquisite. In the rich variety of their content and expression they present the essence of Zen. No systematic ordering is intended, as that might cramp the free movement of the spirit. At the beginning, a few representative pieces are offered: Bodhidharma's meeting with Emperor Wu, culminating in Hsüeh-tou's verse, "Holy truth—open expanse!" (Case 1); Chao-chou's remark on the opening verse of the *Shinjinmei* [Trust in Mind], "The real Way is not difficult. It only abhors choice and attachment" (Case 2); and the third case concerning the great master of the T'ang period, Ma-tsu. To read the *Blue Cliff Record* in its given sequence and be guided by the spirit and imagination of the lively commentary Gundert has provided is to find a sure, albeit not easy, entrance into one of the foremost examples of religious world literature.

What happened to the *Hekiganroku* in China is not entirely clear. It met with great acclaim when it was first published during the lifetime of Yüan-wu (1128), only later to fall prey to the fanatical zeal of his successor, Ta-hui Tsung-kao, who burned every copy of the work he could find and destroyed the printer's blocks. As a result, the work fell out of use until some two hundred years later, when the lay Buddhist Chang Ming-yüan gathered together all available copies and brought out a new edition in 1300. It is not known precisely what motivated Ta-hui to act as he did. Miura and Sasaki surmise that he was afraid the work made things too clear and thus would present an obstacle to Zen practice. Gundert also excludes any "base motivation" and blames Ta-hui's decision on an unruly, unbridled temperament. As we have seen, "opposition to written tradition ... is rooted in the essence of Zen." Perhaps it was the work's own "beauty of expression" that had destined it to the flames. In any case, the whole event, difficult as it is to understand, underlines the fact that Zen allows no written work, no matter how profound and polished, to take the place of practice and experience. The eventual republication of the *Hekiganroku* gave rise to a long string of commentaries in both Chinese and Japanese.

Our knowledge of koan practice in the Soto school is limited. The dialectical design of the Five Ranks was taken over into the koan method and increasingly employed in Zen practice. The line of Ts'ao-shan Pen-chi, in which the Five Ranks came to full expression, had disappeared early on. The Soto school was carried on under the direction of Tung-shan's disciple, Yün-chü Tao-ying (d. 902), though tradition has it that his master had not entrusted him with the Five Ranks. Yün-chü was named after the mountain location of the monastery where he was active for more than thirty years within a large community of followers. Cases of enlightenment played an important role in the guidance he provided his disciples. We do not know whether his early successors in the Soto school took a stance against the use of koan. The Soto masters T'ou-tzu I-ch'ing (1032–1082) and Tan-hsia Tzu-ch'un (d. 1119) both edited koan collections of one hundred cases.

During the Song period it was Hung-chih Cheng-chüeh (1091–1157) who put the Soto school in the limelight. Hung-chih's visit to Yüan-wu, mentioned above, suggests that at least in his early years he was not opposed to the koan practice of the Rinzai school. As a master he earned recognition and attracted a large following. Because of his success in restoring religious discipline after the decline it had suffered during the disturbances of the previous century, he came to be known as the "Patriarch of the Renewal of Mount T'ien-t'ung." He lived on this mountain for some thirty years, and for this reason the sources sometimes call him T'ien-t'ung Cheng-chüeh. His literary gifts are evident in his two collections from the ancients, each a hundred cases with accompanying verses, *Juko hyakusoku* (Chin., *Song-ku pai-tse*) and *Nenko hyakusoku* (Chin., *Nien-ku pai-tse*), both of which enjoyed great popularity in his school. His understanding of Zen practice differed from that of his colleague from the Rinzai school Ta-hui Tsung-kao, who engaged him in a rather bitter controversy. The question whether Cheng-chüeh's views disagreed only with those of his opponent or whether he was also in opposition to the great masters of the T'ang period remains moot.

The second largest koan collection of the Song period is known by its abbreviated title, the *Shoyoroku* (Chin., *Ts'ung-jung lu*, [Book of Equanimity]). It appeared about one hundred years after the *Hekiganroku* and was modeled after it. The work was assembled by the Soto master Wansong Hsing-hsiu (1166–1246), a member of the line of Yün-chü but not a direct successor to Hung-chih. The basis of his work was a group of one hundred cases and verses from Hung-chih Cheng-chüeh's *Juko hyakusoku*. He lectured on Hung-chih's work at the small monastery of Shoyoan, the "Hermitage of Composure." Between the text of the cases and their verses he inserted intermediary notes, giving a fivefold structure to each koan. Five cases were taken from sutras, but the greater part of the collection is made up of cases from the masters of the T'ang period and from the Five Houses. The same names and sometimes the same episodes and words found in other koan collections appear in Wan-song's collection. Often the *Keitoku dentoroku* serves him as a source. Wan-song's rather formidable volume first appeared in 1224, nearly a century after the *Hekiganroku*. The cases of the *Shoyoroku* have become part of Zen's koan tradition.

The *Mumonkan*, a collection of "forty-eight cases of enlightenment of the Buddhas and patriarchs," appeared at the end of the Song period (1229) and represents the most mature of the koan collections. This volume has its own independent character, different from every other in the genre. With an evident disregard for literary quality, the cases use short, unembellished sentences to enter directly into what is essential, to what makes the koan what it is. Each case consists of only three parts (in addition to the title): the text of the case, a critical commentary by Master Wu-men, and the verse, which is less a poem than a simple pair of loosely linked lines. The main contents of the koan are given clear and thematic expression. Many of the episodes, conversations, and dicta appearing in the forty-eight cases are very well-known in Zen history.

The *Mumonkan* is the work of a single editor, Master Wu-men Huik'ai (1183–1260), a successor of Wu-tsu Fa-yen from the Yang-ch'i line of the Rinzai school. He does not, however, belong to the well-known line carried on by Wu-tsu Fa-yen's famous successors Yüan-wu K'o-ch'in and Ta-hui Tsung-kao, but to an historically somewhat obscure branch referred to in the *Mumonkan* only through mention of Yüeh-an Shan-kuo, whose eyes, Master Wu-men tells us, were like meteors and whose acts like lightning (Case 8).

In Wu-men Hui-k'ai, the Dharma heir of Yüeh-lin Shih-kuan (1143–1217), we have another powerful thirteenth-century representative of Lin-chi's Chinese Zen. Wu-men's practice was shaped through and through by the use of koan. The intensity of his own enlightenment is evident in the following verses composed in the afterglow of his experience:

> A thunderclap under a clear blue sky!
> All beings on earth have opened their eyes.
> Everything under the sun has bowed at once.
> Mount Sumeru jumps up and dances the *san-t'ai.*

His work is the direct expression of his own experience. In his foreword he testifies to the close bond between this sacred text in his personal life:

> In the summer of the first year of Shao-ting [1228], I, Hui-k'ai, was the head of the monks at Lung-hsiang in Tung-chia. The monks begged me for instruction. Finally I took up the koan of the ancient masters and used them as brick-bats to knock at the gate in guiding the monks in accordance with their capabilities and types. I have noted down these koan and they have now unwittingly become quite a collection. There are now forty-eight of them, which I have not arranged in any order. I will call the collection the *Mumonkan,* "The Gateless Barrier."

In his postscript, Wu-men Hui-k'ai explains his title, *The Gateless Barrier,* by appealing to the Zen master Hsüan-sha Shi-pei (835–908), a disciple of the famous Hsüeh-feng I-ts'un at the end of the T'ang period. "Have you not heard," he writes, "what Hsüan-sha said, 'No-gate is the gate of emancipation; no-mind is the mind of the person of

Tao'?" Emancipation and selflessness are the two terms that best characterize the religious efforts of Zen masters in their approach to the *Mumonkan* collection. To the Zen student, seeking enlightenment by selfless, spontaneous practice, they show the no-gate that leads to emancipation. Hui-k'ai was in the prime of his life when the *Mumonkan* was first published. His biography reports his later residence in various monasteries. He received numerous tokens of esteem from the emperor of the Southern Song dynasty, including the title "Zen Master of the Buddha Eye."

A rich and concentrated masterpiece, the *Mumonkan* has also met with extraordinary success and received widespread attention in the West. Although the *Mumonkan* differs markedly from the *Hekiganroku*, both collections are considered the primary representative expressions of the Zen koan. The difficult task of translation is aided by detailed Japanese commentaries that clarify complex expressions or popular usages. Given the deep linguistic roots in China, these collections stand as a challenge and opportunity for professional Sinologists—at least for those who have not limited their scholarship to the Chinese classics. Japanese Zen masters make rather free use of the koan, according to their particular understanding of Zen. More than any other writings in Zen literature, these koan texts have been approached and analyzed from a vast array of perspectives and have presented scholars with the challenge of deepening and enriching our understanding of the Zen experience.

Aspects of the Koan Method

In assessing koan practice, one should keep in mind that one is dealing with a method that leads to enlightenment, not with enlightenment itself. In this regard it is worth recalling the distinction that the Japanese Buddhist scholar Ui Hajuku, commenting on the development of Zen, drew between "doctrine" and "aids" on the way to enlightenment, "Doctrine" he takes to refer to the theoretical material of the sutras, while "aids" refers to the paradoxical words and actions, the beatings and shoutings, and the koan method. He finds both elements present in Zen from the beginning. Prior to Ma-tsu and the great masters of the T'ang period more emphasis was placed on doctrine and less on aids, but the opposite became the case as time went on. According to Ui, however, it would be misleading to judge Zen on the basis of the relationship of these two elements, since both have no more than a relative value in the Zen scheme of things. The importance of the aids is often inflated among followers of Zen precisely because they are so distinctively Zen. This easily leads to a depreciation of basic Buddhist teachings. Finally, Ui points out that the two elements are by no means mutually exclusive, but that each actually conditions the other: aids are rooted in Buddhist doctrine and presuppose it, while many doctrinal statements are used as koan exercises.

Koan practice became an essential element of Zen self-understanding. Far from being just one practice alongside many others, koan practice is as important as "sitting in mediation" *(zazen).* Not a few Zen masters, both past and present, have argued that without koan practice it is impossible to come to deeper realization. But although koan practice belongs to the essence of Zen, this practice did not develop with the T'ang masters but during the Song period, when there were already signs that the energy of the Zen movement had begun to decline. If the early Zen masters had reached enlightenment spontaneously out of their own original insights, Zen now had a suitable and effective method by which anyone could attain enlightenment with relative certainty. D. T. Suzuki's assessment of this development is most perceptive:

> Aristocratic Zen was now turned into a democratic, systematized, and to a certain extent, mechanized Zen. No doubt it meant to that extent a deterioration; but without this innovation, Zen might have died out a long time before. To my mind it was the technique of the koan exercise that saved Zen as a unique heritage of Far Eastern culture.

The usual way to answer the question of what a koan is is to offer a few typical examples. In the preceding pages, we have already met with koan of different kinds—cases of enlightenment, conversations, strange happenings, paradoxical sayings of the Zen masters, as well as dialectical formulas—and have pointed out the koan-like features of these various literary forms. The function of a koan is to serve as a means on the way to enlightenment. They are not ends in themselves, nor do they make any claim to express the inexpressible. As Master Wu-men remarks in his preface to the *Mumonkan,* koan are like "bricks to bang on the door with." This functional character of the koan does not preclude the possibility of defining them; it only makes clear that it is their function that is decisive, and that this can be expressed in many different ways.

The procedure is more or less as follows: The master gives the student a koan to think about, resolve, and then report back on to the master. Concentration intensifies as the student first tries to solve the koan intellectually. This initial effort proves impossible, however, for a koan cannot be solved rationally. Indeed, it is a kind of spoof on the human intellect. Concentration and irrationality—these two elements constitute the characteristic psychic situation that engulfs the student wrestling with a koan. As this persistent effort to concentrate intellectually becomes unbearable, anxiety sets in. The entirety of one's consciousness and psychic life is now filled with one thought. The exertion of the search is like wrestling with a deadly enemy or trying to make one's way through a ring of flames. Such assaults on the fortress of human reason inevitably give rise to a distrust of all rational perception. This gnawing doubt, combined with the futile search for a way out, creates a state of extreme and intense yearning for deliverance. The state may persist for days, weeks, or even years; eventually, the tension has to break.

This psychic process may be compared to shooting an arrow from a tightly drawn bow. In his renowned *Zen in the Art of Archery,* Eugen Herrigel gives the process a fitting psychological description. He explains his problem to the master:

> When I have drawn the bow, the moment comes when I feel:
> unless the shot comes at once I shan't be able to endure the
> tension. And what happens then? Merely that I get out of
> breath. So I must loose the shot whether I want to or not,
> because I can't wait for it any longer.

To this the master replies:

> The right shot at the right moment does not come because
> you do not let go of yourself. You do not wait for fulfillment,

but brace yourself for failure. So long as that is so, you have no choice but to call forth something yourself that ought to happen independently of you, and so long as you call it forth your hand will not open in the right way—like the hand of a child. Your hand does not burst open like the skin of a ripe fruit.

As in archery so also in the koan exercise, everything depends on the proper attitude. Only when the attentive mind is relaxed, free from purpose and ego, and fully devoted to the task can it open up of itself.

In his early works Suzuki describes this psychological process in terms of the law of accumulation, saturation, and explosion. Although the psychological concept underlying this model may be partly outdated, it helps to clarify the process and to reveal the danger inherent in it. Accumulation and saturation, when they are in a state of high tension, can by themselves do great harm. An even greater danger is that the premature explosion, more like the detonation of a bomb than the opening of the skin of a ripe fruit. There are plentiful examples from the past and present showing how the practice of koan can lead to a bad end. It is not without good reason that Zen masters sound their warnings. The suppression of reason can throw one's psychic life out of balance. As with the therapeutic process of modern psychiatry, the inviolable dignity of the person sets limits to the use of the koan. The two processes are not dissimilar. In the Zen practice called "private interview" *(dokusan)*, in which the student makes a progress report to the master, situations may arise that are like those that can take place in the psychotherapist's office. The student utters broken, incoherent words and gives expression to other spontaneous reactions.

The structure of the koan led C. G. Jung to identify the "great liberation" in Zen with the emancipation of the unconscious. Under the enormous psychological strain of trying to force a solution for the insoluble koan, enlightenment is experienced as the dawn of a new reality in which the boundaries between the conscious and the unconscious disappear, so that the conscious and unconscious alike are laid open. The Zen disciple realizes the totality of human nature in its primal unity, prior to all discrimination and division. Jung's analysis can shed light on the psychological structure of koan practice.

It was especially because of its psychological implications that the koan method of Zen stirred up great interest when it became known in the West. There is ample support for such psychological interpretations in the history of Zen during the T'ang and the Song periods. Of course, we cannot be sure just how much the Zen masters themselves recognized or intended the psychological effects of their methods. Their main concern was to bring their disciples to a genuine experience, and that experience necessarily implied a break with the student's ordinary state of consciousness. The masters knew only too well that their students were imprisoned by the world of things around them, rendering homage to a naïve realism and convinced that the knowing subject perceives and knows the world of objects. The jolt produced by the koan can shake students from this state of consciousness and propel them into a sudden awakening that will help them move from a world of multiplicity to a world of oneness. In their essence, therefore, the koan are grounded in Mahayana's unitive vision of reality.

The connection between koan and Mahayana, clear from the beginning, was later elaborated and illuminated by the systematization of the cases into categories in the school of Hakuin (1685–1768). In this regard, Ruth Fuller Sasaki has observed:

> The koan is not a conundrum to be solved by a nimble wit. It is not a verbal psychiatric device for shocking the disintegrated ego of a student into some kind of stability. Nor, in my opinion, is it ever a paradoxical statement except to those who view it from outside. When the koan is resolved it is realized to be a simple and clear statement made from the state of consciousness which it has helped to awaken.

This state of consciousness grasps the unity of reality as Mahayana understands it. The purpose of practice is to clear away every trace of duality. All the koan are meant to serve this same purpose. Thus the metaphysical and religious role of the koan in Zen Buddhism is every bit as important as its psychological structure.

During the early period of Zen history there was no established method for using koan. In the reports that have come down to us from the Song period there are indications of beginnings, and even of well-formed patterns, of stylization. We can notice, for instance, differences in accent corresponding to the different styles of the various masters. A frequent practice was to determine some kind of device that would serve as a focus for the practitioner's attention and energies. The koan would be compressed, as it were, into a single word, which the students would then take along wherever they went, constantly mulling it over in their consciousness. The classical example of this is the word *nothing* (Jpn., *mu;* Chin., *wu*) in the first case in the *Mumonkan,* a word that was meant to lead the student beyond objective reasoning and toward ultimate unity.

The dialogue between master and disciple—an indication of their close relationship—also plays an important role in Zen Buddhism. This relationship represents an integral part of Asian religious culture in general. In India, the spiritual guide or guru exercised great influence; in ancient China, there was the teacher of wisdom, who was also the teacher of practical living. All this indicates that from the beginnings of Zen Buddhism a close master-disciple relationship was fostered. This relationship became especially evident in the development of methods for koan practice during the Song period. Since the time of Hakuin and his disciples, the "private interview," or institutionalized conversation between master and disciple known as *sanzen* in the Rinzai sect and later also as *dokusan,* also became part of standard koan practice. The interview was surrounded with much ceremony, and during special periods of practice would take place once a day, sometimes more. In these private interviews students would give an account of their experiences, both positive and negative. Hence, they served as a preventive device against dangerous deviations.

Martin Buber was strongly impressed by the master-disciple relationship in Zen and gave special attention to those koan that centered around some form of interaction between master and disciple. The depth of insight that he perceived in these koan allowed him, he felt, to compare them to the "legendary anecdotes" of Hasidism. The similarity is really only external. The main concern of the koan is concentration, irrationality, and nonduality, while Jewish rabbis seek to make their students aware of another, hidden Thou. The literary genre and aims are completely different.

The use of koan in Zen Buddhism is a unique phenomenon in the history of religion; nothing like it exists in other religious traditions. Developed in China, koan testify to an authentically Chinese mentality, particularly in the way they are rooted in real life. If Zen can be called the Chinese expression of Buddhism, then koan are the most Chinese dimension of Zen. There are of course different ways to understand the practice of the koan, just as individual koan allow for different interpretations. Witness the Zen practitioners of the Song period themselves, whose whole lives revolved around the koan and who contended fiercely with one another regarding their proper use.

THE TWO MAINSTREAMS OF ZEN

Two focal figures mark the middle of the Song period: Ta-hui Tsung-kao, Yüan-wu's Dharma heir who was the staunch defender of authentic koan practice in the Rinzai school, and Hung-chih Cheng-chüeh, who guided the Soto school on its path of enlightenment. Though friends, the two men differed in their notion of what constituted proper Zen practice. Hung-chih was possessed of considerable poetic talent and produced an important literary work. He loved sitting in meditation and committed himself zealously to the practice. The koan collection he edited indicated that he both knew and valued koan practice, though in his preaching and writing he urged a form of practice that scarcely mentions the koan. As his method grew in popularity and began to attract a large following, it aroused the opposition of Ta-hui, who warned against this "heterodoxy" that he called "silent-illumination Zen" (Jpn., *mokusho zen;* Chin., *mo-chao ch'an*). On Ta-hui's lips the words had a contemptuous ring to them, since as a follower of Lin-chi he rejected all forms of sitting motionless in silence.

Hung-chih responded to the attack. In a short, perceptive work of only 288 characters, entitled *The Seal of Silent Illumination* (Jpn., *Moku-shomei;* Chin., *Mo-chao ming*), he disclosed the true meaning of his Zen way. In his view, silent illumination was the most authentic expression of the tradition that had come down from the Buddhas and the patriarchs: To one who forgets words in silence reality is clearly revealed. Already in this sentence, taken from the beginning of the work, we meet the characters for "silence" and "illumination." Silence is the stillness that grounds the enlightened mind, whose natural ability to "shine" is revealed in silence. Reality reveals itself to those sitting in silent meditation without leading them to look on things as objects of intellection. Enlightenment is like the mirror-quality of the enlightened and resplendent Buddha mind:

> One who has attained silent enlightenment belongs to the house of our tradition; silent enlightenment ascends to the heights and penetrates deep into the abyss.

Ta-hui was resolute in his opposition:

> Recently a type of heterodox Zen (Jpn., *jazen*) has grown up in the forest of Zen. By confusing the sickness with the remedy, they have denied the experience of enlightenment. These people think that the experience of enlightenment is but an artificial superstructure meant to attract, so they give it a secondary position, like branches or leaves on the tree. Because they have not experienced enlightenment, they think others have not either. Stubbornly they contend that an empty silence and a musty state of unconsciousness is the original realm of the absolute. To eat their rice twice a day and to sit without thoughts in meditation is what they call complete peace.

In this well-known passage, which is clearly leveled against Hung-chi's "silent-illumination Zen," Ta-hui singles out for criticism the passivity of what he sees as a totally false form of practice. Zen practitioners should not, he argued, pass their days in lifelessness like "cold ashes or a withered tree." The emptiness of Zen meditation is not a dead, lifeless emptiness. As much as he could, Hung-chih rejected these unjust accusations. In the heat of the argument, he disdainfully referred to the one-sided practice of Ta-hui as "koan-gazing Zen" (Jpn., *kanna-zen*; Chin., *k'an-hua ch'an*). Both epithets, "silent-illumination Zen" and "koan-gazing Zen," though devised as detractions, eventually found their way into history as designations for the two sharply opposing positions.

The heart of the controversy was the koan. For Ta-hui, koan practice was required of each and every Zen student as the surest path to the attainment of enlightenment, and he urged his students to persevere zealously in their practice of the koan:

> Just steadily go on with your koan every moment of your life. If a thought rises, do not attempt to suppress it by conscious effort, only renew the attempt to keep the koan before the mind. Whether walking or sitting, let your attention be fixed upon it without interruption! When you begin to find it entirely devoid of flavor, the final moment is approaching, do not let it slip out of your grasp. When all of a sudden something flashes out in your mind, its light will illumine the entire universe and you will see the spiritual land of the Enlightened One fully revealed at the point of a single hair, and the great wheel of the Dharma revolving in a single grain of dust.

No other Chinese Zen Master understood so completely or promoted so vigorously the use of koan as Ta-hui. Koan were the pivot around which all his teaching revolved. For Ta-hui, the koan really allows doubt to break through:

> The thousand and ten thousand doubts that well up in your breast are really only one doubt, all of them burst open when doubt is resolved in the koan. As long as the koan is not resolved, you must occupy yourself with it to the utmost. If you give up on your koan and stir up another doubt about a word of scripture or about a sutra teaching or about a koan of the ancients, or if you allow a doubt about worldly matters to come up—all this means to be joined to the evil spirit. You should not too easily agree with a koan solution that you have discovered, nor should you think about it further and make distinctions. Fasten your attention to where discursive thinking cannot reach. Make sure that you do not allow your mind to run off, like an old mouse that ran into the horn of an ox.

Enlightenment draws meaning and value from doubt:

> Many students today do not doubt themselves, but they doubt others. And so it is said: "Within great doubt there necessarily exists great enlightenment."

What is important for the koan is not literary beauty or deep intellectual paradox. The koan makes its central point through doubt. Doubt bores into the mind of the practitioner and leads to enlightenment.

Ta-hui preferred the koan on "nothing," which in his view was able to cultivate doubt better than any other koan. He warns against the conscious desire for enlightenment and presses for the removal of all imagination and discursive thought, in order then to recommend expressly the koan on "nothing":

> A monk once asked Master Chao-chou, "Has a dog the Buddha nature or not?" Chao-chou said, "Mu!" (Chin., *wu*).

Ta-hui explains:

> This one character is the rod by which many false images and ideas are destroyed in their very foundations. To it you should add no judgments about being or non-being, no arguments, no bodily gestures like raising your eyebrows or blinking your eyes. Words have no place here. Neither should you throw this character away into the nothingness of emptiness, or seek it in the comings and goings of the mind, or try to trace its origins in the scriptures. You must only earnestly and continually stir it [this koan] around the clock. Sitting or lying, walking or standing, you must give yourself over to it constantly. "Does a dog have Buddha nature?" The answer: "Mu." Without withdrawing from everyday life, keep trying, keep looking at this koan!

In stressing the intense practice of the koan on Mu, Ta-hui appealed to Wu-tsu Fa-yen, the teacher of his own master, Yüan-wu K'o-ch'in. Ta-hui looked back to this pioneer of rigorous koan practice after having burned the *Hekiganroku,* the work of his own master. Most likely he destroyed the text because he found that its literary beauty was preventing students from the painful struggle with the koan on nothingness, which for him was the only true koan.

That this koan about the absolute nothingness of the Buddha nature that transcends being and nonbeing assumed such an important place in Zen history is due in no small measure to the simple fact that Wu-men Hui-k'ai placed it first in the *Mumonkan.* As mentioned in his preface and postscript, Master Wu-men strongly desired to transcend by negation. This opening koan, which he entitled "Chao-chou's Dog," is one of the few koan to which he appended a long commentary. In a powerful demonstration of his own understanding of the koan, Wu-men locates the essence of the koan in its ability to stir up doubt. The character *mu* is, as he explains, "the gateless barrier of the Zen school." "Do you not wish to pass through this barrier?" If so,

> Then concentrate yourself into this "Mu," with your 360 bones and 84,000 pores, making your whole body one great inquiry. Day and night work intently at it. Do not attempt nihilistic or dualistic interpretations. It is like having bolted a red hot iron ball. You try to vomit it but cannot....
>
> Now, how should one strive? With might and main work at this "Mu," and be "Mu." If you do not stop or waver in your striving, then behold, when the Dharma candle is lighted, darkness is at once enlightened.

Ta-hui's teaching that doubt is an essential element of the koan remained normative throughout Chinese Zen from the end of the Song period. Kao-feng Yüan-miao (1238–1295), a respected master from the Yang-ch'i line of the Rinzai school who was active well into the Yüan period (1260–1368), described this sense of doubt in his highly acclaimed text *The Essentials of Zen.* The three essential features are "a great root of faith" (Jpn., *daishinkon*), "a great tenacity of purpose" (Jpn., *daifunshi*), and "a great feeling of doubt" (Jpn., *daigijo*). He compares this feeling to the anxiety of a criminal who is in suspense as to whether the heinous crime will be found out or not. All three essential features are indispensable for success in Zen practice.

The Rinzai school dominated Chinese Zen during the Song period. By the end of the era it had absorbed all the other houses and lesser movements with the exception of the Soto school, where the influence of Hung-chih survived. Historians of Zen Buddhism usually focus on the opposition between Hung-chih's "silent illumination Zen" and Ta-hui's "koan-gazing Zen." It is easy to look on the controversy as a continuation of the confluict between the Northern and Southern schools. Indeed, many of the passages in Ta-hui's abusive attacks against the quiet sitting practiced by the disciples of silent illumination are reminiscent of Shen-hui's assaults on the "quietism" of the Northern school. Yet there are serious problems with an approach that tries to divide the whole of Zen history from the time of Bodhidharma to the present into two main opposing orientations. The facts of the matter are much more nuanced.

In the first place, the sources at our disposal are too slanted to supply us with certain knowledge of the teachings and practices of the Northern school. At the same time, our understanding of the Zen school during the Song period is incomparably clearer and more complete. Hung-chih's position aligns him with the House of Ts'ao-tung, whose founders—Tung-shan, Ts'ao-shan, and Yün-chü—support the Soto school. These three masters in turn stand in a continuous line with the great masters of the T'ang period. According to its own self-understanding, the Soto school belongs to the Southern school of Chinese Zen and, like all Zen schools, reveres the Sixth Patriarch, Hui-neng. Hung-chih's "silent-illumination Zen" is well rooted in authentic Zen tradition.

The differences in concrete practice between the Rinzai and Soto schools are undeniable, and they come up again and again both in the controversy between Hung-chih and Ta-hui and in subsequent tensions. The Rinzai adherents reproach the Soto school for its tendencies towards passivity. Only to sit in mediation, they say, dulls the mind into inactivity and engulfs it in a sleepy twilight. This may happen, counter the Soto adherents, but is it necessarily the case? Authentic Soto teachers cultivate an extremely alert and objectless form of meditation. Moreover, koan are used in the Soto school, albeit not in the same dynamic style as in the Rinzai school. The manner of meditation in Soto is more calm, but it certainly does not exclude the experience of enlightenment.

The second criticism that Ta-hui directed against Hung-chih has to do with the experience of enlightenment in Zen (Jpn., *satori*). The Rinzai school aims at a sudden experience that effects a profoundly reorienting conversion. The quickest and surest way to this kind of experience is through the extreme tension-in-doubt produced by the koan exercise. Both koan and *satori*, say the Rinzai followers, are neglected by the Soto school. The criticism is not entirely fair. Soto also recognizes sudden enlightenment, for which koan practice can be extremely helpful; not a few of its masters underwent powerful, shattering experiences. And yet, both *satori* and koan practice are understood differently. For the Soto school the practice of *zazen* is primary. In addition it speaks of a quiet experience of depth that is carried through one's daily activities and is in no way inferior to sudden *satori*. The most outstanding example of this approach of the Soto school is Dogen (1200–1253), the Japanese Zen master who experienced the great enlightenment personally, saw the figure of Buddha during *zazen*, and taught how to bring this experience into one's everyday life. Far removed from any kind of quietistic passivity, Dogen was given over constantly to a transcending denial by which he strove for an ever more perfect realization of the absolute.

Despite all the differences and contradictions, the two schools of "silent-illumination Zen" *(mokusho-zen)* and "koan-gazing Zen" *(kanna-zen)* considered one another genuine forms of Zen Buddhism. Documents from the time tell us of friendly, cordial relations between Hung-chih and Ta-hui. When Hung-chih died in the monastery of Mount T'ien-t'ung, which through his persevering efforts had become one of the important centers of Zen Buddhist monasticism, Ta-hui hastened to attend the funeral rites of his deserving colleague, and we can be certain that Hung-chih would not have hesitated to show the same respects to Ta-hui.

In the two movements represented by Hung-chih and Ta-hui we have the two main currents of Zen that were to be transplanted from China to Japan. One bridge reached from Ta-hui, Hui-k'ai, and Kao-feng to the Japanese Rinzai school, where, half a millennium later, Hakuin would be drawn to the teaching on the Great Doubt and the Great Enlightenment and would give koan practice its definitive form. The other bridge stretched from Hung-chih to Dogen, who, while wrapped up in his study and trying to lay the foundations for the school of Zen he so highly esteemed, would awaken to the Great Experience under his master, T'ien-t'ung Ju-ching (1163–1228).

In one form or another, tendencies to pluralism are present in every period of the Zen movement. Sometimes they are precipitated by the special personalities of influential masters; often they are the result of particular group orientations or historical circumstances. An incredibly rich variety of practices and types of experience have developed over the ages. The development carries on and is especially productive in our own times; there is no telling where it will lead in the future. But towering over this variegated landscape of the history of Zen are the schools of Rinzai and Soto, embodied in the two great figures of Lin-chi and Dogen. Numerous further developments and new forms fall more or less into one or the other of these two most important expressions of Zen. The divergence, rooted in China, was to become still more pronounced and colorful in the Zen Buddhism of Japan.

FIVE HOUSES OF ZEN

Heinrich Dumoulin

DURING THE SECOND HALF of the T'ang period and the period of the Five Dynasties, family traditions took shape within the Zen movement that would come to be known in Zen history as the "Five Houses." The term was first used by Fa-yen Wen-i (885–958), who mentions four of the houses in his treatise *Shumon jikki-ron* (Chin., *Tsung-men shih-kuei lun*):

> When Ts'ao-tung (Jpn., Soto) knocks, the answer comes immediately; Lin-chi (Jpn., Rinzai) is like the breath of people calling each other; Yün-men (Jpn., Ummon) is the meeting of box and lid; the unity of light and dark, square and circle in Kuei-yang (Jpn., Igyo) is the edge that cuts the stream. All of them are the echo of a voice from the valley; their agreement is as tight as fingers clasped together.

Though certain features of four houses are given here—the house of Fa-yen would complete the list—these are hardly what we would call their defining characteristics.

To begin with, any attempt to determine a time frame for the Five Houses runs into insurmountable problems. In their life and work, some of the founding fathers of the houses belong to the Zen movement of the T'ang period, which is the fountainhead of Chinese Zen. It was only in the later chronicles that they came to be classified as the Five Houses. Furthermore, by the beginning of the Song period (perhaps earlier in the case of the House of Kuei-yang) three of the houses had already dissolved. Only the rival traditions of Lin-chi and Ts'ao-tung continued strongly throughout the Song period. The survival of the Five Houses is captured in the popular expression "The Five Houses and the Seven Schools," the latter indicating the two new lines of Yang-ch'i (Jpn., Yogi) and Huang-lung (Jpn., Oryu) that arose in Lin-chi's school at the beginning of the Song period. Chronologically, the Five Houses link the Zen masters of the T'ang period with the Zen movement of the Song period.

The Zen chronicles of the Song period offer abundant materials on the Five Houses. The most significant source of information, the *Ninden gammoku* (Chin., *Jen-t'ien yen-mu*), was compiled by Hui-yen Chih-chao, a monk of the school of Lin-chi who specialized in the history of the Five Houses. Understandably, he places the House of Lin-chi on the top of his list and devotes two of his six volumes to it; treatments of the houses of Yün-men, Ts'ao-tung, Kuei-yang, and Fa-yen follow. The sequence of course varies throughout Zen literature. The ordering we shall be following is based on the fact that the House of Kuei-yang is the earliest and, like the House of Lin-chi, belongs to the line of Ma-tsu, while the houses of Ts'ao-tung, Yün-men, and Fa-yen fall in the tradition of Shih-t'ou, the other great disciple in the third generation after Hui-neng. The House of Fa-yen was the last to develop and may have been the least significant of the five.

It is important to bear in mind that these "houses" do not signify different schools or orientations but rather different family traditions or styles that developed naturally among the masters and then were given preference in a circle of disciples. The style marking the two houses that were strongly influenced by the tradition of Ma-tsu is called "great potential–great action" (Jpn., *daiki daiyu*; Chin., *tai-chi ta-yung*). A great potential will necessarily break forth in sudden, grotesque, but always meaningful action. Thus in the House of Kuei-yang there developed different forms of expression, from simple koan stories to easily understood symbolism. The possibilities of expression were even richer in the House of Lin-chi, which made abundant use of dialectical formulas. The House of Ts'ao-tung is famous for the precision and care with which all things were done. This house developed the important formula of the "Five Ranks." The metaphor of the box and the lid alluded to above nicely fits the style of the House of Yün-men. In the methods of the House of Fa-yen, psychological concerns are blended with the worldview of Kegon.

The following presentation will review the differences in Zen practice within the Five Houses, differences that—and this should be stressed—did not diminish the inner cohesion of the Zen movement after Hui-neng.

Kuei-yang: Experience in Action

Life in a Zen monastery centers around experience—the sudden, direct encounter with reality. The faculty for such experience can announce itself in a thousand different ways and can be expressed in forms that are convincing, often shocking, and at times profoundly penetrating. The House of Kuei-yang offers a broad, impressive selection of such expressions. Its particular style, however, gives clear preference to action and silence over words.

The House of Kuei-yang took its name from the two mountains Kuei (Hunan Province) and Yang (Chiang-hsi Province), where the temples of its founders were located. Kuei-shan Ling-yu (777–853) was appointed head of the new Ta-kuei Monastery by his master, Pai-chang, in a rather unusual way. The master placed a water jug in front of the disciples and asked: "If you can't call this a water jug, what do you call it?" Kuei-shan kicked over the water jug and walked away. The wordless gesture revealed his enlightened state.

The most prominent of Kuei-shan's disciples were Yang-shan Hui-chi (807–883) and Hsiang-yen Chih-hsien (d. 898), both of whom were deeply bound to their master and were as brothers to each other. Indeed, the chronicles praise the familial atmosphere in the House of Kuei-yang. This particular trait is evident in the story of Hsiang-yen's enlightenment, which for a number of reasons ranks among the most famous Zen stories. Master Kuei-shan questioned Hsiang-yen about his original being before his birth. Unable to answer, he implored his master for help, only to be told that he must find the answer for himself. In vain Hsiang-yen searched through the scriptures. Finally, he burned all his books and withdrew into solitude in order to devote himself entirely to this question. One day, while weeding the garden, he heard the clatter of a falling tile. The startling sound awakened him to enlightenment.

According to the report of the chronicle, Hsiang-yen returned to his hut, washed, burned incense, and bowed in the direction of Master

Kuei-shan's dwelling. Then to record his enlightenment, he composed the following lines:

> With one stroke, all previous knowledge is forgotten.
> No cultivation is needed for this.
> This occurrence reveals the ancient way
> And is free from the track of quiescence.
> No trace is left anywhere.
> Whatever I hear and see does not conform to rules.
> All those who are enlightened
> Proclaim this to be the greatest action.

These verses are found among the collected sayings of Kuei-shan, together with two other stanzas that Hsiang-yen composed on the same occasion. His fellow disciple and brother in the Dharma, Yang-shan, criticized the first stanza for being too dependent on the master's style and not directly expressive of personal experience. So Hsiang-yen composed these lines:

> My poverty of last year was not real poverty.
> This year it is want indeed.
> In last year's poverty there was room for a piercing gimlet.
> In this year's poverty even the gimlet is no more.

Perhaps Hsiang-yen was thinking of the philosophical notion of "emptiness" from the Wisdom sutras. In any case, this was the occasion on which Yang-shan is said to have spoken the famous line: "You may have grasped the Zen of the Perfected One, but not even in a dream have you seen the Zen of the Patriarchs." In response, the following verse poured forth from Hsiang-yen's lips:

> I have my secret
> And look at you with twinkling eye.
> If you do not understand this
> Do not call yourself a monk.

As the Chinese author Chang Chung-yüan correctly explains, these three poems indicate different levels of inner realization. While the first poem describes the experience in artistically stylized form, the second evinces signs of an intellectual belaboring. In the third poem, the allusion to the twinkling eye as an expression of an inner state is authentic Zen. With great joy Yang-shan reports to Master Kuei-shan that Brother Hsiang-yen has grasped the Zen of the Patriarchs.

The Zen style of the House of Kuei-yang is characterized by action and silence, both of them intimately bound up with one another. This is evident in Yang-shan's first meeting with the master. When asked who he was, he simply walked through the hall from west to east and then stopped, without saying a word. Movement from west to east symbolizes the transition from bodily ability or potentiality to function or action. Or again, when asked where he had just come from, Yang-shan replied, "From the fields." And when Kuei-shan wanted to know how many people were there, Yang-shan drove his mattock into the ground and stood motionless. Kuei-shan continued: "Today there are many people on the southern mountain cutting grass." Yang-shan took up his mattock and left. Action and silence flow together to give expression to experience. Kuei-shan respected this style of his disciple Yang-shan and held it in high regard, referring to it as "swordplay."

The relation between substance (potentiality) and function is illustrated in a quaint conversation between the master and his disciple during the tea harvest. Kuei-shan said to Yang-shan: "All day I have been listening to your voice as we picked tea leaves, but I have not yet seen you yourself. Show me your real self." Yang-shan shook the tea tree. The master commented, "You have achieved the function but not the substance." When Yang-shan asked his master what he himself had achieved, the master remained silent. Thereupon Yang-shan remarked, "You, Master, have achieved the substance but not the function." What this exchange implies is the unity of potentiality and action, substance and function.

Kuei-shan and Yang-shan exemplify what Zen calls the practice of the enlightened. Both have effected a breakthrough; both have attained the enlightenment experience and live in contact with the realm of the transcendent. As they go about their daily rounds of work and monastic duties, both their silence and their words manifest a state of enlightenment.

Like Kuei-shan and Yang-shan, Hsiang-yen is numbered among the illustrious masters of his time and is also the subject of many well-known stories, perhaps the most popular being the account of the "Man up in a Tree." A man hanging by his teeth from a branch high up in a tree is asked why Bodhidharma came from the West. With graphic precision, the scene depicts the hopelessness of the human condition and was taken up into the *Mumonkan* as a koan for use in Zen practice.

The House of Kuei-yang contains a treasury of valuable traditions. One of these is the use of "perfect marks" (Jpn., *enso*; Chin., *yüan-hsiang*), or more concretely, "circular figures." The circle is one of the eternal forms revered by peoples of all times and cultures, symbolizing the admired and longed-for perfection of being. The image seems first to have been used in Zen by National Teacher Nan-yang Hui-chung, a disciple of Hui-neng. The *Keitoku dentoroku* tells of a disciple who, upon returning to Master Nan-yang after a pilgrimage, drew a circular figure on the ground in front of the master, bowed, and stood there waiting. "The master spoke: 'Do you want to become a Buddha or not?' [The disciple] replied, 'I cannot rub my eyes.' The master said, 'I am not equal to you.' The disciple did not answer." In this exchange, master and disciple alike display great modesty, the disciple because he cannot clear the illusion from his eyes, and the master because he places himself in a position inferior to his disciple. And in the middle of the whole episode lies the circle.

In a passage dealing with Kuei-shan, the chronicle reports a similar encounter:

> The master asked a newly arrived monk what his name was. The monk said, "Yüeh-lun [Full Moon]." The master then drew a circle in the air with his hand. "How do you compare with this?" he asked. The monk replied, "Master, if you ask me in such a way, a great many people will not agree with you." Then the master said, "As for me, this is my way. What is yours?" The monk said, "Do you still see Yüeh-lun?" The master answered, "You can say it your way, but there are a great many people here who do not agree with you."

Circles and full moons express perfect enlightenment, the original face one had before one was born, or the cosmic Buddha body. The disciples know full well that they are far from such perfection. This may also be the reason why Zen masters are wont to draw the circle, the most enduring and pervasive of all Zen symbols, whose form they dash off with incomparable skill and always in such a way the powerful brush stroke never returns precisely to the point where it began. Does this mean that in every expression there must always remain room for imperfection?

According to the chronicles, Yang-shan seems more than anyone to have cultivated the symbolic use of the circle. The *Ninden gammoku* relates that Tan-yüan Ying-chen, the Dharma heir of National Teacher Nan-yang Hui-chung, had transmitted to Yang-shan the method of ninety-seven circles, by means of which the latter attained enlightenment. A detailed explanation of the circular figures is also given, including specific information on characters and hatchmarks to be set inside the circles to give them their specific meanings.

In the section on Yang-shan, the *Keitoku dentoroku* reports: "As the master sat there with eyes closed, a monk came and stood quietly by his side. The master opened his eyes and drew a circle on the ground. Within the circle he wrote the character for water, then looked back at the monk. The monk said nothing." By tracing the character of one of the four elements within the circle, the master specified the nature of the circle. A few lines further, but not necessarily in the same context as the preceding episode, the chronicle has a paragraph on divination, something highly esteemed in China:

> Once the master asked a monk what he knew besides Buddhism. The monk said that he understood the divination techniques in the *Book of Changes*. The master lifted his fan and asked, "Which one among the sixty-four hexagrams is this one?" The monk was unable to reply. The master answered for him, "It is the great potentiality of thunder and lightning and now it is transformed into the destruction of earth and fire."

Throughout Mahayana Buddhism the symbolism of the circle has taken on a variety of different forms. One can hardly speak of dependencies here. Zen is no stranger to the symbol. It was used as a means of promoting enlightenment. The practice of the circle was developed particularly in the Kegon school. We cannot know for certain precisely how Yang-shan and his disciples used and interpreted circles. At a later stage in Zen history circles must have enjoyed widespread use, so much so that they met with opposition. Even as a "preliminary artificial means" (Skt., *upaya-kausalya*; Jpn., *hoben*), it was argued, circles can be harmful because they veil the true nature of reality—the absolute emptiness and formlessness of all things. The symbol of the circle was not recognized as a legitimate way for striving toward Zen enlightenment.

In early source materials, the House of Kuei-yang is presented as authentic Zen. Its founder, Kuei-shan, depicted the ideal of the enlightened person in Taoist tones that were familiar to the masters of the late T'ang period, especially to Lin-chi: "Like autumn waters, clear and still, pure and undisturbed, unmoving [Chin., *wu-wei*; Jpn., *mui*], quiet and deep, unhindered, such a person is called a person of the Tao, a person without trouble [Chin., *wu-shih*; Jpn., *buji*]."

LIN-CHI: THREEFOLD AND FOURFOLD FORMULAS

If it is difficult to neatly locate the period of the Five Houses within the history of Chinese Zen Buddhism, there are even greater problems with situating the school of Lin-chi (Jpn., Rinzai). Its founder, Lin-chi, was prominent within the Zen movement during the T'ang period. During the Song period, the growth of the Rinzai school in southern China represented a whole new phase within Zen. The time between, covering several generations of Zen, lies in darkness. The successors of Lin-chi from the third to the sixth generation carried on the spirit of their founder in northern China without attracting much attention. The special traits of this school—shouting and beating—were the direct inheritance of the peculiar style of its founder. In the previous chapter we tried to communicate something of the essence of Lin-chi's Zen, basing ourselves primarily on the classic work of the school, the *Rinzairoku*. Although this work is imbued with the spirit of Lin-chi, it did not take final shape until many years after his death. The many dialectical and didactic formulas scattered throughout the text were probably editorial glosses added during the tenth and eleventh centuries in the House of Lin-chi. It seems that Feng-hsüeh Yen-chao (896–973) and Fen-yang Shan-chao (947–1024) devoted extensive energies to work on these texts. It is further possible that many of the texts are of later origin. In any case, the threefold and fourfold formulas are distinctive of the House of Lin-chi.

The most important dialectical formula in the House of Lin-chi, "the four alternatives" (Jpn., *shiryoken*; Chin., *ssu-liao-chen*), describes four positions regarding the subject-object relationship. Lin-chi is said to have presented the following at one of his evening conferences:

> Sometimes I take away man and do not take away the surroundings; sometimes I take away the surroundings and do not take away man; sometimes I take away both man and the surroundings; sometimes I take away neither man nor the surroundings.

These four alternatives or positions regarding subject and object represent an ascending grasp of reality. The formula is based on the well-known four propositions of Indian Buddhist logic: being, nonbeing, neither being nor nonbeing, both being and nonbeing (Skt., *catuskotika*; Jpn., *shiku fumbetsu*; Chin., *ssu-chü fen-pieh*). In terms of content, they correspond to the four levels of reality (Skt., *dharmadhatu*, Jpn., *hokkai*) in the Kegon school. In the first and second stages illusion is overcome first by the subject and then by the object. That is to say, all clinging to subjective intellectual perception and to the objective world is repudiated. The third stage negates both subject and object, but differentiation still obtains. This posture of negation corresponds to the state of consciousness achieved in extreme concentration. Only in the fourth stage, which affirms the transcendence of the opposition between subject and object, does all confrontation between subject and object cease. Reality is comprehended in its ultimate oneness. In this formula the philosophy of the Middle Way Madhyamika and the metaphysics of the Kegon school flow together.

Questioned further by one of his monks, Lin-chi offered a concrete metaphor for each of the four statements. His image for the first reads:

> The spring sun comes forth covering the earth with brocade;
> A child's hair hangs down, white as silken strands.

Nature expands. The white hair of a child implies a paradox. The second image is different:

> Mandates of the sovereign are spread through the world;
> The general had laid the dust of battle beyond the frontiers.

With his own home not far from the border, Lin-chi had an existential feel for such imagery. He continues with the third image:

> No news from Ping and Fen,
> Isolated away from everywhere.

Ping and Feng were names of distant regions. In the third stage, concentration is a matter of total seclusion. Finally comes the fourth and crowning image:

> The sovereign ascends [his throne in] the jeweled palace;
> Aged rustics are singing.

On the highest level of consciousness one sees reality as perfect and all-encompassing. The metaphor is reminiscent of the tenth image in the famous Oxherding pictures, in which the enlightened person, sharing what has been given him, enters the marketplace and stands in the middle of life in all its reality. Typical of Zen, the addition of these colorful images lends concreteness to the four abstract statements of the dialectical formula. The formula not only aids in instruction but also in practice; like a koan, it can stir the searching mind.

Another fourfold formula in the *Rinzairoku* deals with conversations or encounters between guest and host, or between student and teacher. Its purpose is to teach the proper way to converse. For Lin-chi the proper didactic procedure in conversational intercourse was most important. In his opening remarks he speaks of the many different and strange situations that can develop during practice:

Followers of the Way, the view of the Ch'an school is that the sequence of death and life is orderly. The student of Ch'an must examine [this] most carefully.

When host and guest meet they vie with one another in discussion. At times, in response to something, they may manifest a form; at times they may act with their whole body; or they may, by picking up a tricky device, [make a display of] joy or anger; or they may reveal half of the body; or again, they may ride upon a lion [Manjushri] or mount upon a lordly elephant [like the bodhisattva Samantabhadra].

Four conversations follow illustrating (1) the superiority of the student or (2) of the teacher, (3) the equality of both partners in control of the situation, or (4) a student-like state of confusion on both sides. The text reads:

1. A true student gives a shout, and to start with holds out a sticky lacquer tray. The teacher, not discerning that this is an objective circumstance, goes after it and performs a lot of antics with it. The student again shouts but still the teacher is unwilling to let go. This is a disease of the vitals that no doctoring can cure: it is called "the guest examines the host."

2. Sometimes a teacher will proffer nothing, but the instant a student asks a question, robs him of it. The student, having been robbed, resists to the death and will not let go: this is called "the host examines the guest."

3. Sometimes a student comes forth before a teacher in conformity with a state of purity. The teacher, discerning that this is an objective circumstance, seizes it and flings it into a pit. "What an excellent teacher!" exclaims the student, and the teacher replies, "Bah! You can't tell good from bad!" Thereupon, the student makes a deep bow: this is called "the host examines the host."

4. Or again, a student will appear before a teacher wearing a cangue [the heavy wooden collar worn as punishment by criminals] and bound with chains. The teacher fastens on still more chains and cangues for him. The student is so delighted that he can't tell what is what: This is called "the guest examines the guest."

Lin-chi closes the discourse with this admonition:

Virtuous monks, all the examples I have brought before you serve to distinguish demons and point out heretics, thus making it possible for you to know what is erroneous and what is correct.

This guest-host pattern was highly valued in the Rinzai school; it illustrates the teaching methods that were in vogue when the Discourses of Lin-chi were redacted and that were to be used in years to come. We really do not know whether the formula, as seen in the text cited above, can be traced back to Lin-chi or not. In the opinion of Demieville, the four conversational alternatives "smack of the scholasticism of the Song period." Yanagida argues that another guest-host formula in the text, similar but more complicated in its propositional style, was a later addition.

In the first book of the *Ninden gammoku*, which deals with Lin-chi, the master makes use of a formula that does not occur in the *Rinzairoku* to describe the fourfold pattern of relationships obtaining between light and activity (Jpn., *shishoyu*). Sometimes light precedes activity; sometimes activity precedes light; sometimes light and activity are simultaneous, sometimes they are not.

Lin-chi's "four types of shouting" (Jpn., *shikatsu*), listed in the *Rinzairoku* ("Critical Examination," sec. 20), are most likely a later addition. The well-known passage reads:

Sometimes a shout is like the jeweled sword of the Vajra King; sometimes a shout is like the golden-haired lion crouching on the ground; sometimes a shout is like a

weed-tipped fishing pole; sometimes a shout doesn't function as a shout.

In each of the four types of shouting we see characteristics of enlightenment. The sword cuts through all false notions. The lion crouched in
ambush suddenly pounces on its prey. Just as a weed-tipped pole is used
to probe fish from the bottom and attract them, so does the master use
shouting to test his students. Paradox and transcending power are manifest in the fourth roar.

Lin-chi's much-discussed threefold formula, known as the "Three
Statements" (Jpn., *sanku*), appears in the *Rinzairoku* in conjunction with
two other threefold formulas, the "Three Mysteries" (Jpn., *sangen*) and
the "Three Essentials" (Jpn., *sanyo*). None of these is explained ("Discourses," sec. 9). After the proclamation of the Three Statements, the
master adds only this: "Each statement must comprise the gates of the
Three Mysteries, and the gate of each mystery must comprise the Three
Essentials." The textual data at our disposal do not allow for much clari-
fication here. The English, French, and Japanese translations show a wide
divergence of interpretation. As Ruth Fuller Sasaki rightly observes,
"This is one of Lin-chi's most enigmatic discourses…. The exact meaning of Lin-chi's 'Three Statements' is not clear." She reports further that
the Three Statements, the Three Mysteries, and the Three Essentials are
interpreted variously as the Buddha, the Dharma, and the Tao (Way); or
as the three Buddha bodies—*dharmakaya, sambhogakaya, nirmana-
kaya*—or as the three principles of Chinese Buddhist philosophy—*li*
("principle"), *chih* ("wisdom"), and *yung* ("functioning"). Yanagida
concludes that "the meaning of the Three Mysteries and the Three
Essentials is not very clear," pointing out numerous attempts at explanation in later Zen literature. Demieville finds the Three Statements
"richly mysterious."

To single out these formulas and make them too central would be to
paint a false picture of the House of Lin-chi. For while Lin-chi, with his
grounding in Mahayana metaphysics and his well-honed speculative
powers, delighted in dialectical statements, his primary concern was concrete realization and experience. The formulas were but an aid to practice. In a sense, they were a bridge between the spontaneous outbursts of

Zen masters of the T'ang period and the highly stylized koan practice of the Song period. Given the state of the historical sources, it is not possible to define the individual phases of this development. After becoming the most influential school of its time, the House of Lin-chi contributed significantly to the spiritual awakening that occurred during the Song period and that was in fact the last high point of Chinese culture to be influenced decisively by Buddhism.

TS'AO-TUNG: "THE FIVE RANKS"

The House of Ts'ao-tung (Jpn., *Soto*) takes its name from an abbreviated combination of the graphs of its two founders, Tung-shan Liang-chieh (807–869) and Ts'ao-shan Pen-chi (840–901), each of whom received their names from the mountains on which their respective monasteries stood. We do not know for sure when the house first took this name, though there are indications that it was soon after the death of Ts'ao-shan. Like the House of Lin-chi, it survived to develop into one of the most important schools or sects of Chinese Zen Buddhism.

Tung-shan was not yet ten years old when he left his parental home for a local temple to begin what was to be a restless monastic life. During his study of fundamental Buddhist teachings he demonstrated such extraordinary intellectual acumen that his teacher decided to send him to the experienced master Ling-mo (747–818), one of the many disciples of Ma-tsu. Ordained at the age of twenty, he studied for a short time with the two famous masters Nan-ch'uan Pu-yüan (748–835) and Kuei-shan Ling-yu (771–853) before becoming a disciple of Yün-yen T'an-sheng (780–841), whose line of succession he carried on. Through Master Yün-yen he was able to "comprehend the sermons of inanimate things," which in Zen does not refer to the miraculous powers of Buddhist saints, who are said to hear with their eyes and see with their ears, but to knowledge of the undifferentiated identity of animate and inanimate beings in the unity of Buddhahood. Many of the exchanges between Tung-shan and his master have been preserved in Zen literature.

After these years of study, Tung-shan visited the temples of China where he became acquainted with the leading representatives of the age. These encounters with Zen masters from various traditions gave him a broad appreciation of the rich diversity of Zen doctrine and method at the time. His long years of wandering came to an end when he entered the monastery on Mount Tung at the age of fifty-two to devote himself totally to the guidance of his disciples, among whom Ts'ao-shan and Yün-chü Tao-ying (d. 902) were the most distinguished.

Tung-shan is a typical representative of southern Chinese Zen. Born south of the Yangtze River (in Chekiang Province), he spent his entire life in southern China, whose gentle climate gave his personality a different quality from that of Lin-chi, who was reared in rough northern climes. A person of literary gifts, he was fond of teaching through the medium of poetry. He shared this love of poetry with his master, Yün-yen, who asked him at the time of his departure:

> "When will you return here?"
> "When Your Reverence has a dwelling place, then I'll
>   come."
> "Once you have gone it will be difficult for us to meet," said
>   the master.
> "It will be difficult not to meet," returned Liang-chieh.
> Then Liang-chieh said, "Your Reverence, a hundred years
>   from now, if someone were to ask me, 'Can you draw a
>   portrait of your master?' how should I reply?"
> "Only answer him, 'Just *this* it is,'" said Yün-yen.
> Liang-chieh remained silent for a time. Then Yün-yen said,
>   "In undertaking this matter you must investigate
>   minutely." Liang-chieh still had some doubts.
>   Later, when Liang-chieh was crossing a stream, he saw
> his reflection in the water, and [at that moment] completely
> realized the meaning of [Yün-yen's] words. He composed
> this verse:
> Seeking it from others is forbidden.
> For thus it becomes further and further estranged.
> Now that I go my way entirely alone,
> There is nowhere I cannot meet it.
> Now it is just what I am,
> Now I am not what it is.

Thus one must understand,
Then one accords with True Suchness.

In poetic style typical of Tung-shan, these verses express the Mahayana view of the oneness and equality of reality and the self. Tung-shan also put into verse the well-known formula of the Five Ranks (Jpn., *goi*; Chin., *wu-wei*), which his master Yün-yen is supposed to have entrusted to him as a secret teaching. Among the disciples of Tung-shan, it was Ts'ao-shan who preserved this precious teaching, elaborating and perfecting it in the process. His character and interests being totally different from those of his fellow disciple Yün-chü, Ts'ao-shan loved to study. From early youth he became acquainted with the teachings of Confucianism and continued his studies even after entering the Buddhist monastic life with parental permission at the age of eighteen. His time of study with Tung-shan was brief (probably from 865 to 868). Only two conversations with his master have been handed down, one dating from the time of his arrival and the other from his departure. He traveled little. For thirty-five years he dwelled in quiet contemplation in the two monasteries at Ts'ao-shan and Ho-yü-shan, where he applied his keen mind to penetrating the meaning of the Five Ranks. The chronicles list the names of nineteen of his disciples. Within four generations, however, his line had become extinct.

Yün-chü, the other important disciple of Tung-shan, had little or no interest in the dialectic of the Five Ranks. He directed his efforts toward the immediate experience of enlightenment, which he incarnated in an exemplary ethical life. Before devoting himself to Zen, he had studied the monastic discipline (Vinaya). He came to Tung-shan two years before the arrival of his colleague Ts'ao-shan but remained in training under the master longer, as numerous records of their conversations attest. Yün-chü enjoyed higher esteem than any of Tung-shan's disciples. The many excellent students later to emerge from his school establish him as one of the most important and influential figures of the age. Thanks to his disciples and spiritual heirs, the Ts'ao-tung school was carried on in China and its line of tradition transmitted to Japan.

The Five Ranks of the House of Ts'ao-tung represent the most important dialectical formula in all of Zen Buddhism. Master Hakuin sees in it the "main principle of Buddhism and the essential road of *sanzen* [Zen practice]." In contradistinction to the other fivefold formulas in Buddhist philosophy based on ontological-psychological analysis—one thinks of the *Abidharmakosa* or the doctrine of *vijnaptimatra*—all five ranks of Ts'ao-tung express various aspects of one and the same thing: the fundamental identity of the Absolute (or universal One) and the relative (or phenomenal many). The formula of the Five Ranks originated in Mahayana metaphysics but was given a Chinese form. Given its affinity with the *I Ching (Book of Changes)*, we may speak of it as an expression of Chinese philosophy. The basic concepts stem from Tung-shan, who in turn was building on foundations laid by Shih-t'ou and other Zen masters of the T'ang period. But it was Ts'ao-shan who grasped the core of the master's teaching and gave it its final form.

The classical statement of the fivefold formula appears in five stanzas that can be traced back to Tung-shan and Ts'ao-shan. The first line of every stanza is composed of three Chinese graphs that serve as a title or indication of the essential content of the rank in question. This is the work of Tung-shan, who may have received the formulations verbally from his master Yün-yen. The next three lines make use of poetic metaphors to present the meaning of the rank. On the basis of recent research, we can attribute them to Ts'ao-shan. Since each of the stanzas expresses the same view of enlightenment from a different perspective, one may also speak of them as "Five Ranks."

The two key concepts in the fivefold formula—*cheng* and *p'ien*, in Japanese, *sho* and *hen*—signify literally, "the straight" and "the bent." They refer to what is absolute, one, identical, universal, and noumenal set up in tension with what is relative, manifold, different, particular, and phenomenal. They are related to the corresponding notions of *li* (Jpn., *ri*; absolute principle) and *shih* (Jpn., *ji*; appearance) in Chinese philosophy, and are also referred to as the dark and the light, depicted respectively by a black circle and a white circle. Tung-shan explains "the straight" as follows: "There is one thing: above, it supports heaven; below, it upholds earth. It is black like lacquer, perpetually in movement and activity." The straight is also the foundation of heaven and earth and of all being. But this absolute is dynamic, constantly in motion. The perceiving mind cannot lay hold of the straight and grasp it as an object. In

Buddhist terminology, it is the true emptiness, without duality, of which the metaphysics of Perfect Wisdom *(prajnaparamita)* speaks.

The absolute becomes manifest in appearances, in "the bent" or light. Absolute and phenomenal cannot be separated; they are identical, one. The absolute is the absolute in relation to the relative, and the relative is relative in relation to the absolute. Therefore, the relative-phenomenal is also called "marvelous being" (Jpn., *myou*) because it is inseparable from "true emptiness" (Jpn., *shinku*). The saying "the marvelous being of true emptiness" or "the true emptiness of marvelous being" expresses the quintessence of the enlightened view of reality.

The following translation of the five stanzas can give only an approximate sense of their deep meaning:

> The Bent within the Straight [Jpn., *shochuhen*]:
> In the third watch of the night
> Before the moon appears,
> No wonder when we meet
> There is no recognition!
> Still cherished in my heart
> Is the beauty of earlier days.
>
> The Straight within the Bent [Jpn., *henchusho*]:
> A sleepy-eyed grandam
> Encounters herself in an old mirror.
> Clearly she sees a face,
> But it doesn't resemble hers at all.
> Too bad, with a muddled head,
> She tries to recognize her reflection!
>
> The Coming from within the Straight [Jpn., *shochurai*]:
> Within nothingness there is a path
> Leading away from the dusts of the world.
> Even if you observe the taboo
> On the present emperor's name,
> You will surpass that eloquent one of yore
> who silenced every tongue.

The Arrival at the Middle of the Bent [Jpn., *henchushi*]:
When two blades cross points,
There's no need to withdraw.
The master swordsman
Is like the lotus blooming in the fire.
Such a man has in and of himself
A heaven-soaring spirit.

Unity Attained [Jpn., *kenchuto*]:
Who dares to equal him
Who falls into neither being nor non-being!
All men want to leave
The current of ordinary life,
But he, after all, comes back
To sit among the coals and ashes.

Two approaches stand out from the vast literature aimed at interpreting the meaning of the Five Ranks. One is primarily concerned with the philosophical content of the formula, the other with its psychological and literary meaning. Ever since Hakuin used the text of the Five Ranks to conclude the final version of his system of koan, its dialectical formula has been considered the crowning achievement of literature on the koan.

Given the close historical connections between the Chinese Zen Buddhism of the Five Ranks and the worldview of the Kegon school, the insights of this latter may aid us in understanding the spiritual meaning of the fivefold formula of the House of Ts'ao-tung. The teaching of the four Dharma realms (Jpn., *shi hokkai*) attributed to the Kegon patriarch Ch'eng-kuan (737–838) provides a direct point of entry. The central notions in this teaching, *shih* (appearance) and *li* (principle), correspond to the key words *p'ien* (the bent, off-center) and *cheng* (the straight, true). The basic thesis, that there is a mutual penetration of all things in the whole of reality, is the same in both positions. The difference is that the Kegon school takes a more philosophical approach, while Zen disciples seek realization through practice. In neither case should the thesis be understood statically. Each of the formulations attempts to present the flowing stream of reality by stressing a different aspect of it.

Kegon philosophy begins with the realm of *shih* (Jpn., *ji hokkai*), in which all things (Skt., *dharma*) exist in mutual dependence through the causal efficacy of the Dharma realm (Jpn., *hokkai engi*). In the second realm, *li* (Jpn., *ri hokkai*), the principle or absolute, is the reality of all things. In comparing the four Dharma realms with the Five Ranks, we find that the first two ranks correspond to the first Dharma realm of *shih*. The identity of the straight (absolute) and the bent (relative) acknowledged in the first two ranks of the Zen formulation is considered under two aspects. First, multiplicity is seen in sameness; all diverse things and events are in their essence the same, formless and empty. Emptiness is undisturbed by any subjective element. Already on this first level, an enlightened viewpoint is present. But Zen practice, of necessity, presses on. The second aspect of the Five Ranks sees the whole in every individual thing; that is, the multiplicity of things is penetrated by the essential principle. The Japanese Buddhologist Kato Totsudo explains both the distinction and the connection between the ranks:

> While on the first rank, the vast multiplicity of things appears to be contained within the natural law of true being-as-it-is, from the perspective [the second level] the law of being-as-it-is is seen to be active in every individual thing in the world of appearances. If the first rank approaches the world of appearances from their true nature, the second uses appearances to arrive at their true nature.

The bipolarity of the two ranks is clearly expressed in symbolic imagery: the first rank is represented by a circle with its top half darkened and the second by a circle with the bottom half darkened.

The third of the Five Ranks—"Coming from within the Straight"—corresponds to the second realm in the Kegon scheme, that of *li*. The relative is not mentioned. The absolute stands in its naked absoluteness. At the same time, the potentiality of the absolute for the relative is expressed in the graph for "middle" or "in." The absolute is pregnant with all possibility, like the seed prior to the first sprouting of its germ. The title and verse of this level admit of different interpretations. In focusing attention on the absolute's transcendence of all opposition, all the opposites are removed at this level. "Fire and ice stand alongside each other in a common absoluteness, spring flowers bloom in the fall, the cow...made of mud...can low...the wooden horse whinnies." Yet even in this perspective the absolute retains its potential for relating to the relative. The dynamic significance of the graph *lai* ("coming, emerging") is of critical importance for fully understanding this third rank. The absolute is poised, as it were, on the verge of entering the world of appearances. "'Arriving at Sameness' is not a final state; this 'Arriving at Sameness' demands a simultaneous 'Leaving Sameness'; thus a dynamic circle of movement between arriving at and departing from sameness should take place." This interpenetration is confirmed by other possible translations of the title line. "The Coming from within the Straight" stresses the dynamic element. "Sameness in the Middle" emphasizes the absolute's transcendence of all opposites. However it is interpreted, the radical absolute of the third rank is bound inseparably to potentiality. Its symbolic representation is a blackened circle (the absolute) surrounded by a white circle (potency).

Textual traditions offer two variants for the title of the fourth rank; both of them make good sense. We adopted the reading *henchushi*, "Arrival at the Middle of the Bent." The alternative reading, *kenchushi*, "Arriving in Mutual Integration," has sameness and difference arriving together. The advantage of this latter title is that it corresponds neatly to the third Dharma realm of the Kegon schema, the realm of the "uninhibited interpenetration of *li* and *shih*" (Jpn., *riji muge hokkai*).

The reading *henchushi* focuses on the diversity of the ten thousand things. It is characteristic of Mahayana thought to mark off the boundaries of the world of diversity in this way. Again, Kato Totsudo states it well:

> The point here is to take life in all its rich variety just as it is, with its ten thousand opposites, and to go along with whatever circumstances require, embracing things after their own inclination or according to chance, letting things be rather than getting in their way, and thus allowing each and every thing, each and every appearance, to pursue a meaning and purpose distinct from my own.

The term *li* (absolute) does not appear in the title line of the fourth rank, but is certainly present in its content. Just as the absolute cannot exist without a potentiality for the relative, so the relative cannot exist without the absolute. By viewing phenomena, mutual conditions, and powers in their own relative form, we see the absolute revealed in pure relativity. Tung-shan likens this process to two fencers with swords bared, neither of whom can force the other to yield; or again, to the lotus blossom unharmed in the midst of the flames. In the symbolism of this rank, the relative is located as the middle of the absolute.

In the original rendering of the title line, "Arrival at the Middle of the Bent," the relationship of opposition between the third and fourth ranks is evident. Even though the title lines of each mention only one pole explicitly—either the absolute or the relative—the other is clearly implied. This device serves to preserve the full force of the formula's symmetry. The second, middle graph of all the title lines is the same: *chu*. In the first two ranks it is translated simply as "in," signifying the mutual penetration of the relative and the absolute. In the next two ranks it is better rendered as "middle," since the sense is that both poles exhibit a dynamic that transcends opposition.

The fifth rank crowns the entire schema, pointing to the oneness of unrestricted interpenetration in a freedom that surpasses all opposition. This rank corresponds to the highest Dharma realm in the Kegon scheme, namely, the realm of the mutual penetration of *li* and *shih*. The fifth rank also corresponds to the fourth Dharma realm of the unrestricted inter-penetration of all phenomena (Jpn., *jiji muge hokkai*). Here the Kegon worldview that lives within Zen comes fully into its own: the "harmonious interplay between particularities and also between each particularity and universality creates a luminous universe." The stanza of the fifth rank indicates a "return to fusion." The one "who falls into neither being nor nonbeing"—the enlightened individual—"comes back to sit among the coals and ashes." The symbol of the fifth rank is the darkened circle.

The basic formula of the Five Ranks underwent certain changes within the House of Ts'ao-tung, without however in any way diminishing its dialectical character. The dialectic between the two poles, *li* and *shih*, remained intact. In his research of this question, Alfonso Verdu examines the important concrete changes expressed in the following three formulas: the "Five Ranks of Merit" (Chin., *kung-hsün wu-wei;* Jpn., *kokun goi no ju*), the "Five Ranks Regarding Lord and Vassal" (Chin., *chün-ch'en wu-wei;* Jpn., *kunshin goi*), and the "Secret Meaning of the Five Ranks" (Chin., *wu-wei chih-chüeh;* Jpn., *goi shiketsu*), which is linked to the formula of the "Manifestation of the Mystery of the Five Ranks" (Chin., *wu-wei hsien-chüeh;* Jpn., *goi shiketsu*), which is linked to the formula of the "Manifestation of the Mystery of the Five Ranks" (Chin., *wu-wei hsien-chüeh;* Jpn., *goi kenketsu*).

The formula of the "Five Ranks of Merit," which is attributed to the old Master Tung-shan, introduces a new perspective by thematizing an ethical, ascetical development that differs from the noetic orientation of the basic formula. In any case, it is uncertain whether the insights of full enlightenment are present already on the earlier ranks or only on the fifth rank of perfection.

The formula of the "Five Ranks Regarding Lord and Vassal" is preceded by a lengthy explanatory commentary by Ts'ao-shan. As symbols of the "straight" and the "bent," lord and vassal represent respectively the absolute element of reality *(li)* and the phenomenal element *(shih).* The third rank of the formula is described as "the lord alone" and the fourth as "the vassal alone." The opposition between these two ranks supports the *henchushi* reading of the fourth rank even though the word for the absolute is not actually used. Later, the fourth rank was given various interpretations by different commentators.

The third formula is simpler in its dialectical structure. The middle ranks (the third and fourth) are without potentiality; they indicate simply sameness and diversity. All fivefold formulas of ranks or states lead to the same goal—perfect unity in total interpenetration. "This is the Hua-yen world of *li-shih wu-ai* (Jpn., *riji muge*)," Verdu concludes, "where the 'form' is equally the void as the void is the 'form.' Word and nonword are but the discriminative mind—aspects of perfect identity in itself."

This Chinese predilection for formulas and numerical schemes accompanied by diagrams and figures is by no means limited to Zen or even Buddhism in general, but reaches back to early Chinese antiquity. The principal symbol for the Five Ranks—light and dark in the form of circles, where light signifies the phenomenal world and dark the noumenal world—is also to be found among the scholars of the Kegon school. The real roots of the diagrams, however, are to be found in the *Book of Changes*, which had been analyzed for several generations and applied in a variety of ways. It seems that in the case of the Five Ranks, Ts'ao-shan, who composed the poetic verses, also drew the diagrams. Such symbols formed an important part of Zen history, responding to the need for visible signs or images, a need that was especially strong during the Song period and was to lead to the remarkable artistic accomplishments of Japanese Zen.

The influence of the Five Ranks extended beyond the House of Ts'ao-tung. The eminent Rinzai master Fen-yang Shan-chao (947–1024) was the first in the House of Lin-chi to make use of the Five Ranks of the House of Ts'ao-tung. The explanatory verses he composed are included in his koan collection, which makes up the second volume of the three-volume *Fun'yoroku*, edited by his disciple Shih-shuang Ch'u-yüan (986–1039). This work represents the first significant koan collection in Chinese literature.

Little is known of Ts'ao-shan's disciples. His line disappeared in the fourth or fifth generation. Yün-chü Tao-ying and his immediate followers carried on the House of Ts'ao-tung but showed little interest in the Five Ranks. Only with the revival of the school in the twelfth century did disciples again give attention to the importance of the fivefold formula. From this developed a number of commentaries of mixed value. The Five Ranks became part of the general Zen heritage.

Yün-men: "The One-Word Barriers"

Like the House of Ts'ao-tung, the houses of Yün-men and Fa-yen belong to the main line of Shih-t'ou, within which divisions had begun already during the first generation after Shih-t'ou. While the House of Ts'ao-tung was formed around the disciple Yüeh-shan Wei-yen, a second line traced its way via T'ien-huang Tao-wu (748–807), Lung-t'an Ch'ung-hsin, and Te-shan Hsüan-chien (782–865) down to the famous master Hsüeh-feng I-ts'un (822–908), a prominent figure at the end of the T'ang period. To Hsüeh-feng the two houses of Yün-men and Fa-yen are indebted for their common origin. Together they typify the Zen movement during the Five Dynasties period (907–960) and form a bridge to the following Song dynasty.

During the period of the Five Dynasties, the North was torn by the ravages of war while the South enjoyed peace and order. Many of the politically independent provinces set themselves up as small kingdoms and enjoyed a general state of well-being that often included a highly developed intellectual culture. For the houses of Yün-men and Fa-yen there were numerous advantages to such a social and political situation. Yet despite all they had in common, the two developed their own distinct characteristics.

Yün-men Wen-yen (864–949) was one of the most eminent Zen personalities of his time. He holds an important place within Zen literature and has been the subject of many stories in the Zen chronicles and the koan collections (eighteen related cases appear in the *Hekiganroku* alone, five in the *Mumonkan*). Born in Chia-hsing (southwest of Shanghai), Yün-men entered religious life at an early age, studying and observing the Buddhist monastic rule (Vinaya) until, driven by the desire for higher wisdom, he took up the itinerant life. He attained enlightenment while with Ch'en Tsun-su (Mu-chou Tao-tsung or Tao-ming, an eccentric disciple of Huang-po who practiced an extremely rigorous form of Zen in Mu-chou. Three times Yün-men asked his master for instruction in the highest truth. The third time, Mu-chou (so called because of his place of residence) threw him out of the gate and shut it so suddenly and with such force that it caught Yün-men's leg and broke it. In the extreme pain Yün-men attained enlightenment.

Mu-chou sent him to Hsüeh-feng, the most illustrious Zen master of the time. After spending a number of years with this master, Yün-men became his Dharma heir. He then set out as a wandering monk, visiting a number of well-known Zen masters until he ended up in Shao-chou, a southern city in Kuang-tung Province where a viceroy from the family of Liu had assumed control after the fall of the T'ang dynasty. The powerful Liu gave full protection to Yün-men. Following the death of the abbot Ju-min, the prince decreed that Yün-men become head of the Reiju-in monastery (Chin., *Ling-shu-yüan*). Later, another ruler from the Liu family built him the monastery of Kotaizen-in (Chin., *Kuang-t'ai ch'an-yüan*) on Mount Yün-men. This accounts for his name: the geographical name of the mountain was extended to the monastery and the founding abbot, who then passed into Zen history as Master Yün-men. The region ruled by the family of Liu in South China and known as the Kingdom of Nan-han became the site of important cultural and artistic developments. In such a milieu, the House of Yün-men flourished and produced some of the most lofty artistic works of Chinese Zen.

On Mount Yün-men the master gathered a large number of disciples and guided them on the path toward enlightenment. Just as he himself had to pay a great price to attain enlightenment, his disciples were not spared the same demands. It was part of his regular practice to strike them with his staff and frighten them with sudden shouts. His special style consisting of short, sharp answers came to be known as the "one-word barriers." Zen literature abounds in such "one-word" retorts, especially in the collected sayings of Yün-men (Jpn., *Ummonroku*) and in the *Nin-den gammoku*. Consider the following exchanges:

> "What is Zen?"—"That's it."
> "What is the way?"—"Grab it."
> "What is Yün-men's sword?"—"Patriarch."

Or again, to a monk who asks about a sword so sharp that it would cut a hair blown across its blade, the only reply given is "Bones."

The following three examples are taken from the *Ninden gammoku*:

> "What is the eye of the True Dharma?"—"Everywhere."

> "He who kills his father and kills his mother confesses before the Buddha. But where shall one confess who kills the Buddha and the patriarchs?"—"Obvious."

> "What is the meaning of the Patriarch's coming from the West?"—"Master."

Not all the answers consist of one graph; sometimes there are two, three, or more. But the answers are always extremely pregnant and incisive. What is more, the same question may occasion different answers.

The breadth and heart of Yün-men's pithy retorts stand out clearly in the contrast between a case from the *Mumonkan*:

"What is the Buddha?"—"A shit-stick."

and one from the collected sayings of Yün-men:

> "What is the pure Dharma body?"—"A flowerbed of peonies."

The last example reflects Yün-men's aesthetic sense in his ability to see the purity of the cosmos in the beauty of nature. All the same, the genuine Zen master makes no difference between "pure" and "impure." When talking about the Buddha nature of reality, Yün-men can find expressions whose concreteness are in no sense inferior to those of Lin-chi.

Yün-men's curt answers were meant to aid practice, to spur insight, and thus to promote realization. Not only his punchy one-syllable retorts, but also his more extended conversations and stories came to be used as koan. Yün-men discovered the classical mode of expression for the eternal Now of time-transcending enlightenment. The sixth example in the *Hekiganroku* illustrates the point well:

> Yün-men addressed the assembly and said: "I am not asking you about the days before the fifteenth of the month. But what about after the fifteenth? Come and give me a word about those days."
> And he himself gave the answer for them: "Every day is a good day."

This koan has received many different interpretations. Certainly, its main message is clear and speaks to everyone, not just to students of Zen. But the story also touches on a deeper, veiled mystery—the mystery of time. The Japanese Zen master Yasutani Hakuun explained that the previous fifteen days signify the time of practice from the full awakening of the desire for truth until the time of ultimate comprehension in experience. The Now of enlightenment is as perfect as the full moon at the halfway mark of its cycle. Just as the moon wanes and becomes dark, so during the fifteen days following enlightenment the consciousness of the awakening, which still lingers in the mind as a residue, fades and disappears. Enlightenment then means "every day," and the "every day" means enlightenment. Hence the very distinction between before and after is rendered useless. Reality is one single Now. This Now or today is every day. "Every day is a good day." A good day is nothing special. Gundert ponders, "Is there, in the grayness of an ordinary everyday that contains nothing special, something very special? And again, might this something very special not itself be everyday?" One has the sense that this koan is a pearl of great price.

Tung-shan Shou-ch'u (d. 900) is the best known of Yün-men's disciples. Continuing his master's use of "one-word barriers," he distinguished between "dead words" that contain rational intention and "living words" that are not bound by reason. His best-known short answer has been preserved in case 18 of the *Mumonkan*. To a monk who asks him, "What is the Buddha?", he replies: "Three pounds of flax." The moment of Tung-shan's enlightenment also came to be the subject of a koan. The *Mumonkan* relates the story as follows in case 15:

> When Tung-shan came to have an interview with Yün-men, Yün-men asked, "Where have you been recently?" "At Ch'a-tu, Master," Tung-shan replied. "Where did you stay during the last *ge* [retreat] period?" "At Pao-tzu of Hunan," replied Tung-shan. "When did you leave there?" "On the twenty-fifth of August," Tung-shan answered. Yün-men exclaimed, "I give you sixty blows with my stick!" The next day Tung-shan came up again and asked the master, "Yesterday you gave me sixty blows with your stick. I do not know where my fault was." Yün-men cried out, "You rice bag! Have you been prowling about like that from Chiang-his to Hunan?" At this Tung-shan was enlightened.

Whether Tung-shan actually received these blows is not clear from the wording of the text. Commentators disagree on this point. The editor of the work, Wu-men Hui-ka'i (1183–1260), however, criticizes Yün-men's gentle handling of Tung-shan and attributes the fall of the House of Yün-men to such manifestations of weakness.

The House of Yün-men made a considerable contribution to Chinese culture. Its founder, Yün-men, has been called the "most eloquent of the Ch'an masters." Paradoxically, this master had a great fear of words, and yet thanks to his enlightenment he could "stand unharmed in the midst of flames." From him emanated the "light" of which he said, "All people have it within themselves, but when they seek after it, it is all darkness." In this ever-present, dynamic light one finds the secret of Yün-men's powerful language. During the early Song period, the House of Yün-men flourished, and together with the House of Lin-chi exercised a considerable influence on the upper classes of Chinese society.

The highpoint of this development comes with Hsüeh-tou Ch'ung-hsien (980–1052), the poet of the hundred verses of the *Hekiganroku*. His own master and Yün-men's successor, Chih-men Kuang-tsu (d. 1031), was also a poet. We have already noted how the Rinzai master Fen-yang used poetry to express enlightened wisdom. Hsüeh-tou surpassed all of these poetic predecessors. As a master, he enjoyed great popularity and attracted many disciples. Among his work is a collection of some 250 poems. His work reached its highest level in the verses that he composed for cases he himself had selected, mostly from the *Keitoku dentoroku* and the collected sayings of Yün-men. His goal was to forge the essence of the masters' words and deeds into poetic form. In this way, he laid the foundations for the *Hekiganroku*, which, in the words of a Chinese Zen disciple, represents "the foremost scripture containing the beliefs of our faith." In this koan collection we have the epitome of poetic achievement in Zen literature. Through his writings, Hsüeh-tou contributed to the restoration of the House of Yün-men, which had fallen into a state of decline at the time. The house did not survive, however, as an independent school; during the Song period it was absorbed into the powerful Rinzai school.

FA-YEN: THE INTERPENETRATION OF ATTRIBUTES

The House of Fa-yen, the last of the Five Houses, was short-lived. The name Fa-yen derives from the posthumous title its founder was given by his friend and patron, Prince Li Ching (916–961), a local lord in South China. Fa-yen Wen-i (885–958), the founder of the last of the Five Houses, centered his activity in a politically and culturally important center in the South, located on the site of present-day Nan-ching. Many disciples came to the monastery of Seiryo-ji (Chin., *Ch'in-liang-ssu*) to hear this master so well versed in both the Chinese and Buddhist classics; with confidence they entrusted themselves to his sure and gentle guidance. His psychological insight and clever versatility were widely reputed.

Despite his high intellectual cultivation, Fa-yen adopted an authentically Zen style and passed it on as such to his followers. While he did not pounce upon his students and strike them with his staff, he did give them answers of extraordinary precision and power. His favorite method was pure Zen—simply to repeat the words of a question or remark, without any explanation. An illustration from the *Keitoku dentoroku* gives an idea of the method at work. Fa-yen asked his companion, Shao-hsiu, what this saying of the ancients meant: "A slight differentiation causes a separation as between heaven and earth." Shao-hsiu replied: "A slight differentiation causes a separation as between heaven and earth." The master asked: "How can your interpretation hold good?" Shao-hsiu asked: "What is yours?" The master replied: "A slight differentiation causes a separation between heaven and earth." Numerous such examples have come down to us in the writings of Zen, as well as a large number of striking answers in the typical Zen style. For example:

> "What should one do during the twelve hours of day and night?"—"Every step should tread on this question."

In offering his students such teachings and responses, Master Fa-yen stood in the best of Zen tradition.

In the House of Fa-yen, the Kegon worldview occupied an even more prominent place than it did in other Zen schools. The master studied Kegon scriptures intensively, and had his disciples read the works of the patriarchs Tu-shun (557–640) and Fa-tsang (643–712). Fa-yen well understood the interpenetration of the six attributes of being: totality and differentiation, sameness and difference, becoming and passing away. These attributes, illustrated by a circle, represent different aspects of reality that are neither identical nor different. Fa-yen explains:

The meaning of the six attributes of Kegon is that within sameness there is difference. For difference to be different from sameness is in no way the intention of all the Buddhas. The intention of all the Buddhas is both totality and differentiation. How can there be both sameness and difference? When a male body enters *samadhi*, a female body is indifferent to it. When there is indifference terms are transcended. When the ten thousand appearances are utterly bright, there is neither reality *[li; Jpn., ri]* nor appearance *[shih; Jpn., ji]*.

By contemplating a circle in which the six attributes are written, one can come to an experience of this doctrine of oneness.

The basic insight of the Kegon school concerning "difference in sameness" and "sameness in difference" is illustrated in an episode from the life of Fa-yen, recorded in characteristic Zen style, that was later to become a famous koan in the *Mumonkan* collection:

> The monks gathered in the hall to hear the great Fa-yen of Ch'ing-liang give *teisho* [instruction in Dharma] before the midday meal. Fa-yen pointed to the bamboo blinds. At this two monks went to the blinds and rolled them up alike. Fa-yen said, "One has it, the other has not."

Wu-men comments that the master may have failed—a comment intended to push students more deeply into the koan's meaning. If the surface of the episode communicates "difference in sameness," its underside contains "sameness in difference." What matters is that one overcomes duality.

Fa-yen carried on the methods of the T'ang Zen masters. He loved paradoxes and aimed at inducing sudden enlightenment. Thus his bonds with the heritage of the Zen tradition are undeniable. Moreover, a brief overview of his school reveals that it planted the seeds for later developments in Chinese Zen Buddhism.

Fa-yen's Dharma heir, T'ien-t'ai Te-shao (891–971), continued to guide the House of Fa-yen, but not along a straight Zen line. After he had achieved enlightenment and acquired a significant following, he turned to the teachings of the T'ien-t'ai school, which, after the confusion of the time of the Five Dynasties, had suffered considerable decline in popularity. Enjoying the favor of the local prince, T'ien-t'ai Te-shao was appointed to the office of regional teacher in the southern princedom of Wu-yüeh, a center and catalyst for cultural development during the Song period. His two disciples, Yung-ming Yen-shou (904–975) and Tao-yüan (dates unknown), played important roles, in very different ways, in subsequent Zen history.

Yung-ming introduced a development that truly bore fruit only later. This "famous and enthusiastic syncretist" was ahead of his time in attempting a comprehensive synthesis of all Buddhist teachings. This he proposed in his extensive work, the *Sugyoroku* (Chin., *Tsung-ching lu*). He recited the *Lotus Sutra* and combined the recitation of the name of Amitabha Buddha (Jpn., *nembutsu*; Chin., *nien-fo*) with his Zen practice. Listed as the first patriarch of the Pure Land school during the Song period, the magnanimous and learned Yung-ming may be considered the pioneer of the unification movement between Zen and the *nembutsu* tradition, a movement that was later to gain the upper hand in Chinese Buddhism.

Tao-yüan's work, on the other hand, was to become a cornerstone in the history of genuine Chinese Zen. The chronicle he compiled, the *Keitoku dentoroku*, marks, with its extensive account of all the Zen masters and their projects, the close of a certain period in the history of the formation and expansion of Zen in China. At the same time, it provided a wealth of materials that laid the foundations for the so-called koan-Zen that was soon to develop. Most of the koan in the collections stem from Tao-yüan's chronicle either directly or indirectly. Unfortunately, we known very little of his activity. In the House of Fa-yen, especially through Fa-yen's work, the *Shumon jikki-ron*, the period of the Five Houses was brought to clear self-consciousness. Fa-yen proved to be such a convincing advocate for his house that even the preeminent Confucian Chu Hsi, otherwise no friend of Buddhism, could offer him nothing but unequivocal praise.

The roots of the Five Houses of Chinese Zen reach back to the era of transition during the second half of the T'ang period. This was the time of the great and original Zen masters, in whose lineage the Five Houses were formed. Without introducing any essential changes, the houses articulated particularities and differences that would influence the further development of Zen history. The Five Houses also formed a bridge to the second flowering of Chinese Zen during the Song period.

The "Short-cut" Approach of K'an-hua Meditation

Robert E. Buswell, Jr.

Two of the earliest Ch'an masters to use *kung-an* in instructing their students were Yün-men Wen-yen (d. 949), the founder of the Yün-men school, and Fen-yang Shan-chao (947–1024), who revived what was at that time a moribund Lin-chi school. Fen-yang himself compiled three separate collections of *kung-an* in his *Record*: one hundred "old cases" *(ku-tse)* with explanatory verses by Fen-yang; one hundred original *kung-an* by Fen-yang himself, to which he appended his own answers; and one hundred old cases with Fen-yang's alternate answers.

It is of course the Lin-chi school that is most closely associated with the use of *kung-an*, and the majority of *kung-an* anthologies belong to that school. The largest of these anthologies is the *Blue Cliff Record (Pi-yen lu)*, compiled in final form by Yüan-wu K'o-ch'in (1063–1135), a tenth-generation Lin-chi successor who belonged to the collateral Yang-ch'i lineage of that school. The *Blue Cliff Record* itself is an expansion and elaboration of an earlier work by Hsüeh-tou Ch'ung-hsien (980–1052) entitled *One Hundred Cases and Verses to the Old [Cases] (Po-tse song-ku)*, a collection of one hundred anecdotes concerning earlier Ch'an masters to which Hsüeh-tou appended explanatory verses and annotation. Some sixty years later, Yüan-wu added his own introductory "pointers" to each case along with further explanation of, and commentaries to, both the case and Hsüeh-tou's verses, to form his larger anthology. A typical case in the *Blue Cliff Record* begins with a "pointer" by Yüan-wu to direct the student toward the important issue raised in the *kung-an*; this is followed by the *kung-an* itself, with Yüan-wu's interlinear notes, and a concluding commentary to the verses, also

by Yüan-wu. A more complex genre of literature can hardly be imagined, rivaling any of the exegetical commentaries of the doctrinal schools.
These collections of stories, most of which were compiled during the
Song dynasty, constitute one of the largest bodies of writings of any of
the Chinese schools of Buddhism. Any pretense Ch'an may have still
retained about being a teaching that "did not rely on words and letters"
was hardly supportable given the rapid proliferation of such anthologies
within different teaching lineages.

The compilation of *kung-an* collections, with their distinctive language and style, illustrates the tendency in Song dynasty Ch'an toward
refined literary activity, which was termed "lettered Ch'an"(*wentzu*
Ch'an). These literary endeavors helped to bring Ch'an into the main-
stream of Chinese cultural life and also led to a fertile interchange
between Ch'an and secular *belles lettres*. But this tendency toward
greater and greater erudition was also anathema to later teachers in the
Lin-chi school; if Ch'an "did not rely on words and letters," what was the
need for these massive anthologies of Ch'an works? Yüan-wu's own successor, Ta-hui Tsung-kao (1089–1163), vehemently lashed out at Song
wen-tzu Ch'an, as epitomized in his teacher's *Blue Cliff Record*, for fos-
tering, he claimed, the mistaken idea that Ch'an was merely clever repar-
tee and elegant verse. In perhaps the ultimate expression of contempt for
this literary type of Ch'an, Ta-hui, according to legend, tried to keep the
Blue Cliff Record out of circulation by having the xylographs from which
it was printed burned.

Unfortunately the notoriety of Ta-hui's provocative action with
regard to his teacher's writings has tended to obscure the revolutionary
step made by Yüan-wu in the use of *kung-an*. Yüan-wu was apparently
the first to teach that *kung-an* were not simply the dead records of an
exchange between ancient Ch'an masters, and thus suitably the focus of
literary endeavors. Rather, they should be used as if they were directly
pointing to the mind of each and every individual—that is, as a statement
of immediate, contemporary relevance guiding one toward enlightenment. As Yüan-wu warns in his Hsin-yao *(Essentials of Mind):* "Do not
look for the living roads in the words and phrases, bury yourself in the
kung-an of the ancients, or make a stratagem for living in the ghost cave
or beneath the dark mountain. It is important only to access awakening

and have profound realization." Despite the number of *kung-an* that had been compiled in anthologies like his own *Blue Cliff Record*, Yüan-wu insisted that any one case represented all other cases, since each was a presentation of a Ch'an master's enlightened mind. Hence, a single *kung-an* contained all the past and present teachings of Buddhism and Ch'an and was sufficient in itself to bring the student to awakening. As Yüan-wu states: "If one generates understanding and accesses awakening through a single phrase [i.e., the *hua-t'ou*], a single encounter, or a single object, then immeasurable, innumerable functions and *kung-an* are simultaneously penetrated."

This change in the concept of the *kung-an* was crystallized with Yüan-wu. And with Ta-hui fully elaborating the viewpoint of his teacher, *kung-an* emerged not as literary foils but as contemplative tools for realizing one's own innate enlightenment. Hence, through the influence of Yüan-wu and Ta-hui the proliferation of *kung-an* collections eventually slowed as the need to consider a multitude of ancient cases in the course of one's training was obviated in the radical reduction of Ch'an meditation to looking into *(k'an)* but a single *kung-an*.

Chung-feng Ming-pen (1263–1323), a Yüan dynasty Ch'an monk in the Mi-an branch of Yüan-wu's line, describes the use of the *kung-an* as a catalyst for enlightenment in one of the most renowned passages of Ch'an literature:

> The *kung-an* is something that can be used only by men with enlightened minds who wish to prove their understanding. They are certainly not intended to be used merely to increase one's lore and provide topics for idle discussion. The so-called venerable masters of Ch'an are the chief officials of the public law courts of the monastic community, as it were, and their collections of sayings are the case records of points that have been vigorously advocated. Occasionally men of former times, in the intervals when they were not teaching, in spare moments when their doors were closed, would take up these cases and arrange them, give their judgment on them, compose verses of praise on them and write their own answers to them. Surely they did not

do this just to show off their erudition and contradict the
worthy men of old. Rather . . . they stooped to using expedient means in order to open the wisdom eye of men of later
generations, hoping thereby to make it possible for them to
attain the understanding of the great dharma for themselves in the same way.

In *kung-an* investigation, according to Ta-hui, rather than reflect over
the entire *kung-an* exchange, which could lead the mind to distraction,
one should instead zero in on the principal topic, or most essential element, of that exchange, which he terms its "critical phrase" *(hua-t'ou)*.
Ta-hui called this new approach to meditation *k'an-hua* Ch'an—the
Ch'an of observing the critical phrase—and alleged that it was a "short-
cut" leading to instantaneous enlightenment.

The distinction between *kung-an* investigation as a pedagogical tool
and *k'an-hua* practice as a meditative technique can be illustrated by
examining the *kung-an* Ta-hui most often taught: the *wu* (J. *mu*) of
Chao-chou (J. Joshu) Ts'ung-shen (778–897).

Once a monk asked Chao-chou, "Does a dog have Buddha-nature or
not?" Chao-chou replied "No!" *(wu)*.

The entire exchange between Chao-chou and his pupil would constitute the *kung-an*, while its "critical phrase," or "principal topic" *(hua-
t'ou)*, would be just the word "no." Because Chao-chou's answer
contradicts the most fundamental tenet of sinitic Buddhist doctrine,
which insisted that the Buddha-nature is innate in all sentient beings,
investigating the reply "no" provides a jolt to the students' ordinary
ways of thinking. Single-minded attention to that one word "no" then
creates an introspective focus that eventually leads the meditator back to
the minds' enlightened source—a process that Ch'an terms "tracing back
the radiance emanating from the mind." Once the student has recovered
his mind's source by this counter-illumination, he will know the intent
with which Chao-chou made his response—and, by extension, the
enlightened mind that framed that intent—and will consummate in himself the very same state of enlightenment. Looking into the *hua-t'ou* thus
leads to the non-dual, enlightened source of the mind from which all discriminative thought arises. The adept can then act as Chao-chou and will

understand all the *kung-an* intuitively. Hence, in this new method, *hua-t'ou* practice seeks to emulate the enlightened mind of previous masters, not to explain (by literary means) the meaning of their remarks. It is as if the student were instructed to pattern his mind after that of the enlightened master who appears in the *kung-an* until they think as one.

It may seem curious that Lin-chi Ch'an, after developing a style of teaching that was less reliant on conceptual explanation, should ultimately embrace a contemplative technique that explicitly employs words, especially when compared with standard Indian meditative approaches that made no recourse to language, such as following the breath or visualizing the parts of the body. It is therefore worth reiterating that Ch'an considered the *hua-t'ou*, or meditative locutions, to be "live words" *(huo-chü)*, because they lead to awakening, and the conceptual teaching of the doctrinal schools "dead words" *(su-chü)*, because they led only to intellectual understanding. Yüan-wu warns: "Examine the live word; don't examine the dead word. One who adheres utterly to the live word will not forget for an eternity of eons. One who adheres utterly to the dead word will never be able to save himself. If you want to take the patriarchs and Buddhas as your masters, you must clearly choose the live word." Cha'n words, such as those that appear in a *hua-t'ou*, were thus conceived of as a form of spiritual homeopathy, using a minimal, but potent, dosage of the "poison of words" to cure the malady of conceptualization. Hsü-yün (1840–1949), a renowned Ch'an master of the Chinese Republican era, explains:

> The message of the Ch'an sect prior to the T'ang and Song dynasties was contained in one phrase of half a line, "understand the mind, see one's nature" which brought realization of the path. The transmission from master to disciple involved nothing more than "stamping" [the master's] mind on the mind [of his disciple]. There was no other technique. Ordinarily, the disciple would ask for instruction and the master would reply. [The master] just used the appropriate technique to release [the disciple] from his bonds, as for an illness one prescribes medicine.

After the Song period, the capacity of people degenerated, and while they were taught, they wouldn't do anything. For example, if told to "renounce everything," or "do not have thoughts of good and evil," they would not renounce anything, and thought not of the good, but only of the evil. At that time, the patriarchs and teachers, from unavoidable necessity, *selected a method that used poison to counteract poison* [emphasis added]. They taught students to investigate the *kung-an* and to observe the *hua-t'ou*.

A *kung-an* or *hua-t'ou* was therefore conceived of as nothing more than an expedient; there was absolutely nothing arcane or mystical about it. Its purpose was simply "to open up the eyes of patched-robed monks of this world." Anything in fact could serve the same purpose as the *hua-t'ou* in catalyzing the experience of awakening; a story of an ancient master's enlightenment, the scriptures of Buddhism, even the ordinary activities of day-to-day life. As an expedient, the *hua-t'ou* had no ultimate meaning, and there was no specific, predetermined answer to the *kung-an* such as the Japanese Rinzai tradition is commonly portrayed as expecting.

The reader might wonder at this point whether calling the *hua-t'ou* an expedient contradicts the Lin-chi claim that *k'an-hua* Ch'an is a sudden approach to enlightenment. This is not the case. One common simile for sudden cultivation, which Ta-hui uses in his own writings, is that of an archer shooting arrows at a target: even though it may take thousands of attempts before his aim is accurate and he is able to hit the bull's-eye consistently, it is the same act of shooting that is repeated time and again. The repeated observation of the *hua-t'ou* (shooting the arrows) will catalyze awakening (hitting the target consistently) but that result does not occur after progressive development through a series of stages. It is worth noting that much of traditional Chinese apprenticeship took place in the same way, learning to do the whole job properly over a long period of time rather than mastering a series of smaller steps. Ta-hui himself is extremely careful to avoid any implication that *k'an-hua* Ch'an involves any sort of graduated progress. Ta-hui does mention different experiences that are engendered by observing the *hua-t'ou*, such as perplexity, bursting, power, and interfusion. But while such experiences may be called "constantly illuminating in silence" or "a person who experiences the

Great Death," or "an event that occurs before your parents are born," or "an event that occurs before the void-eon," Ta-hui warns that these are merely different perspectives from which *hua-t'ou* investigation may be described depending on the aspiration and talent of the individual, not stages that are invariably undergone on the way toward enlightenment.

Further, while the conceptual form of a *hua-t'ou* may involve linguistic convention, it is still a "live word" because it is designed to lead to an experience of ultimate validity. Hence it is not the expedient that renders a soteriology either sudden or gradual, but the attachment thereto. As Ta-hui says, "While one can access the path through the gate of the expedients, it is a sickness to conserve expedients and not discard them." If anything, Ta-hui views *hua-t'ou* as a "sudden" expedient, intended to catalyze an equally "sudden" awakening.

The purpose of the *hua-t'ou*, then, is to enable the student to transcend the dualistic processes of thought in a single moment of insight, without requiring that he "progress gradually through a series of steps or stages." For this reason Ta-hui refers to *k'an-hua* Ch'an as a "short-cut" approach to meditation:

> If you want to understand the principle of the short-cut, you must in one fell swoop break through this one thought—then and only then will you comprehend birth and death. Then and only then will it be called accessing awakening....You need only lay down, all at once, the mind full of deluded thoughts and inverted thinking, the mind of logical discrimination, the mind that loves life and hates death, the mind of knowledge and views, interpretation and comprehension, and the mind that rejoices in stillness and turns from disturbance.

Any kind of intellectualization of the *hua-t'ou*, any attempt to understand it in terms of ordinary conceptual thought, was repeatedly denied by Ta-hui. The significance of this warning becomes especially clear when Ta-hui's intimate associations with the powerful Song intelligentsia are taken into account. Ta-hui admonished these members of this elite class that the intellectual abilities they had cultivated throughout their careers could themselves become the most implacable of obstacles to enlightenment.

> Nowadays the literati *(shih-ta-fu)*, despite a hundred attempts or a thousand tries, are never able to experience direct penetration of this matter. This is solely due to the fact that their natures are too clever and their opinions too multifarious. When they meet a master of our school, as soon as he opens his mouth and flaps his tongue they immediately presume that they understand. Therefore it would actually be much better for them to be stupid, without so much evil understanding and evil awareness.... The clever are actually obstructed by their cleverness, and can't gain a sudden breakthrough.

Ta-hui repeatedly cautions his learned students not even to try to resolve the *hua-t'ou*; instead they should just give up the conceit that they have the intellectual tools that would allow them to understand it. This admonition Ta-hui reiterates in his advice on how to proceed with the contemplation of several different *hua-t'ou*. With reference to Yün-men's "dry shit stick," Ta-hui warns, "When you examine this, don't use your usual intelligence and perspicacity." Discussing Chao-chou's "cypress tree in the courtyard," Ta-hui remarks, "Suddenly with regard to this cypress tree, the mind and mind-consciousness will come to an end and the breath will stop. This is where the *[hua-]t'ou* is penetrated." Ta-hui has even listed some eight defects in the examination of Chao-chou's "no," several of which involve the use of the rational mind to determine the meaning of the *hua-t'ou*. Thus there is nothing that the student can ultimately understand about the *hua-t'ou* as long as he employs his habitual processes of thought; in perhaps the ultimate paradox, it is only when he finally abandons all attempts to understand the *hua-t'ou* that its real significance becomes clear.

In these descriptions of the central place that nonconceptualization occupies in *k'an-hua* Ch'an, we have further intimation of the subitist character of this approach to meditation. *K'an-hua* Ch'an is termed a "short-cut" because it does not require a gradual unfolding of truth, but can be understood in a single instant of insight. Echoing Ma-tsu's conception of a cultivation that is simultaneously perfected in one overwhelming experience of awakening, Ta-hui too says: "Understanding one is understanding all; awakening to one is awakening to all; realizing one is realizing all. It's like slicing through a spool of thread: with one stroke all its strands are simultaneously cut. Realizing limitless teachings is just the same: there is no sequence whatsoever." There is nothing that need be developed; all the student must do is simply renounce both the hope that there is something that can be achieved through the practice as well as the conceit that he will achieve that result.

This state beyond hope, where "there is no place to put one's hands and feet," Ta-hui remarks, "is really a good place." It is a "good place" because it is there that conceptualization is brought to an end: "Without debate and ratiocination they are at a loss, with no place to put their hands and feet." Only then can the student make the all-important transition from the conditioned to the unconditioned, which is likened to a death-defying "leap off a hundred-foot pole." One need only recall the role of no-thought as the access to final realization-awakening to see how thoroughly that earlier account of meditation has been subsumed by the *hua-t'ou* technique.

The leap off the hundred-foot pole from the conditioned to the unconditioned is perhaps the quintessential expression of what Ch'an means by a sudden style of cultivation and meditation. Sudden cultivation demands that there be no hint of any sequence of practices that would lead the student from one stage to another, progressively abandoning defilements and cultivating wholesome actions, until he achieves perfect purity of mind. The jump off the hundred-foot pole suggests the radical nonattachment, even to one's own body and mind, that Buddhism has always expected as a prerequisite to enlightenment. Ch'an does not deny that it might take time for one to build up the courage necessary to take that ultimate plunge. But its lack of sequence at least freed it from charges of being gradualistic.

Ta-hui's interpretation of "sudden cultivation" is perhaps even more radical than was Ma-tsu's earlier description based on spontaneity. Both claim that total relinquishment, which is final enlightenment, cannot be achieved by undertaking any kind of practice. But whereas

Ma-tsu stresses the need "to be free of defilement" and "spontaneous,"
Ta-hui refuses even to posit the necessity of maintaining an undefiled
state, which the ordinary person might find daunting. For Ta-hui, nothing at all need be perfected to achieve enlightenment: not purity, not
samadhi or prajna, not even the bare faith of Lin-chi. Ta-hui insists
instead that the practice must begin and end amid the typical afflictions
of ordinary life—especially ignorance, delusion, insecurity and stress.
K'an-hua Ch'an in fact encourages the student to foster all the confusion and perplexity he can muster, for it was expected that the ordinary
person, when first faced with the *hua-t'ou*, would indeed be puzzled as
to its significance. This puzzlement is what Lin-chi Ch'an terms the
"sensation of doubt" *(i-ch'ing)*, and building that sensation is the main
purpose of investigating the *hua-t'ou*. This peculiar Ch'an emphasis on
doubt had a rather long history by Ta-hui's time. One of the earliest
usages of the term appears in the enlightenment poem of Lo-han Kuei-
ch'en (867–928), the teacher of Fa-yen Wen-i (885–958), who refers to
enlightenment as shattering the "ball of doubt" *(i-t'uan)*. Ta-hui's
grandteacher, Wu-tsu Fa-yen (1024?–1104), also taught his students to
keep the great ball of doubt. But it was Ta-hui who drew out the full
implications of this idea, making it the core of his approach to formal
meditation practice.

Doubt is the perplexity the student feels from his inability to resolve
the riddle of the *kung-an*. Doubt acts as the force that pressures the mind
to break out of the complacency engendered by its habitual ways of
thinking. Doubt places the person at a disconcerting loss, for he soon finds
that his ordinary ratiocinative processes are inadequate to the task of
penetrating the *hua-t'ou*. Because the person ordinarily assumes that he
is "in control" (a notion attacked in Buddhism's virulent critiques of the-
ologies positing an eternal self, or *atman*), the insecurity created by the
hua-t'ou becomes frustrating and unnerving, a feeling likened to "a mos-
quito atop an iron ox." But it is precisely this sensation of doubt that *hua-
t'ou* are intended to produce, and after it is present, their purpose is
fulfilled.

When doubt becomes unqualified, it and the *hua t'ou* become indis-
tinguishable; as the Korean Son monk T'aego Pou (1301–1382) says,
"The doubt and the *hwadu (hua-t'ou)* fuse into one." From this point

continued investigation of the doubt-cum-*hua-t'ou* will eventually trap the mind in an unmoving state of perfect concentration. That is to say, when the sense of frustration over one's inability to resolve the *hua-t'ou* through ordinary logic has brought an end to random thought, intense one-pointedness of mind is engendered, which eventually produces the experience of no-thought. Ta-hui compared this state of being existentially, implacably "stuck" to a rat stuck in the narrowing taper of a cow's-horn trap, burrowing ever deeper to get at some oil placed inside its tip, until finally the rat is caught.

The power of doubt in cutting off conceptualization is stressed repeatedly by Ta-hui: doubt is that state of perplexity "where intellect cannot operate and thought cannot reach; it is the road through which discrimination is eradicated and theorizing ended. [Doubt makes the mind] puzzled, frustrated, and tasteless [i.e., lacking in any intellectual interest]—just as if you were gnawing on an iron bar." Kao-feng Yüan-miao (1238–1295), a Yüan dynasty master in the Mi-an branch of the Lin-chi school, and teacher of Chung-feng Ming-pen, clarifies how doubt leads to a state of no-thought:

> As the sensation of doubt is perfected little by little, there then is no mind that initiates actions. And once there is no mind that initiates actions, the objects of thought are then forgotten. This ensures that the myriads of conditions naturally expire, but without bringing them to an end. The six windows [of the senses] are naturally calmed, but without calming them. Without countering the dust [of sensory objects] one suddenly accesses the no-mind Samadhi.

Ta-hui interprets the story of Bodhidharma's instruction to his disciple Hui-k'o (487–593) as a paradigm of the way Ch'an statements are intended to frustrate the mundane mind of the student so thoroughly that they serve as a catalyst for supramundane awakening. Bodhidharma first instructed Hui-k'o, "Bring all conditioning to rest outside, and keep the mind without panting inside." "But," Ta-hui explains, "Hui-k'o quoted texts and thereby sought certification. For this reason, Bodhidharma rejected each and every one of his statements; finally, when there was no place left [for Hui-k'o] to use his mind, he was able to step back and consider [those words]…. Suddenly, all conditioning was ended, and he then saw the moon and forgot the finger."

As the story illustrates, the sensation of doubt must become all-consuming. In such a state, all the perplexities of everyday life are rolled into one existential "great doubt" *(ta-i)*, produced through examining the *hua-t'ou*. As Ta-hui says, "Whether a thousand doubts or a myriad doubts, they are all just one doubt. If you break through your doubt concerning the *hua-t'ou*, then a thousand or myriad doubts are all abruptly destroyed."

Ta-hui viewed the unique rhetoric of Ch'an in the same way. In the only *kung-an* ascribed to him personally, he illustrates the distinctive use of Ch'an language.

> If you call this a bamboo comb, you are stuck to it. If you don't call this a bamboo comb, you have turned your back to it. Don't speak, but don't stay silent. Do not cogitate and do not guess. Do not shake your sleeves [in disapproval] and walk out. Anything you do is wrong…. Once I was likened to an official who confiscated all of someone's wealth and property and then demanded still more. I find this analogy particularly sublime. Truly, I demand that you hand over everything. When you have nowhere to escape, you will have to beg to take the road of death. Throwing yourself into the river or jumping into fire, you will die when your time comes. Only after you are dead will you gradually come back to life.

Because mental stress and existential quandary were exactly the states that Ta-hui sought to foster through *k'an-hua* Ch'an, it is no surprise that he embraced ordinary life as the ideal venue for Buddhist meditation practice. Alluding to the simile drawn by Vimalakirti, the quintessential Mahayana lay adept, he says, "The high plains do not produce lotus flowers: it is the mud of the lowlying marshlands that produces these flowers." But Ta-hui's vision of the ordinary, afflicted condition of humankind as the way to enlightenment is a radical departure even for Mahayana Buddhism. Ta-hui saw the world as the ideal training ground for religious practice because it provided a plethora of situations in which frustration, doubting, and insecurity would appear—all weapons in the arsenal of *hua-t'ou* meditation. Moreover, the obstacles facing the householder were so ubiquitous and seductive (sex, wealth, fame, and so on, ad infinitum) that a person who was able to withstand them developed a tremendous "dynamism" or "power" that was far superior to that of a sequestered monk, who faced few obstacles in his daily practice and so needed to expend only a modicum of effort to overcome them.

For Ta-hui, dynamism plays a pivotal role in consummating the process of *hua-t'ou* investigation because it is the energy that shakes the student loose from everything he had identified with previously. And again, it is by living in the world, yet remaining detached, that one develops dynamism: "As soon as you become aware of gradually conserving power in the midst of the dusty afflictions of daily life, this then will be where you gain power. This is how you achieve Buddhahood and become a patriarch." If, on the other hand, the student permits himself to become entangled in worldly affairs, he loses his dynamism by allowing his energy to become dissipated in mundane distractions and wandering thoughts.

Given the prominent place of faith in earlier Ch'an thought, as exemplified by Lin-chi, it is rather striking the extent to which Ta-hui has deemphasized faith in favor of doubt. While there are passages in Ta-hui's writings where he does acknowledge the role of faith as a support of practice, he seems on the whole to have had a rather poor opinion of the prospects of the ordinary person attempting to rely on faith. More typically, Ta-hui maintains that practice has its inception in doubt, is enhanced through dynamism and the application of effort, and develops into faith only as those preceding factors mature. In his "directive" to the nun Miao-yüan, for example, Ta-hui says: "If you want to transcend birth and death and cross the sea of suffering, you must raise straight the banner of effort. Directly beneath it, faith will become sufficient. Only where this faith has become sufficient will the event take place of transcending birth and death and crossing the sea of suffering."

To succeed in *hua-t'ou* practice, a strong sense of urgency about one's practice, rather than faith, is what is first required. In a refrain found frequently in his writings, Ta-hui says: "You should constantly paste the two words 'birth' and 'death' on your forehead. Whether drinking tea or eating rice, when sitting or lying down, when directing the servants, when coordinating your household affairs, when happy and when angry, when walking and when standing, when entertaining guests—[throughout all these events those two words] must not be removed." Ta-hui even goes so far as to dismiss the need for faith, since diligent practice will corroborate the teachings of Buddhism whether one begins by believing them or not. Ta-hui's emphasis on the place of effort eventually became the "great zeal" discussed by Kao-feng Yüan-miao in his *Essentials of Ch'an (Ch'an-yao)*, a synopsis of Ch'an practice that enjoyed a wide currency in the post-classical Ch'an schools of the Yüan and Ming dynasties. In that text great faith, great zeal, and great doubt are treated together as the "three essentials" of *k'an-hua* Ch'an.

> Through the application of effort, then, the doubt engendered by the *hua-t'ou* becomes so intense that all distracting thoughts come to an end. When this condition is reached a final "burst" is all that is needed to catalyze the experience of enlightenment. In other words, when the "one great doubt" produced with reference to a single *hua-t'ou* becomes the locus around which all other doubts accumulate, intense pressure is generated on the meditator's intellectual processes and on his own sense of self-identity and self-worth. The coalescence of all the meditator's thoughts and actions into that doubt—which resonates with the connotation of "absorption" (samadhi) in Sino-Indian Buddhism—produces the power (here, almost the courage) necessary to abandon himself seemingly to ultimate disaster: his own personal destruction. When the student's consummate dynamism carries him beyond the point where he can cope with the pressure created by the doubt, the doubt explodes, annihilating the student's identification with body and mind. While ordinary language may be unable to describe this achievement, it is an experience that is readily available to all; Ta-hui compares it to "a man drinking water: he himself knows whether it is cold or warm."

The explosion of the doubt destroys the bifurcating tendencies of thought as well. Whereas previously all of one's experiences were seen to revolve around one's self, and interpreted as either self or other, through *k'an-hua* practice the mind opens into a new, all-inclusive perspective from which the limiting "point of view" that is the ego is eliminated. Awareness now has no fixed locus. The distinctions ordinarily perceived between self and other disappear, and consciousness expands infinitely, encompassing the entire universe both spatially and temporally: "Throughout boundless world systems, oneself and others are not separated by as much as the tip of a hair; the ten time periods of past and present, from beginning to end, are not separate from the present thought-moment."

This expansive vision restores the perfect clarity of mind, and all actions become expressions of the enlightened mind:

> A patriarch [Bodhidharma] said, "If mind and conscious-ness are quiescent and extinct, without a single thought stirring, this is called right enlightenment." Once enlightenment is right, then throughout the twenty-four hours of your daily activities, when seeing forms, hearing sounds, smelling scents, tasting flavors, feeling sensations, or knowing mental objects, whether walking or standing, sitting or lying down, where speaking or silent, active or still, there's nothing that is not clear.... Once you've attained purity, when active you manifest the function of clarity, and when inactive you return to the essence of clarity.

In seeing the macrocosm of the universe reflected in the microcosm of the individual, the Ch'an conception of enlightenment is framed in terms evocative of the *summum bonum* of Hua-yen philosophy, the "multivalent interfusion of all phenomena." Moreover, as the consummation of a practical subitism, the *k'an-hua* technique epitomizes the Chinese conception of the immanence of enlightenment within the mundane world.

K'an-hua Ch'an may thus be viewed as one of several products of the sinification of Buddhism, whereby the highest reaches of Buddhist spirituality were made accessible to Chinese adherents of both lay and monastic persuasions. Its evolution was prompted by critiques of Sino-Indian meditative concepts and hastened by the rhetorical and pedagogical experimentation that occurred during the middle Ch'an period. The *k'an-hua* technique, as standardized during the classical Ch'an period, exemplifies the Hung-chou conception of a "spontaneous" practice which is perfected not through a graduated regimen of cultivation but through instantaneous insight; and Song accounts of *hua-t'ou* investigation purport to be a definitive enunciation of the soteriology of sudden awakening—sudden cultivation, in which all traces of "gradualism" have been rigorously excised. *Hua-t'ou* meditation thus emerges as a practical application of the subitist teachings that had been the hallmark of the Ch'an school since early in its history.

K'an-hua Ch'an became virtually synonymous with Lin-chi practice from Ta-hui's time onward, and the approach was transmitted to Korea within a generation and, some decades later, to Japan. Understanding the theoretical foundations of this technique is therefore vital not only for drawing out the wider implications of the meaning of sudden enlightenment in Chinese Ch'an, but also for comprehending the subsequent evolution of Ch'an throughout East Asia. In the final analysis, *k'an-hua* Ch'an did not evolve because of the degeneration of the pristine message of some elusive Ch'an "golden age," but instead was the consummation of forces set in motion centuries before, propelled by the sudden-gradual debate.

KOAN PRACTICE

William M. Bodiford

MEDIEVAL SOTO MONKS and nuns mastered the depths of Zen enlightenment, the trivial moments of daily life, and the routine activities of monastic training through the language of the Chinese Ch'an patriarchs as recorded in koan texts. This specialized idiom allowed Zen teachers and students to describe different approaches to practice, various states of meditation, and fine distinctions between points of view or levels of understanding. More important, koan study—like ordination rituals and funeral ceremonies—encapsulated Zen transcendence in tangible forms, expressed it in concrete performances, and allowed it to be communicated easily to monks, nuns, and laypersons. For clerics and villagers alike this body of Zen praxis fused together the symbolic transmission of the Buddha's enlightenment, its embodiment in the words and actions of the Zen master, with the worlds lived and imagined, both inside and outside the monastery. While koan training, ordination rituals, and funeral ceremonies comprise only three of the Zen practices performed by medieval Soto monks, each proved indispensable for the rapid growth of Soto institutions and the religious efficacy of these institutions within rural society.

Today leading Soto scholars regard the medieval period of Soto history as the dark ages *(ankoku jidai)* when "true Soto" Zen practices were all but forgotten. They cite the rapid institutional expansion as evidence of rampant compromise with folk religious customs. They abhor a perceived overemphasis on koan training as a deviation from Dogen's method of Zen practice. Certainly it is true that few medieval Soto temples produced significant doctrinal commentaries on Dogen's writings, and most temples served the religious needs of local patrons in ways that no longer attract much empathy. Modern criticisms by Soto leaders,

however, do an injustice to the religious world of their medieval predecessors who neither abandoned Zen practice nor lost their religious identity. In fact, medieval Soto monks engaged in koan training, ordination
rituals, and funeral ceremonies to emulate and identify themselves with
Zen traditions, to preserve their sectarian identity, and ultimately to
transform Zen monastic rituals in ways that more readily met a variety
of social and religious needs.

It is also true that Dogen criticized certain aspects of koan training.
But there is no doubt that Dogen himself trained in and taught his students systematic methods of koan investigation. His teachings cannot be
comprehended without intimate knowledge of Chinese koan; he quotes
more than 580 of them. An investigation into Dogen's approach to koan
training, its methods and psychology, or its ultimate significance within
his overall conception of Zen practice is beyond the scope of this study.
Nor would it contribute significantly to our present task, which is to see
how koan training functioned in the context of medieval religious life.
The average Soto monk in medieval times enjoyed neither Dogen's educational background nor his linguistic skills. The vast majority could not
follow in Dogen's footsteps and travel to China, study directly under a
Chinese teacher, or immerse themselves in a Chinese cultural environment. Other means had to be developed to preserve and transmit the distinctive features of the Chinese approach to Buddhist training that
Ch'an represented. In many ways the mysterious sophistication and
religious potency of Ch'an language proved the most irresistible feature
of all.

KOAN STUDY IN EARLY JAPANESE ZEN

The Japanese adoption of Zen as a Chinese-style religious institution
entailed the mastery of the literary and artistic fashions of Song dynasty
China, not just religious adjustments. All the trappings of Zen monastic
life, from the architecture and decoration of monastic buildings to the
proper etiquette of washing one's face, were more foreign to Japanese
monks than the practice of sitting in meditation. Koan training proved
to be no exception to this general pattern. The proper form and conduct
of the teaching process had to be mastered just as much as the religious

content conveyed by the koan. Moreover, the koan were taught and written in a specialized language even more foreign than the literary Chinese employed in traditional Buddhist scriptures.

Scholars typically explain the development of koan discourse as a Chinese rejection of abstract Indian terminology in favor of simple, concrete expressions. It is ironic, therefore, that this "direct" idiom required prodigious amounts of intellectual accomplishment and textual investigation by Japanese students of Chinese Ch'an. Even native Chinese did not achieve spontaneity of expression in the paradoxical idiom of classical Ch'an without great familiarity with Ch'an literature. As non-native speakers of Chinese, the Japanese acquired that spontaneity only after long struggle. By the time of the Southern Song dynasty (twelfth century) not only had a large corpus of Ch'an scripture with many standardized genres been created, but the practice of alluding to secular Chinese literature had also become widely practiced. Like other Chinese literati, Ch'an masters were expected to master the art of prosody and compose verse freely for all occasions. Collected verse, especially verses commenting on the famous koan, comprised one section of most Song period recorded sayings. Even Dogen adhered to this custom. His *goroku* includes his Chinese-language verses on ninety selected koan. The ability to read such poetic comments with full comprehension of the literary allusions was attained only by well-educated Japanese monks. Even fewer ever expected to compose their own verses.

Initially Japanese Zen students had to confront the obstacle of studying under teachers who spoke only Chinese. Many Japanese monks failed to bridge this barrier. Buddhist pilgrims returned from China carrying more of China's material culture than its spiritual one. Even Chinese teachers who came to Japan rarely learned more than a few words of Japanese. The Chinese Ch'an master I-shan I-ning (1247–1317), who arrived in Japan in 1299, refused to accept Japanese students unless they were able to demonstrate their proficiency in Chinese. Evidence suggests that Japanese monks who mastered Chinese pronunciation and who could quote Chinese literary proverbs generally won more ready acceptance from their Chinese teachers in Japan.

The Zen inherited by these Japanese students continued to be taught in imitation of the same Chinese syntax and stereotyped norms. Teacher and disciple exchange questions and answers in Chinese word order. Successful understanding of a koan had to be attested to by the student's supplying a proper "appended verse" *(jakugo)* selected either from Ch'an or secular Chinese literature. At the officially sponsored Zen temples—the ones belonging to the *Gozan* (Five Mountain) system—senior monks were expected to excel at composing Chinese verse in the complex style of matched counterpoint lines (usually alternating in four and six character combinations) known as *bien-li wen*. For these monks, mastering the intricacies of Chinese prosody became a major occupation. Only the brightest, most studious monks could hope to succeed within the confines of the *Gozan*. Monks of less scholastic inclination turned to the non-*Gozan* affiliated Zen monasteries, the *rinka*, where they gradually developed more accessible methods of koan instruction.

Thanks to the pioneering investigations of D. T. Suzuki and Tamamura Takeji, the broad outlines of koan study as developed within *rinka* lineages are fairly clear. It had three main features: a standardized koan curriculum, a standardized set of answers based on stereotyped Chinese sayings, and a standardized method of secretly guiding students through the curriculum of koan and answers. By standardizing and simplifying each of these, the early *rinka* teachers not only lessened the amount of memorization required for koan study by non-native speakers of Chinese but also ensured the preservation of the koan system for later generations of students. Koan training systems based on these three characteristics appeared within many lineages, both Soto and Rinzai, and through the modifications imposed by Hakuin Ekaku (1685–1768) have continued to the present in Japanese Rinzai Zen.

The koan curriculum differed in each *rinka* lineage, but within any particular lineage every generation of students proceeded through a set series of koan, more or less in an invariable order. By repeating the same series of koan in each generation, both teacher and student were freed from the burden of having to confront vast numbers of Zen texts. When a student later became a Zen teacher and began instructing his own disciples, he merely had to follow the examples set by his own teacher. Innovation was neither required, nor, it seems, widely practiced. Although each lineage had its own techniques for koan study, most curriculums followed a threefold division. For example, the Daio lineage centered at

Daitokuji placed particular emphasis on the koan of the *Blue Cliff Record* (*Hekiganroku*; Ch. *Pi-yen lu*). In this lineage the curriculum consisted of the following sequence: the initiatory koan (known as *heki-zen*), the koan of the *Hekiganroku* (known as the *hekigan*), and the koan to be studied afterwards (the *hekigo*). A few other lineages concentrated on koan taken from just three texts: the *Blue Cliff Record*, the *Record of Lin-chi* (*Rinzairoku*; Ch. *Lin-chi lu*), and the *Koans of Wu-men* (*Mumonkan*; Ch. *Wu-men kuan*). These three levels were known as the first, second, and third barriers (*shokan, ryokan,* and *sankan*).

The most common threefold divisions classified koan not on any textual basis but according to content. In these curriculums, the three types or levels of koan (known as the *sanmi* within the Soto lineages) usually consisted of the categories of: "Ultimate Truth" (*richi*), "Devices" (*kikan*), and "Reality Itself" (*kojo*). The division of Zen koan into these three categories is found even in the earliest Japanese accounts of koan and might well have been based on Chinese precedents. For example, Enni Ben'en wrote: "[one must] directly transcend the *richi* and *kikan* of the Buddhas and patriarchs. Transcending the Buddhas' *richi* is passing through the forest of brambles. Transcending the patriarchs' *kikan* is penetrating through the iron mountain and steel wall. Then for the first time one will know the fundamental *kojo*." And Nanpo Shomyo (1235–1308), the founder of the Daio lineage, wrote:

> Although the number of koan is said to be only one thousand seven hundred, actually the mountains and rivers, the great earth, the grasses and trees, the forests—whatever is seen by the eyes, whatever is heard by the ears—all of these are koan. Within our school, [koan] comprises three meanings. These are *richi, kikan,* and *kojo*. The first, *richi*, are the heart [i.e., essence] or nature indicated by the truthful words preached by all Buddhas and taught by the patriarchs. The next, *kikan,* are the displays of compassion by the Buddhas and patriarchs: the twisting of one's nose, the twinkling of an eye. In other words it is, "The stone horse wading in the water." The last, *kojo*, are the direct words of the Buddha, the true form of all reality, all without differentiation. This is

what is meant by the sayings: "The sky is the sky, and the
earth is the earth"; "Mountains are mountains, and water
is water"; "Eyes are horizontal, and the nose is vertical."

According to Nanpo, the first type of koan consists of responses to
metaphysical or doctrinal questions, the second type included accounts
of the illogical statements or extraordinary teaching methods (shouts
and beatings) used by famous Zen teachers, and the last type included the
stories of how famous teachers had used or described common objects or
situations. These three categories of koan correspond to the standard
Buddhist technique of describing reality or enlightenment in terms of its
nature, its functions, and its appearances. But whereas traditional
Buddhist descriptions relied on philosophical terminology, koan language employs vivid examples of each category.

The second distinctive feature of the Japanese koan training techniques is the systematic use of stereotyped Chinese phrases to analyze
or answer each koan. The roots of this practice probably date to the very
first Japanese attempts to overcome the barrier of the Chinese language.
The course of its growth, however, can be gauged only from the sporadic
criticisms of this practice that appear in the writings of major *Gozan*
teachers. Wu-hsüeh Tsu-hsüan (Jpn. Mugaku Sogen, 1226–1286), who
arrived in Japan in 1279, lamented the tendency of his Japanese students
to compile lists of sayings from Zen texts. Tsu-hsüan admonished his
students not to reuse the words of others without knowing the experience for oneself, a practice that he described as less beneficial than merely
reciting the Buddha's name. Likewise, Muso Soseki termed the tendency
of Japanese monks to identify Zen sayings with Zen enlightenment an
insane delusion. According to Soseki, many "self-styled men of the Way"
(*donin;* i.e., *rinka* monks) failed to acquire sufficient learning. He criticized these monks for devoting too much time to meditation instead of
to reading Zen texts and studying Chinese classics. These monks, Soseki
asserted, skimmed Zen texts not for the meaning but only to glean the
supplemental sayings *(betsugo)* or alternative responses *(daigo)* that
past masters had supplied for various koan.

At *Gozan* monasteries koan texts were studied in a scholastic fashion. At *rinka* monasteries, however, the predominant form of koan study

was the memorization of a set number of stereotyped sayings. These sayings, generally known as "appended words" *(agyo)*, were used to summarize or explain each segment of a koan text. In the course of his koan training a student learned not only the expressions favored within his own lineage but also exactly what types of situations fit each expression. Unlike *Gozan* monks, who might compose their own Chinese verse, *rinka* monks merely had to select an appropriate phrase from a limited set of "appended words." This means that the same Chinese phrase was used on separate occasions to describe very different experiences. Regardless of a student's own understanding, little individuality or creativity was expected in his responses to a koan.

This emphasis on imitation is generally credited with causing a gradual decline in the vitality of medieval koan training. Whether or not such a decline occurred, on the positive side reliance on stereotyped phrases—which simplified the linguistic demands of the koan method at a time when Chinese learning was not widespread—ensured the survival of the koan system. Repetitive use of Zen sayings did not necessarily stifle individuality. It probably resembled the drills used in modern foreign language instruction, which teach students how to use a large vocabulary of new terms correctly even before they fully understand the literal meaning of each word. The stereotyped answers gave Zen students the means to acquire rapid fluency in Zen expression. Certainly hackneyed imitation by beginner monks would have lacked inner depth or conviction. Yet many monks who blindly memorized Zen expressions must have experienced a deeper inner resource as their practice matured.

The third feature of koan training at *rinka* temples was teaching through private initiation into the proper series of responses for each koan. Private instruction has always been a key element of organized Zen monastic life. The earliest Chinese monastic code (i.e., the *Ch'an yüan ch'ing-kuei,* 1103) provides full instructions for the ceremony of Entering the Master's Quarters *(nyusshitsu),* during which all the monks assembled at the abbot's building and then entered one by one. Medieval *rinka* lineages, however, practiced an informal private instruction, conducted in secret only for selected individual students, who would visit the abbot's quarters alone. In purpose and content these secret sessions were completely different from the sessions conducted as part of the group ceremony. During the regular visits to the abbot's quarters, the teacher counseled and encouraged each member of the community of monks, one at a time. The secret instruction sessions, however, were limited to senior disciples who would inherit their teacher's dharma lineage. For these disciples alone the teacher conducted lengthy initiations into the entire koan curriculum and into that lineage's own set of questions and answers used for each koan.

Secret manuals recording the koan curriculum exist for several lineages. The more detailed of these manuals are nearly complete textbooks of both the koan curriculum and the standardized answers taught in that particular lineage. In Rinzai lineages these manuals are known as *missanroku* and *missancho* (Records of Secret Instructions). In Soto these texts are referred to as *monsan*, a word that appears to be an abbreviation of the more descriptive term *monto hissan* (the secret instructions of this lineage). The development of these koan manuals is obscure. No early texts survive. The earliest extant texts (sixteenth century) contain frequent references to earlier, well-developed traditions. The practice of secretly initiating students into particular questions and answers for each koan, therefore, probably has early roots. It must have co-evolved with the first two features of Japanese koan study as a method to ensure the faithful transmission of the standardized curriculum and stereotyped answers.

Certainly, the copying of koan manuals was practiced by the time of Ikkyu Sojun (1394–1481). In his "Self Admonitions" (*Jikaishu*, ca. 1461), Ikkyu assailed the exaggerated importance Zen monks attach to dharma succession and their equating of initiation into koan answers with attainment of that succession. Ikkyu focused the brunt of his attacks on Yoso Soi (1376–1458), a fellow Daio-line Rinzai monk known for his successful campaign to rebuild Daitokuji. Ikkyu accused Yoso of having obtained contributions from the merchants by selling them the questions, answers, and verses for the koan taught at Daitokuji. These merchants (even as laymen) could then claim to be full Zen masters with knowledge of all the traditions handed down within the Daio line. Evidently, the possibility of being initiated into the esoteric lore of Zen language proved extremely tempting even to worldly merchants.

THE BEGINNINGS OF SOTO KOAN LITERATURE

Fixed koan curriculums appeared within Soto lineages at least as early as the end of the fourteenth century. One Soto koan manual (i.e., *monsan*) states that Gasan's disciple Tsugen Jakurei found it necessary to forbid his disciples to teach koan without authorization. One biography reports that secret instruction in koan was common during Tsugen's lifetime. Other evidence supports the accuracy of this chronology. The earliest extant *monsan* text, the *Enso monsan*, purports to be a 1396 copy by Mugoku Etetsu (1350–1430), a disciple of one of Tsugen Jakurei's disciples. Baisan Monpon (a contemporary of Tsugen) prescribed the study of *wato* (Zen words; i.e., koan) in his monastic regulations. During this same period, between 1397 and 1411, a Soto temple in Kyushu published a woodblock edition of the *Hekiganroku*, the premier koan collection.

By this period Rinzai and Soto monks studied koan at each other's temples. Sometimes *Gozan* monks joined Soto temples after becoming dissatisfied with the *Gozan* emphasis on literary pursuits. Likewise, many Soto monks (especially those of Giin's line) studied in *Gozan* temples in order to learn the intricacies of Chinese prosody. But to study with monks in other *rinka* lineages was much more common. To illustrate the connections between medieval Rinzai and Soto, Tamamura Takeji cites the example of Shochu Shotan (d. 1492), a Rinzai monk, and Chikuba Kotaku (1419–1471), a Soto monk.

Shochu inherited the koan curriculum of the so-called Genju line of *rinka* Rinzai Zen from his master Yuho Toeki (n.d.). Nonetheless, Shochu remained unsatisfied with his level of attainment and studied under other teachers. In 1433 he spent seven days on sacred Mt. Kiyosumi praying to Kokuzo bodhisattva to complete his mastery of Zen. He then climbed Mt. Fuji in order to select his next Zen teacher by means of ritual divination. The teacher selected was Daiko Myoshu (d. 1437), a Soto master of the Tsugen lineage. Shochu studied under Daiko until he inherited the entire koan curriculum of the Tsugen line. After Daiko's death Shochu continued training under several other Soto masters, all of whom belonged to the same subfaction within the Tsugen line as had Daiko.

Then Shochu met Chikuba Kotaku, a Soto teacher in a different subfaction of the Tsugen line. Chikuba, like Shochu, had studied koan in several different lineages. He had inherited the koan curriculum of the *rinka* Daio line from Ikkyu Sojun. After Shochu and Chikuba met, they decided to study under each other. In other words, the Rinzai monk Shochu taught the secrets of his Soto koan curriculum to the Soto master of a different line. In exchange, the Soto monk Chikuba taught the secrets of his Rinzai koan curriculum to a Rinzai master of a different line. In essence, each became dharma heir to the other, learning the secrets of their own style from a monk nominally affiliated with the other.

From this example and others, Tamamura asserts that by the fifteenth century the distinctions between Rinzai and Soto had totally broken down, that Zen monks remained aware only of the rivalries between different lineages, and that two Soto lineages would have been as distant from each other as if one had been Rinzai and the other Soto. Tamamura's characterization is accurate insofar as every lineage had its own secret teachings. In terms of self-awareness and religious goals, however, monks in both Zen traditions typically exaggerated even small differences between Rinzai and Soto. In studying koan, the training methods taught were not necessarily similar. Bassui Tokusho, for example, had been extremely critical of Soto teachers, stating that their intellectual approach to koan training prevented them from even dreaming of the depths of the realization taught in Rinzai lines.

In some cases koan manuals authored by Rinzai monks apparently did become confused with the writings of Soto patriarchs. Two texts in particular, the *Kenshoron* (Treatise on Perceiving Reality) attributed to Dogen and the *Himitsu shobo genzo* (Secret *Shobo genzo*) attributed to Keizan, appear to have originated in the Hotto line of the Rinzai monk Kyoo Unryo. Kyoo obtained access to the writings of Dogen and Keizan when he served as abbot of Daijoji. Biographies state that Kyoo also authored several Zen texts, including *Kana kenshosho* (Japanese-Language Treatise on Perceiving Reality) and *Shobo genzogo* (*Shobo genzo* Koans). It cannot be proved that Kyoo texts are the same as the ones now attributed to Dogen and Keizan, but a recently discovered manuscript (copied ca. 1486) suggests that they are probably related. This texts quotes Hotto-line monks such as Shinchi Kakushin and Bassui Tokusho as well as various Chinese masters on techniques for concentrating on koan in ways that will arouse doubt *(gidan)* and induce an insight into reality *(kensho)*. It also includes an essay attributed to Dogen, titled *Kenshoron*. This essay, still attributed to Dogen, also has been preserved at various Soto temples, but under the same title as Kyoo's treatise, *Kana kenshosho.*

A similar example of confusion over titles and authorship appears in the biography of Keizan Jokin compiled by the Rinzai monk Mangen Shiban, which states that Keizan wrote a text titled *Shobo genzogo*— again the same title as Kyoo's text. Soto records mention no such title. But Keizan is cited as the author of a commentary on ten Chinese koan titled *Himitsu shobo genzo* (Secret *Shobo genzo*). Significantly, this *Himitsu shobo genzo* was found among the Hotto-line manuscripts just mentioned. Also significant is the fact that not all versions of this text cite Keizan as author. Some Soto lineages secretly transmitted copies of the same set of ten Chinese koans under the title *Jusoku shobo genzo* (Ten-Koan *Shobo genzo*), but without any reference to Keizan.

These examples suggest that koan texts passed from one *rinka* lineage to another. The outside origin of these teachings, however, could not be acknowledged. Instead, the texts borrowed respectability associated with the names Dogen and Keizan. A similar process of borrowing the authority of ancient patriarchs can be observed in most of the secret koan literature passed down within medieval Soto. This literature defies easy summation, but it cannot be ignored. It presents us with a gold mine of information regarding what Soto monks studied and how; what institutional, pedagogical, and ritual structures mediated the koan experience; what religious or doctrinal interpretations were applied to koan; and the general flow of monastic rituals and medieval institutions.

Medieval Soto Koan Literature

In addition to the secret koan manuals *(monsan)* mentioned earlier, extensive records of medieval koan study exits in secret initiation documents *(kirikami)* and in transcriptions of monastic lectures *(kikigak-isho)*. A brief review of each of these genres reveals the features and limitations of the literature as historical sources as well as the nature of Zen training in late medieval Soto.

Koan Manuals (Monsan)

Monsan detail the curriculum, questions, and expected responses for each koan. Each medieval Soto lineage regarded the questions and answers that had been devised by their own past masters as closely guarded secrets. Possession of a completed record of a particular lineage's koan curriculum was seen as proof of succession to that dharma line. *Monsan*, therefore, were transmitted in secret. One *monsan* explained this process by distinguishing between two types of private instruction sessions offered during the biannual ninety-day training period. During the morning session *(chosan)* the Zen master met privately with all the monks one-by-one, regardless of lineage affiliations. Mornings were termed *Yang*, the "open instructions," the "revealed word." Meetings during the evening *(yasan)* were termed *Yin*, the "private matters," the "secret words." Only future dharma heirs received evening instruction.

At present most of the *monsan* available to scholars belong to lines descendant from Tsugen Jakurei (i.e., the largest Soto faction). These texts often cite answers from other Soto lineages, thereby indicating that the Tsugen faction held no monopoly on koan initiations. Within this faction, different branch lineages exhibit wide variation in both curriculum and answers for the koan. The branch lines descendant from Ryoan Emyo (1337–1411) emphasized nonverbal responses (i.e., *kikan*), whereas the branch lines descendant from Sekioku Shinryo (1345–1423) emphasized analysis (i.e., *richi*). Consider, for example, the answers for the koan concerning Shakyamuni Buddha holding up a flower (the first koan in the *Jusoku shobo genzo* mentioned above). Student monks within the Ryoan line imitated the walk of a small child to express the meaning of the holding up of a flower, whereas the Sekioku-line teachers merely explained that the meaning of the koan is within the person holding the flower, not within the flower itself.

In general, *monsan* follow a standard question-and-answer format. First the koan is identified by name only. Following each name, there are one, two, or a series of questions to be asked by the teacher (usually introduced by the word *shi*). The questions might include requests to explain the meaning of key terms in the koan, to provide an appropriate Chinese verse or phrase *(agyo* or *jakugo)* that would express that same meaning, to explain *(seppa;* abbreviated as *ha)* the meaning of that Chinese phrase, or to sum up the basic meaning or purpose of the koan as a whole *(rakkyo* or *hikkyo).* After each one of these questions the expected response is indicated. Occasionally, a text might explicitly indicate that the student monk *(gaku)* is to respond. More often, the text indicates that the teacher substitutes *(dai)* for the monk.

In Chinese Ch'an literature, the term *dai* ("in place of") usually introduces an alternative answer to an old question or introduces the master's own answer for a question to which no monk in the assembly would respond. In medieval Soto koan literature, however, *dai* always indicates that the teacher is supplying the correct answer in order to instruct his student, not in order to replace the answer in the original text. An example will clarify this distinction between these two uses of *dai*. The *Blue Cliff Record* contains the following koan:

> Yun-men [Jpn. Unmon], lecturing the assembly, said: "The old Buddha and the bare pillar intermingle. What functioning is this?"
> Speaking for *(dai)* himself [he answered]: "In the southern mountains, clouds arise; in the northern mountains, rain falls."

In the Soto *monsan* this incident is cited by the title "Unmon's old Buddha [and] bare pillar." The *monsan* lists the following questions and answers:

> Teacher *(shi):* "As for the old Buddha?"
> Substituting *(dai)* [for the student]: "This one person."
> Teacher: "As for the bare pillar?"
> Substitute: "A five-foot object [of perception]."
> Teacher: "When the rains disperse and clouds draw
>   together?"
> Substitute: "The very burning away of body and mind
>   *(shinjin* [i.e., subject and object])."
> Teacher: "An appended verse *(jakugo)*?"
> Substitute: [in Chinese]

"The night moon glitters in the cold pool;
"The autumn wind penetrates the skull bone."
Teacher: "Explain *(seppa)* [its meaning]."
Substitute: "Mind and object are one."

Throughout this entire session the student monk apparently would have made no response. The students expected only to become conversant with the many nuances of each koan. They did not have to create new responses. The surviving *monsan* reveal few, if any, signs of the students struggling with each koan on their own.

Soto Koan study, however, was not confined to linguistic analysis. Ryoan-line *monsan* repeatedly call for physical gestures in response to the teacher's questions, as in the following passage:

What is "Tozan's 'The inanimate preach the dharma'?"
Student's [nonverbal response]: Cough, [then] sit. Wait,
  saying nothing. [Then,] Thump the cushion two or three
  times.
Teacher: "That's still too weak."
Student's [nonverbal response]: With fists, strike the
  straw mat.
This is the teaching *(san)* of Tokuo [Horyu].

Often the answers alluded to terms or concepts taught only in Soto lineages. For example, the same Ryoan-line *monsan* just cited also includes the following sequence:

Question: "How does [one] sit atop a hundred-foot pole?"
Substitute: "Sitting in [total] forgetfulness."
Question: "How does [one's] whole body appear in all
  directions?"
Substitute: "Jumping up; falling down."
Question: "A verse?"
  "*Shinjin datsuraku*
  "*Datsuraku shinjin.*"

This commentary asserts that Zen meditation, in and of itself, is the experience of the totality of existence as enlightenment. The "top of a hundred-foot pole" is a common Zen expression for the goal of Zen training, or enlightenment. In this case, that enlightenment is conceived of as the activity of sitting in Zen meditation without any special mental effort. Although sitting normally is static, in this passage it is paired with the activity of one's body becoming manifest everywhere. This means that Zen meditation is the experiencing of all reality as a dynamic momentness (jumping up and falling down), or as *shinjin datsuraku*, the phrase that Dogen used to describe the experience of Zen meditation.

Another *monsan*, from a different line within the Ryoan faction, begins with a historical definition of the Soto line and then differentiates proper Soto practices from other styles of Zen. In its emphasis on sectarian identity it explicitly cites Dogen as the authority behind the Soto approach to koan study:

> The Soto school derives from the line of Shih-t'ou, [which in turn] derived from the first patriarch, Bodhidharma. The sixth patriarch, master Huineng, while working as a rice polisher within the assembly of the fifth patriarch, Hunjen, considered this matter [i.e., enlightenment] day and night without interruption even while drinking tea or eating rice. As his exertion *(kufu)* gradually matured, he naturally penetrated into [the realm of] fundamental wisdom. This "penetrating" *(tonyu)* does not refer to his having smashed through all objects [of perception]. Without loss of the realm of objects, he attained the mind of wisdom. This "mind of wisdom" *(shinchi)* is the [realization of one's] original face without thought of good, without thought of evil [i.e., reality itself, beyond mundane thoughts]. When Ch'ing-yuan grasped this doctrine, the sixth patriarch accepted him as [his disciple]. Shih-t'ou, then, was the successor to Ch'ing-yuan. From the teachings bequeathed by them there must not be even the slightest deviation....
>
> Showing off with shouts and with [blows of the] staff are great hindrances. Among the ancients, [only] one in ten

thousand believed in such practices. Since the first Japanese patriarch, Master Dogen of Eiheiji, had strongly rejected these, [likewise] how much more [strongly] should [the] unlearned monks of this later age who have not yet forgotten [their worldly] knowledge and who have not yet cast off [their] discriminating intellect [do so]. If one believes in such practices, not only will he fall like an arrow into hell, but he also will completely lose the true teaching [i.e., Buddhism]. People born into this corrupt, turbulent end of the final age [of Buddhism], having minds full of dreams and delusions, should merely sit in meditation according to the old [Zen monastic] codes. Throughout the twelve periods of the day, they should realize this matter [i.e., enlightenment] through *shinjin datsuraku*.

The fact that this text encourages monks to practice Zen meditation according to the old monastic regulations is noteworthy. Modern Soto scholars usually assert that observance of regulated sessions of Zen meditations gradually disappeared in medieval Japan until revived in the early eighteenth century after the arrival of Ming-dynasty Chinese monks. This *monsan* demonstrates, however, that meditation according to the old regulations continued to be advocated in medieval Soto.

Initiation Documents (Kirikami)

After *monsan*, the second prime source for descriptions of medieval Soto koan training is the *kirikami* traditionally handed down within many Soto lineages. *Kirikami* (literally "paper strips") vary in length from single sheets to bound volumes. They record secret instructions for the performance of ritual. In medieval Japan, *kirikami* were used at all levels of society for teaching almost any endeavor centered on private master-disciple lineages, such as theatrical performance, poetry composition, martial arts, secret religious practices, and especially Buddhism.

Soto *kirikami* generally performed two functions. First, mere possession of them served as yet another testament to one's religious authority. Second, they supplemented the Chinese monastic codes *(shingi)* that governed Zen monastic life. Whereas the Chinese codes regulated the operation of large monasteries as a whole, *kirikami* describe procedures for the private rituals conducted by the abbot alone, such as techniques for performing consecrations, funerals, transfers of merit, dharma transmissions, and precept initiations. *Kirikami* also differ from Chinese codes in that while the latter reveal the influence of Chinese social customs and beliefs, *kirikami* reflect Japanese folk beliefs and magical practices.

Kirikami depict many aspects of koan study, since koan initiation was an important monastic ritual. These koan initiation documents treat the same subject matter as the full-length *monsan* described above. In contrast to the *monsan*, they are more narrowly focused and of shorter length. Some describe the correct series of questions and answers for just a single koan (often referred to as *sanwa*). The *sanwa* documents were not part of the general training curriculum but were reserved for special occasions. Within some lines, for instance, each new dharma heir was instructed in a series of questions and answers regarding the legendary first Zen transmission when Shakyamuni Buddha help up a flower *(nenge)* and his disciple Mahakashyapa smiled.

Even *kirikami* concerning other types of rituals or the meaning of ritual implements often adapted the same question-and-answer format as used for koan study. For example, one *kirikami* that describes the seven main Zen monastic buildings (which the abbot toured both during his inauguration ceremony and as part of his daily ritual) begins as follows:

> Teacher: "First, the abbot's building?"
> Substitute: "Prior to the Great Ultimate (*taikyoku*) [there is] the abbot's building."
> Teacher: "Nothing exists prior to the Great Ultimate. How can [you] say that the abbot's building exists?"
> Substitute: "This answer means that the master dwells in the place of non-being."
> Teacher: "A verse?"
> Substitute:
> "No bright brightness;
> "In the dark, no darkness."
> Teacher: "Next, the storehouse?…"

The document continues in the same format for each of the seven buildings. Likewise, another initiation document describes an incense burner as a symbol of the fleetingness of life:

> Teacher: "The evaluation *(sadame)* of an incense burner?"
> Student's [nonverbal response]: Points at his own body.
> Teacher: "As for the burning incense?"
> Answer: "Exhalations and inhalations."
> Teacher: "A verse?
> "Within one wisp of burning [incense];
> "Grasp this mind."

These *kirikami* in koan-style, question-and-answer format are especially noteworthy because they demonstrate the large degree to which the use of appended verses *(agyo* or *jakugo)* dominated religious training in medieval Soto Zen. All objects of daily use and all aspects of monastic life were analyzed from the standpoint of Zen dialectics in order to imbue them with a secret significance. The special language and techniques of koan study extended beyond meditation training to permeate the attitudes of medieval Soto monks toward all religious practices, so that even rituals adapted from non-Zen traditions were redefined in terms of Zen concepts.

As in the case with the *monsan* cited above, many *kirikami* invoked the authority of Dogen or his Chinese teacher, Ju-ching. Passages such as "the hundred twenty items listed in these certificates [are] the dharma bequeathed at T'ien-t'ung [i.e., Ju-ching's monastery], [they are] the secrets of Dogen" are commonplace. Whether or not teachings or rituals could be traced back to these men, such was the symbolic power of the idealized "transmission from China" that medieval Soto monks sincerely believed their own practices to be faithful reenactments of this ancient paradigm. Here is a *kirikami* regarding the staff held by a Zen teacher while lecturing:

> The teacher [Ju-ching] asked: "What is this one stick?"
> Dogen replied: "Everyone is [so] endowed."
> The teacher said: "[Be] endowed! Look!"
> Dogen replied: "No-mind."

The teacher said: "Transcend words."
Dogen stood up...

When the student Zen monk stood up he not only beheld Dogen, but transmuted through ritual he became the Dogen of his own generation.

Transcription Commentaries (Kikigakisho)

In contrast to the secret records in *monsan* and *kirikami*, texts known as *kikigakisho* contain transcriptions of open lectures on koan presented at medieval Soto monasteries. The practice of producing bound editions of informal transcriptions seems to have begun at *Gozan* monasteries. Between the fourteenth and sixteenth centuries *Gozan* monks transcribed numerous lectures on the classics of Chinese secular literature. At Soto monasteries very few lectures on secular literature occurred. Instead Soto monks focused on Zen texts, especially on koan collections. Transcriptions of these comments offer many insights into medieval Zen life because they often convey minute details of the circumstances of each day's lecture. In spite of their historical value, however, records of medieval Zen lectures (especially informal transcriptions) have suffered a low literary reputation that has inhibited their study and publication.

Japanese linguists only recently began publishing medieval Zen *kikigakisho* (which they term *shomono*) when they discovered in them phonetic transcriptions of medieval colloquial Japanese. The characteristics of a transcription commentary are well illustrated by the *Ninden genmokusho*, a record of lectures of Senso Esai on the *jen-t'ien yen-mu* (Jpn. *Ninden genmoku*; Guidelines for Gods and Men) delivered between 1471 and 1474. Three transcriptions exist, each probably recorded separately. Two of the transcriptions are similarly terse, in that the content of Senso's remarks is expressed in as few words as possible with no words separating the commentary from the original text or from mention of contemporaneous events. They resemble a modern college student's lecture notes rather than a complete transcription.

In contrast to these, the third version is very detailed, extending to more than three times the length of either of the other two. The sources for each portion of the transcription are identified in full and the quotations are in the form of complete sentences. The differences between this third version and the other two are so striking that normally it would suggest that they must represent different series of lectures on the same text. However, careful comparison of the contemporaneous events mentioned in all three versions reveals that each recorded the same lectures given at the same time and place. The differences between each version, therefore, must have resulted not from different source lectures but from different scribes, one of whom took more detailed notes.

The majority of medieval Soto *kikigakisho* record lectures not on Zen treatises such as the *Jen-t'ien yen-mu*, but on koan collections. The *Blue Cliff Record* and *Koans of Wu-men* were widely studied. Transcriptions of Senso Esai's lectures exist for both. Most Soto teachers, however, rather than following a standard koan collection, chose koans for their lectures according to their own inclinations. Koans were selected mainly from the above two collections and from the *Zenrin ruiju* (Ch. *Ch'an-lin lei-chu*, 1307), an exhaustive Chinese encyclopedia of koan and verses used by Chinese teachers to comment on them. The *Shoyoroku* (Ch. *Tsung-jung lu*, 1223), a koan collection compiled by two Chinese Ts'ao-tung teachers, also occasionally appears in quotations.

Whether lecturing on Zen treatises, koan collections, or their own selected topics, medieval Soto teachers followed the same question-and-answer format used for private koan initiations. First, the teacher identified the topic or recited the koan. Then, with a question, he invited *(satsu)* the assembled monks to recite a verse summing up the meaning of that topic. Occasionally monks responded, but more often the teacher supplied his own verse in place of *(dai)* the monks. Finally, some teachers also explained *(seppa)* the meaning of the verse. Usually, however, only the teacher's verse comments were recorded. For this reason, some teachers also conducted a second series of lectures on the same koans, in which they explained the meaning of the verses they had previously delivered.

For example, there are two versions of koan lectures by Kokai Ryotatsu (d. 1599). The first, *Kokaidai* (Kokai's Alternate [Verses]), lists only the names of each koan in full with Kokai's questions and verse answers. The second, *Kokaidaisho* (Kokai's Alternate-[Verse] Commentary), lists only the names of each koan, each of which is accompanied by a full account of Kokai's explanations of each of his verses. When the teacher lectured on the verses *(dai)* originally given by someone other than himself, the resulting transcription usually would be titled with his own name and the word *saigin* (reexamination).

Even though the question-and-answer format was the same, crucial differences separate the answers recorded in *monsan* or *kirikami* and those appearing in *kikigakisho*. The answers in the first group represent secret teachings that remained the same from generation to generation. In the *kikigakisho*, however, the koan selected, the questions asked, and the answers each represent the mood and character of a given teacher at a particular moment. Although the teachers usually gave their own answers, the students were free to attempt (and some transcriptions include) individual interpretations. For a monk the attempt to respond freely in front of the whole assembly could be a crucial step in his training. In one case, Daian Shueki (1406–1473) accepted Zengan Tojun (d. 1495) as his dharma heir after the latter had been the only one able to give a suitable answer to a question posed to the entire assembly.

The questions and verse answers often commented as much on the day's events as on the koan in question. For example, Senso Esai's verse comments in the *Ninden genmokusho* that were given on the seventeenth day of each month always contained a reference to the attributes of Kannon, the bodhisattva for whom special services were conducted on that day. Likewise, Senso's concluding verse given at the end of one ninety-day training session (after which the monks were free to travel again) ordered: "Go! Go! Don't look back. What a small place [this is] on the great earth." Another version of Senso's *Ninden genmokusho* notes that the lecture began just as the monks had finished reciting the monastic code. The date given in the text is the twenty-first, the day of the month on which the monks jointly recited the rules governing conduct in the monastery library *(shuryo)*. Immediately after this recitation, everyone returned to the monks' hall for another period of meditation. If this is the recitation referred to in the transcription, then the meaning of Senso's concluding verse for that day's lecture becomes easy to understand. Senso had asked: "What is the intended meaning of the ancient patriarchs?" and then answered, "The great assembly [of monks] meditating in the [monks'] hall." This answer directed the monks to leave the

TABLE 2.

COMPARISON OF ANNUAL LECTURE DATES IN MEDIEVAL SOTO

Events Dates	Goroku Fusai Zenkyu (1347–1408)	Kikigakisho: Ryonen Eicho (1471–1551)	Kokai Ryotatsu (D. 1599)	Daien Monsatsu (D. 1636)
Saitan (first day of New Year)				
1:1	yes	yes	yes	yes
Gensho (first moon)		*Soan* (end of winter training session)		
1:15	yes	yes	yes	yes
Nehan (Buddha's Nirvana)				
2:15	yes	—	—	—
Kashaku (admittance of new monks)				
3:28	—	—	yes	yes
Bussho (Buddha's Birthday)				
4:8	yes	yes	yes	yes
Hi' i (adjustment of monastic seniority)				
4:13	—	—	—	yes
Ketsuge (start of summer training session)				
4:15	yes	yes	yes	yes
Yasan hajime (first evening instruction)				
4:18	—	—	yes	yes
Tango (midsummer)				
5:5	yes	yes	yes	yes
(full moon)				
5:15	yes	—	yes	yes
Kankin (sutra recitation)				
5:28	—	—	—	yes
(full moon)				
6:15	yes	—	yes	yes
Kankin (sutra recitation [for the dead])				
7:1	—	—	yes	yes
Shichiseki (night of the cowherd and weaving maid stars)				
7:7	—	—	yes	yes

Events Dates	Goroku Fusai Zenkyu (1347–1408)	Kikigakisho: Ryonen Eicho (1471–1551)	Kokai Ryotatsu (D. 1599)	Daien Monsatsu (D. 1636)
Kaige (end of summer training session)				
7:15	yes	yes	yes	yes
Chushu (night of the harvest moon)				
8:15	—	—	yes	yes
Dogenki (memorial for Dogen)				
8:28	—	—	—	yes
Chinjuki (service for protective spirits)				
9:19	—	—	—	yes
Kairo (opening of hearth)				
1:1	yes	—	yes	yes
Darumaki (memorial for Bodhidharma)				
1:5	—	—	yes	yes
Ketto (start of winter training session)				
1:15	—	yes	yes	yes
Nyujo (Buddha's trance)				
12:1	—	—	yes	yes
Rohachi (Buddha's enlightenment)				
12:8	yes	yes	yes	yes
Nisoki (memorial for second patriarch)				
12:10	—	yes	—	—
Toji (midwinter)				
12:22	yes	yes	yes	—
Joya (New Year's Eve)				
12:30	yes	yes	yes	—

Sources: *Fusai osho ju Noshu Shogakuzan Soji Zenji goroku,* fasc. 1, in SZ, vol. 5, *Goroku,* 1:123–129; Ishikawa Rikizan, "En'o chuko Ryoan dai osho hogo' ni tsuite," 68–72 [note: Additional events are probably included in the original text, but not reported fully by Ishikawa]; Kokai Ryotatsu, *Kokaidai,* unpublished manuscript in Komazawa University Library; and Kagamishima Genryu, "Kaidai," in *Daien daisho,* 2, Zenmon Shomono Sokan, 3:336–337. A dash (—) indicates that the event in question does not appear in the source cited.

library and return to the monks' hall for meditation. Answers such as these represent a conscious effort by the teachers to make the koan seem relevant to the monks' daily situations.

Because of the spontaneity they record, *kikigakisho* in many ways represent a Japanese counterpart to the *goroku* (recorded sayings) genre of Ch'an literature that had developed in China. As with the early Ch'an records, the Japanese *kikigakisho* record the colloquial language of the time, with many slang and nonliterary expressions. Both types of texts record concrete comments of a living teacher as he delivered his lectures and responded to students' questions. Finally, *kikigakisho* resemble the late style of *goroku* developed in the Song dynasty in that the lectures comprising the original source material invariably were delivered according to the monastic calendar described in the Chinese monastic codes (see table 2). The regular occurrences of lectures during the ninety-day meditation training sessions is particularly noteworthy. These lectures demonstrate that Zen training continued at Soto monasteries uninterrupted by the civil disturbances of fifteenth- and sixteenth-century Japan.

Medieval *kikigakisho*, however, differ from Chinese "recorded sayings" in several ways. First, Japanese Zen teachers traditionally wrote their own *goroku* in imitation of the genre produced in China. Only addresses composed in Chinese were included. Because of this artificial process, Japanese *goroku* often reveal very little of either the Zen teachings or the personalities of their authors. Second, in *kikigakisho* the emphasis or point of the lecture lies not in the topic as a whole but only in the concluding verse that sums up each koan. Often the same topic or same koan was brought up repeatedly, but depending on the circumstances of that particular day the teacher (or students) asked different questions and answered with different verses. For example, Ryonen Eicho invariably began each ninety-day training period *(ango)* during one nine-year period (1519–1528) by questioning *(satsu)* his students on the meaning of this same line from the Sutra on Perfect Enlightenment *(Engakukyo):* "By great perfect enlightenment make yourself into a temple [wherein] body and mind abide *(ango)* in true knowledge of the undifferentiated [i.e., the absolute]." The quote remained the same, but his questions and answers always differed.

Medieval Soto literature leaves no doubt that in the fifteenth and six-teenth centuries koan study had permeated every aspect of Soto Zen training. Each lineage had its own koan curriculum. Rituals and doctrines were taught in koan format, with questions answered by stereotyped phrases. Teachers lectured on Zen texts and individual koan as a means of teaching students how to apply these phrases to any and all situations. Soto koan Zen centered on the analysis and creative use of concluding phrases of stereotyped Chinese verse, the alternate sayings *(daigo)*, and appended words *(agyo or jakugo)*.

Medieval Soto Zen practice, however, was not limited to koan train-ing. Rituals originally intended for inside the monastery, such as precept ordinations and funerals, forged essential links uniting the communities of Zen monks to their lay supporters. These areas, the subjects of the fol-lowing chapters, represent major departures from Zen practice in Dogen's time. Yet perhaps because they have continued to play a major role in retaining lay allegiance down to the present day, modern Soto leaders typically attempt to reconcile these practices with Dogen's teach-ings rather than to renounce them.

THE NATURE OF THE RINZAI (LINJI) KOAN PRACTICE

Victor Sogen Hori

D.T. Suzuki's early works (notably his *Essays in Zen Buddhism, Second Series*, 1953) and Miura and Sasaki's *Zen Dust* (1966) were for a very long time the only major resources available in non-Asian languages for research into the Zen koan. In recent years, however, a rich bounty of material has appeared. At the level of basic texts, in addition to a steady stream of translations of the traditional "recorded sayings" of the Zen masters from which koan cases were originally derived, numerous koan collections, some of them newly created in the West, have also been published in translation. At the scholarly level, major philosophical and historical studies on the nature and development of the koan have appeared. Despite all these efforts, there is still no philosophical agreement on the nature of the koan, and indeed little factual information on the actual conduct of koan practice. Before we attempt to describe the capping-phrase practice, we need a clear picture of the Rinzai koan practice in general.

A RELIGIOUS PRACTICE

To begin with, like all Buddhist practices, Rinzai koan practice is religious in nature. This point seems to be forgotten in current accounts. Popular descriptions of the koan as "riddles" or "paradoxes" make it seem as if the Zen practitioner is interested in little more than the solving of intellectual puzzles. Those interested in enhancing the spontaneity of athletic or artistic performance tend to focus on Zen as a training technique for attaining a state of consciousness in which "the dancer is one with the dance" (Gallwey 1974, Sudnow 1978). Scholars who study

117

Zen as a language game give the impression that the practitioner is basically learning a new set of rules for language (Sellman 1979, Wright 1992). Others insist that the notion of religious experience (Proudfoot 1985), or Zen experience (Sharf 1995A, 1995B), is a concept manufactured and manipulated for ideological reasons, depicting the practitioner as primarily engaged in some form or other of cultural politics. Critics who suggest that the koan is a form of "scriptural exegesis" (Sharf 1995A, 108) give the impression that the Zen koan practice differs little from scholarship in general. These kinds of interpretations of Zen practice are misleading at best. The koan practice is first and foremost a religious practice, undertaken primarily not in order to solve a riddle, not to perfect the spontaneous performance of some skill, not to learn a new form of linguistic expression, not to play cultural politics, and not to carry on scholarship. Such ingredients may certainly be involved, but they are always subservient to the traditional Buddhist goals of awakened wisdom and selfless compassion.

In saying this, I am making a normative statement, not a description of fact. The fact is, in most Rinzai monasteries today, many of the monks engage in meditation and koan practice for a mere two or three years in order to qualify for the status of *jushoku* (resident priest), which will allow them to assume the role of a temple priest. For many of them, engagement with the koan may indeed consist in a little more than the practice of solving riddles and learning a ritualized language, a fraction of the full practice. In the full practice the Zen practitioner must bring to the engagement the three necessities of the Great Root of Faith, the Great Ball of Doubt, and the Great Overpowering Will *(daishinkon, daigidan, daifunshi)*. The koan is an artificial problem given by a teacher to a student with the aim of precipitating a genuine religious crisis that involves all the human faculties—intellect, emotion, and will.

At first, one's efforts and attention are focused on the koan. When it cannot be solved (one soon learns that there is no simple "right answer"), doubt sets in. Ordinary doubt is directed at some external object such as the koan itself or the teacher, but when it has been directed back to oneself, it is transformed into Great Doubt. To carry on relentlessly this act of self-doubt, one needs the Great Root of Faith. Ordinarily, faith and doubt are related to one another in inverse proportion: where faith is strong, doubt is weak; and vice versa. But in Zen practice, the greater the doubt, the greater the faith. Great Faith and Great Doubt are two aspects of the same mind of awakening *(bodaishin)*. The Great Overpowering Will is needed to surmount all obstacles along the way. Since doubt is focused on oneself, no matter how strong, wily, and resourceful one is in facing the opponent, that opponent (oneself) is always just as strong, wily, and resourceful in resisting. When self-doubt has grown to the point that one is totally consumed by it, the usual operations of mind cease. The mind of total self-doubt no longer classifies intellectually, no longer arises in anger or sorrow, no longer exerts itself as will and ego. This is the state that Hakuin described as akin to being frozen in a great crystal:

> Suddenly a great doubt manifested itself before me. It was as though I were frozen solid in the midst of an ice sheet extending tens of thousands of miles. A purity filled my breast and I could neither go forward nor retreat. To all intents and purposes I was out of my mind and the *Mu* alone remained. Although I sat in the Lecture Hall and listened to the Master's lecture, it was as though I were hearing from a distance outside the hall. At times, I felt as though I were floating through the air. (*Orategama III*, Yampolsky 1971, 118)

In this state, Hakuin happened one day to hear the temple bell ring. At that moment the ice shattered and he was thrust back into the world. In this experience, called the Great Death *(daishi ichiban)*, the self-doubt is finally extinguished and the Great Doubt is transformed into Great Awakening. As Ta-hui says, "Beneath the Great Doubt, always there is a great awakening."

Kensho, the experience of awakening, is more than merely the state of concentrated *samadhi*. When the Great Doubt has totally taken over the self, there is no more distinction between self and other, subject and object. There is no more differentiation, no more attachment. This is merely *samadhi* and not *kensho*. *Kensho* is not the self's withdrawal from the conventional world, but rather the selfless self breaking back into the conventional world. It is only when this *samadhi* has been shattered that a new self arises. This self returns and again sees the things of the world as objects, now as empty objects; it again thinks in differentiated categories and feels attachment, but now with insight into their emptiness.

Again, I am speaking in normative terms. The particular aspects of Zen koan practice on which scholars have concentrated their attentions—its nondual epistemology, its ritual and performance, its language, its politics—are aspects. They are facets of a practice whose fundamental core is a religious practice.

KOAN: INSTRUMENT OR REALIZATION?

Most commentators take the approach that the koan is an *upaya*, an instrument, that deliberately poses a problem unsolvable by the rational mind in order to drive the mind beyond the limits of rationality and intellectual cognition. This approach views the koan as a psychological technique cunningly designed to cause the rational and intellectual functions of mind to self-destruct, thus liberating the mind to the vast realm of the nonrational and the intuitive. Powerful personal accounts of spiritual quest make it seem that the koan is not a text to be studied for its meaning as one would study an essay or a poem, but rather an existential explosive device with language merely serving as the fuse.

Part of the problem with many such instrumentalist approaches is that it deprives the koan itself of meaning. The koan, it is said, cannot be understood intellectually; it gives the appearance of being meaningful only to seduce the meaning-seeking mind to engage with it (Rosemont 1970). This interpretation ignores the mass of evidence contradicting the idea that the koan is no more than a meaningless, blunt psychological instrument. It is hard to think that the shelves of heavy volumes of koan commentary produced through the centuries and the lectures in which Zen teachers expound at length on the koan are all occupied with a technique that is in itself nonsense. It is much more sensible to begin from the assumption that koan disclose their own meaning (though not necessarily an intellectual one), once they have been properly understood.

A second difficulty is that in trying to demonstrate how the koan overcomes the dualisms and false dichotomies created by the conventional mind, the instrumental approach introduces dualism and dichotomy back into the picture again. The awakened mind, it is said, has transcended the dualistic dichotomizing of conventional mind and resides in a state of nonduality. The awakened person is thus freer than the average person in being able to choose to act either in the conventional dualistic way or in the awakened nondual way. But the dichotomy between duality and nonduality, conventional thinking and awakened mind, is itself a duality. Rather than being free from dualistic thinking, the awakened mind ends up more tightly locked into dualistic thinking, incessantly forced to choose between being conventional or being awakened.

A much better way of approaching the koan is by way of the "realizational" model, a term I have borrowed from Hee-jin Kim (1985). The practitioner does not solve the koan by grasping intellectually the meaning of "the sound of one hand" or "original face before father and mother were born." Rather, in the crisis of self-doubt referred to above, one experiences the koan not as an object standing before the mind that investigates it, but as the seeking mind itself. As long as consciousness and koan oppose each other as subject and object, there are still two hands clapping, mother and father have already been born. But when the koan has overwhelmed the mind so that it is no longer the object but the seeking subject itself, subject and object are no longer two. This is "one hand clapping", the point "before father and mother have been born." This entails a "realization" in the two senses of the term. By making real, i.e., by actually *becoming* an example of the nonduality of subject and object, the practitioner also realizes, i.e., *cognitively understands*, the koan. The realization of understanding depends on the realization of making actual.

This realizational account of the koan solves several problems. On the one hand, it helps explain how the solution to a koan requires the personal experience of "the sound of one hand" or of "one's original face." On the other, it allows us to see the koan as not merely a blunt or meaningless instrument, useful only as means to some further end, but as possessed of a meaningful content of its own which can be apprehended intellectually.

"Zen Experience"

If an instrumentalist approach deemphasizes the meaning of the koan and overemphasizes the experiential aspect, there are scholars on the other end of the spectrum with the opposite approach. Robert Sharf, for example, writes:

> The koan genre, far from serving as a means to obviate reason, is a highly sophisticated form of scriptural exegesis: the manipulation or "solution" of a particular koan traditionally demanded an extensive knowledge of canonical Buddhist doctrine and classical Zen verse. (Sharf 1995A, 108)

In claiming that the solving of a koan is an exercise in scriptural exegesis, Sharf also argues against the traditional claim that one must necessarily have a *kensho* experience before one can understand Zen. His position is that the idea of *kensho* experience has been manufactured and manipulated for ideological purposes by Buddhist modernists (Sharf 1995A, 1995B, 1995C). While it is not possible in this essay to deal with all the details of his position, I feel it necessary to comment on the principal question at stake here.

What does it mean to say that Zen can only be known by experience? The term "experience" needs examination. The ordinary question, "Have you had any experience of living in a foreign country?" usually means nothing more than "Have you ever lived in a foreign country?" "Having experience of" is a loose idiom for describing things one has done or undergone. In a more academic context, however, "experience" has at least two specialized meanings, that are often confused with one another. We may distinguish them as Experience 1: learning or knowing firsthand; and Experience 2: having pure consciousness.

Experience 1 does not entail any epistemological claims about the nature of experience. It simply denies that what is known has been known secondhand, relying on someone else's account. This idea is at work, for instance, in the question, "How do you know it is hot in Indonesia? Have you experienced it for yourself or have you just heard about it from another?" Experience 2, in contrast, does make epistemological claims about the nature of experience. It presupposes a distinction between the rational and the intuitive, the intellectual and nonintellectual, the cognitive and the noncognitive. Its adjective form, "experiential," connotes all these—intuitive, non-intellectual, noncognitive. To experience something in this sense means to have a direct apprehension without any intellectual or conceptual activity. The experience is "pure" precisely to the extent that there is no intellection or conceptualization going on. This idea is at work in the claim, for example, that "mystical experience is not something you attain by thinking. You have to experience it." Although both thinking and experiencing are firsthand, only the latter can be said to be pure.

If "not founded on words and letters" means that Zen must be experienced, we have to ask: Experienced how—as Experience 1 or as Experience 2? If Experience 1, then the claim that Zen must be experienced is true but trivial. If Experience 2, then the claim is important but false.

If the claim that Zen must be experienced amounts to the statement that one must learn or come to know Zen firsthand, then hearing about it or reading a description of it written by someone else does not count as experience. In this sense, the idea that Zen is "not founded on words and letters" really amounts to saying that it is "not founded on the words and letters of another." But there is nothing uniquely Zen about this. Vast areas of human life cannot be experienced vicariously but can only be learned or known or accomplished firsthand. In fact, Zen teachers often point out parallel examples from everyday life. I recall a lecture in which the Zen master spoke of five things that people have to do by themselves and for which no one can substitute: eat, sleep, urinate, defecate, and attain *satori*. Although the Zen tradition puts great emphasis on the fact that Zen is "not founded on words and letters" and must be experienced, this claim does not require the concept of a "pure experience."

At the same time, there are many who interpret the dictum that Zen is "not founded on words and letters" to mean that "Zen experience" is Experience 2, pure in the sense of being totally without intellectual or conceptual activity. Elsewhere I have argued that the very notion of a "pure experience" is shot through with conceptual problems, and that the reason for its popularity is that it is used ideologically to promote a kind of individualism: in the same way that there is supposed to be a state of nature in which individuals lived in freedom before society arose to compromise it, so also there is supposed to be a pure consciousness before conceptual thinking and social conditioning arose to defile it (Hori 2000).

But even if the notion of "pure experience" were intelligible, the realization of a Zen koan would not be experience in this sense. Within the experience of the nonduality of subject and object, there is still intellectual cognition. Ordinary perception presupposes conceptual activity in order to remain clear and intact. One sees the world through concepts like "here," "there," "tree," "table," "red," "loud," "bowl," "book," etc. Without these concepts to inform our perception, we would not be able to recognize these flesh-colored things as "hands," to interpret those lines on the wall as a "door," to hear that shrilling sound as a "telephone." All seeing that has meaning is "seeing-as," seeing according to concepts. Without the investment of conceptual activity in perception, the phenomenal world would become a blur of amorphous patches of color, sounds that we would not recognize as speech, sensations without meaning. Zen awakening does not cause perception to lose its crisp, clear form and dissolve into such shapeless forms and cacophonous sounds. The mind of a Zen master is not booming, buzzing confusion. The fact that the world continues to be clearly perceived and that one's surroundings can still be described in ordinary language indicates that the experience associated with Zen awakening cannot be a "pure experience."

The experience of realization in a koan is indescribable, but only in the very ordinary sense in which *all* immediate experience is basically indescribable. The resistance of the koan to words is no stronger than the resistance of the aroma of a cup of coffee to verbal expression. The traditional Zen expression of this fact is *reidan jichi*, "Know for yourself hot and cold." To know the sensation of hot and cold is one thing; to explain it to one who does not know it is another. The experience of the realization in koan is not intrinsically indescribable, but only indescribable relative to the repertoire of experiences of the people conversing. When I speak of the aroma of a cup of coffee and the sensation of hot and cold, other people know what I am talking about because they, too, have smelled coffee and felt the sting of hot and cold. But if I should speak of the taste of durian fruit, the Southeast Asian fruit with the nauseating smell and the wonderful taste, few Western readers will understand what I am talking about.

If one attempts to describe the realization of a koan to one who has not had the experience, communication naturally fails, and one reverts to saying that it is "not founded on words and letters." But just as any two people who share an experience can talk about it, so there can be discussion about the experience of insight into the Zen koan. (There is, however, a social prohibition against talking about Zen, which may discourage such discussions from actually taking place.)

So it is quite true that Zen can only be known by experience (in a quite ordinary sense of experience), but this does not imply that Zen is some "pure experience" completely devoid of intellectual activity. A corollary to this conclusion is this: there can be meaningful language about Zen but only between people who have shared its experience. Two aspects of meaning are conjoined in meaningful discourse: *reference*, the object, event, or experience that a word or statement denotes; and *sense*, the significance of a linguistic expression. (The classic example of the distinction is that of "the morning star" and "the evening star," which have different senses but the same reference, namely the planet Venus.) One who is not a connoisseur of wine does not know what "oakiness" *refers* to in wine tasting and therefore does not understand the *sense* of a statement such as, "This wine is too oaky." The same could be said of the entire vocabulary of aesthetic and technical appreciation: words like "highlights," "nose," "fruitiness" in wine tasting; "lushness" and "restraint" in the sound of the strings in music appreciation; "gracefulness" in hockey; "intelligence" in boxing; and so forth. When one does not know the *reference* of these terms in experience, one cannot understand the sense of any statement using them.

Many expressions, "splitting migraine," "the pain and pleasure of childbirth," "prolonged melancholia," "the shame of being old," refer to special or particular experiences that many people have never had, and perhaps never will. But few will claim that these experiences are some special class of experience "not founded on words and letters." Because all of us had some general experiences of "headache," "pleasure," "melancholy," and "shame," we can understand the general sense of these special expressions without having a particular reference for "splitting migraine" or "pain of childbirth" in our repertoire of experiences. The experience of the Zen unity of self and other, however, is so unusual that it does not fall under any more general class. In this case, without one's own experience, one has no point of *reference* for the "sound of one hand" or "original face," and therefore one cannot understand the *sense* of the expressions in which such locutions are used: "Divide the sound of one hand into two"; "How old is the sound of one hand?"; "Make the sound of one hand stand upside down." That does not mean that the language of Zen is meaningless. It is *senseless* only to those who have not had the experience to which it *refers*.

IDEOLOGICAL USE OF EXPERIENCE

Sharf and other scholars have argued that the notion of "religious experience" is an epistemological category created as a useful tool in cultural politics. Sharf writes:

> Nishida, Suzuki, Hisamatsu, and their followers, like Schleiermacher, Otto, and James before them, were reacting to the onslaught of Enlightenment values. They sought to reframe our conceptions of the religious such that a core of spiritual and moral values would survive the headlong clash with secular philosophy, science, and technical progress. They were thus led to posit an "essential core" of religion, conceived of as a private, veridical, ineffable experience inaccessible to empirical scientific analysis. (Sharf 1995A, 135)

That is, those who have described the core of religion as the ineffable experience of the numinous, or of the sacred, or of *satori*, implicitly draw a self-serving line between, on the one hand, those people who have had religious experience (like themselves, practitioners of a religion) and are therefore empowered to be judges of truth and falsehood in matters of religion, and, on the other hand, those people who have not (like the secular and scientific critics of religion) and are therefore incapable of distinguishing truth from falsehood in matters of religion. I do not mean to deny that the notion of "religious experience" has been used in the ideological way described here, to anoint certain persons with the authority to speak on religious matters and disenfranchise others. But "religious experience" is not the only fabled beast lurking in the ideological woods. "Empirical scientific analysis," also known as "academic objectivity," is another such epistemological concept. Proponents not only claim it exists but also use it to draw a self-serving line between those who have it (like themselves, academic scholars) and are therefore empowered to be the judge of true and false, and those who do not have it (like practitioners of religion) and are therefore incapable of distinguishing the true and the false. In this conflict over who has authority to speak on matters religious, both sides posit epistemological entities, "religious experience" and "scientific objectivity," and both sides claim possession of it to grant themselves authority and to disenfranchise the other. In this conflict, it sounds like two hands clapping, but underneath it is really only one.

It is not necessary to get entangled in this debate to make a more important point: simply because a concept has been used in a political or ideological context does not mean that it has no epistemological value. Sharf's criticism leaves one with the impression that because he has shown that the notion of Zen experience has been used politically, this implies that there is no such thing as genuine Zen experience as traditionally described. What are the grounds for such a stark either/or assumption? There are any number of concepts like gender, color of skin, and religious creed, that have been used as political and ideological tools, but that does not mean that they are empty concepts without real content. Even though the notion of religious experience may be used for ideological purposes, that does not of itself imply that there is no genuine religious experience.

Intellectual Interpretation of the Koan

As generation upon generation of Zen teachers have stated, it is a mistake to think that one can solve a koan merely by analyzing it intellectually. Nevertheless Zen has an intellectually comprehensive vocabulary for discussing the many aspects of Zen awakening. Part of this intellectual vocabulary is technical and philosophical, most of it is symbolic and metaphorical. Some of the technical vocabulary is described in a later chapter: the initial awakening, *honbun* (the Fundamental), dynamic action, verbal expression, Five Ranks, the Ten Precepts, the arousing of compassion for all sentient beings, the straight and the crooked, and so on. The vast majority of the verses and phrases of the capping phrase collections, however, uses symbol and metaphor.

Sometimes the connection between technical vocabulary and symbolic expression is explicitly drawn. For instance, in the headnotes of several verses, the editor of the Zenrin Kushu (ZRKS) uses the technical term *honbun*, "the Fundamental," to explain the graphic symbolism of the verses. In the examples below, the words inside parentheses are translations from the headnotes.

> *Jurai kokoro tetsu ni nitari*
> Originally his heart resembles iron.
>   (ZRKS 5.209n: Originally, the sturdy man; the Fundamental.)
> *Kokufu fuite mo irazu*
> The black wind blows but cannot enter.
>   (ZRKS 5.313n: A *wato* about the Fundamental.)
> *Myoju ten'ei o zessu*
> The bright pearl is beyond all cloudiness.
>   (ZRKS 5.379: This verse uses the bright pearl to illuminate
>   the Fundamental.)

Other metaphorical expressions for the Fundamental have been repeated so often, they are now Zen clichés: "sound of one hand," "original face," "Mu," "the great matter," "the point of Bodhidharma's coming from the West," etc.

But such examples of technical terminology are uncommon. Most often, the Zen phrase books use metaphorical language without explanation, expecting that the reader will have, or will develop, the eye to see through the metaphor to the underlying meaning. Take, for example, the following three phrases referring to the nonduality of subject and object:

Hinju ittai.	Guest and host are one.
Riji funi.	Principle and fact are not two.
Banbutsu ichinyo.	The ten thousand things are one.

This sort of explicit labeling using philosophical terminology is said to "stink of Zen." The Zen tradition rather prefers to use colorful symbolic language.

Hi ochite tsuki imada noborazu.	The sun has set but the moon has yet to rise.
Ikke no fushi.	Father and son in one house.
Itto ichidan.	One sword [cuts into] one piece.

The image in the final line is particularly interesting. The usual expression is *Itto nidan*, "One sword [cuts into] two pieces," but here the sword of Zen cuts into a single piece, symbolizing a discrimination that is nondual. The metaphorical language is much more striking than the dry technical language.

Although it is true that one can only grasp a koan by becoming it, that one cannot grasp a koan merely through intellectual understanding, nevertheless there is an intellectual language, both technical and symbolic, for talking about the many aspects of Zen awakening. Intellectual understanding of the koan and the experience of the nonduality of subject and object are not opposed to each other, the one excluding the other. Without realization of the point of the koan, there can be no intellectual understanding of the koan. With realization comes understanding.

Capping-phrase collections are expressions of Zen awakening in language. The awakening of Zen can only be realized personally; it is "not founded upon words and letters." That is the gold of Zen. But to convey that awakening to others, one must use language. To sell the gold of Zen, one must mix it with sand.

BIBLIOGRAPHY

Gallwey, W. Timothy. *The Inner Game of Tennis.* New York: Random House, 1974.

Kim, Hee-jin. "Introductory Essay: Language in Dogen's Zen." *Flowers of Emptiness: Selections from Dogen's Shobogenzo* Lewiston and Queenston: Edwin Mellen Press. 1–47, 1985.

Miura, Isshō and Ruth Fuller Sasaki. *Zen Dust: The History of the Koan and Koan Study in Rinzai (Lin-chi) Zen.* Kyoto: The First Zen Institute of America, 1966.

Proudfoot, Wayne. *Religious Experience.* Berkeley: University of California Press, 1985.

Rosemont, Henry, Jr. "The Meaning Is the Use: Koan and Mondo as Linguistic Tools of the Zen Masters." *Philosophy East and West* 20: 109–19, 1970.

Sellman, James. "The Koan: A Language Game." *Philosophical Quarterly* 7. Supp.: 1–9, 1979.

Sharf, Robert H. "The Zen of Japanese Nationalism." *In Curators of the Buddha,* ed. by Donald S. Lopez. Chicago: University of Chicago Press. 107–60. Originally published in *History of Religions* 33: 1–43, 1995.

———— "Buddhist Modernism and the Rhetoric of Meditative Experience." *Numen* 42: 228–83, 1995.

———— "Zen and the Way of the New Religions." *Japanese Journal of Religious Studies* 22: 417–58, 1995.

Sudnow, David. *Ways of the Hand: The Organization of Improvised Conduct.* Cambridge: Harvard University Press, 1978.

Suzuki, Daisetz T. *Essays in Zen Buddhism, Second Series.* London: Rider, 1953.

Wright, Dale S. "Rethinking Transcendence: The Role of Language in Zen Experience." *Philosophy East and West* 42: 113–38, 1992.

Yampolsky, Philip. *The Zen Master Hakuin: Selected Writings.* New York: Columbia University Press, 1971.

THE STEPS OF KOAN PRACTICE

Victor Sogen Hori

IN THIS CHAPTER, we will consider the stages involved in koan practice as well as some of the technical terminology that accompanies it. The aim is to present a general picture of the overall training career of full-time practitioners engaged in the koan curriculum.

KOAN AND MEDITATION: ENDS OR MEANS?

Although many beginning monks take "passing" the koan to be the goal of their practice and see meditation as merely the means to that goal, Rinzai teachers caution against this way of thinking. Monks begin and end their daily activities with a period of *zazen* sitting in the *zendo*. From within a period of *zazen*, monks proceed to the main hall to chant sutras. From within *zazen*, they go to meals, to *samu* work, and to begging. After returning from the day's activities, they return to the *zendo* for another period of *zazen*. When they go to bed at night, they are still in a period of *zazen* that is not ended until the ringing of the bell the next morning. Ritually speaking, therefore, *zazen* is the one fundamental activity of the monastery, the center from which all else is done.

Zazen is far from being just the means to passing the koan. The ritual structure of monastery life makes it clear that it is rather the other way around: one works on a koan in order to do meditation.

Monasteries vary somewhat in their meditation schedules, but most continue to maintain the traditional schedule of two training terms in summer and winter, each containing three or four major *sesshin* (a week of intensive meditation practice), and a number of minor *sesshin* filling out the rest of the year. Three *sesshin* a month is common. In addition, regardless of the *sesshin* schedule and unless there is some special reason, the bell for *sanzen* (meeting with the *roshi* or Zen master) is put out each morning so that monks may confront the roshi over their koan at least once a day. In stricter monasteries, monks can expect several hours of meditation and at least two *sanzen* every day throughout most of the year.

The initial koan given to monks, known as *shokan* or "the First Barrier," is usually either Hakuin's *Sekishu onjo* (the Sound of One Hand) or Joshu's *Mu* (Mumonkan Case 1). Some temples begin with *Honrai no menmoku* (the Original Face, Mumonkan Case 23). The Chinese glyph *kan* in *shokan* can also mean "gate," so that *shokan* could also be translated "First Entry." I prefer to render it "barrier" to emphasize the difficulty involved in passing through it. Monks are expected to get their first insight, or *kensho*, into the Fundamental through meditation on one of these koan. It may take anywhere from half a year to several years to do so. The term *kensho* needs fuller attention than we will be able to give it here. It contains several layers of meaning in Japanese and, to complicate matters still further, has entered the English language, where Western expectations have given it a new and independent career. Suffice it to remark here that no monk can pass his first koan without demonstrating *kensho*. Some academics have surmised that passing a koan is a form of "scriptural exegesis" presupposing considerable prior study of Buddhist texts. From my own experience as a monk in the Daitoku-ji monastery, I can testify that indeed very few of my fellow monks could be described as intellectuals or as learned in Buddhist teachings. In any case, once past the first barrier, the monk needs further training before he can arrive at and articulate his first insight.

Sassho, Checking Questions

A single koan usually breaks down into parts, the initial "main case" *(honsoku)* and numerous "checking questions" *(sassho)*. *Sassho* perform two functions. First, by means of these questions the roshi can confirm the monk's original insight into the Fundamental and gauge the depth of that insight. Second, the checking questions push the monk to broaden his insight beyond the Fundamental into particular instances of it. For example, the First Barrier koan "Sound of One Hand" and "Mu" are typically followed by checking questions such as "What is the Sound of One Hand from in front and from behind?" or "Divide Mu into two." The number of questions ranges anywhere from twenty to a hundred or more, depending on the teaching lineage of the roshi. Checking questions serve the roshi as a quick way to uncover deception. The required initial responses to koan have become fixed over time, and monks sometimes learn the required responses through hearsay. To confirm that the insight is actually the monk's own and not something he is repeating second-hand, all the roshi need do is confront him with a few of these checking questions.

Whichever of the two (Sound of One Hand or Mu) the monk receives initially, the novice monk will most likely receive the other of the pair immediately afterwards, so that his entire first year or more is taken up with these two koan and their *sassho*.

The Inzan and Takuju Schools

Once past the First Barrier koan, practice in Rinzai monasteries follows one of two patterns, depending on whether the teaching roshi belongs to the Inzan school or the Takuju school. Inzan Ien (1751–1814) and Takuju Kosen (1760–1833) were the direct disciples of Gasan Jito (1727–1797), who himself was a direct disciple of Hakuin Ekaku (1686–1769). All monasteries and roshi presently teaching in Japan associate themselves with one or the other of these schools. The two teach basically the same body of koan and both consider themselves to be transmitting the Zen of Hakuin. But the Inzan school is thought to be sharper and more dynamic in style, while the Takuju school is thought to be more meticulous and low-keyed.

In the Takuju school, Takuju monks work systematically through the *Mumonkan*, beginning with Case 1, advancing to Case 2, Case 3, and so on. On completion of this text, they work on a number of cases from the *Katto-shu*, and then move on to the *Hekigan-roku*, whose cases they also take up in order, Case 1, Case 2, and so on. In contrast, monks in the Inzan lineage receive koan from a variety of collections— *Mumonkan*, *Hekigan-roku*, *Katto-shu*, *Chin'u-shu*—in what appears to be random order. In fact, however, the order is fixed, so much so that a monk transferring from one Inzan school roshi to another need merely tell the new roshi his last koan in order for the new roshi to know where to continue without leaving any gap or requiring any repetition of work already done.

It is commonly said that, compared to Inzan monks, Takuju monks receive many more *sassho* or checking questions after passing the main case and are asked to provide more *jakugo* (capping phrases). To accommodate the large number of *sassho* and *jakugo* assignments, the *sesshin* schedule in a Takuju monastery often includes more *sanzen* sessions with the roshi, as many as seven a day. Over the years, the two schools have developed slightly different bodies of Zen verses and phrases from which to draw *jakugo*. The verses and phrases that make up [the volume from which this chapter was drawn] have been taken from two modern collections, Tsuchiya Etsudo's *Zengoshu* and Shibayama Zenkei's *Zenrin kushu*, in order to encompass the practice of both schools.

The two schools are not so divided as to prohibit the occasional crossover of traditions. A monastery's style of koan practice will depend on the roshi teaching there at any given time, and although most monasteries have become associated in the course of generations with a particular school, occasionally a *honzan* headquarters of one of the schools will ask a roshi from the other to take over one of its monasteries. From time to time, a particularly gifted roshi will make it a point to train under several teachers, learning the style of both schools in order to be able to give instruction in either of them. In addition, many roshi seem to know that particular koan are treated differently in the other school, and this knowledge is passed along in their own teachings of those koan.

Koan Taikei, THE KOAN SYSTEM

Both the Inzan and Takuju schools teach the koan system attributed to Hakuin, although it should be noted that there are some grounds for doubting that he was the creator of the present koan system. Since we are more concerned with the present use of the system, there is no need to go into these historical questions here.

When people speak of Hakuin's koan system, they usually are referring to a five-fold division of koan:

Hosshin	*Dharmakaya* or Dharma-body
Kikan	Dynamic Action
Gonsen	Explication of Words
Hachi nanto	Eight Difficult-to-Pass
Goi jujukin	Five Ranks and the Ten Grave Precepts

This five-fold division seems to have evolved from earlier classification systems. It is known that the Japanese Zen monk Shoichi Kokushi (Ben'en Enni, 1202–1280) had systematized koan into categories, but there is some disagreement as to whether he used three or four. The Zen monk and scholar Akizuki Ryomin describes three categories: *Richi* (Attaining the Principle), *Kikan* (Dynamic Action) and *Kojo* (Directed Upwards) (Akizuki 1987, 77). Others add a fourth category: *Koge* (Directed Downwards) (Ito 1970, 36). Nanpo Jomyo (1235–1309), the monk who brought the Yogi branch of Rinzai Zen to Japan from China, also divided koan into three categories: *Richi, Kikan,* and *Kojo* (Akizuki 1987, 77–78; Asahina 1941, 49–50).

Akizuki notes, however, that in Hakuin's system the original fifth category was not *Goi jujukin* (Five Ranks and the Ten Grave Precepts) but *Kojo.* He faults the Zen roshi Asahina Sogen for first substituting *Goi jujukin* as the fifth category, lamenting the fact that both Zen roshi and lay writers have blindly followed his lead (Akizuki 1987, 82). The lack of agreement on precisely what the five categories are has carried over into English-language accounts of Hakuin's system. Miura and Sasaki present Hakuin's system with *Goi jujukin* as the fifth category (ZD, 62–76), while Shimano gives *Kojo* (Directed Upwards) as the fifth category and *Goi jujukin* as a sixth category (Shimano 1988, 79–80). No systematic survey has been conducted to determine what system the majority of Rinzai teaching-roshi in Japan now follow, but my general impression is that *Goi jujukin,* and not *Kojo,* is usually considered the fifth category.

A complete list of all the categories of koan in use would have to include not only *Kojo* but two others as well. At very advanced stages of koan practice, a monk might receive:

> *Kojo* (Directed Upwards)
> *Matsugo no rokan* (Last Barrier)
> *Saigo no ikketsu* (Final Confirmation).

I will discuss each of these in greater detail below. Since descriptions of Hakuin's five stages are readily available in English, I will restrict myself to an abbreviated account of his system here.

Hosshin (Dharmakaya) Koan

The *Hosshin* koan reveal the *dharmakaya*, the Dharma-body, or the Fundamental. Asahina Sogen Roshi explains:

> The simple explanation of Dharma-body, given by the ancients, is that one takes the dharma and makes oneself one with it, but this is just what we mean by true reality *(shin-nyo)*, by Dharma-nature, by Buddha-nature, by awakening *(bodai)*, by nirvana, by the original body of the universe. For the Zen practitioner, it means one's own mind nature. In more concrete terms, it is the subject *(shujinko)* of our seeing and hearing, of all our consciousness…
>
> The Zen practitioner by illuminating Dharma-body seeks to illuminate himself, to emancipate himself from life-and-death, and to attain unhindered freedom. The *Richi* koan, the *Kikan* koan, the *Kojo* koan and all other koan attempt nothing more than to illuminate Dharma-body and radiate freedom through becoming one with the realm of Dharma-body. (Asahina 1941, 56)

The Dharma-body koan are the koan on which a monk experiences an initial awakening, *kensho* or *satori*. The First Barrier koan, the Sound of One Hand, and Joshu's Mu fall within this first group. As we see in the formula "If you awaken to *hosshin*, then there is not one single thing" *(Hosshin kakuryo sureba ichi motsu mo nashi)*, the realm of *hosshin* is the realm of the undifferentiated and unconditioned. It is useful, at least provisionally, to think of *Hosshin* koan as those that introduce the undifferentiated and the unconditional. (Like many other Zen terms, *hosshin* has also a second sense in which the undifferentiated is identical with the differentiated and the unconditioned with the conditioned.)

Kikan (Dynamic Action) Koan

The *Kikan* or Dynamic Action koan open up the realm of the differentiated and the dynamic in Zen. The character *ki* in *kikan* is difficult to translate. Originally it denoted a weaver's loom, and in both Chinese and Japanese it is used today in compounds to signify machinery or anything mechanical. In Buddhism it has its own technical meanings, which differ from one branch to the next. Within Zen it has come to be used as a synonym for *hataraki* (working or functioning), and in its wider connotations carries the sense of spirit, dynamism, action, or flair. In general, it implies action rather than stillness and involvement rather than detachment, as, for instance, in the term *zenki*, which refers to the dynamic activity of the awakened person in the concrete situations of daily life.

Taken together, *Hosshin* koan and *Kikan* koan reflect the traditional Chinese contrast between substance *(tai)* and function *(yu)*. The *Hosshin* or "Body of the Buddha" koan take one to the realm of the ultimate and unconditioned. But it is all too easy to get stuck there, in a condition that Zen calls *deiri no kyuin*, "a worm in the mud" (mud being a metaphor for *satori*). Kikan koan pry the monk out of the suffocating *satori* of the undifferentiated and the unconditioned, returning him to the everyday phenomenal world of self and things, of conventionality and discrimination. *Kikan* koan show that the Fundamental is not merely still and tranquil but also active and dynamic, not only empty and undifferentiated but also full of distinctions and differentiation. To learn this is said to be more difficult than the attainment of the original *satori*, as we see in the following verse.

> *Nehan no kokoro wa akirameyasuku,*
> *Sabetsu no chi wa irigatashi.*
> To clarify the mind of nirvana is easy,
> But to enter the wisdom of discrimination is hard.

Gonsen (Explication of Words) Koan

Gonsen koan bring to light the fact that while the Fundamental is "not founded on words and letters," it is nevertheless expressed through words and letters. Gonsen koan can be quite long, so that even memorizing them in order to recite them in the presence of the roshi can be a major task in itself. Despite the fact that a special category exists for verbal expression, in my opinion the Gonsen koan do not present any problem with words and language that is not common to all koan. In every koan, the Zen practitioner faces the problem of breaking through the surface of words and letters—which may appear to be speaking of something else entirely—to the Fundamental beneath. In this sense the problem of how to express in words and letters what is purportedly not founded on words and letters arises in every koan and is part of the very nature of koan practice (see Hori 2000 for a fuller discussion).

Hachi Nanto (Eight Difficult-To-Pass) Koan

Hakuin selected eight particularly dreadful koan that he said would give the Zen practitioner chest pains and stomachaches. He urged his monks to risk their lives in order to pass these locked barriers and attain Zen awakening (Akizuki 1987, 89). These Hachi nanto koan, as they are known, are considered a major test for Zen monks, though there seems to be some disagreement about what these koan are supposed to teach and what their importance is in the overall koan curriculum. Miura states that one who has completed the Nanto koan understands "jiji mege hokkai, the Dharma world where each thing interpenetrates and harmonizes perfectly with every other thing without any hindrance whatsoever, the realm of complete effortlessness" (ZD, 61). This description makes it seem as if the point of the Nanto koan is to attain the fourth Hua-yen dharma-dhatu. Akizuki, in contrast, argues that the teachers of antiquity created the Nanto koan to show practitioners that after satori there was also the realm of discrimination and differentiation (which is the function of Kikan koan), and then after that, the work of saving sentient beings (Akizuki 1987, 88). I might add that I myself have heard a roshi remark quite bluntly that the Nanto have no significance beyond the fact that Hakuin found them difficult to pass.

Despite this range of opinion about the function of the *Nanto* koan, most Zen teachers accept a more or less standard explanation, according to which the initial stages of the koan curriculum are designed to bring the monk to awakening and then to deepen it, while the more advanced stages are meant to cut the monk's attachment to his own awakening and arouse compassion for others. This latter function is attributed to *Nanto* koan in the version of the curriculum where the fourth and fifth categories are *Nanto* and *Kojo*. I cite Asahina Sogen Roshi's account of the *Nanto* koan:

> Once a person feels he has attained some degree of satori, he becomes satisfied with the Dharma joy of this new world and thus it is hard for him to make any further advance. In the history of Zen, there are many who at this stage have sat down in self-satisfaction and stopped here. Such people think themselves fine as they are and therefore have no ability to help other people. Indeed on closer reflection, [we see that] they have not even saved themselves. The *Nanto* are a painful stick to the one who undertakes them. They make one know what it means to say, "Atop the mountain, another mountain." ... That precious satori, which one got by going here, going there, doing this and doing that—[these *Nanto* koan] take that *satori* and crush it like tree leaves into dust. Zen people call this "the house destroyed and the family scattered." "Holding onto nothing" has been replaced by "absolutely nothing to lose." (Asahina 1941, 61–62)

The *Nanto* koan, then, are meant to throw the Zen practitioner back into crisis, releasing another Great Doubt, one that is directed not against the conventional self, but against the self that got created with *satori*.

The cycle of attaining awakening and then cutting it off is described in numerous Zen verses, such as the following:

> *Bompu moshi shiraba, sunawachi kore seijin,*
> *Seijin moshi shiraba, sunawachi kore bompu.*
> An ordinary person knows it and becomes a sage;
> A sage understands it and becomes an ordinary person.

> *Tsuchi o nigitte kin to nasu koto wa nao yasukarubeshi,*
> *Kin o henjite tsuchi to nasu koto wa kaette mata katashi.*
> To take earth and turn it into gold may be easy,
> But to take gold and turn it into earth, that is difficult indeed.

There is uncertainty now about which eight koan are included in Hakuin's list. Miura and Sasaki in *Zen Dust* (1966, 57–61) mention the following five koan:

Nansen's Flower (*Hekigan-roku* Case 40)
A Buffalo Passes the Window (*Mumonkan* Case 38)
Sozan's Memorial Tower (*Katto-shu* Case 140)
Suigan's Eyebrows (*Hekigan-roku* Case 8)
Enkan's Rhinoceros Fan (*Hekigan-roku* Case 91)

Shimano (1988, 78–79) gives as an example:
The Old Woman Burns the Hut (*Katto-shu* Case 162).

Asahina Sogen (1941, 62–63) gives as additional examples:
Goso Hoen's "Hakuun Said 'Not Yet'" (*Katto-shu* Case 269)
Shuzan's Main Cable (*Katto-shu* Case 280).

Akizuki (1987, 90–91) adds:
Nansen Has Died (*Katto-shu* Case 282)
Kenpo's Three Illnesses (*Katto-shu* Case 17).

Together these give us ten koan for Hakuin's list of Eight Difficult-to-Pass koan.

Goi (Five Ranks) Koan

The fifth category, *Goi jujukin*, contains two subcategories, koan of the Five Ranks and koan dealing with the Ten Grave Precepts. The term "Five Ranks" is an abbreviation of "Tozan's Five Ranks." Tozan Ryokai (Tung-shan Liang-chieh, 807–869) was the teacher of Sozan Honjaku (Ts'ao-shan Pen-chi, 840–901). The two were cofounders of the Soto

School of Zen, the name "Soto" representing a combination of the first characters of each of their names. For the Japanese Rinzai school, however, Tozan's Five Ranks are presented in a work authored by Hakuin called *Tojo goi hensho kuketsu,* "The Five Ranks of the Crooked and the Straight: The Oral Teachings of the [Monk] who Lived on Mount To." This work is included in the handbook called *Zudokko (The Poison-Painted Drum),* which is one of the standard possessions of practicing monks.

The *Goi* koan do not introduce the monk to anything new. Rather, they require the monk to systematize all the koan that he has passed, using the classification system of Tozan's Five Ranks. The ranks are:

Shochuhen	The Crooked within the Straight
Henchusho	The Straight within the Crooked
Shochurai	The Coming from within the Straight
Kenchushi	The Arrival at Mutual Integration
Kenchuto	Unity Attained.

In Asahina's explanation (1941, 64), *sho* "is emptiness, is truth, is black, is darkness, is principle, is *yin*," while *hen* "is form, is vulgar, is white, is brightness, is fact, is *yang*." Miura and Sasaki have translated *shoi'i* and *hen'i* as "Real" and "Apparent," but I prefer to render them as "Straight" and "Crooked" in order to avoid the implication that "Real" is more real than "Apparent." The practicing monk has met the pair *sho'i* and *hen'i* in koan practice long before he reaches the Five Ranks. In fact, the distinction between the Fundamental and its particular instantiations, as seen in the First Barrier koan and its particular *sassho* checking questions, is basically the same distinction as that between *sho'i* and *hen'i*. Koan almost always divide into two or more parts that invariably see the koan from the two sides of *sho'i* and *hen'i*. Some commentators claim that the philosophical background of Mahayana Buddhist thought stands behind Zen, and indeed this is one of those places in which that background emerges into clear relief in that the distinction between *sho'i* and *hen'i* can easily be taken as the Zen transformation of the Two Truths.

Although the Five Ranks is associated with Tozan Ryokai, the idea of five ranks or positions must have grown out of the Chinese theory of Five Elements or Five Forces. The article on Tozan's Five Ranks in the

Mochizuki bukkyo daijiten dictionary of Buddhist terms describes the connections that various commentators have found between the Five Ranks and everything from yin-yang thought to hexagrams of the *I Ching* and Chou Tun-i's diagram of the Supreme Ultimate (Mochizuki 1958, 3864–9). Few useful commentaries on the Five Ranks exist in English. The best starting point is still Chapter Seven of Miura and Sasaki's *Zen Dust*, which contains a slightly abbreviated translation of Hakuin's account of the Five Ranks, *Tojo goi hensho kuketsu*. One can also consult Luk 1961, Powell 1986, Chang 1969, Lai 1983, and Tokiwa 1991.

Of particular interest for many readers will be the relationship between the Five Ranks and the *I Ching*. Since the Five Ranks are constructed from two elements, one positive and one negative (Straight and Crooked, Lord and Vassal, Real and Apparent), it is easy to pair them with hexagrams in the *I Ching*, which themselves are composed of combinations of *yin* and *yang* lines. In fact, Hakuin's own account of the Five Ranks, *Tojo goi hensho kuketsu*, begins with a diagram of Hexagram 30, Fire upon Fire, but for some reason this diagram has been omitted from the English translation in Miura and Sasaki's *Zen Dust*. Some of the final koan connected with the Rinzai Five Ranks also treat the hexagrams of the *I Ching*. In working on these koan, the monk is expected to prepare a set of six woodblocks with *yin* and *yang* faces to be used in the *sanzen* room when he meets the roshi.

Juju Kinkai (The Ten Grave Precepts)

Juju kinkai, the Ten Grave Precepts, are the precepts against taking life, stealing, misusing sex, lying, intoxication, speaking ill of others, praising oneself, covetousness, anger, and reviling the Three Treasures. The Ten Grave Precepts bring Hakuin's koan system to completion, since the final end of Rinzai koan practice is not benefit for oneself but benefit for others. Asahina notes that in these koan the practicing monk must embody the precepts as *Hosshin*, realize their dynamic activity as *Kikan*, express them in words as *Gonsen*, penetrate them completely as *Nanto*, thoroughly understand their theoretic rationale in the *Goi*, and then practice them faithfully in daily life as *Juju kinkai*. At the same time, he regrets that these koan come at the end of a long system of training, since most monks who begin koan practice leave their training in mid-course without having come to the Ten Grave Precepts (Asahina 1941, 70).

In English there are only a few comments on the Ten Grave Precepts koan, none of which reflect the way they are taught in Japanese Rinzai training. In their chapter on the Ten Grave Precepts, Miura and Sasaki merely list the precepts and cite a passage from monastery *Admonitions* (ZD, 73–76). Shimano observes that the point of these koan is to get past the habit, especially marked in the West, of always seeing things as either good or bad, and to move to the "ultimate standpoint" beyond the dualistic view of killing or not killing. He places strong emphasis on nonduality, on "no killer and no one to be killed," on "realization of oneness" (Shimano 1988, 80–81). Aitken takes the opposite tack, emphasizing the standpoint of the conventional. His lectures on the Ten Grave Precepts rarely use the language of oneness, replacing it with examples of drunken men in hotel rooms, woman chasers in the sangha, and a cranky mother with a demanding daughter (Aitken 1984, 3–104). In Rinzai koan training, both the *sho'i* and *hen'i* (straight and crooked, nondual and dual) aspects of the Ten Grave Precepts are given equal emphasis, and the precepts as a whole are presented not merely as rules to guard human behavior against the tendency to wrong-doing, but also as positive expressions of the bodhisattva's practice of "the *samadhi* of freedom in the other," *tajiyu zammai*.

Kojo (Directed Upwards)

In the curriculum that seems to be most widely adopted today, the fourth and fifth categories are *Nanto* (Difficult to Pass) and *Goi jujukin* (Five Ranks and the Ten Grave Precepts). As we remarked earlier, in what Akizuki claims was the older original koan system, the fifth category was *Kojo* (Directed Upwards). Today this category no longer seems to have a well-defined function. In the older curriculum where the fourth and fifth categories were *Nanto* and *Kojo*, the *Nanto* koan would simply have been eight koan considered extremely difficult to pass, and the *Kojo* koan would have had the special function of ridding the monk of any "stink of Zen" and of attachment to his awakening.

The variety of different translations of the term *Kojo* merits comment. I have translated it literally as "Directed Upwards" in view of the fact that Shoichi Kokushi adds the further category *Koge*, "Directed Downwards." Shimano translates *Kojo* as "Crowning," but I find this misleading in that it implies a kind of finality or completion. Akizuki (1987, 91), writing in Japanese, uses the English term "nonattachment" to explain the function of *Kojo*. Mohr (1999, 317–18) translates it as "Going beyond," which I find far better in that it implies an open-endedness. *Kojo* is a reminder that not even the attainment of *satori* or *kensho* is final, that there is "Atop the mountain, another mountain." After the task of reaching *satori* comes that of ridding oneself of *satori* and working for the salvation of others. This is *Kojo*. The saying "When you reach the top of the mountain, you must keep going" seems to imply just this sort of further ascent. But the second mountain one has to climb after arriving at the *samadhi* summit of freedom for oneself *(jijiyu zammai)* begins with a descent downhill, back into the valley as it were, to cultivate for others the *samadhi* of freedom *(tajiyu zammai)*. The final stage of practice is to leave the mountain to work for the benefit of all sentient beings, and of this stage of practice there is no end.

Matsugo no rokan, the Last Barrier; Saigo no ikketsu, the Final Confirmation

Not much has been written about these last koan, and needless to say, Zen priests and monks are reluctant to speak of them in public. The Last Barrier koan is given to the monk as he leaves the monastery. Akizuki gives as examples "Sum up all of the Record of Rinzai in one phrase!" and "Hakuin's 'Not yet'" (1987, 96). But since the monk is leaving the monastery, he is not meant to pass this koan immediately, but rather to carry it constantly with him and to try again and again to see through it right to the bottom. Finally, some roshi assign a last koan called *Saigo no ikketsu*. I have not been able to discover much about this koan but suspect that it is an alternate name for *Matsugo no rokan*.

Shotai Choyo, Long Nurturing of the Sacred Fetus

The formal koan training completed in the monastery does nothing more than create a "sacred fetus." A monk who has completed the koan training is not yet ready to step out into the world and take on a public role. He must first complete another stage called *Shotai choyo* (sometimes pronounced *Seitai choyo*), the "long nurturing of the sacred fetus." This period of withdrawal after the completion of the koan curriculum is also known as *Gogo no shugyo* or "post-*satori* training." (There is some ambiguity in the use of the term, since the same term may also refer to all training after initial *satori*.) As explained in the lectures that roshi give to their monks, a monk who has completed the koan curriculum leaves the monastery for several years, hiding his identity as a monk, in order to engage in some activity completely unrelated to monastery practice. The great example is Daito Kokushi, the "beggar under the bridge." Zen lore has it that after his *satori*, he lived for twenty years with the beggars under the Gojo Bridge in Kyoto, giving his *satori* time to ripen before he went on to found the Daitoku-ji temple. Daito Kokushi's disciple, Kanzan Egen, it is said, withdrew to the mountains of Ibuka in present-day Gifu Prefecture, where for eight years he tended cattle and tilled the fields (Miura and Saski 1966, 325). In his *Mujintoron (Discourse on the Inexhaustible Lamp)*, Torei Enji cites the long maturation periods of numerous past masters: Hui-neng, the Sixth Patriarch, went south for fifteen years; Nansen Fugan resided for thirty years in a hermitage (where monks eventually gathered and argued about a cat that Nansen had killed); Daibai Hojo ate pine needles and wore clothes made from lotus stalks for thirty years; Yogi Hoe spent twenty years in a dilapidated hut where snowflakes bejewelled the floor in the winter (Torei 1989, 451–74). During this period of ripening the monk is said to learn to apply the awakening he attained in formal monastery training to the concrete situations of daily life, and he does this by deliberately extinguishing all self-consciousness of *satori*.

The phrase "long nurturing of the sacred fetus" resonates with profound nuances. The term "sacred fetus" itself looks as if it originated in Taoist practices of longevity and immortality, since the point of Taoist inner alchemy practice is to combine breath, vital force, and spirit to create a sacred fetus which is then nurtured through further discipline into immortality. The practice of withdrawing from society also has clear associations with the broader image of the recluse or hermit in Chinese culture. This individual withdrew from public life not because he was incapable of functioning in the world, but because he found the world too disordered for a person of principle to exercise his talents properly. He chose seclusion in order to nourish himself, all the better to reemerge and assume public responsibility at a later time, when a proper leader had appeared and the time was ripe (Vervoorn 1990). A legendary example of this is Chu-ko Liang in the *Romance of the Three Kingdoms*. This master scholar and strategist of war lived in deep seclusion until Liu Pei, the last scion of the Han Empire, visited him three times and was able to persuade him to come forth and join him in the attempt to reestablish his empire (Brewitt-Taylor 1959, 385–407). Reclusion thus symbolizes the fact that, while capable of handling power and rank, the hermit is not attached to these things but puts his self-cultivation and the welfare of people first. Similarly, in *Shotai choyo*, the Zen practitioner who has finished his formal training engages in an informal training in which he thoroughly detaches himself from his accomplishments and willingly assumes anonymity for service to others.

Personal Reflections

I conclude this short account of the so-called koan system with a number of supplementary remarks. In day-to-day monastic life, the several categories of koan make little difference to the practicing monk. Monks themselves do not know to which category the koan they are presently working on belongs. The categories of koan are useful to senior monks, who need to reflect on the koan system as a whole, but monks in the thick of practice seldom speak of *hosshin, kikan, nanto,* or the like.

Moreover, the formal categories of the koan system give the impression that every koan can be assigned to a single category, but in fact *hosshin, kikan,* and *gonsen* point to aspects found in all the koan that every practicing monk easily recognizes even without the formal description. In every koan the monk must grasp the koan itself *(hosshin)*, experience its dynamic working *(kikan)*, and use language to express what is "not founded on words and letters" *(gonsen)*. In the same way, the *jakugo* assignments are actually a *gonsen* exercise, even though the word may never be used.

Japanese Rinzai Zen is often criticized, even by its own monks, for allowing the koan practice to calcify into a rigid formalism. It is not uncommon to hear Rinzai practice faulted for being little more than a ritual recapitulation of koan responses that the mere passage of time has baptized as orthodoxy. There is some truth to this, but in defense of the practice, I would add that in my own case I never felt anything but admiration for the teachers of the past who had devised a system of training that time and again forced me to plunge deep into *zazen* to find an answer from a place in myself I did not know existed. The fixed response to a koan resembles the fixed patterns of movements in the martial arts called *kata*. One practices them again and again until they become movements of power, executed precisely and without deliberation. As for whether there are "correct answers" to the koan, Zen teachers insist that before one engages in the practice a koan may appear to have a fixed meaning, but that after one has completed the practice, that koan has no meaning at all, fixed or otherwise.

BIBLIOGRAPHY

Aitken, Robert. *The Mind of Clover: Essays in Zen Buddhist Ethics.* San Francisco: North Point Press, 1984.

Akizuki, Ryomin. *Koan: A Practical Introduction to Zen.* Tokyo: Chikuma Shobo, 1987.

Asahina, Sogen, *Zen Koan.* Tokyo: Yōzankaku, 1941.

Brewitt-Taylor, C. H., trans. *Romance of the Three Kingdoms.* Rutland and Tokyo: Charles E. Tuttle, 1959.

Chang Cung-yuan, "Interfusion of Universality and Particularity." *Original Teachings of Ch'an Buddhism: Selected from The Transmission of the Lamp.* New York: Random House, 41-57, 1969.

Hori, Victor Sōgen. "Koan and Kenshō in the Rinzai Koan Curriculum." In Heine, Steven and D. S. Wright, eds. *The Koan: Texts and Contexts in Zen Buddhism.* Oxford: Oxford University Press, 280–315, 2000.

Ito, Kokan. *Zen and the Koan.* Tokyo: Shunjusha (1970, 36).

Lai, Whalen, and Lewis R. Lancaster, eds. *Early Ch'an in China and Tibet.* Berkeley: Berkeley Buddhist Studies, 1983.

Luk, Charles. *Cha'n and Zen Teaching.* 3 vols. London: Rider, 1961.

Miura, Issho and Ruth Fuller Sasaki. *Zen Dust: The History of the Koan and Koan Study in Rinzai (Lin-chi) Zen.* Kyoto: The First Zen Institute of America, 1966.

Mochizuki, Shinko, ed. *Mochizuki Buddhist Lexicon, Revised Edition.* Tokyo: Sekei Seiten Kanko Kyokai, 1958.

Mohr, Michel. "Hakuin." In *Buddhist Spirituality 2: Later China, Korea, Japan and the Modern World.* Edited by Takeuchi Yoshinori with James W. Heisig, Paul L. Swanson, and Joseph S. O'Leary. New York: Crossroad Publishing, 307–28, 1999.

Powell, William F., trans. *The Record of Tung-shan.* Honolulu: University of Hawai'i Press, 1986.

Shimano Eido. "Zen Koans." In *Kraft 1988,* 70–87, 1988.

Tokiwa, Gishin. "Hakuin Ekaku's Insight into 'The Deep Secret of Hen (Pian)-Sho (Zheng) Reciprocity' and His Koan 'The Sound of a Single Hand.'" *Journal of Indian and Buddhist Studies* 39/2: 989–93, 1991.

Torei, Enji Zenji. *Discourse on the Inexhaustible Lamp.* Comments by Daibi Zenji, trans. by Yoko Okuda. London: Zen Centre, 1989.

Vervoorn, A. *Men of the Cliffs and Caves: The Development of the Chinese Eremitic Tradition to the End of the Han Dynasty.* Hong Kong: The Chinese University Press, 1990.

JAPANESE KOAN STUDY

DOGEN AND KOANS

John Daido Loori

DOGEN AND THE TWO SHOBOGENZOS

RELATIVELY UNKNOWN during his lifetime in Kamakura Japan, Eihei Dogen is now considered to be one of the most remarkable religious figures and teachers in the history of Zen, as well as an outstanding philosopher, mystic, and poet. His works have had a tremendous impact, not only in Japan and within the Soto School of Zen Buddhism, but also in the West.

Dogen is best known for his monumental work, the *Kana* or *Japanese Shobogenzo*, a collection of ninety-six essays composed in Japanese between the years 1231 and 1253. Based on Dogen's profound religious experience and enriched by his philosophical and literary gifts, the *Shobogenzo* or *Treasury of the True Dharma Eye* is a unique expression of the Buddhist teachings. Several English translations of and commentaries on the *Shobogenzo* are in existence today, and scholars and practitioners alike share the ever-increasing body of information on Dogen's life and work.

Not as popular as Dogen's *Kana Shobogenzo* is his *Mana* or *Sambyakusoku Shobogenzo (The Shobogenzo of Three Hundred Koans)*, a collection of three hundred cases that Dogen collected during his travels in China from 1227 to 1230. This seminal work, which was to influence all of Dogen's other teachings, remained in obscurity for many centuries. It wasn't until 1934 that it was rediscovered and made available to the general public by Professor Tokuju Oya, and only recently was its authenticity finally verified.

The *Mana Shobogenzo*, unlike Dogen's other writings, was written in Chinese. And though these three hundred cases were culled largely from Zen texts of the Song era—*The Blue Cliff Record (Hekiganroku)*, and *The Book of Equanimity (Shoyoroku,* also translated as *The Book of Serenity)*—unlike the koans in these collections, they are not accompanied either by a title or commentary, yet Dogen used them frequently as seeds for his other writings, particularly the *Kana Shobogenzo* and the *Eihei Koroku.*

However, because Dogen was an outspoken critic of koan study, some people insist that he would never have collected or used koans. What seems closer to the truth is that he opposed the *superficial* treatment of koans, not koan introspection itself. Legend has it that before he left China to return to Japan, the young Dogen stayed up all night and hand-copied *The Blue Cliff Record.* Dogen's early teachers, Eisai and Myozen, both taught koan introspection. In fact, Dogen received Rinzai transmission in the Oryu line from Myozen before leaving for China, and though that lineage died out in both China and Japan, it is preserved within the Soto school to this day.

Dogen's teachings themselves require a solid understanding of Chinese koan literature. As William Bodiford points out in his *Soto Zen in Medieval Japan,* Dogen used "more than 580 koans" in his writings. In the *Kana Shobogenzo* alone, Dogen elaborates on fifty-five koans, quoting them in their entirety, and he refers to some of them more than two hundred and eighty times. In the *Eihei Koroku,* ninety-nine koans are quoted, and one hundred and nine are mentioned at least briefly. Clearly, we can no longer assert Dogen was flatly opposed to koans.

Dogen knew about the formulaic method of koan study prevalent in both the Soto and some lineages of the Rinzai School where, instead of having to "see into" a koan, practitioners could simply memorize the answers. He also knew of Dahui's *huatou* method (literally, "head-word"; see also Buswell's essay in this volume) of working with koans. This method emphasized seeing into the main point of a koan, but did not delve into its subtler details.

In contrast to these approaches, Dogen's study and understanding of koans had much more breadth and depth. Using a linguistic style unparalleled in the history of koan literature, Dogen addressed both the key phrases of each case, as well as the secondary—yet equally important—points nestled in the dialogues. He frequently examined koans from the perspective of the Five Ranks of Dongshan (J. Tozan). And he pointed out the questions that should be addressed in each case, challenging practitioners to examine them deeply.

These three characteristics of Dogen's approach to koan introspection—his unique use of language, treatment of the Five Ranks of Dongshan and meticulous study of all aspects of a koan—set Dogen's writings on koans far apart from the traditional commentaries available in the Zen literature. They make a careful comparative reading of Dogen's *Kana Shobogenzo* and his other writings with the Song-Dynasty collections extremely valuable to modern koan practitioners.

To fully appreciate Dogen's treatment of koans, it is critical to differentiate between koan study and formal koan introspection in the context of a vital teacher-student relationship. Koan study tends to rely on the intellect. It aims to shed light on the basic Buddhist teachings communicated in the koan in a similar way that a teacher will comment on a case in a *teisho* or formal discourse, clarifying the koan's key points. In koan introspection, students sit with the koan in zazen, letting go of trying to solve or understand it. They embody it as a whole body-and-mind experience. The teacher then tests the students' direct insight in *dokusan*, private face-to-face interviews.

Dokusan demands that one directly and dynamically present one's own realization. Because of this, it can be said that there is no one answer to a koan. Seeing into a koan requires the embodiment of a certain state of consciousness. It is this direct seeing into a koan that the teacher looks for and tests to determine the clarity of the student's insight. And it is this direct insight that is at the heart of realization.

In my own training, my first encounter with Dogen's singular way of dealing with koans happened within that intimate teacher-student relationship. Maezumi Roshi asked me to work with a set of miscellaneous koans I had already passed through with a previous teacher. I refused. Instead of arguing with me, Maezumi Roshi instructed me to sit shikantaza. Soon after, I came across Dogen's "Genjokoan" ("The Way of Everyday Life") and brought a few questions about it into face-to-face teachings. Maezumi encouraged me to sit with Dogen's lines in zazen, treating them as koans. With time, reading other chapters of the *Kana Shobogenzo*, I began to develop a deepening appreciation of the way Dogen presented koans with an unprecedented degree of depth and scope. Later still, as my traditional koan training evolved, it became increasingly clear to me that Dogen was a true master of the koan form, offering an amazing vista of the Buddhadharma through his koan treatment.

As a Zen teacher, my chief interests in the two *Shobogenzos* are Dogen's unique way of commenting on koans in the *Kana Shobogenzo*, as well as the choice of koans he collected in the *Mana Shobogenzo*, especially as they may affect contemporary Western practitioners.

DOGEN'S UNIQUE COMMENTARY STYLE

Dogen is a master of language. It is impossible to study his writings and not be moved by the poetry and creativity of his words. He brings to each koan his literary sophistication, an extensive familiarity with Buddhism, and an unparalleled appreciation of the dharma. In his teachings, he always communicates on multiple levels: with discursive language, poetic imagery, and with "intimate words," *mitsugo*. Intimate words are a direct pointing to the truth, meant to be grasped in an instant and absorbed intuitively rather than in a linear, sequential way. Dogen uses all of these methods freely to transmit his understanding. His teachings have the "lips and mouth" quality that characterized the style of Chinese masters Zhaozhou (J. Joshu) and Yunmen (J. Unmon), teachers who used live, "turning words" to help practitioners see into their own nature.

Another aspect of Dogen's unique treatment of koans is his use of the Five Ranks of Master Dongshan to illuminate different perspectives available within a koan. The Five Ranks—first delineated by Dongshan and elaborated on by his successor Caoshan (J. Sozan)—are a formulation of the coming together of dualities. The first rank is "the relative within the absolute." This is emptiness: no eye, ear, nose, tongue, body, or mind. The second rank is the realization of that emptiness, and is referred to as "the absolute within the relative"—the realm in which the enlightenment experience, or "kensho," occurs. Yet absolute and relative are still dualistic. The third rank is "coming from within the absolute." No longer in the abstract, the whole universe becomes your very life itself and, inevitably, compassion arises. Dongshan's fourth rank is "arriving at mutual integration," the coming from both absolute and relative. At this stage, the absolute and relative are integrated, but they're still two things. In the fifth rank, "unity attained," there is no more duality. There is just one thing—neither absolute or relative, up or down, profane or holy, good or bad, male or female.

Dogen never explicitly talks about the Five Ranks, except to summarily dismiss them, yet he definitely engages them in a way that reflects a singular understanding and appreciation of their method. In "Sansuikyo" ("The Mountains and Rivers Sutra") for example, he writes:

> Since ancient times wise ones and sages have also lived by the water. When they live by the water they catch fish or they catch humans or they catch the Way. These are traditional water styles. Further, they must be catching the self, catching the hook, being caught by the hook, and being caught by the Way.

Then, Dogen introduces one of the koans from the *Mana Shobogenzo*, Case 90 ("Jiashan Sees the Ferryman"), and comments on it:

> In ancient times, when Chuanzi suddenly left Yaoshan and went to live on the river, he got the sage Jiashan of the flower-in-river. Isn't this catching fish, catching humans, catching water? Isn't this catching himself? The fact that Jiashan could see Chuanzi is because he is Chuanzi. Chuanzi teaching Jiashan is Chuanzi meeting himself.

This passage is presenting the first two of the Five Ranks. The line, "The fact that Jiashan could see Chuanzi is because he is Chuanzi" is the relative within the absolute (or the absolute containing the relative), the first rank. The line "Chuanzi teaching Jiashan is Chuanzi meeting himself" is the absolute within the relative, the second rank.

Although Dogen had some reservations about the Five Ranks, it was not because he did not find them true. He simply did not want them to become a formula—a mere intellectualization or abstraction. Dogen did not use them in the way they were taught conventionally. He wanted them to be realized face-to-face in koan introspection between teacher and student.

"Catching the self," "catching the hook," "being caught by the hook," "being caught by the way" are all expressions of the interplay of opposites—specifically about how that tension works within the teacher-student relationship. So, "Chuanzi teaching Jiashan is Chuanzi meeting himself" is "the teacher teaching the student is the teacher meeting him or herself."

Again, in "Katto," Dogen writes about Bodhidharma's transmission of the marrow to Huike (J. Eka):

> You should be aware of the phrases "You attain me; I attain you; attaining both me and you and attaining both you and me." In personally viewing the ancestors' body/mind, if we speak of there being no oneness of internal and external or if we speak of the whole body not being completely penetrated, then we have not yet seen the realm of the ancestors' present.

For Dogen, the relationship of a teacher and student is *katto*, a spiritual entanglement, which, from his perspective, is a process of using entanglements to transmit entanglements. "Entanglements entwining entanglements is the buddhas and ancestors interpenetrating buddhas and ancestors." This is an expression of the merging of dualities. This is the relationship between Jiashan and Chuanzi. It is the relationship between Bodhidharma and Huike. And it is the relationship to which Dogen directs himself whenever he expounds the non-dual dharma in the koans he is using.

Next we have Dogen's meticulous treatment of all aspects of a koan. As I mentioned before, commentaries on many of the koans that Dogen deemed important and that were included in his *Mana Shobogenzo* can be found in the classic Song collections. When we compare the commentaries of these collections with Dogen's commentaries in the *Kana Shobogenzo*, we find that the truth—the dharma—of these koans is consistently presented by each commentator, and yet, there is a unique quality to Dogen's expression of the Zen truth that sets his treatment of koans in a class by itself.

For example, a brief look at Case 105 of the *Mana Shobogenzo*, "The Hands and Eyes of Great Compassion," will help to illustrate Dogen's depth of understanding and expression. This koan appears in two fascicles of the *Kana Shobogenzo*: in "Daishugyo" and in "Kannon." The same koan appears as Case 89 in the *Blue Cliff Record* and as Case 54 in the *Book of Serenity*:

> Yunyan asked Daowu: "How does the Bodhisattva of Great Compassion [Kannon] use so many hands and eyes?"
> Daowu said: "It's just like a person in the middle of the night reaching back in search of a pillow."
> Yunyan said: "I understand."
> Daowu said: "How do you understand it?"
> Yunyan said: "All over the body are hands and eyes."
> Daowu said: "What you said is all right, but it's only eighty percent of it."
> Yunyan said: "I'm like this, senior brother. How do you understand it?"
> Daowu said: "Throughout the body are hands and eyes."

Taking up only a few of the points in this rich koan, we find the following. In the *Blue Cliff Record* commentary, Yuanwu refers to the 84,000 arms of Kannon Bodhisattva as symbolic arms and says, "Great Compassion has this many hands and eyes. Do all of you?" With this question he challenges the reader to consider the statement from the point of view of intimacy.

When he addresses "reaching back for a pillow in the middle of the night," he asks the question, "[In this activity] tell me, where are the eyes?" But, whereas Yuanwu deals with the phrase "the night" only briefly, Dogen comments on it extensively, since it is a pivotal point of the koan.

Yuanwu also deals with Yunyan's "all over the body are hands and eyes" and Daowu's "this is all right, but it is only eighty percent of it" and "throughout the body are hands and eyes." He asks the question, "But say, is 'all over the body' right, or is 'throughout the body' right?" Then he himself indirectly answers this with the statement "Although they seem covered with mud, nevertheless they are bright and clean," implying that although Daowu and Yunyan may appear to be having "a conversation in the weeds" (are intellectualizing), in fact they are both expressing clearly the truth of the activity of Great Compassion.

Yuanwu then concludes by saying that practitioners who think that Yunyan's response must have been wrong while Daowu's was right are caught up in words and phrases and have not yet realized the truth.

In the *Book of Equanimity*, Wansong begins his commentary with a quote: "Li Ao asked Ehu, 'What does the Great Compassionate One use a thousand hands and eyes for?' Ehu said, 'What does the emperor use public officials for?'" This exchange seems to imply that the thousand hands and eyes of Great Compassion are meant to facilitate the bodhisattva's functioning in the world. It is a reasonable and logical conclusion, but it entirely misses the truth of this koan.

He then quotes a couple of stories that are perhaps intended to illustrate the principles presented in the koan, but they do not in any way clarify them for the reader. They just introduce more entanglements of words and ideas. He does agree with Yuanwu about the identity of Yunyan and Daowu's understanding, refuting the notion that one is clearer than the other.

Let us look now at Dogen, who begins his treatment of the koan by extolling the virtues of both Yunyan and Daowu, and immediately establishing their unity with each other. He then presents the identity of Kannon Bodhisattva and Yunyan, and the uniqueness of Yunyan's understanding of Kannon. He says: "Kannon is present in Yunyan who has been experiencing it together with Daowu. And not only one or two Kannons, but hundreds of thousands of Kannons are experiencing the same state as Yunyan."

Then, speaking of the 84,000 hands and eyes of great compassion, Dogen makes clear that they are not limited to any number. He says, "They are indeed beyond the bounds of countlessness and limitlessness." The limitlessly abundant hands and eyes are clearly the state of consciousness that Yunyan and Daowu are experiencing together. With a unique twist Dogen says, "Yunyan is asking Daowu, 'The use [of the hands and eyes] does what?'" He is asking the reader to consider how Kannon uses her manifold hands and eyes and to ask, "Does what, moves what, expresses what?"

Dogen then uses Daowu's answer, "She is like a person in the night reaching back for a pillow," to launch into an exhaustive exploration of "in the night." He asks us to examine the difference between "nighttime as it is supposed in the light of day" and "the nighttime as it is in the night. In sum, we should examine it as that time which is not day or night."

Then he becomes even more specific. He says, "This nighttime is not necessarily only the nighttime of the day and night of human beings and gods." The night that Dogen is speaking of is in the realm of the absolute, the non-dual state of consciousness in which body and mind have fallen away. Extending this concept of night into the matter of searching for a pillow he says, "You should understand that the expression used here by Daowu does not concern taking a pillow, pulling a pillow, or pushing a pillow. If you try to deeply understand what Daowu means when he speaks of 'reaching behind at night for a pillow,' you must examine it with night eyes. Look at it carefully."

The remainder of the koan is subjected to the same kind of close scrutiny, functioning within various levels of understanding and addressing subtleties that were not presented in the *Blue Cliff Record* and *Book of Equanimity*. This koan is only one among the many examples of the unique style and profound insight that Dogen brings to the understanding of classical koans.

THE THREE HUNDRED KOANS AND THEIR RELEVANCE TO MODERN ZEN PRACTICE

All we have dealt with so far would be of little more than theoretical interest to us, were it not for the relevance that Dogen's teachings have for contemporary western practitioners. In addition to Dogen's style and insight, a critical aspect of his treatment of koans is how the particular cases he selected can assist practitioners to examine important areas of spiritual practice in the twenty-first century. Among these areas are the moral and ethical teachings of Zen, the teacher-student relationship—as illustrated in case 90 quoted above—and social activism.

Over the years, in developing my own commentaries of the *Mana Shobogenzo* koans, I have attempted to present Dogen's dharma heart as it is manifested in this particular time, this place, and these circumstances, as well as address issues that were not dealt with in the past for various political, social, or cultural reasons. One example is Case 227 of the *Mana Shobogenzo*, "Priest Xixian's, I Am Watching":

> Xixian Faan of Lushan was asked by a government officer, "When I took the city of Jinling with an army troop, I killed countless people. Am I at fault?"
> Xixian said, "I am watching closely."

A Japanese master commenting on this koan said:

> As Buddhists we take a precept not to destroy life. The government officer was worried since his position involved him in ordering the killing of many people. That his actions were sinful, of course. If we judge his conduct, he committed many sins, but he was unable to avoid this in carrying out his duty. Master Xixian recognized the difficult circumstance of the officer's life, and so he wouldn't say that his actions were sins. He just said that he was always watching reality. In reality it is difficult at times to categorize the conduct of others as good or bad. Reality is very severe. Master Xixian recognized the officer's life was in reality very severe so that he himself was just watching the real situation. In reality, situations are usually complex. We must recognize the existence of such a fact. It is sometimes difficult to criticize or to affirm. If we see a snake crawling toward a baby and we are too concerned with following the precepts exactly we may hesitate too long to save the baby. At the moment of the present we must be free even from the precepts to act as the circumstances demand.

My own view is somewhat different. The commentary I added to this case reads:

> Priest Xixian's response, "I am watching closely" is at once fat-headed and misguided. He has missed an opportunity to

cause an evil that has already arisen to be extinguished, and to cause good that has not arisen to arise. Both he and the general deserve thirty blows of my stick.

Governments and rulers are traditionally driven by power, politics, and money, and are usually not inclined toward clear moral commitments. However, for a Zen priest to avoid taking moral responsibility when asked is inexcusable.

Enlightenment without morality is not yet enlightenment. Morality without enlightenment is not yet morality. Enlightenment and morality are non-dual in the Way. One does not exist without the other. The truth is not beyond good and evil as is commonly believed. It is rather a way of living one's life with a definite moral commitment that is practiced, realized, and verified within the realm of good and evil itself, yet remains undefiled by them.

Setting aside impostor priests and phony followers, you tell me, how do you transform watching into doing, the three poisons into the three virtues? More importantly, what is it that you call yourself?

How far are we willing to go to justify our position? Gary Snyder once wrote: "Institutional Buddhism has been conspicuously ready to accept or ignore the inequalities and tyrannies of whatever political system it found itself under. This can be death to Buddhism because it is death to any meaningful function of compassion. Wisdom without compassion feels no pain." Or, "Enlightenment without morality is not yet enlightenment. Morality without enlightenment is not yet morality."

The consequences of not engaging the wisdom of honest, raw practice are that real lives suffer, people die, our fragile and wondrous planet is treated poorly. We need to challenge and encourage one another to realize our clarity and compassion. That is our imperative.

For me, the comparative use of the two *Shobogenzos* and Dogen's other writings, along with the traditional koans in our koan introspection, is a very practical—and crucial—endeavor. While this kind of study has opened up new possibilities in the training of western Zen students by addressing their natural philosophical and psychological inclinations, it has not abandoned the heart of the dharma transmitted from Shakyamuni Buddha to the present.

We are incredibly fortunate to have access to Master Dogen's outstanding body of work. We should not waste the opportunity to study it. And, as he himself said often, we must study exhaustively. Because ultimately, no matter how many hundreds of koans we pass through, if they do not change the way we relate to the rest of the world, then they are nothing but meaningless intellectual exercises. We must *realize* these koans, and we must actualize them in everything that we do. That is the only way we will truly transform our lives.

Keizan, Koans, and Succession in the Soto School

Francis Dojun Cook

Editor's Note: The following are excerpts from Francis Dojun Cook's Introduction to The Record of Transmitting the Light *by Keizan Jokin. They are intended to provide a context for the style and format of this unique koan collection, as well as present some background information on Keizan, named "Great Patriarch of Japanese Zen." Following this essay is a sample case koan from the collection dealing with Sixth Ancestor Dajian Huineng's enlightenment.*

The Record of Transmitting the Light (*Denkoroku* in Japanese) is a type of literature that can be called "spiritual genealogy." Like ordinary genealogies, it traces the history of a family, locating its origins in some ancestor long ago and tracing the ancestor's descendants down through successive generations to the present. This accomplishes several goals that are important for the family: It provides a panoramic view of the continuity of a line rooted in distant antiquity; it records the exploits and special distinctions of each generation; it provides a basis for family pride and style; and, perhaps most important, it provides a strong sense of family identity. Together, these things create a sense of rootedness, as well as continuity and identity through history.

But unlike traditional family genealogies tracing a genetic bloodline, the *Record* traces a spiritual bloodline. Thus, the fifty-three generations recorded in Keizan's work are not related by blood but rather by spiritual kinship in which the inheritance of each generation is one of spiritual endowment and authority.

Keizan took it as his task to trace the genealogy of the Soto line of Zen Buddhism, which was his "family." The founding ancestor to which Keizan's line is heir was the Buddha Shakyamuni, who passed on his spiritual endowment and authority to his own spiritual son, Mahakashyapa, who, in turn, passed it on to his spiritual son, Ananda, and so on, through twenty-eight generations in India, twenty-two generations in China, and two generations in Japan, ending with Zen Master Koun Ejo, the fifty-second patriarch of the family. In the process of recording these generations, Keizan discusses the spiritual struggles and victories of such well-known figures in Buddhist history as Mahakashyapa, Ananda, Ashvaghosa, Vasubandhu, Bodhidharma, Huike, Qingyuan, Dongshan, and Dogen, along with a number of others in the Indian line who are unknown outside Buddhist genealogies of this kind. Thus, the *Record* shows a straight and unbroken line of descent starting from the Buddha and continuing through India, China, and Japan, ending with Ejo, who was Keizan's own spiritual grandfather. Keizan omits any mention of himself out of modesty, although he was the fifty-fourth patriarch of the family, and he also does not include his predecessor and spiritual father, Tettsu Gikai, who was still living and whose inclusion Keizan apparently felt was inappropriate. Gikai is only mentioned briefly in the account of Ejo as having established the family at Daijo Monastery.

At the heart of the *Record* lie such genealogical matters as transmission, succession, and inheritance—words that are encountered frequently in the text. There are also the related matters of continuity, legitimacy, and authenticity. The structure of each chapter is fairly uniform. The current patriarch of the family is wandering about teaching, or is an abbot of a monastery, and he is searching for a suitable individual to inherit his authority. He encounters a young man of unusual commitment and talent who has forsaken secular life and seeks enlightenment. After some passage of time, during which the young man struggles valiantly and single-mindedly, he achieves enlightenment, often during an encounter with the patriarchal master. The master confirms the awakening and recognizes the younger man as a fit successor. Thus, the younger man succeeds the older in a process that has continued unbroken over many generations. The point of such a narrative is that at any point in the chain of successors, an individual can demonstrate his legitimacy and his claim to the family name by proving that his predecessor was so-and-so, whose own claims derive from his own predecessor, and so on back to the founding ancestor. Ultimately, Shakyamuni himself, as the founder of the family, is the ultimate legitimator of all subsequent successors.

There are other Zen genealogies besides Keizan's *Record*, each with its own structure and purpose, and there are also genealogies in traditions outside Zen, such as Pure Land and Huayan. However, Keizan's *Record* is unique within this genre of literature. Each of the fifty-three chapters begins with a koan case *(hon soku)*, which records the master's awakening in a dialogue with his master, upon hearing some remark made by his master, or upon pondering some spiritual problem. The short introductory case is then followed by a story *(kien)* about the master, including his birthplace and parentage, religious yearnings as a youth, home departure and tonsure, spiritual struggle, awakening, and succession to the title of patriarch. The main purpose of this section is that of providing the circumstances surrounding the awakening experience announced in the preceding koan case. This latter section is often the occasion of stressing the master's special virtues and abilities, his unique fitness to become a patriarchal successor, and his later success as a Zen teacher. Occasionally, especially in the accounts of the Indian patriarchs, the master is shown exhibiting marvelous supernatural powers in an atmosphere charged with the miraculous and fabulous. This section can be lengthy in the case of particularly important pivotal figures such as Bodhidharma, or it can be perfunctorily brief in cases where the background information on an individual is practically nonexistent. At any rate, the material for this section of a chapter is not Keizan's own invention but rather was drawn from the other genealogies such as the Chinese *Jing De Chuan Deng Lu (Keitoku Dentoroku)* and *Wu Deng Hui Yuan (Goto Egen)*, which were Keizan's two main sources. Hence, these stories were well known in the Zen tradition and could be found elsewhere. However, a comparison of Keizan's telling of these stories and their presentation in other sources shows the author editing, abbreviating, expanding, shifting emphasis, and otherwise exercising a critical choice in what to include or exclude.

The third section of each chapter consists of Keizan's commentary on either the main case or, rarely, on the second section. This section, named *nentei* in many modern editions, is very similar to the traditional teisho given by the master to his monks. Neither the *teisho* nor the *nentei* is a simple explanation or discussion *about* the koan case, but rather functions as an occasion for the master to speak "from the heart," to explore the case from an enlightenment perspective. Such an occasion may stimulate the monk's own spiritual search and provide pointers for the individual who is prepared to understand as a result of considerable practice and his own inquiring spirit. Keizan's talks, like the classical *teisho*, provide him with the opportunity to guide practice, exhort, correct, and encourage, as he clarifies the import of the koan case. I have given this section of a chapter the more familiar heading of *teisho* in order to alert the reader to the nature of the section.

[...] The fourth and final section of each chapter is a short verse, usually made up of two lines of seven ideographic characters each or, occasionally, of four lines of five characters each. These verses are the occasion for Keizan to present the gist of the introductory koan, to summarize his remarks in the commentary section, and to express his appreciation and praise for the koan case. These verses are excellent examples of the highly literary nature of Zen and the literary tastes of Zen masters, and, at the same time, they serve the reader by providing a handy reference for the interpretation of the main case and Keizan's commentary. In a word, the verse is the case and its commentary in a poetic nutshell.

[...] The success of the Japanese Soto tradition from the fourteenth century on was, as historians agree, due in no small part to Keizan's efforts to make it widely known and practiced. His historical importance in Japanese Buddhism consists of his success in making Soto Zen a popular religion. Some of this success was due to the incorporation of elements of liturgy and practice from outside of Zen, and there is little doubt that had Soto retained the austere, noncompromising, eremitical style associated with Dogen, it would not have become the school with the large following and numerous temples and priests that it has become in recent centuries. Keizan's important place in this development is enshrined in his title, Taiso, the "Great Patriarch," which places him almost as high as the founder, Dogen, the Koso, or "Eminent Patriarch."

It is often said that if Dogen were the father of Japanese Soto, Keizan was the mother.

Perhaps the *Denkoroku* did play some part in this great expansion and the eventual success of Soto Zen in becoming an accepted part of the Japanese religious establishment. By demonstrating that Soto held a legitimacy and authority based on a Dharma succession that could be traced all the way back to the Buddha in India, Keizan could counter any claims that his tradition was a mere upstart and interloper; he could achieve a standing of legitimacy and acceptability in the eyes of secular authorities who were often closely allied politically with the older, established traditions; and he could win acceptance among a population already increasingly proselytized by the growing Pure Land and Nichiren traditions. In so doing, the *Record* served as a certificate of respectability in the same way any genealogy does.

However, this should not be construed as implying that the *Record* was composed merely as an expedient tool designed to win acceptance for Keizan's tradition among a hostile or indifferent audience. While its structure and content indicate that it also had that purpose, its primary function seems to have been to celebrate the "light" of its title. Two facts support this conclusion. First, the fifty-three chapters of the text were delivered orally on formal occasions to a community of monks. It was not presented to the court or to the military powers as a document supporting a claim. In fact, no evidence indicates that it was ever presented to authorities as a kind of petition or memorial. The place of presentation (Daijo Monastery), the audience (Zen monks), and the contents of the text support a conclusion that the primary purpose of the text was to instruct and encourage monks. A second point is that the *Denkoroku* does not appear to have been widely known outside Soto monasteries until the mid-nineteenth century, when it was first printed and circulated widely. Thus, from the first, its audience seems to have been the Soto priesthood. It provided them with an authoritative review of the essentials of Soto Zen teachings; reminded them of the seriousness of their vocation and the need to practice hard; and, at the same time, in documenting their genealogical heritage, provided them with a sense of confidence, pride, and legitimacy.

All these functions of the text are based on the evidence of the existence of the "light" of the title. It is likened to a pearl that is bright and lustrous without need of carving and polishing, a vermilion boat so beautiful that no artist could capture its beauty in a painting, the wind that circulates everywhere and shakes the world but cannot be seen or touched, and an icy spring so deep that no traveler can make out its bottom. The occurrence of such epithets and figures of speech throughout the text shows the author not only recording a transmission from master to disciple, in which the disciple realized finally the existence of the "Undying Lord of the Hermitage," but also expressing his profound reverence for this light in the heightened emotional language of poetry.

[…] It is this light that is mentioned in the title of Keizan's *Record* as being transmitted from Shakyamuni through fifty-two generations to Ejo and, by implication, to Tettsu Gikai and Keizan himself. Whatever else may be said about one's essential nature, it is the self as the brilliant light of clear and alert knowing of events that most clearly concerned Keizan. He emphasizes this aspect of the self in chapter after chapter, saying that it is "a thoroughly clear knowing," an "alert knowing," "a clear and distinct, constant knowing" and "a perfectly clear knowing," "boundless clarity and brightness" and "just alertness," to mention just a few instances from the text.

We learn from the *Record* that [the] True Self or essential nature is the origin of all things and remains their imperishable essential nature, and among humans it takes the form of a capacity for knowing events clearly, without delusion. This clear knowing always lurks just beneath the surface, so to speak, whether the individual is wise or foolish, learned or ignorant, a genius or a simpleton. However, among all these, it remains obscure and nonfunctioning if the individual is not awakened to its existence. For most of humankind, it is obscured by delusion in the form of a tendency to discriminate between "self" and "other," by conventional and habitual patterns of interpreting experience, by stereotyped reactions to events, by grasping experience from the perspective of the ordinary self obsessed with fear and craving, by filtering experience through the lens of some philosophical position or ideological perspective, and so on. In short, what passes among us for clear understanding of our experience is, according to Keizan, a clouded, distorted, darkened misunderstanding. When we really become aware of this truth, and at the same time become aware of this clear light within us, we awaken and become

Buddhas. If we do not, then, says Keizan, we remain bound to the prison of this world and transmigrate endlessly in the six paths, falling repeatedly into the clutches of "Old Yama," the Lord of the Dead.

This light is none other than wisdom, insight, or the impeccably clear knowing known throughout Buddhist history as *prajna*, a term that Keizan himself uses occasionally in the text. Prajna is not a special, privileged, "correct" way of knowing events but rather is the knowing of events in the total absence of all viewpoints and perspectives. Thus, while it is a mode of knowing, it is a knowing that does not filter experience through a pre-existing set of assumptions about the nature of an experience. So thoroughgoing is the demand to eliminate *all* perspectives that not even something such as a "Zen position" or "Buddhist perspective" is considered a legitimate filter. Thus, as Nagarjuna insisted in the second century, all perspectives and positions must be abandoned so that events are encountered and responded to from what might be called a perspective of no perspective or a positionless position.

Western philosophers in modern times have concluded that such a perspectiveless perspective is impossible and, indeed, the crisis in contemporary philosophy and theology is a result of the growing consensus that all knowledge is necessarily conditioned by culture, physiology, and personality. Thus, it is argued, we can never know events as they truly are, apart from our interpretation of them, because we can never transcend those factors that condition our experience of events. We are necessarily and forever locked within our minds, and our minds are conditioned. On the other hand, Buddhism has claimed for well over two thousand years that a pure, unconditioned way of knowing is indeed possible and we can know events just as they are, undistorted by culture or personality. This claim, in fact, is the tacit assumption at the bottom of Keizan's text. Keizan, like all his predecessors, saw without doubt that this way of knowing is innate in all of us, and that although it has been obscured by various conditioning factors, like a precious jewel buried in a heap of excrement, it can be uncovered and found. This assumption is, in fact, the sole rationale for Zen practice.

Zen practice, consisting primarily of zazen and koan study, is a process of digging down through the various layers that cover the light of clear knowing, a kind of spiritual archaeology, so to speak. In human beings, these layers are made up of such things as concepts, symbols, language, categories, habits, ideological presuppositions, and the natural, innate tendency to divide the world into "self" and "not self." Some layers are made up of the acquired, some of the innate, but all are perceived in Buddhism as similar to the layers of excrement that obscure the precious jewel of clear knowing. Once these layers are removed, a way of knowing is recovered that functions without conventional concepts and categories of thought, which, according to all schools of Buddhism, superimpose a meaning on events that does not belong intrinsically to them. To experience events as they truly are, one must experience them without the least bit of personal or cultural meaning added to them. This kind of knowing might best be called "no mind," a term favored by some Zen masters. "No mind" is not confusion, uncertainty or blankness, but, rather, an extremely clear knowing freed of all conceptualization and symbolization.

This kind of knowing is said to be innate, basic, and prior to ordinary discriminative, conceptualizing knowing. It is prior because it is the root and origin of the latter, which arises from the more basic, prior consciousness in the form of a bifurcation into a knowing aspect and a known aspect. The consequence of this split is two-fold. On the one hand, consciousness becomes *self*-conscious, so that human beings are not only aware of an experience but can also be aware of being aware. On the other hand, what are thought to be events or things "out there," external to the mind, are in reality only the mind's ideas of events. Thus, rather than knowing an event as it truly is in itself, what we know is our idea about the event. This latter is the known aspect of mind, or mind as its own object. Consequently, as Western thinkers admit, we are ordinarily locked within our own minds and have no access to the true and real. Buddhists also admit that this is the case ordinarily, but that the subject/object split can be healed and the mind restored to its original form. This is awakening or enlightenment and is the professed objective of Buddhism.

Since this awakening is, by definition, the ability to know events just as they are, apart from interpretation, assumption, and emotional reaction, then it follows that there is really no "correct" way of knowing events that stands in opposition to a "false" way. The religious and existential problem is not a matter of having wrong ideas about events so much as it is having any idea at all. Any interpretive mechanism is, as an interpretation, a distortion, even a "Buddhist" interpretation, and so enlightenment can never be a matter of replacing bad ideas with good ones. Consequently, the kind of pristine knowing that is Keizan's concern should not be mistaken as being a superior "Zen" way of looking at things that replaces a defective way of seeing them. Pristine knowing is not a point of view.

This is the light that Keizan celebrates and appreciates in his *Record* and the kind of knowing that the master looks for in the disciple. The good teacher is one who recognizes it in the student when he sees it, and since it is absolutely essential that teachers possess this form of knowing, the student who convincingly displays it becomes the master's successor through what is considered a transmission. The fifty-three chapters of Keizan's work show clearly that succession is never based on mere mastery of Buddhist doctrine, the displaying of doctrinal correctness, or the adherence to sectarian orthodoxy, but is based on this kind of unconditioned, unprejudiced knowing that Keizan likens to a brightness greater than the sun and moon combined. Shakyamuni found it and passed it on to Mahakashyapa, who passed it on to Ananda, and so on down the generations to Dogen and then Ejo in Japan. This is Keizan's story and the foundation of his own position as Great Patriarch of Japanese Soto Zen.

Authorship of the *Record* is attributed to Zen Master Keizan Jokin, the first patriarch of the Soji-ji branch of Japanese Soto Zen and the fourth patriarch of Japanese Soto Zen. Most older secondary sources list his birth date as 1268, but recent scholars have argued for a date of 1264. Assuming the latter date to be correct, this means that Keizan was born eleven years after the death of the great founder of Japanese Soto Zen, Zen Master Eihei Dogen. Keizan was born in modern-day Fukui Prefecture, know at the time as Echizen Prefecture, and he was a member of the great and powerful Fujiwara family that had been at the center of Japanese politics for many centuries.

His secular history is nonexistent, since he took up the religious life at a very early age, either in his eighth or thirteenth year. Apparently, he was heavily influenced to seek religion by his mother, who had suffered from the time she was quite young and had sought solace and help from the merciful bodhisattva Kannon. At any rate, he seems to have made the short journey to Eihei-ji monastery while still a boy. There, he became a student of the third patriarch in Dogen's line and then current abbot of the temple, Tettsu Gikai. Keizan records that at the age of twelve, he received the precepts from the still living former abbot and second patriarch, Koun Ejo.

At the age of seventeen, he left Eihei-ji to travel from monastery to monastery to meet various teachers and be tested by them, a practice that went back hundreds of years in China and that survived in Japanese Zen circles. His first stop was nearby Hokyo-ji where the abbot was Jakuen, as he was called in Japan, a Chinese monk who had followed Dogen back to Japan when Dogen returned from China in 1227. Jakuen had studied Zen under Dogen and then under Dogen's successor, Ejo, and now he was abbot of Hokyo-ji.

Keizan stayed awhile with Jakuen, impressing the Chinese master so much that even though there were many followers at the monastery, Jakuen made Keizan the *ino* (the head priest who oversees all personal affairs within the monastery), a high honor indeed, since the position was always reserved for monks who had trained a long time and who were recognized as being proficient in all temple matters. However, Keizan only stayed for a short time and then continued his travels, eventually studying with a series of teachers such as Egyo and Kakushin. This was to be a fruitful and fateful study, for these teachers were Rinzai masters who combined Zen practice with the esoteric practices found in Shingon Buddhism and the esoteric branch of Tendai Buddhism. This eclectic approach seems to have influenced Keizan, who later incorporated some of these same practices in his monasteries. He even climbed Mount Hiei and studied for a while in the great Tendai monastic complex there.

In the end, he returned to Eihei-ji and his teacher Tettsu Gikai. However, by this time, some historians claim, there was very serious turmoil at the monastery. A dispute had broken out among the monks, and Gikai, the abbot, was at the center of the dispute. Scholars have studied this dispute from several angles and have arrived at differing theories as to the essence of the controversy. The exact nature of the dispute cannot be stated with any degree of certainty, if indeed it actually took place, but what seems to be clear from traditional accounts is that a large faction of monks questioned Gikai's qualifications as abbot. They wanted Gikai out, but Gikai also had his own supporters, and so two factions fought over who would be the abbot. The anti-Gikai faction triumphed, and Gikai was forced to leave Eihei-ji, to be succeeded by the fourth abbot, Gien. Gikai founded a new monastery, Daijo-ji, and became its first abbot, to be followed a little later by his student Keizan. Thus Keizan became the second abbot of Daijo-ji, a monastery with which he would be strongly associated throughout his mature years.

In 1294, at the age of thirty, he had his great awakening when he heard Gikai use the old Zen phrase, "Ordinary mind is the Way." The following year, he inherited Gikai's Dharma and became his successor. The next few years were spent teaching at Joman-ji, a temple in Tokushima Prefecture. It was about this time that he first met Gasan Joseki, who was to become one of his greatest disciples and his successor. In 1298 he returned to Daijo-ji to assist the aging and ailing Gikai, and it was in this capacity as assistant to Gikai that he began the fifty-three talks of the *Denkoroku* in the winter of 1300. Two years later, he became the second abbot of Daijo-ji. He had granted the seal of approval to Gasan the year before, and the following year he also granted it to Meiho Sotetsu, thus acquiring his two greatest successors and laying the foundation for the future development of his branch of Soto Zen.

Keizan was the abbot at Daijo-ji from 1302 to 1311. Gikai died in 1309 at the age of ninety-one, and two years later, Keizan turned the monastery over to his disciple and successor Meiho and started a new monastery named Joju-ji. The final decade and a half of his life was spent establishing a number of new monasteries, such as Joju-ji, Yoko-ji, and Koko-ji, acting as abbot and establishing what he considered proper practice at all these places. His biggest accomplishment, probably, was the founding of Soji-ji, in Noto, through which in later centuries passed a long succession of illustrious Soto abbots and scholar-priests. It became the headquarters monastery of Keizan's wing of Soto Zen, Eihei-ji becoming the other headquarters in a system of dual headquarters that has lasted until today and makes Soto Zen unique in Japanese Buddhism. This is the heritage of the great dispute at Eihei-ji that resulted in a dual abbacy. Keizan died at Yoko-jin in 1325 at the comparatively young age of sixty-one.

...[Keizan] was, primarily, the first patriarch of his own branch of Soto Zen and the fourth patriarch in Dogen's line. With the destructive internal dispute at Eihei-ji in the late 1200s and Gikai's banishment, Soto Zen split into two branches, to be known later as the Eihei-ji branch and the Soji-ji branch. Gien assumed the position of fourth abbot of Eihei-ji when Gikai left, but the damage was great, and supporters abandoned the monastery and the practice declined. Gikai, meanwhile, founded Daijo-ji and became its first abbot. When Keizan succeeded him as abbot, in effect a new branch of Soto was established that persists to the present day. Thus, the two branches went their respective ways with their own respective succession of abbots. Keizan's title of "Great Patriarch" reflects both his place in the growth of Soto and his position as the founder of the Soji-ji branch of Soto.

Finally, Keizan wrote the *Denkoroku*, regarded in Soto circles almost as highly as Dogen's *Shobogenzo*. He also composed an important work on monastic discipline, the Keizan Shingi; a commentary on the Chinese Zen classic, *Xin Xin Ming*, entitled *Shinjin Mei Nentei*; two works on Zen meditation, the *Sankon Zazen Setsu* and *Zazen Yojin-ki*; and a record of his life and achievements, the *Tokikki*. However, none of these is of the quality of the *Denkoroku*. This work is unique in structure and purpose among all similar Zen spiritual genealogies. And while it cannot be said to be the literary equal of Master Dogen's peerless work, it is nevertheless of excellent literary quality. However, equally important, it is a sustained presentation of a remarkable man's understanding of the religious life, a valuable religious document from the Zen past, and a prime source for understanding the nature of Soto Zen Buddhism.

ANCESTOR DAJIAN HUINENG

Keizan Jokin

Translated by Francis Dojun Cook

FROM *The Record of Transmitting the Light*

Case

The thirty-third patriarch, [China's Sixth Patriarch,] was Zen Master Dajian [Huineng]. He worked in the rice-hulling shed at Huangmei. Once, Zen Master Daman [Hongren] entered the shed and asked, "Is the rice white yet?" The master answered, "It's white, but it hasn't been sifted yet." Daman struck the mortar three times with his staff. The master shook the sifting basket three times and entered the Patriarch's room.

Circumstances

The master's family name was Lu. His ancestors were from Fanyang. His father was named Xingtao. In the first quarter of the seventh century, [Xingtao] was demoted and sent to Xinzhou in the far south, where he finally settled. [Huineng's] father died and his mother took care of him. While he was growing, the family was very poor and the master earned a living chopping and selling wood. One day he went to the city with a bundle of kindling and he heard a customer reciting the *Diamond-cutter Sutra [Vajracchedika-prajna-pararamita Sutra]*. When the customer reached the place where it said, "You should raise the unsupported thought," [Huineng] was awakened. He asked the customer, "What scripture is this? From whom did you get it?" The customer replied, "This is the *Diamond-cutter Sutra* and I got it from the Great Master Hongren, at Huangmei."

The master spoke to his mother at once about looking for a teacher so he could find the Dharma. He went directly to Shaozhou and visited a lofty-minded man named Liu Zhiliu and they became friends. The nun Wujin Cang was Zhiliu's mother-in-law and she was always reciting the *Nirvana Sutra*. The master listened to her for a while and then told her what it meant. The nun picked up a scroll and asked about some words. The master said, "I can't read." The nun marveled at this and said to the village elders, "Huineng has the Way. We ought to invite him [to stay] and support him." So, the people competed to greet him and pay their respects.

There was an old temple nearby by the name of Baolin. The people all got together, rebuilt it, and invited the master to stay there. The four groups [of male and female monastics and lay people] gathered in droves. It quickly became a place where the Dharma flourished. One day, the master suddenly thought, "I am seeking the great Dharma. Why stop halfway?" He left the next day and went to the caves in the western part of Zhangluo Province. There he met Zen Master Zhiyuan, whom he asked for help. The master said, "When I look at you, I see an expression that is quite superior, not at all like that of ordinary people. I hear that the Indian Bodhidharma has transmitted the Mind Seal to [Hongren] Huangmei. You should go there to see him and become certain."

The master thanked him and left, going directly to Huangmei, where he visited Zen Master Daman. The Patriarch asked him, "Where are you from?" The master replied, "I come from Lingnan." The Patriarch asked, "What are you looking for?" The master answered, "I just want to become a Buddha." The Patriarch said, "People from Lingnan have no Buddha nature. How can you expect to become a Buddha?" The master answered, "Among people there are northerners and southerners, but can that be true of Buddha nature?" The Patriarch realized that he was an unusual person and sent him to the rice-hulling shed. Huineng bowed and left. He went to the rice-hulling shed where he toiled at the mortar day and night without letup for eight months. The Patriarch, realizing that the time had come for passing on [the Dharma], told the monks, "The True Dharma is hard to understand. Don't just pointlessly remember what I say and make that your responsibility. I want each of you to compose a verse that shows what you understand. If the words display the truth, I will confer the robe and the Dharma."

At the time, Shenxiu, senior monk among more than seven hundred monks, was conversant with both Buddhist and non-Buddhist learning and was admired by everyone. They praised him, saying, "If not the honorable Xiu, then who?" Shenxiu caught wind of this and thought no more. When he finished composing his verse, he went several times to the master's room to present it, but he felt unsure and broke out in a sweat. He could not present it. He tried fourteen times in three days but could not present the verse. Then he thought, "It would be better if I write it on the wall. If Hongren sees it and says it is good, I will appear and say it is mine. If he says it is unsatisfactory, I will go into the mountains and spend my time there. What kind of path can I practice just accepting the homage of others?" That night around midnight, when no one could see him, he took a lamp and wrote a verse on the wall of the South Hall, presenting his understanding. Here is the verse:

> The body is the tree of enlightenment;
> The mind is like a bright mirror-stand.
> Wipe it clean over and over,
> And do not let the dust gather.

The Patriarch was walking around and saw the verse. He knew it was Shenxiu's verse and praised it saying, "If later generations practice in accordance with it, they will get excellent results." He made everyone memorize it. The master was pounding rice and heard someone reciting the verse. He asked another monk, "What are these phrases?" The other monk said, "Don't you know? The master is looking for an heir and everyone has to compose a verse about Mind. These sentences were composed by the senior monk Shenxiu. The master praised them highly. He will surely pass on the Dharma and robe [to Shenxiu]." The master asked, "How does the verse go?" The other student recited it for him. The master was silent for a while and then said, "It's really excellent, all right, but it's not quite perfect." The other monk shouted at him, "What does a simpleton like you know? Don't talk crazy!" The master replied, "Don't you believe me? Then I'll add a verse to it." The student just looked at him and laughed. That night, the master took a young servant boy with him to the hall. The master held a lamp and had the servant add a verse next to Shenxiu's. It said,

Enlightenment is essentially not a tree;
The bright mirror is not a stand.
From the beginning, not a single thing exists;
Where can the dust collect?

When they saw the verse, everyone in the monastery said, "This is the verse of a living bodhisattva." Everyone praised it loudly. The Patriarch knew it was Huineng's verse and said, "Whoever wrote this has not yet seen his [original] face," and erased it. Consequently, the other monks totally ignored it. During the night, the Patriarch secretly went to the rice-hulling shed and asked, "Is the rice white?" The master answered, "It's white, but it hasn't been sifted yet." The Patriarch then struck the mortar three times with his staff and the master shook the sifting basket three times and entered the [Patriarch's] room.

The Patriarch said, "Buddhas appear in the world for the sake of the one great matter and guide people according to their faculties. Finally, such things as the ten stages, three vehicles, and sudden and gradual [enlightenment] become teachings. Moreover, [the Buddha] conferred the unsurpassed, extremely subtle, intimate, perfectly marvelous true Treasury of the Eye of the True Dharma on his senior disciple, the Venerable Mahakashyapa. It has been transmitted successively from patriarch to patriarch up to Bodhidharma in the twenty-eighth generation. When he came here, he found Great Master Huike, and it was [eventually] passed on to me. Now, I pass on the Dharma treasure and robe that have been transmitted. You must guard them well and not allow [the Dharma] to perish."

The master knelt and received the robe and Dharma and asked, "I have now received the Dharma, but on whom should I confer the robe [later]?" The Patriarch replied, "Long ago, when Bodhidharma first arrived, people lacked faith, so he transmitted the robe to show that one had obtained the Dharma. Faith has matured now, but the robe will become a point of contention, so let it stop with you and not be passed on. You had better go away and hide. Wait for the right time before you teach. It is said that the life of a person who has received the robe hangs by a thread." The master asked, "Where should I hide?" The Patriarch said, "Stop when you get to Huai; hide a while when you reach Hui."

The master prostrated himself before the Patriarch, took the robe and left. There was a ferry at the foot of Mount Huangmei and the Patriarch personally escorted him there. The master bowed and said, "You should go back. Since I have found the Way, I should cross over myself." The Patriarch answered, "Though you have already found the Way, I still have to cross over." So saying, he took the pole and crossed over to the other shore. The Patriarch returned alone to the monastery without anyone finding out.

After that, the Fifth Patriarch no longer entered the hall [to give Dharma talks]. If monks came and questioned him, he said, "My Way is gone." They would ask, "Who has received the robe and Dharma?" and the Patriarch would answer, "An able [*neng*] has acquired it." The monks reasoned, "The workman Lu's name is *neng* [able]," but when they called on him, he was missing. They realized that he had acquired [the robe and Dharma] and set out after him.

At that time, there was [a monk] named Huiming who had aroused the thought of enlightenment after having been in the army, and he became their leader. He followed the master and overtook him in the Dayu Range [of mountains]. The master said, "This robe symbolizes faith. It is not something to compete for with force." He placed the robe and bowl on a rock and hid in some grass.

When Huiming arrived and tried to lift them, he could not do it, try as he may. He said trembling greatly, "I came for the Dharma, not the robe." Huineng emerged and sat on the rock. Huiming bowed and said, "Please, workman, explain the essentials of the Dharma for me." The master said, "Not thinking of good, not thinking of evil, at the very moment, what is your original face?" Hearing these words, Huiming was greatly awakened. Then, he asked, "Is there a secret meaning beyond the secret words you have spoken just now?" The master answered, "What I have said to you is not secret. If you reflect inwardly, the secret is there within." Huiming said, "Although I dwell at Huangmei, I have not yet looked within and discovered my own face. Now, I have received your teaching and I am like someone who drinks water and knows for sure whether it is warm or cold. You are now my master." The master said, "If it is as you say, we both have Huangmei [Hongren] for a master." Huiming bowed gratefully and withdrew.

Later, when [Huiming] was an abbot, he changed his name from Huiming to Daoming, to avoid using the first part of the master's name [out of respect]. When someone came there to practice, he always sent him to practice with the master.

After receiving the robe and Dharma, the master hid himself among hunters in Xixian. After ten years, on the eighth day of the first month of 676, he moved to the far south where he encountered Dharma Master Yinzong lecturing on the *Nirvana Sutra* at Fa Xing Temple. He lodged in the hallway. The wind was blowing a banner and he heard two monks arguing, one saying it was the banner that was moving, and the other saying that it was the wind moving. They talked back and forth but did not hit on the truth. The master said, "If a lowly layman may interrupt your lofty discussion, it is neither the banner nor the wind that is moving; it is your minds that are moving." When Yinzong heard about this discussion, he was astonished and thought it was quite remarkable. The next day, he summoned the master to his room and asked about the meaning of the banner and wind. The master explained the principle fully and Yinzong arose involuntarily, saying, "You are definitely not an ordinary person. Who are you?" The master then told him of the circumstances of receiving the Dharma, concealing nothing. Thereupon, Yingzong made the bow of a student and asked for the essentials of Zen. He told his own followers, "I am a thoroughly ordinary man, but I have just met a living bodhisattva." He then pointed to the layman Lu in the group and said, "There he is." Then he asked that the robes of faith that had been transmitted be brought out so that everyone could pay homage to them.

On the fifteenth of the same month, all the well-known monks were called together so that [Huineng] could have his head shaved. On the eighth day of the second month, he received the complete precepts from Precept Master Zhiguang of Faxing Temple. The platform used for giving the precepts had been established earlier in the Song Dynasty by Tripitaka Master Gunabhadra. He had predicted, "Later there will be a living bodhisattva who will receive the precepts on this platform." Also, near the end of the Liang Dynasty, Tripitaka Master Paramartha had planted two *bodhi* trees beside the platform with his own hands, telling the monks, "A hundred and twenty years from now a greatly awakened man will appear and expound the unexcelled Way beneath these trees and liberate innumerable beings." After taking the precepts, the master taught the Dharma teaching of the Eastern Mountain, just as had been foretold so long ago.

The next year, on the eighth day of the second month, the master suddenly said to the monks, "I do not want to stay here anymore; I am going to return to my former dwelling." Accordingly, Yinzong and more than a thousand monks and lay people escorted him back to Baolin Monastery. Weiju, the governor of Guangzhou, invited him to turn the wheel of the Dharma at Dafan Temple and also received the formless precept of Mind. Huineng's followers recorded his talks, calling them the "Platform Scripture," which is well known. Then he returned to Caoxi Monastery and showered down the rain of the great Dharma. His students numbered over a thousand. At the age of seventy-five, he died sitting in dignity in zazen.

Teisho

When the transmission took place, like water passed from one container to another without a drop being spilled, [Hongren] asked, "Is the rice white yet?" These grains of rice are surely the marvelous sprouts that will become a King of Dharma, the life-roots of both sages and ordinary people. Once planted in wild fields, they grow even without weeding. Husked and polished, they take on no impurity. However, though this is how they are, they are still unsifted. If they are sifted, they pervade inside and outside, and move up and down. When the mortar was struck three times, the rice grains were scooped out of the mortar spontaneously and the functioning of Mind was suddenly bared. When the rice was sifted three times, the [spirit of the] Patriarch was transmitted. Since then, the night when the mortar was struck has not brightened, the day of transmission has not darkened.

It seems that the master was a wood cutter from Lingnan and was the workman Lu in the rice-hulling shed. In old times, he wandered in the mountains earning a living with an ax. Even though he had not studied the ancient [Buddhist] teachings and illuminated his mind, still, just by hearing one sentence from the scriptures about raising an unsupported thought, he finally ended up in the rice-hulling mill with a mortar and pestle. Although he never practiced Zen, raised Dharma questions, or experienced awakening [in the usual manner], by working diligently for eight months, he illumined the mind as a bright mirror that is not a stand. In the middle of the night, the transmission took place and the lifeblood of successive patriarchs was transmitted. Though it was not necessarily the result of many years of effort, it is clear that for just a brief period he put forth the utmost effort. The achievement of the Way by all Buddhas cannot essentially be measured in terms of long and short time periods. How can you grasp the transmission of the Way by patriarchal teachers through such distinctions as past and present?

Moreover, for ninety days this summer [during the *ango*, training period], I have spoken of this and that, commenting on the past and present, and explaining the lives of the Buddha patriarchs with wild and gentle words. I have gone into the subtle and fine [which words cannot describe] and treated you all like sons and grandsons, and more, besmirching the Zen tradition and displaying our shame. Consequently, you may think that you have penetrated the truth and acquired power, but you do not seem to have accorded intimately with the intentions of the patriarchs. Your behavior is not at all like that of our wise predecessors. Because of causes in past lives and good luck, we have been able to meet. If you single-mindedly make an effort in the Way, you will achieve the Way, but many of you have not yet reached the other shore. You have still not peeked into the profound heart of the matter. It has been a long time since the Buddha went away. You have not completed your work in the Way, and life is slipping away, so why wait until tomorrow? Summer is over and fall begins. You will be taking off in all directions, scattering here and there as always. How can you recklessly memorize a word or a half a sentence and call that my Dharma or my Way, or hang onto a piece of knowledge or half an understanding and think that this is the Way of the Mahayana? Even if you have acquired power sufficiently, the shame of our family is still exposed. How much less should you preach the Dharma pretending to be something you are not and spouting nonsense! If you really want to reach this realm, do not vainly waste time day or night or recklessly misuse your minds and bodies.

Verse

> Striking the mortar—the sound was loud, echoing beyond time
>   and space;
> Sifting the clouds—the silver moon appeared, and the night was
>   deep and clear.

Hakuin Ekaku and the Modern Koan System

Philip Yampolsky

HAKUIN WAS BORN IN 1686 to a commoner family of low status, in Hara, in present-day Shizuoka Prefecture. He was a Kanto man (that is, he came from an eastern district closer to Edo than to Kyoto), and although he turned back to Kyoto Zen for his teaching, he remained always an independent, active proponent of the popular-type, mass-appeal Buddhism that had arisen in Edo with such men as Shido Bu'nan and Suzuki Shosan (1579–1655). At an early age he turned to Buddhism, although he describes a period when he lost his faith in its efficacy and devoted himself to secular literature. This period is reflected in his voluminous writings in both Chinese *(kambun)* and Japanese, which demonstrate his wide knowledge of Chinese literature and the various popular Japanese genres of the time. At the age of twenty-two he set out to pursue his studies in earnest, visiting various temples and gaining what he believed to be a degree of awakening. Toward the end of his twenty-fourth year he visited the Zen Master Shoju Rojin (Dokyo Etan, 1642–1721). Shoju was the heir of Shido Bu'nan, who was in turn the heir of Gudo Toshoku. Gudo was in the Myoshin-ji tradition and traced his Zen ancestry to Kanzan, Shuho, and Nampo. Hakuin stayed with Shoju only eight months; all we know of this Zen master we know from Hakuin, who quotes him extensively. Hakuin most probably did not receive Shoju's sanction of his understanding of Zen; he himself writes that it was not until much later that he awakened to the import of Shoju's teaching. Hakuin never visited Shoju again; nor did he make mention in his writings of his connection with Shoju until after the latter's death. It is nevertheless accepted that Hakuin was Shoju's heir, and thus of the O-To-Kan line of transmission.

After leaving Shoju, Hakuin wandered about from temple to temple, practicing and perfecting his Zen. When he was thirty-two he returned to his temple, the Shoin-ji in his native town of Hara. Here he devoted himself to teaching a growing band of disciples. He frequently traveled about Japan, using the donations he received for preaching and lecturing to print the large number of works he composed and to support the disciples who studied under him. He passed away in January of 1769.

Whatever suspicions one may entertain about the authenticity of Hakuin's lineage, these have little bearing on the type of Zen he taught. Hakuin insisted that, for Zen meditation practice, the practitioner must have three basic qualities: an overriding faith, a great doubt when facing the koans, and a strong aspiration and perseverance. The student's first task was to see into his own true nature *(kensho)*. To this end Hakuin championed the *Mu* koan and later in his life the *Sekishu no onjo*, the "Sound of the Single Hand," a koan which he himself devised. The method by which koans are to be solved is, of course, by disciplined *zazen*, or meditation sitting, accompanied by private interviews with the teacher *(sanzen)*, in which the Master gives guidance and eventually sanction to the student's understanding of a particular koan. But this is only the first step. In his *Yasen kanna* Hakuin quotes the famous Song Master Ta-hui Tsung-kao (Daie Soko, 1089–1163) as having stated that he had experienced eighteen great awakenings and an uncountable number of small ones during his lifetime. Thus, once the initial awakening has been obtained, the student must go on with the practice after awakening. This unremitting practice is, in effect, the koan system.

It is difficult to obtain an exact picture of the early role of the koans in Japan. We know that they were used by Shuho Myocho (Daito Kokushi), for a koan collection compiled by him remains. Surely they played a significant role in the teachings of the early Zen masters who came from China. That koans were used throughout the Muromachi and Momoyama periods is demonstrated by the many records of koan interviews *(missancho)* that remain. Exactly how they were used or in what number is not certain, but records indicate a system of approximately three hundred koans, centering around the *Pi-yen lu* koan collection. Reference is found to a system involving the study of one hundred koans before beginning the *Pi-yen lu (hekizen)*, then the hundred koans in the

Pi-yen lu, and a hundred koans after the *Pi-yen lu (hekigo)*. It is unclear just what this system involved, and the "hundred koans" in each instance appears to be an approximate number. Also involved was the custom of requiring the student to add verse comments, drawn mainly from Chinese poetry, indicating his understanding of a particular koan. This custom was maintained, in a modified form, in the Zen taught by Hakuin.

With the spread of the Rinzai schools throughout the country there came a tendency to devise a form that would have a greater popular appeal. This type of Zen made little use of the koan and at times even rejected it. It was against this kind of Zen that Hakuin revolted, at least in terms of its suitability for the practicing monk. Although Hakuin devoted considerable effort, particularly in his writings, toward the lay world, for the monastery environment he insisted on a strict and lengthy term of study, centering on the koan.

The exact details of the koan system Hakuin used are not clearly known. As mentioned earlier, it emphasized the use of the *Mu* koan and later the Sound of the Single Hand for the initial awakening, with an intensive program of koan study for the practice after awakening. This program was later organized by Hakuin's disciple Torei and by the latter's disciples Inzan Ien (1751–1814) and Takuju Kosen (1760–1833) into a formalized system of koan study. There are variations in the methods used by Inzan and Takuju, but essentially they are compatible. The programs of study require a progression through a specified series of koans. Frequently the order and type of the koan will vary. As the student's understanding advances, koans investigated at an earlier stage may be investigated again, until eventually those few who survive the intensive, rigorous, and exhausting course of study are themselves sanctioned as teachers. Then follows a period of several years' self-imposed isolation until the student is ready to emerge as a teacher.

In addition to the formal meditation, the practitioner is required, together with the body of monks, to live in an extremely regulated monastic atmosphere, with set rules for proper procedure in all his activities. An important feature of the monk's life is the work period in which the temple buildings and grounds are cared for, vegetables grown, and other tasks accomplished. This work, as Hakuin conceived it, was part of the koan study. Thus he emphasized practice in the midst of activity, be it in the work of the temple or in the bustle of the lay world. In *Orategama* we read:

> I am not trying to tell you to discard completely quietistic meditation and to seek specifically for a place of activity to carry on your practice. What is most worthy of respect is a pure koan meditation that neither knows nor is conscious of the two aspects, the quiet and the active. This is why it has been said that the true practicing monk walks but does not know he is walking, sits but does not know he is sitting.
>
> For penetrating to the depths of one's own true self-nature and for attaining a vitality valid on all occasions, nothing can surpass meditation in the midst of activity.

[…] Hakuin recognizes the need for a Buddhism directed toward the people in general. Although his chief preoccupation was with the monks who were studying under him, he also showed a major concern for the common people, as well as for the spiritual welfare of the feudal lords and their retainers. He addressed works to each of these three groups. Directed toward the monks are books designed principally as aids to their study: *Kaian koku go* contains verse comments on the *Daito-roku* [Record of Daito]; the *Sokko-roku kaien fusetsu* consists of lectures on the *Hsü-t'ang-lu* [Record of Hsü-t'ang]; the *Keiso dokuzui* comprises Hakuin's own recorded sayings, in the traditional style of such works; other books are chiefly autobiographical statements designed to encourage his students.

His advice to various feudal lords makes up much of his writing. This advice is given in letter form, with the same passages often repeated in two or more letters. When printed, several letters are usually grouped together under various titles, generally the names of unpretentious plants and flowers. Not all of these letters, however, are addressed to feudal lords; two in the well-known *Orategama* are directed toward a nun of the Hoke (Nichiren) Sect and an ailing priest. Much of the material contained in them deals with the efficacy of the Zen Hakuin preaches, but some works are cautionary expositions on the functions of a good ruler, conventionally Confucian in tone. He advocates a humane government and the proper treatment of the farmers. But no matter what the principal subject of the letter may be, Hakuin invariably adds passages extolling the virtues of his own school of Buddhism.

Orategama Zokushu

Hakuin Ekaku

Translated by Philip Yampolsky

Letter in answer to the question: Which is superior, the Koan or the Nembutsu?

IN YOUR RECENT LETTER you ask whether the calling of the Buddha's name is of any help to continuous and uninterrupted true meditation, and whether the calling of the name is one with the meditation on Chao-chou's *Mu*. Your kind letter inquires whether there are any particular deficiencies in either of the two methods.

When you kill a man, is it the same thing if you kill him with a sword or with a spear, or are there any particular drawbacks in the two methods? How does one answer such a question? Certainly the sword and spear are two different weapons, yet can we call the killing itself two things? In the past Tadanobu used a chess board to pursue an enemy, Shinozuka ripped loose a board from a ship's deck and used it to beat someone, the Empress Lü used poisoned wine to kill the [Chao King Liu] Ju-i, Hsüan-wu unfastened a lute string and used it to garrote a lady of pleasure, Kuan Yü brandished the dragon sword, and Chang Fei took up the viper club. The sword and the spear are two, but the duality lies only in the skill or clumsiness, the honesty or dishonesty, of the person who wields them.

So it is with the study of the Way. Whether you sit in meditation, recite the sutras, intone the *dharani*, or call the Buddha's name, if you devote all your efforts to what you are doing and attain to the ultimate, you will kick down the dark cave of ignorance, destroy the evil bandits of the five desires, smash the illumination of the Great Perfect Mirror, penetrate to the true status of the perfect knowledge of the Four Wisdoms, and attain to the understanding of the Great Matter. The content of the practices may vary but what difference is there in the goal that is reached?

191

Say there are two men whose strength and physical makeup are the same. Each is equipped with strong armor and sharp weapons and they engage each other in battle. Yet one does not possess a strong determination. He doubts and he fears; he does not know whether to fight or to run away. He cannot decide whether to live or to die, whether to advance or to retreat. His eyes waver, his footwork is unsteady; confused, he does not know what to do. The other does not consider danger. It matters not who is strong and who weak. His whole body is concentrated, his eyes fixed, his teeth gritted, and with valiant spirit he presses forward. Which man will win is as obvious as the palm of your hand. It is perfectly clear that no matter what odds he encountered, the second man would win every time. Suppose two armies were facing each other. One army has a hundred thousand troops, all mercenaries paid with gold and silver. The other has but a thousand men, trained in virtue and loyalty, their determination wedded with benevolence. To set these thousand men against the hundred thousand would be like loosing a fierce tiger against a flock of sheep. It all comes down to the worthiness or lack of worth of the generals in command. What can differences in strength or the amount of weapons possibly have to do with it?

The same thing applies to concentrated meditation. Supposing you have one man who is occupied with the koan of Chao-chou's *Mu* and another who devotes himself exclusively to the calling of the Buddha's name. If the meditation of the former is not pure, if his determination is not firm, even if he devotes himself to the koan for ten or twenty years, he will gain no benefit whatsoever. The man who calls the Buddha's name, on the other hand, should he call it with complete concentration and undiluted purity, should he neither concern himself with the filthy mundane world nor seek the Pure Land, but proceed determinedly without retrogression, he will, before ten days have passed, gain the benefits of *samadhi*, produce the wisdom of the Buddha, and achieve the Great Matter of salvation in the very place he stands.

What is salvation *(ojo)*? It all comes down to the one thing—seeing into your own nature. The *Sutra* states the vow: "Until all those who repeat my name ten times in their desire to be born in my land are born there, I shall not accept true enlightenment." Where is "my land?" Is it not the innate self-nature with which you yourself are endowed, standing bright and clear before your eyes? If you have not seen into your own nature it will not be easy for you to see this land. Yet nowadays those who practice the Pure Land teaching recite the name daily a thousand times, ten thousand times, a million times, but not one of them has determined the Great Matter of salvation. Don't they realize that Amida Buddha refused to accept true enlightenment? Still more, don't they realize that one instant of thought is this very Paradise of Salvation? Why wait then for ten repetitions of the name?

For this reason the Buddha has said that for the valiant man, becoming a Buddha is in an instant of thought; for the indolent man, Nirvana will take three *asankheya* kalpas. It should be known that those who think that the *Mu* koan and the recitation of the Buddha's name are two different things belong to the class of evil heretics. How sad it is that the Pure Land practitioners today are unaware of the basic aspiration of the many Buddhas. They believe only that the Buddha is in the Western Land and are unaware that the Western Land is the basis of their own minds. They are convinced that through the power of the recitation of the Buddha's name they will somehow leap through space and after they are dead be reborn in the Western Land. But although they spend their whole lives in painful struggle, they will not be able to achieve their vow to be reborn there. Know then that "in all the Buddha lands everywhere there is the Law of the One Unique Vehicle." This is why it has been said: "The Buddha body fills the Dharmakaya; it appears before all sentient beings everywhere." If the Buddha were only in the Western Land it would not be possible for him to appear before all sentient beings everywhere. And if he does appear before all sentient beings everywhere, then he cannot be only in the Western Land. How sad indeed that, although it is as obvious as the palms of their hands that the pure, true body of the Tathagata stands in all its brilliance clearly before their eyes, people are all unable to see him because their eye of wisdom is blinded. Unspeakable indeed!

Isn't it said: "His brilliance illumines the world in all directions"? But do not understand this to mean that the brilliance and the world are two different things. If you are awakened, the worlds in all directions, grass, trees, and lands are perfected and at once are the true body of the pure light of the Tathagata. If you are deluded, the true body of the pure light of the Tathagata is perfected, but in error is made to be the world in all directions, grass, trees, and lands. That is why the *Sutra* says: "If you see me as form or seek me as sound, you are practicing the ways of the heretic and will never be able to see the Tathagata."

The true practitioner of the Pure Land doctrine is not like this. He does not contemplate birth, he does not contemplate death; his mind does not falter or fall into error. Reciting the name of the Buddha constantly, he has reached the state where the mind is undisturbed. The Great Matter appears suddenly before him and his salvation is determined. Such a man can be called one who has truly seen into his own nature. His own body is the limitless body of Amida, the treasure trees of seven precious gems, the pond of the eight virtues. His own mind is illumined and radiates before his eyes. He has penetrated to the understanding that mountains, rivers, the great earth, all phenomena are the rare and mysterious Sea of Adornment. The ultimate, in which there is complete concentration in calling the name, in which not an instant of thought is produced, and in which the body and life are cast aside is known as "going" (o). The place where *samadhi* is perfected and true wisdom makes its appearance is known as "being born" (jo). The welling-forth of this absolute principle in all its clarity, the immovable place in which he [the true practitioner] stands, not one fraction of an inch apart [from true understanding], is "the welcoming of Amida" (raigo). When the welcoming and the rebirth are then and there not two things—this is the true substance of seeing into one's own nature.

Around the Genroku period [1688–1703] there were two Pure Land practitioners, one named Enjo and the other Engu. Each was possessed of the same aspiration and neither of them relaxed one bit in his concentrated recitation of the Buddha's name. Enjo was a native of Yamashiro. His recitation of the name was pure and he had reached the state where his mind was undisturbed. Suddenly he had perfected his *samadhi* and had determined the Great Matter of Salvation. Having attained this state he went to pay a visit to the old Master Dokutan at Hatsuyama in the province of Totomi.

> Dokutan asked: "From what province do you come?"
> Enjo replied: "From Yamashire."
> Dokutan asked: "To what sect do you belong?"

"The Pure Land," Enjo answered.

Dokutan asked: "How old is Amida Buddha?"

Enjo replied: "The same age as I."

"And how old are you?" Dokutan countered.

"The same as Amida," Enjo replied.

Then Dokutan asked: "Then where are you right at this moment?"

Enjo clenched his left hand and raised it a little.

Dokutan was startled. "You really are a true practitioner of the Pure Land doctrine," he added.

Engu also, after not so long a time, perfected his samadhi and determined for himself the Great Matter.

Around the beginning of the Genroku period there was a monk in Akazawa in Izu Province by the name of Sokuo. He also gained great virtue through the power of the recitation of the Buddha's name. I have mentioned here two or three of these Pure Land practitioners; there are many others like them, but I do not have the time to list them one by one. These men in themselves serve as proof of the virtue gained from concentrated recitation of the Buddha's name.

It must be understood that the koan and the recitation of the Buddha's name are both contributing causes to the path that leads to the opening up of the wisdom of the Buddha. The opening up of the wisdom of the Buddha is the main purpose for the appearance of the various Buddhas in this world. In the past the Buddha established expedients; one was called "rebirth in the Pure Land," another "seeing into one's own nature." How can these be two different things! Zen people who have not penetrated to this understanding look at a Pure Land practitioner and think that he is a stupid and evil common person who knows nothing about the Great Matter of seeing into one's own nature. They feel that he is vainly reciting the Buddha's name in the hope of leaping across countless countries in broad daylight in order to be reborn in the Pure Land, and they liken him to a lame turtle that dresses itself up and then expects to jump over to China. They condemn him particularly for not knowing that as far as these countless countries are concerned, the ten evils and the eight wrong views herald the awakening to the wisdom of the Buddha, and that when these evils and heresies are dissipated the very place where one stands is the Pure Land.

The Pure Land practitioner, on the other hand, looks at the Zen man and thinks that here is someone who has no faith in the saving grace of Amida, but pridefully seeks to gain awakening through his own efforts and tries to make the great awakening his escape from birth and death. "Isn't this the most ridiculous of practices? Is this something that we poor mortals of inadequate capacities can accomplish in this degenerate age?" they ask. So they scorn the Zen man and compare him to a duck, that, deciding it will fly to Korea, fits itself with wings, thinking that it can emulate a hawk.

The practitioner of the *Lotus Sutra* berates others, saying: "Our *Sutra* is the basic vow because of which all Buddhas appear in the world, the one direct way by which all the Tathagatas attain to Buddhahood. If you disregard our unsurpassedly wondrous *Sutra* what possible use can there be in reciting the Buddha's name or in practicing Zen? Anyone who, when he sees a specialist in reciting this *Sutra*, says that this specialist has not perfected his understanding of the unique One Vehicle, has not opened up the knowledge of the true form of the various dharmas, and is merely screaming incongruous sounds every day, like frogs croaking amidst the paddy fields in spring, is himself a prater of nonsense, a fool who disregards the golden words concerning the Arjaka tree, and a perpetrator of evil heresies."

Aren't these people aware that the *Lotus Sutra* has leaped over the gradual step-by-step methods of the *Agamas, Vaipulya*, and the rest of the four doctrines and speaks of the essential teaching of the opening up of the Buddha's wisdom? This is why the *Sutra* says: "[The Buddhas] appear in this world to show the Way to the opening up of the Buddha's wisdom." Know then that with the luminescence of perfect understanding, the vow to appear in the world is made. Studying Zen, calling the name, even reading and reciting sutras, are all aids in the path toward seeing the Way. They are like the staves that travelers use to aid them in their journeys.

Among staves there are those made of goosefoot and those made of bamboo. Though the staves are made of different materials they both serve the same purpose—to help the voyager in his travels. Do not say then that the goosefoot staff is good and the one made of bamboo poor. If the voyager loses his perseverance and collapses of fatigue, what use is either staff, no matter of what it is made? It is the same with studying Zen under a teacher. Its essence lies only in the one instant of thought, borne by the fierce perseverance of the practitioner. Don't say: "The koan is good, the calling of the Buddha's name is bad." If the practitioner does not have that valiant will to succeed, neither the calling of the name nor the koan will be of any use whatsoever. They will be of as much value as glasses for a blind man or a comb for a monk.

Supposing there are a hundred people, each fitted out with his own provisions, who wish to go to the capital. But their guide is incompetent and in error leads them to a distant, desolate plain, teeming with wolves and tigers. They spend their days fighting over whose staff is made of better wood, arguing about whose garments are superior, and worrying about the cost of their travels. All they talk about are the staves, all they shout about are the expenses, until they are unable to move one step further. They have spent their time in vain, years have been added to their lives, and their bodies are wearied and exhausted. Finally they fall prey to the wolves and tigers, and in this far and desolate area become idle spirits and wild demons. Thus in the end they never are able to reach the capital. The wise thing to do is to pay no attention to such things as staves and traveling clothes but single-mindedly to advance without losing ground. In this way you will quickly reach the capital. But if you imitate the customs of today by depending upon the power of the Buddha while alive, and hoping to go to the Western Land after you have died, then throughout your whole life you will never be able to achieve *samadhi* and will never be able to determine your salvation. How much less so will you be able to achieve the Great Matter of the true seeing into your own nature.

The Priest of Shinju-an has left a verse:

> More tenuous than figures written on a flowing stream,
> The future of those who depend upon the Buddha.

Even though he has written in this way Ikkyu did not mean that the Pure Land practices are to be despised and the calling of the name to be abjured.

But if you are looking for something that will help you attain continuous uninterrupted true meditation and insight into your own nature, then calling the Buddha's name is fine, but you could as well recite the grain-grinding song instead. Do not think you are going to become a Buddha by deliberately discarding the essentials of seeing into your own nature and turning instead to the virtues gained from calling the Buddha's name.

To put it in the form of a parable, suppose you had a great ship that could hold ten thousand bales of rice. The ship is moored, ready for sailing; a favorable wind is blowing, the oarsmen are ready, their voices raised in song. The captain, his crew, and the helmsman are all in accord and they set out over the waves rowing toward far-off waters, proceeding bravely onward day after day. But wait: the hawser has not been loosened. They cannot cross over the rolling waves, and though each day they exhaust all their efforts, they are still in the harbor from which they started out. It is but a small hawser that binds them, yet it is stronger than ten thousand men.

So it is with the study of the Way. A man may be physically well-endowed, possessed of an enormous vitality, have superb talents, make Ma-tsu and Po-chang his teachers, Nan-ch'üan and Ch'ang-sha his companions, nourish well his valiant energies, advance in his single-minded practice, train himself in pure undistracted meditation, yet if he has not cut off the root of life, he will never attain to the joy where the "Ka" is shouted.

What is this root of life? It is that instant of ignorance that has come down through endless kalpas of time. Evolving through heaven and hell, this evil world and the Pure Land, that the three evil realms and the six evil paths are made to appear is all because of the power of this root of life. Although it is nothing but dreamlike, illusory fancied thoughts, it can block the Great Matter of seeing into one's own nature more effectively than an army of a hundred thousand demons. Sometimes it is called illusory thoughts, sometimes the root of birth and death, sometimes the passions, sometimes a demon. It is one thing with many names, but if you examine it closely you will find that what it comes down to is one concept: that the self is real. Because of this view that the self exists, we have birth and death, Nirvana, the passions, enlightenment. That is why it is said: "If the mind is produced, all things are produced; if the mind is destroyed, all things are destroyed." Elsewhere we read: "[Should a bodhisattva give rise to a notion of] the self, of a man, of a sentient being, this is not a true bodhisattva." The Buddha asked Kashyapa: "What Law do the sons of good families practice so that they can conform with the Law of the Great Nirvana?" Kashyapa answered by mentioning one by one such things as the five precepts, the ten good characteristics, the eighteen differentiating qualities, the six perfections, all the good actions of a bodhisattva, the eight forms of deliverance, the countless Dharma gates, but the Buddha would accept none of his answers. Finally Kashyapa asked the Buddha: "What laws are there that conform with Nirvana?" and the Buddha answered: "The only Law that conforms with Nirvana is the Law of non-ego."

But non-ego is of two kinds. Take a man who is weak in body and mind. He is afraid of everybody, destroys his vitality, and is influenced by all external circumstances. He does not get angry even when reviled; he does not care even if he is rejected but always stupidly plods along getting nowhere. His knowledge advances not one bit and he thinks that the non-ego to which he has attained is sufficient. Such a person is a torn rice bag, bloated from gorging himself on the swill of swine, an ignorant, blind fool. This does not represent the true non-ego. How much less so then for the man who, relying on the power of the calling of the Buddha's name, hopes to "go" to the Pure Land and thus tries to "become" a Buddha! What is this "going"? What is this "becoming"? If it isn't ego, then what is it? Don't say: "This is a view that denies karma." Is this denying or not denying? If you are not a hero who has truly seen into his own nature, don't think it is something that can be known so easily. If you want accordance with the true, pure non-ego, you must be prepared to let go your hold when hanging from a sheer precipice, to die and return again to life. Only then can you attain to the true ego of the four Nirvana virtues.

What is "to let go your hold when hanging from a sheer precipice"? Suppose a man should find himself in some desolate area where no man has ever walked before. Below him are the perpendicular walls of a bottomless chasm. His feet rest precariously on a patch of slippery moss, and there is no spot of earth on which he can steady himself. He can neither advance nor retreat; he faces only death. The only things he has on which to depend are a vine that he grasps by the left hand and a creeper that he holds with his right. His life hangs as if from a dangling thread. If he were suddenly to let go his dried bones would not even be left.

So it is with the study of the Way. If you take up one koan and investigate it unceasingly, your mind will die and your will will be destroyed. It is as though a vast, empty abyss lay before you, with no place to set your hands and feet. You face death and your bosom feels as though it were afire. Then suddenly you are one with the koan, and both body and mind are cast off. This is known as the time when the hands are released over the abyss. Then when suddenly you return to life, there is the great joy of one who drinks the water and knows for himself whether it is hot or cold. This is known as rebirth in the Pure Land. This is known as seeing into one's own nature. You must push forward relentlessly, and with the help of this complete concentration you will penetrate without fail to the basic source of your own nature. Never doubt that without seeing into your own nature you cannot become a Buddha; without seeing into your own nature there is no Pure Land.

Even the world-honored Tathagata, the incomparable great sage of the three worlds who longed to become the guide to all sentient beings, before he entered the Himalaya and saw once into his own nature, was no different from ordinary people, revolving endlessly in the cycle of transmigration, and he himself passed through some eight thousand rebirths. With the coming of the dawn of the great awakening to one's own nature, then are the eyes opened wide to enlightenment. It is an unparalleled ignorance to believe that one can become a Buddha without seeing into one's own nature, or that there is a Pure Land outside of one's own nature.

The Twenty-Eighth Patriarch, Bodhidharma, borne by the living body of the bodhisattva Kannon, endured endless stretches of raging waves to come to China, a land that already possessed the sacred scriptures in abundance, to transmit the seal of the Buddha mind that had been handed down from the Tathagata. Hearing of this, and wondering what Great Matter he had to impart, people wiped their eyes, adjusted their garments, and came longing for instruction. And what he had to teach was only the one thing—seeing into one's own nature and becoming Buddha. Although he set up six gates, including the "Breaking through

Form" and the "Awakened Nature," ultimately they all come down to the one thing—seeing into one's own nature.

But sentient beings are numberless; therefore the gates to the Dharma are numberless. Among them [the Buddha] established one gate, that of rebirth into the Pure Land, as a temporary expedient to rescue Vaidehi from the prison in which she languished. If rebirth in the Pure Land were the pivotal teaching of Buddhism, then Bodhidharma could just as well have written a note of two or three lines and sent it on to China. Would Bodhidharma have endured the painful agonies of the raging waves and risked his life against monster fish to come all the way to China just to say: "Concentrate on the calling of the Buddha's name and you will be reborn in the Pure Land"?

The same was true of the Buddha. At first he lived in the palace of his father Suddhodana and spent time in pleasurable enjoyment with his wives Yasodhara and Gopika. His position was that of a ruler; he possessed the wealth of India, and he believed that at death it would be satisfactory to call the name and be reborn in the Pure Land. One can imagine the state of his mind then, when he discarded his position as king, for six years engaged in arduous ascetic practices and suffered the scorn of the hermit Aradakalama. Later he entered deep into the Himalaya and fell into so intense a *samadhi* that he was unaware of the reeds that were piercing his thigh or the lightning that struck down horses and oxen beside him. His whole body was so emaciated that he looked like a tile bound with rope and his bones stuck to his skin.

Then finally, on the eighth day of the twelfth month, he glimpsed the planet Venus, and then for the first time saw into his own nature and gained a great awakening. At this time he exclaimed aloud: "How wonderful! All sentient beings are endowed with the great wisdom and virtuous characteristics of the Tathagata!" And then he came down from the mountain and expounded in full measure the sudden and the gradual, the intermediate and the complete teachings. At this time he was venerated as the Tathagata, endowed with the ten titles and possessed of the perfect miraculous enlightenment. Is this not what Shan-hui Ta-shih has described in these words: "Suddenly awakening to the source of the mind, the treasure storehouse is opened"? Even though ours is a degenerate age, is this not a splendid example that Buddhists today should venerate? If you look for the essentials and the basic content of the practice that has been transmitted from the Tathagata who appeared in this world through the Patriarchs and sages and all wise men and famous monks, it is nothing other than the principle of seeing into one's own nature.

Rennyo Shonin has spoken about everyday rebirth and rebirth without the welcoming of Amida. When you think about it, is this not the true principle of seeing into your own nature? Even Honen Shonin, who delved deeply into the Tripitaka and read through its five thousand volumes five times, who was worshipped as a living Tathagata by everyone from lord to commoner, always lamented that it was not solely a matter of making the principle clear within the sacred works. Because he had no predecessor who had investigated the basis of the mind in the teachings outside the scriptures, he likened his own state of mind to a line too short to allow the bucket to scoop up the water in a deep well, or to wings too short to fly over the vast reaches of the sky. What is the basis of the mind in the transmission outside the scriptures? Is it not the teaching of seeing into one's own nature? One is indeed struck with awe and veneration to see that not one word uttered by the Taoist sages violates this teaching to the slightest degree. That people today show contempt and scorn for the Great Matter of seeing into one's own nature—a thing for which even the august Honen Shonin, who was venerated and respected by the gods, longed for deeply— is, in my opinion, a serious crime. Of course, for people who do not know of the principle, this cannot be considered so great a crime.

Eshin Sozu, at the age of twenty-four, saying that he wanted to polish the Great Perfect Mirror of his own nature, retired to the vastness of Yokawa and during the day practiced the three sutras of the Lotus and at night called the Buddha's name sixty thousand times. At other times of the day he was not idle, yet it was only when he reached the age of sixty-four that he felt that he had understood the True Reality of his own nature. He is indeed worthy of veneration. When one reaches this state of the realization of True Reality in one's own body, the mountains, rivers, the great earth, all phenomena, grass, trees, lands, the sentient and the non-sentient all appear at the same time as the complete body of the unchanging True Reality. This is the appearance of Nirvana, the time of awakening to one's own nature.

Myohen Sozu of Mount Koya, in the fall of a year when he was in his fifties, entered into a deep *samadhi* of calling the Buddha's name. [That evening] Koya Daishi [appeared before him and] presented him formally with a surplice *(kesa)* of lily-root fiber and a golden leaf of the scriptures [explaining the *samadhi*]. The gist of what he said was: "Pointing only in the one direction of the west is an expedient. If you discard the nine other directions and stop the confused mind and throughout your life call the name of the Buddha, you will gain the great virtue of the opening of the mind's eye." The opening of the mind's eye is of itself seeing into one's own nature.

Even though there are over five thousand rolls of the scriptures spoken by the Buddha, and although he preached on the wondrous meaning of the sudden, gradual, secret, and indeterminate doctrines, nowhere does the Great Matter of seeing into one's own nature appear. This is why the Sutra says: "There is only this one True Reality. Any other is not the True." In all the three periods from the past to the present, there has not been one Buddha or Patriarch who did not see into his own nature. Those sages and wise men who have not seen into their own natures have not achieved the ultimate.

When I was seven or eight my heart turned toward the principles of Buddhism. When I was fifteen I left home to become a monk. From the age of nineteen I began making pilgrimages and when I was twenty-four for the first time I attained insight into my own nature. After this I wandered from monastery to monastery, crossed the thresholds of many good teachers, investigated in detail all the Buddhist scriptures, studied widely the sacred works of Buddhism, Confucianism, and Taoism, as well as the writings of secular literature. I vowed that if I found one teaching that surpassed that of seeing into one's own nature—and these included the works of Lao Tzu, Chuang Tzu, and Lieh Tzu—would without fail accept it and do my best to propagate it. But I am now sixty-five years old and I have yet to find any teaching that excels that of seeing into one's own nature. You may well ask then, "Why waste all this paper and ink writing all these stupid things for others to read?" It is only to help people to see into their own natures that I keep on ceaselessly talking about it. For if you reach that point where your mind is not agitated, then your eyes will open wide with the great joy of awakening.

If you discard the *Mu* koan and, by intoning the name of the Buddha with the power of concentrated recitation of the Buddha's name you can make clear your own nature and penetrate at once to the bones and marrow of the Buddhas and Patriarchs, then this is fine. Even if you cannot see your own nature clearly, by the power of the calling of the name you will without fail be reborn in Paradise. But if what you are really trying to do is to cleverly accomplish both things at the same time, then by all means discard at once the practice of calling the Buddha's name and take up in purity the *Mu* koan. Why do I say this? It is because some two hundred years ago evil and careless Zen followers decimated the Zen monasteries and corrupted the true style of Zen, spreading vulgar and debased heretical understanding.

In the Zen teaching, though "loftiness" is emphasized, even greater loftiness is demanded; in the Zen monasteries "steepness" is venerated, yet even greater steepness is needed. "The vital harbor is always seized," and the sacred and the profane are not allowed through. When one word is uttered the spirit of the three stages is destroyed and the eye of the four rewards is beclouded. When a single phrase is spoken the idle spirits rush away in fear and the wild demons wail in despair. The bowels of the wooden man are rent and the marrow of the iron woman is split. When one encounters a superb Zen student endowed with marvelous qualities and brilliant talents, the koans that are difficult to pass, difficult to understand, difficult to have faith in, and difficult to enter into, are presented to him. Then the true Dharma eye is blinded and the wondrous mind of Nirvana stolen away. The student will pass by the village with the poisoned water without drinking a drop and will devote himself solely to his koan. He will smash the dark cave of emotional considerations; he will pierce the snug nest of conceptual thinking; he will exhaust reason and bring an end to words; he will bring death to his mind and wipe out consciousness. Then suddenly this strange, blind fool, standing neither in the sacred nor in the profane, neither Buddha nor demon, will leap free, and with this repay his deep obligations to the Buddha and the Patriarchs.

Techniques such as these are called the "talons and teeth of the Cave of Dharma" and the "supernatural talisman that wrests life from death." They are of great benefit to people of superior talents. Those of medium or inferior talents leave such things alone and quite disregard them. The people of the Pure Land school, in fact, are opposed to them. But the Pure Land is still a teaching to which veneration is due. Amida Buddha, with the skillful concentrated practice of great compassion, on the basis of his forty-eight vows, was endowed with the three minds and four practices. These techniques were established solely for those of medium and inferior talents and are of benefit to ignorant and stupid beings, enabling them to escape from the ten evils and five deadly sins. Giving primary importance to the golden words "to gather [all sentient] beings and to cast aside none," they make the low important and require still more lowliness, they make the easiness essential and venerate still more easiness. Therefore they tell you: "Even though you have studied well all the teachings of the Buddha, consider yourself an ignorant, illiterate fool, and just single-mindedly practice the calling of the Buddha's name. For these degenerate later days, filled with evil and turmoil, this is a technique that must not be omitted even for a single day."

In Zen it is as though giants were pitted against one another, with victory going to the tallest. In Pure Land it is as though midgets were set to fight, with victory going to the smallest. If the tallness of Zen were despised and Zen done away with, the true style of progress toward the Buddha mind would be swept away and destroyed. If the lowness of the Pure Land teachings were despised and cast aside, stupid, ignorant people would be unable to escape from the evil realms.

Think of the Buddha as the Great King of Healing. He has set up eighty-four thousand medicines to cure the eighty-four thousand diseases. Zen, the teaching schools, Ritsu, the Pure Land are all methods used to treat a disease. Think of these methods as the four classes of people in the world: warriors, farmers, craftsmen, merchants. The warrior is endowed with both knowledge and benevolence. He perfects his command of the military works, protects the ruler, subdues the rebels, and brings peace to the country. He makes his lord like a lord under Yao and Shun, the people like the people under Yao and Shun. He need not show anger, for the people fear him more than the punishment of the axe and halberd, and venerate the severe austerity of his bearing. Indeed he is a beautiful vessel, worthy of respect.

The merchant opens a large store and his ambition is to see it grow by selling his goods, his silks, cottons, grains, fish, and meat. He complies with the demands of everyone, be he monk or layman, man or woman, be he old, young, respectable or disreputable. If the warrior feels envy at the magnitude of the trader's operations and, coveting the tradesman's goods and profits, should try to become a merchant himself, he will discard his capacity for archery and horsemanship, forget the martial arts, and become a laughing stock to his friends. His lord will become enraged and will drive him away. If the merchant, envying the strict dignity of the samurai, girds a sword to his side, mounts a horse and, pretending to be a military figure, rides recklessly about here and there, everybody will laugh at him, and his family calling will be destroyed.

As I said before, if you cannot attain to Zen, then when you face death, try to be reborn in the Pure Land. Those who try to practice both at the same time will be able to obtain neither the fish nor the bear's paw, but instead will cultivate the karma of birth and death, fail to cut off the root of life, and will never be able to attain the joy where the "Ka" is shouted.

When I talk about the similarities of the *Mu* koan and the calling of the Buddha's name, I do not mean that they are not without differences when it comes time to test the quality of the virtue gained and the depth or shallowness with which the Way is seen. In general, for the hero who would seek enlightenment, who would cut off the seepages of emotions and conceptions, and who destroy the film of ignorance that covers the eye, nothing surpasses the *Mu* koan.

The Master Fa-yen of Mount Wu-tsu has said in a verse:

> The exposed sword of Choa-chou
> Gleams brilliantly like cold frost.
> If someone tries to ask about it,
> His body will at once be cut in two.

To all intents and purposes, the study of Zen makes as its essential the resolution of the ball of doubt. That is why it is said: "At the bottom of great doubt lies great awakening. If you doubt fully you will awaken fully." Fo-kuo has said: "If you don't doubt the koans you suffer a grave disease." If those who study Zen are able to make the great doubt appear before them, a hundred out of a hundred, a thousand out of a thousand, will without fail attain awakening.

When a person faces the great doubt, before him there is in all directions only a vast and empty land without birth and without death, like a huge plain of ice extending ten thousand miles. As though seated within a vase of lapis lazuli surrounded by absolute purity, without his sense he sits and forgets to stand, stands and forgets to sit. Within his heart there is not the slightest thought or emotion, only the single word *Mu*. It is just as though he were standing in complete emptiness. At this time no fears arise, no thoughts creep in, and when he advances single-mindedly without retrogression, suddenly it will be as though a sheet of ice were broken or a jade tower had fallen. He will experience a great joy, one that never in forty years has he seen or heard. At this time "birth, death, and Nirvana will be like yesterday's dream, like the bubbles in the seas of the three thousand worlds, like the enlightened status of all the wise men and sages." This is known as the time of the great penetration of wondrous awakening, the state where the "Ka" is shouted. It cannot be handed down, it cannot be explained; it is just like knowing for yourself by drinking it whether the water is hot or cold. The ten directions melt before the eyes, the three periods are penetrated in an instant of thought. What joy is there in the realms of man and Heaven that can compare with this?

This power can be obtained in the space of three to five days, if the student will advance determinedly. You may ask how one can make this great doubt appear. Do not favor a quiet place, do not shun a busy place, but always set in the area below the navel Chao-chou's *Mu*. Then, asking what principle this *Mu* contains, if you discard all emotions, concepts, and thoughts and investigate single-mindedly, there is no one before whom the great doubt will not appear. When you call forth this great doubt before you in its pure and uninvolved form you may undergo an unpleasant and strange reaction. However, you must accept the fact that the realization of so felicitous a thing as the Great Matter, the trampling of the multi-tiered gate of birth and death that has come down through endless kalpas, the penetration of the inner understanding of the basic enlightenment of all the Tathagatas of the ten directions, must involve a certain amount of suffering.

When you come to think about it, those who have investigated the *Mu* koan, brought before themselves the great doubt, experienced the Great Death, and attained the great joy, are countless in number. Of those who called the Buddha's name and gained a small measure of benefit from it, I have heard of no more than two or three. The abbot of Eshin-in has called it the benefits of wisdom or the power of faith in the mind. If you investigate the *Mu* or the Three Pounds of Flax or some other koan, to obtain True Reality in your own body should take from two or three months to a year or a year and a half. The efficacy gained from calling the Buddha's name or reciting the sutras will require forty years of strenuous effort. It is all a matter of raising or failing to raise this ball of doubt. It must be understood that this ball of doubt is like a pair of wings that advances you along the way a man such as Honen Shonin was virtuous, benevolent, righteous, persevering, and courageous. As he read the sacred scriptures in the darkness, if he used to some extent the luminescence of his eye of wisdom, he must, to the extent that this ball of doubt was formed, have attained to the Great Matter in the place where he stood and have determined for himself his rebirth. What a tragedy it was that the robe was too short, so that he could not draw the water from the bottom of the well.

Although there were countless billions of Buddha names and countless billions of dharani, such great Masters as Yang-ch'I, Huang-lung, Chen-ching, His-keng, Fo-chien, and Miao-shi selected, from the vast number of gates to the teaching available, this Mu koan alone for their students to study. Is this not the strong point of the teaching? Consider then that the Mu koan easily gives rise to the ball of doubt, while the recitation of the Buddha's names makes it very difficult to bring it to a head.

Moreover, in the Zen schools of China, the concentrated recitation of the Buddha's name, with the wish to be reborn in the Pure Land, did not exist at all at the time when the Zen monasteries had yet to wither, and the true teachings had yet to fall to the ground. The Twenty-eight Indian Patriarchs, the Six Chinese Patriarchs, their descendants in the transmission of Zen, Nan-Yüeh, Ch'ing-yüan, Ma-tsu, Shih-t'ou, Po-chang, Huang-po, Nan-ch'üan, Ch'ang-sha, Lin-chi, Hsing-hua, Nan-yüan, Feng-hsüeh, Shou-shan, Feng-yang, Tz'u-ming, Huang-lung, Chen-ching, Hui-t'ang, His-keng, and Miao-hsi, all the masters of the Five Houses and Seven Schools, all the monks of the Liang, Ch'en, Sui, T'ang, Song, and Yüan dynasties, they all raised up the teaching style of "steepness" and attached to their arms the supernatural talisman that wrests life from death, chewed and made reverberate in their own mouths the talons and teeth of the Cave of the Dharma. All they were concerned about was to prevent the style of the teaching from falling in the dirt. Day and night they kept in motion relentlessly the wheel of the vow, without slackening for a moment. They never once, even inadvertently, spoke of rebirth in the Pure Land.

But sad, sad! Time passed; lives were lived out. The great teachings withered and vulgar concepts arose; the old songs died out and banalities flourished. Then toward the end of the Ming dynasty there appeared a man known as Chu-hung from Yün-ch'i. His talents were not sufficient to tackle the mysteries of Zen, nor had he the eye to see into the Way. As he studied onward he could not gain the delights of Nirvana; as he retrogressed he suffered from the terrors of the cycle of birth and death. Finally, unable to stand his distress, he was attracted to the memory of Hui-yüan's Lotus Society. He abandoned the "steepness" technique of the founders of Zen and calling himself the "Great Master of the Lotus Pond," he wrote a commentary on the *Amitayus Sutra*, advocated strongly the teachings relating to the calling of the Buddha's name, and displayed an incredibly shallow understanding of Zen. Yüan-hsien Yung-chiao of Ku-shan wrote a work known as *Ching-tz'u yao-yü*, in which he concurred with Chu-hung's views and rendered him great assistance. With this these teachings spread throughout China, overflowing even to Japan, and ultimately reached a state where nothing could be done about them. Even if Lin-chi, Te-shan, Fen-yang, Tz'u-ming, Huang-lung, Chen-ching, Hsi-keng, and Miao-hsi were to appear in the world of today, were to raise their arms, gnash their teeth, spit on their hands, and proceed to drive these teachings out, they would not be able to undo this madness.

This is not meant to belittle the basic teachings of the Pure Land nor to make light of the practice of the calling of the Buddha's name. But not to practice Zen meditation while within the Zen Sect, to becloud the eye to see into one's own nature because of laziness in the study of Zen under a teacher and idleness in one's aspirations, only weakens the power to study Zen. People such as these end up spending their whole lives in vain. Then when the day of their death is close at hand, they begin to fear the endless painful cycle of their births to come, and suddenly decide that they will work to seek rebirth in the Pure Land. Solemnly fingering their rosary beads and reciting the Buddha's name aloud, they tell the ignorant men and women among the laity that this is what is appropriate for untalented people in this degenerate age, and that in this miserable and evil world no superior practice exists. With fallen hair and gap-toothed mouths, they are apt to cry with sincerity, to blink their eyes, and entice men with words that seem to ring with truth. Yet what possible miracle can those expect, who up to now have failed to practice Zen?

People of this sort, while within Zen, slander the Zen teachings. They are like those wood-eating maggots that are produced in beams and pillars and then in turn destroy these very beams and pillars. They must be investigated at once. Indolence when in the prime of life leads to regret and misery in old age. The regret and misery of old age is not worthy of censure. The past need not be blamed, but the idleness and sloth of a young man, this each person must really fear.

Since the Ming dynasty, gangs of this type have become very large. All of them are mediocre and ineffectual Zen followers. Thirty years ago an old monk expressed his dismay, the tears falling from his eyes: "Ah, how Zen is declining! Three hundred years from now all Zen temples will startle the neighborhood by setting up the metal plate, installing the wooden gong, and holding worship six times a day." A fearful prospect indeed! In closing, I have one last word to say. Do not regret losing your eyebrows, but for the sake of your lord raise up the teaching. Do not come to an understanding of the Patriarchs as a *katsu;* do not come to an understanding of the koans as the *dharani.* You're not trying to devour the jujube in one gulp! Why is this a kind phrase? A monk asked Chao-chou: "Does a dog have Buddha-nature? Chao-chou answered: "*Mu!*"

With respect.

THE VOICE OF THE SOUND OF ONE HAND

Hakuin Ekaku

BASED ON THE MODERN JAPANESE ADAPTATION
BY K. YOSHIZAWA
Freely translated by W. S. Yokoyama

*The Sound of One Hand is the famous koan coined by the Japanese Rinzai
Zen master Hakuin (1685–1768). In the spring of 1753, in a letter he wrote
down some of his thoughts on the koan in a rambling essay to a lady named
Tomisato Ken'ei. It has since come to be known by the name Sekishu onjo,
The Voice of the Sound of One Hand; it is also known as Yabukoji.*

*In recent years the essay was compiled in one volume of a new
Hakuin series edited by K. Yoshizawa. Yoshizawa also included a modern Japanese adaptation that can be used as a guide for reading the original. The Yoshizawa version is to be commended for clarifying the logic
of Hakuin's essay, and for supplementing it with materials that clarify
the sources of many of Hakuin's quotations.*—W. S. Yokoyama

A letter requested by Tomisato Ken'ei, a lady attending the retired lord
of Okayama castle

I. INTRODUCTION

Your letter of April 27 came to hand at the beginning of May. In the mean-
time I chanced to meet you at the Ho'unji, I cannot tell you how happy

Source: Hakuin Ekaku 1685–1768, Hakuin Zenji Hogo Zenshu, Vol. 12: *Sekishu onjo, Sankyo
itchi no ben, Hokyo kutsu no ki, Tosen shiko*. Edited and annotated by Yoshizawa Katsuhiro.
Kyoto: Zenbunka Kenkyusho. Readers interested in seeing an English version of the original
essay are referred to the "Yabukoji" chapter of Philip Yampolsky, *The Zen Master Hakuin:
Selected Writings*.

I was! After that I trust you returned to the castle without incident with your retired lord and that you have all been enjoying the utmost good health.

When I talked to you last, you asked me to write a letter of Buddhist instruction on the way to awaken *kensho,* insight into the Buddha-nature in ourselves, indeed a splendid suggestion. I have not forgotten your request in the least, but till now my time here has been taken up with all kinds of things.

Yesterday May 27 was my late mother's fiftieth memorial service, and as it was approaching I was looking about for something meritorious I might do in her honor, and at that time it occurred to me that writing that essay you requested earlier might be just the thing, and so on the night of the twenty-fifth I started in on the project, and had to work on it furiously to make a clean copy to present before my mother's memorial tablet in the altar. That's why it is in this shape, full of omissions and errors as you will find, as I send it on to you.

I intended to ask you not to show this clumsy composition to others, but on second thought, if you read it to others and have them listen to it, perhaps it will be the same as making an offering to the gods.

The first thing I want to say is, as I send you this long document to read full of passages taken from Buddhist scriptures and ancient writings, remember the old saying, "Whatever comes in from that front gate can never be your Family Treasure," that such knowledge as originates from outside yourself can never assist your arriving at a great Satori, the big Awakening. Whatever you do, you must once see for yourself the fact that that buddha-nature you sought for was always yours from the start—there is nothing more important than this.

How can we see for ourselves this fact that buddha-nature was originally ours?

The Buddhist teachings have assumed various forms in the course of explanation: sudden and gradual, greater and smaller vehicle, revealed and esoteric, indeterminate, and so on. But in the realization of the Buddha Way, the most important thing is to evince a valiant heart that presses forward and never falls back. Until you can taste the joy of great Satori, the big Awakening, never fall back—it is in this spirit you must enter into practice.

How can we taste the joy of great Satori? As in the saying, "Under the huge swarm of doubt assailing you lies great Satori," we must scare up a great flock of doubts. Ask yourself, as you read this essay, what is that You that so reads. As you go through your daily routines, as you laugh or cry in response to different events, ask yourself, what is that You that does so? Is this our mind, is this our nature? Is it colored blue, yellow, red, or white? Is it inside, outside, or somewhere in between? The sense of this You is something we have to clearly see for ourselves, and we must strive day in and day out until we realize it so fully as to be able to describe it. Gone is that deluded heart of ours that switches back and forth, every speck of doubt wiped clean, not a single stray thought arises. Where you are neither man nor woman, neither clever nor foolish, neither alive nor dead, that heart of yours is now so exquisitely empty you cannot tell whether it is night or day, so completely has your body and mind melted away—that is the dimension of the spirit you will surely experience time and again.

Even as you experience it there is nothing to fear, and as you press forth seeking in yourself a solution to the obstacles you encounter, suddenly you will break through to the heart source, the fact that this buddha-nature was originally yours, the Truth that your being as such is buddha-nature will dawn on you as clearly as the morning sun, and you will surely taste of a great Joy as never before. This kind of experience can be called *kensho,* seeing the buddha-nature in yourself, or it can be called *ojo jodo,* passage to birth in the Pure Land. Just as there is no buddha outside this buddha-mind of yours, there is no Pure Land outside this buddha-nature of yours. Where all thoughts cease to arise is called the "passage," and at this point there emerges the "birth," the Truth that your being as such is buddha-nature.

Failing to reach such a truth, most Buddhists in the world when passing away seek passage to birth in the Pure Land, and as they do all kinds of practice and perform good deeds, as a result they are born in the highest realms of heaven, or in the human world as emperors or generals or aristocrats with big names from the start. While the majority are born into fortunate circumstances, they know nothing about their earlier episode when passing away and so on. For, outside the mind there is no Pure Land, outside the mind there is no buddha.

To thus have the good fortune to be born in the human world or the heavens above is nothing to covet in the least. Just as an arrow shot into the heavens loses its force and eventually plummets to the earth, even if you are born into the higher heavenly realms, once your lucky power runs out, you are sure to fall into the evil destinies. As this is the situation that prevails in the heavenly realms, there is no reason to covet birth in fortunate circumstances in the human world. The ones born as a human in lucky circumstances have completely forgotten their past good roots, and thinking their pleasant surroundings to be their just desserts, they do not hesitate to take from others and cause injury to life and limb, as if the bad karma they are making holds no consequence for them, but surely they will fall into evil realms in the next world.

The effects of the good deeds piled up in your past life are the reason for the happy circumstances you enjoy in your present life, yet the happy circumstances in your present life will surely make for suffering in the next world. Thus the old saying, "Letting you be deliriously happy in this life is how the Triple World wreaks its revenge on you!"

There are countless teachings that assert that if you get awakened it will save you in the next life, almost all of them makeshift explanations. The highest teaching is simply to get awakened to *kensho*, the insight into the buddha-nature in yourself. In the Lotus Sutra it says much the same thing, "The multiple buddhas like Shakyamuni, knowing that sentient beings have to see the buddha in themselves, thus make their appearances in this world." The Buddhist sutras say that Shakyamuni was reborn 8,000 times in explaining his numerous appearances in this Saha world, but in the end he entered the snowy mountains to do six years of ascetic practice to at last attain buddhahood, thereby proclaiming his first attainment of Supreme Enlightenment, a true Satori without peer. In the Triple World of past and present, there is not a single one among all the Buddhist patriarchs and wise sages who has not attained *kensho*, insight into the buddha-nature in themselves. This being so, there might be tens of thousands of good deeds and practices we can do, but this *kensho*, insight into the buddha-nature in ourselves, does not pale in the least beside them; note this well.

I was 15 when I entered the monastery. Around 22 or 23 I got into a terrible funk, struggling mightily night and day with the Mu koan assigned me. Then in the spring of my twenty-fourth year, one night at the Eiganji sesshin retreat in Takada, Echigo, I happened to hear the tolling of a distant bell and suddenly I awakened. Since then 45 years have passed, and to whomever I have met I have recommended that at least once in their lives they experience *kensho*, insight into the buddha-nature in themselves, and get the power to see clear through the Great Question. Sometimes I told them to give rise to doubts about the source of their own heart or nature; at other times I urged them to work out their own solution to Joshu's Mu koan. I tried all kinds of methods of instruction, and during that time those who variously arrived at kensho were both the old and the young, men and women, priest and layman, I reckon some several dozens of people all told.

And then some five or six years ago, I had an idea and started instructing people to "hear for yourself the Voice issuing from the silent borders of the Sound of One Hand," a major departure from what I had been using up to then, and regardless of whoever I tried it with, everyone found it especially easy to give rise to a swarm of doubts, to easily work out their own solutions as to how to proceed, and I felt that there was a vast difference in the overall effectiveness of this koan. And so now, I exclusively recommend that my students work on hearing the Voice of the Sound of One Hand.

II. THE SINGLE HAND

What do I mean by working out the Single Hand? Now, if you bring your two hands together like this, you will produce a clapping sound, but thrust out a single hand and what sound does it make? In [Confucius's] *Doctrine of the Mean / Zhong yong* it says, "The deeds of heavens have neither sound nor smell"—this is the drift of what I mean. Again in [Zeami's] *Witches Peak / Yamanba*: "From the depths of the empty valley a voice rises, / Wavering like an echo over the trees, / Silently pealing forth its tidings, / Leaving the valley ringing in its wake"—this too conveys the essence of the matter.

The Sound of One Hand is not a sound you hear with the ear. If at all times throughout the day you struggle with the Sound of One Hand, without mixing in any intellectualization and staying aloof of the five senses, without bringing into play any words of logic or explanation, if you pursue it to the bitter end be that where it may, then suddenly you break through to the source of your wandering in this realm of birth and death, to the very source of Ignorance-rooted existence. This is the moment when the Phoenix breaks free from its golden net, when the Crane leaps from its cage. When that happens, the source of our consciousness is shattered, this world of delusion starts to crumble from its source, and you see Truth as she is in all her beauty; your actions supplemented with the wisdom to do, you verify for yourself that now you have power of one endowed with wisdom that truly allows you to see through all things.

When you hear for yourself the Voice of the One Hand, not only do you hear the voices of all buddhas and bodhisattvas and wise sages, you also hear the voices of the hungry pretas, the fighting asuras, and snarling beasts, the cacophony of voices of heaven and hell, all of the myriad voices that there are, were or ever shall be, all of these you hear for yourself. This is the ability of divine hearing.

When you hear for yourself the Voice of the One Hand, you see clear through the real world from the buddha lands in all directions to the six destinies. This is the ability of divine seeing.

When you hear for yourself the Voice of the One Hand, you clearly see as if reflected in a clear mirror the past by which you came floating and sinking from vast kalpas ago, and the future where your life force flows on endlessly. This is the ability to know one's own destiny.

When you hear for yourself the Voice of the One Hand, whatever you are doing, whether enjoying a bowl of rice or sipping a cup of tea, all of it you do in the samadhi of living of one bestowed with the buddha-mind. This is not something you learned from book study or attained from directed practice; it was what you always had with you from before—that is one thing that you realize. Once you realize it, whether it is like the Kegon description of the dharma world or like the Lotus view that there is really only One Vehicle, or as the Great master Fu says, "While holding nothing, hold the bowl in your hands, and while walking, walk along while riding atop the ox," or the words, "Stir the great Yangtze into a thick river of butter, make the thorn thicket into a sandalwood grove," this truth is one that you know clearly for yourself. To know in this way is nothing other than the ability to know the divine realm.

When you hear for yourself the Voice of the One Hand, you know that this [buddha-]mind of ours is of course the [buddha-]mind of all people, as well as the mind of the buddhas and the gods; you can see clear through all minds at a glace without a flicker of doubt. This is the ability to see into the hearts of others.

When you hear for yourself the Voice of the One Hand, you know that, in the [buddha-]mind people originally have, when there is not a speck of Ignorance to be seen then neither is there any speck of birth and death, that when there is no klesa then there is no bodhi, that when there are no sentient beings to deliver then there is not a single Dharma sign to point the way; you realize that the only thing there is is a sheer and crisp silence. This is called the ability to empty oneself of excess baggage.

When you can open your eyes in this way, you realize that all things in the world are the fabled hundred thousand infinite teachings that the buddha has devised, that all things in the world are the buddha as such invested with infinite merits, that all things in the world are the beautifully ornamented buddha land itself. You realize that all of these things are already fully provided within our own hearts, with not the slightest bit of it missing; you realize that all the good deeds you ever needed are already done inside us, and that the fruits of good karma are already ours to enjoy—that is truly something to celebrate.

Truly it is said, the hardest thing gotten is getting born human, the rarest thing met is meeting the Buddha Dharma. Though here and now you're born human and hear the true Dharma, still you're unable to awaken from the dream, and as if living a dream you pursue fame and fortune, you indulge a life of fantasy chasing imaginary things far from reality, and if you end up wasting your entire lifetime in that way, though no one might scold you, once again you must return to your old haunting grounds of the three foul lots, where you will undergo eternities of suffering. Is this not truly unfortunate and pitiful? What you really ought to revile and disdain is that defiled land of this Saha world, what you really ought to fear is the fearful suffering of the three foul lots.

In the Buddha, the most important piece of wisdom is to believe in the law of cause and effect, knowing that there is a life in the world to come and to fear the consequences of suffering there, and any person who has penetrating insight into buddha-mind and buddha-nature that all people basically have, then such a one is to be revered as a buddha, patriarch, or wise sage.

But unfortunately, the average intellectual these days, by dint of having read a little and sat in on a few lectures, think themselves as men who have realized the Truth and they start to refute the law of cause and effect. And when they see people believing in cause and effect to get saved in the next world or practicing and logging up good deeds, they burst out laughing. What are we to make of them?

It may well be said that Man is the Primate of all living things, and the point that makes him different from the beasts is that Man knows that there is a next world and he is afraid of the consequences of suffering there. The intellectuals of today, though, seem to be content with throwing their lot in with the beasts. Of the saintly and wise of the past and present, there is not one who did not believe in cause and effect and who did not fear the consequences of suffering. If the law of cause and effect and the notion of the Triple World were denied, then the view [of Mencius's Wanzhang chapter] that "under the heavens there is no land that is not the king's land, within the borders of the land there is no man who is not the king's subject" would prevail, and temples and priests would simply not be allowed to exist.

Shakyamuni was born the royal prince of the great king Shuddhodana. But deeply aware of the impermanence of the world and fearing the consequences of suffering in the three foul lots of the six destinies, and seeking eternal salvation, he left behind his two beautiful wives, gave up his throne, and became a monk. At first he labored hard to serve a hermit, and then entered the snowy mountain to undergo austerities; he was skin and bones when he opened up his first satori, to become the great guide and teacher of the Triple World.

Princess Chujo was a striking beauty, and among the ladies and ladies-in-waiting in the palace no one could compare with her in looks, so much so that she was a sure choice to proceed to the Prince's inner palace. But after riding into the palace grounds in a jeweled palanquin, she found that the life there was much like the Burning House [the Lotus Sutra talks about], and crying bitter tears she fled the capital in the night and entered

Mount Hibari where, after enduring untold hardships, she at last opened the supreme Dharma eye.

In addition to this case, there were countless others who, though born into fortunate circumstances, feared the consequence of suffering in the next life, and sought the Buddha Way, throwing their entire life into it, leaving behind their loving families and becoming monks.

Those born into a life of luxury can well afford to devote their lives in this way, running off in search of the Way. But for those like us who come from the bottom rungs of society, what point is there to detesting the lives we lead? Even if there were hermits who lived lives spanning tens of thousands of years, it would merely be a waste of time for us to dream of it. Truly people like us are but shadows [cast by lightning flashes]—fleeting, transient existences, are we not? Even then, with no goal in mind, we pass the time plodding along day after day like the blind mule, not even holding up to half a day's practice were we to try, as we squander away these precious months and days of ours. In a perfect hustle and bustle, we let our mind run amok like a squad of mad monkeys, and in the end piling up not the least good cause to our name, we grow old meaninglessly and just waste away into nothing.

In this way we must deeply reflect and give rise to a heart of misgiving.

Most people are at birth changed into one form and at death changed into another; in this way they have been constantly rising and sinking in the world of delusion. But if we give further thought to the matter, what this means is that we did not have enough lucky power to be born in the heavens, nor enough bad karma to land us in hell, and that is why all of us received birth in this defiled land of the Saha world. The differences we observe between the noble and the lowly, the poor and the rich, as well as the clever and the clumsy, the swift and the dull, are all the result of the karma of our previous lives. If you are born into this world a noble aristocrat, that only means you did not have sufficient good merit to be born in the heavens, and if you are struggling in poverty, that means you did not have enough bad karma to land you in hell. The law of cause and effect is truly something to be feared.

This being the case, whoever you are, you should go cap in hand before this Law, and as long as life's breath clings to you, you should strive to make every effort, whatever you may be doing, to hear for yourself the

Voice of the Single Hand. And, once you hear that Sound of the Single Hand and all other sounds and voices cease thereafter, even though you have now cleared two barriers, what all this implies will vary depending on the individual. And so, monks who have arrived at an insight into this great matter will then undergo the long process of Zen interview with this old monk [—that's me!—] who will kindly guide them in the process.

And so, though you may demonstrate that you have passed through the Single Hand koan, you cannot be satisfied to have it over and done with. Whatever credentials you may have to show your insight and understanding—you might be a wise high-ranking priest well-armed with both wisdom and practice—if you fail to understand that the buddha land's law of cause and effect is the reason for the state of awe that the Bodhisattva inspires in us, no matter how completely you may claim to have mastered the abstruse points of the Zen school, you will still unwittingly fall into the rut of the Two-Vehicle doctrine. And there are those who are satisfied with what little wisdom solely benefits themselves alone, who are strangers to the Mahayana way, who do not have a proper grasp of the law of cause and effect, who again end up reborn in the most unexpected places. These cases come down to us from the ancient past, but these again are different from the majority of the cases seen today, the practitioner that falls into the view of nihilism, who thinks that all we have to do is make our minds empty, who thinks that there is no Buddha we need to turn to and no Dharma that has to be explained, and who thinks that Zen is all just a matter of letting ourselves fall into the deep hole of nihilism.

Now, then, what is the buddha land's law of cause and effect as the reason for the state of awe that the Bodhisattva inspires in us? That is what is embodied in the Four Great Vows, it is our putting them into practice. It is our seeking Supreme Awakening, benefiting sentient beings by it, and creating a buddha land in real terms. To do so is the Perfect Means taking us beyond the pitfall of the small output Two-Vehicle model, and to create a Mahayana bodhisattva way in real terms. In the sutras, a complete and clear insight and understanding is portrayed as the Eye, while action and understanding in perfect correspondence with one another is like the Limb, thus Eye and Limb work together, and when Truth and action work together, for the first time you arrive at the spot where Nirvana's treasure lies. And so the Perfect Means shorn of wisdom is like the Limb without the Eye, while wisdom without the Perfect Means is like the Eye without the Limb.

All of the wise sages past and present in every direction, in order to put their finishing touches to the Buddha dharma, have constantly striven to put the Four Great Vows into practice. Whether we speak of Samantabhadra's 10 vows or Amida's 48 vows, each of them was made on the platform of seeking *bodhi*, Awakening, but before they would accept it for themselves, they had to lay into the great Dharma charity work of saving sentient beings.

The Buddha dharma is like a great ocean: the more you enter it, the deeper it gets—this you must know. But the sad thing is, and this is also in part due to the sway of latter-age logic, many of the old roshis who have followings of young monks are saying, "'No thought, no mind: that is buddha,' and so as there is no Buddha to seek outside, there is no Dharma to explain," and they force their young monks to sit like incense smoke rising in the graveyards, making them practice "dead-sitting" zazen, telling them that this is the Zen approach to self-improvement. Since there is no self, there is no Buddha, there is no Dharma, but if you take this reasoning to ridiculous lengths, this will bring great results, they assert. If we examine their line of reasoning, though, we have to ask: how can a fool of a monk who doesn't even know how to read a single letter differ from an ordinary person off the street? In this scenario, such a person would have no energy to pursue the Way, there would be no Zen functioning forthcoming. Such a monk cannot protect and transmit the Buddha dharma or help to push the Zen vehicle along.

Next, there is the monk who boasts his own views but has little wisdom to back it, who thinks the patriarchs and the world in general are ridiculous, who all but howls at night like a mad dog, who goes about badmouthing everyone—this is the kind of colleague we have to work with: a person who simply hasn't gotten it. You can assign this kind of monk to the monk's hall, but all he will do is eat up the food; he is completely useless. In this case, how can you expect our intelligent laymen who are sophisticated and have professional concerns to put their trust in someone like this? How can we expect such a person to explain the greatness of the Dharma to the king or his ministers or those who run the country? This is regrettable. With the loss of the genuine ways of ancient tradition, Zen has been hijacked by a bunch of frauds.

If we think back to the course the school has taken the past 100 years to the present day, the new trends in Zen have not always brought welcome changes. Everywhere Zen has begun to fuse with Nembutsu. Now, when you speak of the Buddha-mind (Zen) school, the reality is that content-wise it is none other than the Pure Land school, the Jodoshu.

That our temple buildings are splendid should not disguise the fact. In the main hall they now use so many noisemaking devices that the blaring voices of the sutra service can be heard far away—it's as if you had walked into a kabuki theatre. It makes you think, "Why, Manjushri's Pure Land and Samantabhadra's dojo must be just like this!" Sitting in his regal chair wearing a big red hat, the great master in purple robes waves his whisk in the midst of incense smoke, looking all awesome and dignified like a living Buddha on display. People, without thinking, put their hands together in reverence and touch their foreheads to the ground; some of them are so moved by the sight that their tears begin to flow. The roshi is said to represent Zen's direct transmission, but in this scenario he has moved closer to Buddha-devil worship.

This kind of colleague is like Maudgalyayana in their divine powers when it comes to pulling the wool over the eyes of parishioners; they rival Purna in their eloquence when it comes to talking people out of their estates. But when we size them up for their true eye, as far as the power of insight into themselves or the energy to pursue the Way goes, of these qualities they have none. As practice progresses, they are unable to settle into that easy and comfortable outlook that comes with satori—"Oh, well, so much for that," they say, as they leave off their practice and let their suffering in birth and death go unresolved; naturally they are unable to come into that easy frame of mind. The absence of any peace of mind becomes their chronic state. This truly portrays the turmoil they feel inside. Even though they have become monks, they are unable to open the eye of the Way, and it is meaningless for them to receive the offerings of charity, and in one tale it is said that after the monk died, he was reborn as a mushroom in the garden of the donor family, and thus returned their act of religious charity.

Hatching all kinds of schemes that disturb the world, these men who ostensibly earn the respect of others know how to play up to parishioners to take the lion's share of offerings, and for their labors they will surely fall into hell in their next lives where their flesh and bones will be minced to bits, and they will be forced to swallow hot molten balls of lead. And when this thought occurs to them, they suddenly panic and, latching onto whatever can save them, they happen to hear that "just one calling of the name of Amida Buddha instantly clears away infinite amounts of bad karma," and so they secretly start fingering a rosary and saying the Nembutsu and so on, praying for passage to the Land of Bliss. Truly pitiful, these colleagues of mine! As they have no power of insight into themselves or power to pursue the Way, they turn to Nembutsu in hopes of salvation. But when we think of the Zen transmission down through the ages of the patriarchs and so on, is it really acceptable that these things be done in the name of our Dharma lineage?

In our transmission of the Light comprising some 1700 patriarchs and teachers, as well as laymen who have interviewed and actually awakened satori, of those who in the end threw themselves on the mercy of Nembutsu seeking passage to the Pure Land, there is not a single one. The reason is, when they first got insight into the Way and attained satori, they saw clear through to the fact that this whole world as such was the Pure Land and that everyone in it was a Buddha. This is called the opening of Buddha wisdom through insight into the Way. The world is the Pure Land, and the people in it are all Buddhas. Once you realize this, what need is there to seek elsewhere for a Pure Land or Buddha?

The great master Nagarjuna occasionally talks about Nembutsu samadhi, but this draws on the abilities of the lower strata of middle grade seekers who, by chanting the Nembutsu over and over again, arrive at a state where, when their hearts are at one and undisturbed, they immerse themselves in a sheer mental image of the Pure Land, and as an indication that they have settled the one great matter of passage to birth, Nagarjuna called this *Nembutsu*. In the Sutra of Contemplation on Infinite Life, in which the consort Vaidehi is imprisoned in the castle dungeon, there is a scene where she seeks the Pure Land and says the Nembutsu, but all this is a [cosmic drama] put on to point out the Perfect Means available [to this kind of seeker].

It is not my intention to criticize the Nembutsu school for promoting exclusive chanting. What I do wish to criticize is those bodies who deposit themselves in the Zen gate who, failing to gain insight into themselves, cannot generate the energy to pursue the Way, and who instead do Nembutsu seeking salvation, thus causing confusion in the Zen creed they follow. If they wish to pursue the Pure Land school, the Jodoshu, let them make a clean breast of it by switching creeds. Let them clank that bell doing Nembutsu day and night for all I care, and if they happen to settle that one great matter, the more power to them. But to put on the lion's skin and to roar not like a lion but to let out a screechy voice like a fox, why that is simply outrageous! Just as a bat is not quite bird, not quite rat, these monks are neither one nor the other. So saying, what has happened to the accomplished Zen master who arbitrated true from false, speaking volumes with just the wave of the whisk, who guided his disciples with a length of bamboo cane? If it is exclusive chanting of Nembutsu they want, one clanker is all they need; they have no use for these tools of the Way they never resort to. Truly it is said that a Dharma master is wise to save his comb!

If that's all the insight you need, why then did Shakyamuni give up the throne and leave the bevy of 3,000 pretty princesses behind? As an Indian prince with a vast fortune at his disposal, all he had to do was wait until old age to chant the Nembutsu and embark on that passage to the Pure Land. At age 19, tearfully leaving his family and spending six years in painful practice and so on—what a sheer waste of his time! And the same goes for his group of 500 disciples who endured painful practices. It is said that Parshva never once lay down to sleep in 40 years. The second great patriarch cut off an arm for the sake of Dharma. Zen master Xuansha [damaged] his leg to see the light, Zen master Linji had to be struck three times by Zen master Huangbo, Yunmen broke his leg, Ciming pierced his thigh with an awl to keep sitting. Would it not have been far easier for them to skip all these painful practices and just chant the Nembutsu for that passage to the Land of Bliss? All the great master Bodhidharma had to do was write a few lines in a letter to the effect, "Just do Nembutsu and you will be born in the Pure Land," and that would have solved everything. Why, all that painful effort could have been avoided, and so it was completely unnecessary for Zen to cross 10,000 li of huge waves to transmit the Dharma of seeing the buddha-nature in yourself—isn't that right?

Why then are the Zen patriarchs and masters of the past completely oblivious of the Land of Bliss? Could it be that the practice in the past was too demanding, whereas now it's a cinch to make the passage to birth? Either way it is mistaken.

At this point, a person named Kanjoshi came forward and said,
"Recently, in both the Rinzai and Soto schools, the monks intensely sitting are urged to realize No Thought, No Mind, but of the Zen monks, there is almost no one among the elderly ones approaching age 70 who is not into Nembutsu. If that's the case, why do you lay into them so vehemently?"

[Hakuin replies:] Truly it is as you say. But, for instance, all things have small beginnings like a river so small you could float a teacup on it, but you must dam it at the source. Though the Min starts off small enough, with no dam to impede it, at length it becomes the mighty Chu-jiang that flows into the great sea. Hakuin is grown old and would never waste his time criticizing others. As I'm personally worried about the problem, I see I've ended up making these rather candid remarks. Though grasses and trees have no voice, when they are moved by the wind, it sounds as if they are moaning.

The other day a certain Buddhist priest came to tell me he had heard that the majority of Zen temples in China had fallen into ruin. Jing shan, Tiantong shan, Jingci si of Hang shou, as well as Zen master Mazu's dojo in Jiangxi, Nanyue, Niutou-shan, and so on—all of them are apparently abandoned. Temples other than Zen ones are also the same, just a bunch of broken-down abandoned buildings, their temple bells now recast into spades and hoes, the temple lands made over into farmland, with no trace of any Buddha statues or scriptures remaining. The only temple that remains standing is where Zen master Cishou once was, but the walls have fallen and the cloister is leaning over on the verge of collapse, grass is growing everywhere and vines have taken over.

In olden days, when Zen flourished, the temples resounded with the noisy accompaniment to the chanting, and here, where strict practice was undertaken, imperial ministers and military leaders lined up to do Zen interviews, but is it the age or is it by imperial decree that, why, not even two or three centuries later, it has all come to this! This is not because of imperial decree. It is because of the Zen/Pure Land fusion, the junk Zen of silent illumination, it is because of these mistaken forms of Zen that we have the result now on our hands. Those demonic parties have done more to tyrannically put down Zen than any political suppression of Buddhism. I say this because, any "down with Buddha, out with Shakya" movement is an attack from the outside, and as long as the tradition is sound on the inside, it will in time restore itself. But when it starts to rust away from within, you can talk about the healing hands of the Buddha all you want, but there is no way to heal this situation. I suppose that our Buddhism in Japan, judging from its present state of affairs, will also start to drift and may eventually disappear altogether one day.

"*Why, if you practice Zen and Nembutsu together, you get the benefits of both rolled into one, like a tiger that has sprouted wings!*"— but this kind of thinking is not to be encouraged. It is the biggest mistake imaginable. To lump Zen and Nembutsu together would be to infect Zen with a fatal disease from which it will die off before long. From the first, Zen was transmitted by the twenty-eighth patriarch of India to the sixth patriarch of China and was passed down bit by bit. It has become the crossbeam of the network of the Eight schools, the great black pillar of Buddhism. Should that crossbeam ever crumble, the entire edifice will also come falling down. All the other schools would also be destroyed. I have no doubt that Chinese Buddhism is a vanishing breed.

Zen is far from simple. Even for someone like Zen's first patriarch, the great master Bodhidharma, who at age eight was shown a valuable pearl and retorted, "That's only a worldly treasure—a truly noble treasure is the Dharma," after leaving home he served Prajnatara for 20 years, until at long last everything he had learned culminated in a deep understanding. It is no easy matter. Shakyamuni once said, "These arhats who are disciples of mine cannot understand the point; only the great bodhisattvas are up to it, and can arrive at an understanding of this point." Truly the Great Matter of Zen is impossible to believe, impossible to enter, impossible to get through, and impossible to explain. And so the Zen patriarchs and teachers spilled their guts out, talking with such urgency as if the house was on fire, hoping to articulate that one statement, the Iron Bit that you can't get to with either chopsticks or beating sticks.

But nowadays, we have these easygoing Zen students; Zen interviews have no effect on them, they have no eye to see into themselves, and putting on airs of how commendable it is and how grateful they are, they do the Nembutsu, saying, "Doing Zen and Pure Land together is just the thing for me." Truly it is just the thing to make you choke on your food, if you ask me.

A superb practitioner, rather, musters up a valiant heart, and not worrying about life or limb, passes through the impossible koan, to take up residence in the deepest reaches of the Zen gate, and with a grip on that koan, gives his strictest attention to practitioners everywhere under the sun, restoring the tradition, once again bringing the Zen creed to life— that is my fondest wish.

When the idea occurred to me the other night, I started to write this Dharma essay under lamplight, and got this far when I suddenly started chuckling to myself. The reason is, I intended to set down the essentials of how you could enter the way of insight, but ended up with a long, drawn-out discussion deploring the weakening of the Zen tradition. Just as a merchant is constantly talking profits, or a woodsman is full of stories about the woods he loves, this old man is the same; for me it is the way of the patriarchs I am worried about. Yesterday I heard from someone that the Zen monasteries in China had become broken down and dilapidated, and all day long I was depressed, and without intending to I wrote about the reason why they are vanishing in this letter. It is just like a worried man who expresses his worried thoughts even in his sleep. This old man in the normal course of the day is really concerned about it, and so harps on it in his letter, so please do not find it nonsensical and not worth reading. My hope is that, if you find it opportune, you might find it helpful to others who are into practice and doing Zen interviews and finding their way.

At all events, once you have heard the Voice of the Single Hand for yourself, spur yourself on with the wheel of the Vow to never give in; set this bodhisattva practice into action, as you put the finishing touches to the Buddha Dharma. Whether monk gone out or layman at home, without this spirit of the Vow, however many good roots you pile up, in the end you cannot escape from wandering lost again in birth and death. Know for yourself the awe the Bodhisattva inspires in us, and even your wandering lost in birth and death as such becomes your ticket to leave it behind. Keep this point well in mind. Also, if you think you have made a little progress with the Single Hand, do not toss it aside, and let me know in a letter.

Please note that it was in the middle of the night when I wrote this, setting down whatever came to mind, forgetting everything else. I see my handwriting is rather wild and unruly, so please don't show it to anyone else!

Modern Koan Commentaries

NINTH KOAN

Sokei-an Sasaki

TWENTY-FIVE ZEN KOANS, MARCH 5, 1938
NINTH KOAN

ONE DAY JOSHU WENT TO SEE the stone bridge with the Head of the monks. Joshu questioned the Head of the monks:

"Who made this stone bridge?"

The Head of the monks answered, "Li-yuan made it."

Joshu said, "When he made it, where did he first put his hand?" The Head of the monks could make no answer.

Joshu said, "We are talking about an ordinary stone bridge. To my question you do not know how to answer—where the builder first put his hand."

This is the koan. Joshu was one of the famous Zen masters of the T'ang Dynasty. He was a native of Central China, near Nan-yiang, between the Yellow River and the Yangtsze, near the China Sea. He died when he was 120 years old—897 A.D.

I cannot record here all those stories about Joshu. I have selected one of the ones which included Nansen whose disciple Joshu was.

When Joshu was a lad under the Osho of Kotsu-in, his head was shaved, but the commandments were not yet given to him.

Later he went to Nansen and paid his homage to the Master while he was taking a rest.

The Master asked, "From where did you take your departure?"

Joshu said, "From the temple of the Lucky Image."

The Master said, "Have you seen the Lucky Image?"

"No, I did not see the Lucky Image, but I saw the reclining Buddha."

The Master said, "Have you a master of your own or not?"
Joshu said, "Yes, I have."
"Where is your master?"
Joshu replied, "In the middle of a severe winter, I bow and pray that the Master may thrive and prosper."
Nansen realized that he was a vessel of dharma and permitted him to become his disciple.

This was the beginning of Joshu's becoming the disciple of Nansen. Nansen was also a famous Zen master. There were five different sects in Zen—five different schools in the Zen sect in the T'ang dynasty: Rinzai, Soto, Hogen, Ikyo, and Ummon schools. Each sect has different attitudes in the expression of its attainment of Zen.

While Rinzai was using his famous shout, Tozan, the master of the Soto school indicated everyday life as what is Zen. One would say to Tozan, "I wish to know," and Tozan would answer, "Take my tea." And Hogen was showing the actual thing always. One would say, "What is the stone upon the mountain?" And Hogen would say, "Oh, it is a stone upon the mountain." Ikyo's attitude was as father to child. Isan and Kyozan were picking tea leaves all day long. Isan was on one side and Kyozan on the other, talking to each other through the tea leaves. Isan questioned Kyozan:

"We have been talking all day long and I have never seen your body yet. I have heard your voice all day long but I haven't seen your body yet."
Kyozan shook the tea tree.
Isan said, "No, no! I made a mistake!"
Kyozan became silent.
Isan said, "I see your body, but I don't see your activity."
And Kyozan shook the tea leaves—such way.

This was the school. The Ummon school was using the lips in speech. If one asked, "What is the mystery of Buddhism?" Ummon would answer one word or one syllable. No one understood the meaning of his answer. These are the five schools of the Zen sect.

But this Joshu's attitude was more like Ummon's school, although he was not of that sect, but he used marvelous speech.

This stone bridge of Joshu was a famous stone bridge made by the governor Li-yuan of Joshu. It is still existing in Northern China. This stone bridge was very beautiful—built like an arch, every stone supporting the other—so every stone must be set at once.

Some novice came to see the bridge of Joshu and hearing of the famous master, he visited him and said:

"I have heard of the fame of the famous stone bridge of Joshu but I saw a plank."

He was saying, "I have heard of the famous Zen master of Joshu, but I saw just an everyday monk."

Joshu answered, "You saw a plank, but you did not see the stone bridge."
The monk said, "What is the stone bridge?"
Joshu said, "You must come closer."
The monk came closer.

Another monk came and said, "I have heard of the fame of the famous stone bridge of Joshu but I saw a plank."
Joshu said, "You saw a plank, not the stone bridge."
The monk said, "What is the stone bridge?"
Joshu said, "Donkeys will come across it."

His answers were so deep it was very difficult to grasp the viewpoint of Joshu.

When Joshu was a lad under the Osho of Kotsu-in, his head was shaved, but the commandments were not yet given to him. As a lad he went to a little temple in his own town and shaved his head, but he was so young that the monk did not give him the commandments. Before they are twelve years old they are not given the commandments. From twelve to twenty years they have the five commandments and from twenty years they are given those two hundred and fifty laws.

234 Sitting With Koans

Later he went to Nansen and paid his homage to the Master while he was taking a rest. Nansen was living near Nanking. So Joshu came down to the south and paid homage to him. Nansen was lying down and when Joshu came, someone led him to Nansen's cell where Nansen was lying on the floor... You must make your own mental picture of this to understand this koan.

The Master asked, "From where did you take your departure?" Joshu said, "From the temple of the Lucky Image." The Master said, "Have you seen the Lucky Image?" This question is like a mouse in the kitchen—you must catch it. This "Lucky Image" is something you must catch. If I said, "God"—you must find it.

"No, I did not see the Lucky Image, but I saw the reclining Buddha." This young boy! The "lying-down Buddha!" Nansen's question was, "Have you seen the mystery of Buddha?" And the answer is, "The mystery of Buddha is in that lying-down Buddha." He means Nansen himself. "You are the lying-down Buddha." He did not say this, but he means it; and Nansen realizes that here is a good young monk! So,

The Master said, "Have you a master of your own or not?" The first question is not so difficult, but the second question—you cannot escape it!

Joshu said, "Yes, I have." "Where is your master?" Perhaps Joshu spread his mat and bowed to Nansen.

Joshu replied, "In the middle of a severe winter, I bow and pray that the Master may thrive and prosper." Nansen realized that he was a vessel of dharma and permitted him to become his disciple. Nansen thinks, "This child is too smart! But you can take sanzen!"

Soon after Joshu left and took the commandments, and then came back to Nansen and stayed a long time. There are many stories of Joshu. I chose this one:

One day Joshu went to see the stone bridge with the Head of the monks. Joshu questioned the Head of the monks. Zen master and disciples—their mind is always on enlightenment. The Master's every word is a question to the student, but the student does not understand; he thinks the Master's words are the usual words, "Good morning," "Good evening," "Good-bye"! But from the Zen master's standpoint, it is different.

"Who made this stone bridge?" The Head of the monks answered, "Li-yuan made it." Joshu said, "When he made it, where did he first put his hand?" A similar koan to this is that koan which you would [sic.] observe always. Indra made the tower which was seamless upon the top of Sumeru Mountain. When he made it, where did he put his hand first? The same koan! God created this universe in one piece. From which corner did he begin his creation of the world? You will answer: "On Monday, this; on Tuesday that; on Wednesday and Thursday this and that; on Friday, the fish; on Saturday the human being, and on Sunday he took a rest!" The same question! And this question was so deep that—

The Head of the monks could make no answer. He could not say a word! I regret I did not tell him that the fish were created on Friday! Then he could make an answer!

Joshu said, "We are talking about an ordinary stone bridge. To my question you do not know how to answer—where the builder first put his hand." Joshu's view of the real state of reality was expressed by this. It is like Tozan's answer to "What is Zen?" Tozan said, "Drink your tea." The novice thinks Zen is very difficult—thinks that through four stages, first samadhi, then prajna, third emptiness, and in the fourth then we attain the mystery of Zen!

We must destroy all these appearances and all this mutability and then in the pure mind you will attain!… Different from the usual idea is that of those giant Zen masters. They take back their eyes, ears, all which belongs to them, and again they observe the world and see nothing which is impure, nothing which is mutable; all is clear, all is beautiful! Their attitude is very wonderful. He affirms nothing; he accepts everything. He does not deny even the cockroach in the kitchen! He accepts everything like the ocean, which swallows clear water and dirty water at the same time.

But first you destroy all your notions and all your sense perceptions and reach, if you so-call it, final nothingness! And then you open your eyes from the inside—open your ear from the inside. When you were born you opened your eyes from the outside—color is there, father is there, and mother, and you never question it. But when you question it—what is it?—you find it is vibration of ether that is color, and vibration of ether that is sound…. So, in the outside, your father, your mother, color,

236 *Sitting With Koans*

is just vibration of ether. Without that there is no father, no mother, no red, green, no light, no darkness.... You question all the five shadows, and then you go through the uttermost bottom of consciousness and nothingness. And you think that is enlightenment. But it is not true enlightenment yet. You must accept all....

This was Joshu's understanding. *"We are talking about an ordinary stone bridge. To my question you do not know how to answer—where the builder first put his hand."*

The monk's attitude was lofty—he could make no answer. Joshu's attitude was different. These koans show the true understanding of Zen.

Prajnatara Recites His Sutra

Nyogen Senzaki

Book of Equanimity, Case 3

Introduction

Monks, go back to the timeless era. There you can see the black turtle run toward the fire and hear the voice of the wordless teaching. Can you recognize the flowers blossoming on the millstone? What kind of scripture will you recite in that region?

Note

Bansho here raises the curtain on that vivid stage where Buddhas and Patriarchs perform their best acts. Western scholars who criticize Buddhism, but are themselves without Zen experience, may be found hooting from their seats under the advertising curtain.

Henceforth, Space in itself and Time in itself sink into mere shadows and only a kind of union of the two can be maintained as self-existent.

Minkowski

We postulate something called "tomorrow" and think of it as a duration separated from "today." But when tomorrow comes, it turns out to be today; and so one postulates another tomorrow, which is nothing but an extension of that tomorrow and this today, and so on, endlessly. We worry about a so-called "hereafter," but our own individual death is not the end of the world! This hereafter is not what we think it is. For example: My present life is the hereafter for someone else who died before me, and in this present life I unwittingly carry on the work of someone else, just as someone else will without question carry on my work after I have died. So why worry about one's own little death! The world is timeless. Past, present, and future are merely names that refer back to the relative perspective these conventions presuppose.

An ancient philosopher once visited the tyrant of Syracuse in Sicily. The tyrant told him all about his plans for the future, his schemes and projected conquests, finally saying to the philosopher: "After all of this has been accomplished, after I have built a city, declared war on Messina, as well as on other countries, and after having conquered them all, then I shall settle down and be happy." This was the tyrant's postwar talk. The philosopher said, "Why don't you settle down now and be happy?"

Those who do not know the region of the timeless that Bansho is pointing to in his Introduction always blame others for their own misdeeds and never examine their own selves; they are thus condemned to engaging in endless conflict among themselves.

In China the black turtle lives in the deep sea, only sometimes coming out of the water to wander onto land. Using his instinct, sooner or later he goes back to the sea. When Bansho speaks of the black turtle's approaching fire instead of water, it is his way of crushing prejudice and *Ideologie*. When he asks, "Can you recognize the flowers blossoming on the millstone?" the reader is being invited to loosen his tight hold on conventional ideas (since flowers do not blossom on millstones!). "The wordless teaching" transcends the music of notes and technique.

Birds are flying creatures, but ostriches, cassowaries, and emus in Australia, as well as kiwis in New Zealand and penguins in Antarctica, cannot fly at all. Fish live in water, but the climbing perch climbs trees and sideways at that, flapping its way up to a height sometimes of five feet or more. On the shores of the Bay of Stilis in Greece there are goats that have the peculiar habit of building large nests in trees. If you ask a child, "Why is a pig so dirty?" you will get the reply: "Because it's a pig!" "A Jap is a Jap" and "A Jew is a Jew" are similar examples of this kind of simple-minded prejudice and Ideologie.

Bansho's monks thought it their business to recite sutras before accepting food, just as Christian ministers pray before dining. This clinging to conventions should have been crushed by the time they reached the Theme of this chapter:

A king of eastern India invited Prajnatara, the teacher of Bodhidharma, to a royal feast, expecting to get a recitation of some kind out of this learned monk. Prajnatara, after having remained silent for a while, began to eat. The king asked, "Why don't you recite the sutras?" The monk replied: "My inhalation does not tangle itself up with the five skandhas; my exhalation goes out freely without becoming ensnared in the chain of cause and effect. Thus I recite a million scrolls of holy scripture."

Buddha Shakyamuni used to call his preaching "turning the Wheel of Dharma." Just like the ancient Indian wheel weapon capable of sweeping the enemy off its feet, so the Buddha's teaching was capable of completely crushing the delusions of man. The spiritual medicine prescribed was always in accordance with the particular sickness to be cured. Buddha's teachings were transmitted verbally from teacher to student, from mouth to ear. The sutras, or holy scriptures, were thus recited by disciples in their original form—Sanskrit or Pali; and, later, in Chinese translations. To recite scriptures without knowing the true meaning of the teaching they contain is like murmuring the pharmacopoeia without having examined the patient! The king in this koan was foolish enough to expect to get—in return for his royal feast—some magical words from the Patriarch, as well as the merit deriving from having fed such a "holy man." Wanshi's and Bansho's monks thought they were followers of the Buddha just because they could recite sutras. It was to combat this clinging to the conventional that the present chapter was written.

The five skandhas are: rupa (form), vedana (sense perception), samjna (thought), samskara (conformation), and vijnana (consciousness). These are the processes through which mind and body, the inner and the outer, the subjective and the objective, interweave. Because Prajnatara is able to breathe in and out without becoming entangled in the five skandhas, he transcends the suffering which is the necessary consequence of attachment to these constituents of consciousness. It was from this same condition of karma-free samadhi that the Buddha himself started turning his Wheel of Dharma. And this condition is the source of all the sutras, or holy scriptures, of Buddhism. *In your meditation you should think nonthinking. Now what is nonthinking? it is to thik nothing. Dogen Zenji.*

A well-known Japanese actor was asked by his understudy: "How is it you say your part on opening night as if you'd already performed it many times?" To which the actor responded: "I first practice it many times in rehearsal, but then try to forget it completely the night before the first performance."

Koans are usually solved when one is not meditating. In true meditation there is nothing to think about—even one's koan should be forgotten. The purpose of koan study is to drive the student into this region of nothingness.

> The rhinoceros takes his walk in the moonlight.
> The wooden horse plays with the spring breeze.
> A pair of cold, blue eyes
> Glares behind the white bushy eyebrows.
> He does not read sutras with those eyes.
> His mind extends into the timeless region.
> No victory without fighting.
> The perfect machine moves with one touch.
> Kanzan forgets his way home;
> Jittoku returns with him, hand in hand.

NOTES

The rhinoceros walks under the moon; no one knows what he wants; he is neither hungry nor thirsty. The Chinese call him a desireless walker. The wooden horse enjoys his freedom, no one can tie him up. The Patriarch lives the same unconcerned life as these two. To reach this stage, however, requires very hard work, a constant battle against the inertia of delusion. (Kanzan is the manifestation of Manjusri, or enlightenment; Jittoku of Samantabhadra, or loving-kindness.)

PASSOVER TEISHO

Soen Nakagawa

DAI BOSATSU ZENDO KONGO JI, APRIL 13, 1974

WHEN MY TEACHER, Yamamoto Gempo Roshi, was about fifty years old, he decided that he wanted to go to Ryutaku Ji to rebuild it. His teacher, Sohan Roshi, did not agree. Sohan Roshi said, "That place is very damp and full of moisture. If you go to such a damp place, with your terrible neuralgia, it will kill you. Though Ryutaku Ji has fallen into disrepair, and there are no longer any monks living there, Hakuin is not subject to such conditions. He cannot be found under his memorial tower; nor is he in any of the monastery buildings. Hakuin is not such a person." To this, Gempo Roshi answered, "It is *because* Hakuin is not such a person that I want to go." Sohan Roshi replied, "If this is the case, then you may go." This is a wonderful Zen conversation.

What is true of Hakuin is true of us all as well: *Because* we are not the kind of person to be found underneath a stone in the Sangha Meadow at Dai Bosatsu Zendo, *therefore* let us make a beautiful Sangha Meadow—a beautiful memorial tower for all Patriarchs. The next time I come to Dai Bosatsu I will bring some of Hakuin's ashes. They are not ashes, exactly. After he had been cremated, one of his disciples found in his ashes something little and round, very beautiful and transparent. When we keep our body and mind pure, when our everyday life is just like a sesshin all the time, our whole being becomes purified. Body and mind are not separated—they are one. It is said that after having been cremated, sometimes such a transparent residue can be found. Of course, if it is not found, that's all right too! But after Hakuin had been cremated, his disciple found this transparent jewel-like residue. This is what I will bring to Dai Bosatsu Zendo next time. *Because* we have no need for such a thing, *therefore* we must have it. All right?

241

In order for this purification to take place, we need a great deal of endurance. Gempo Roshi had an extremely painful case of neuralgia. What he endured in his life was incomparably more painful than what you are going through with your Zazen during this sesshin. He got this condition as a result of working very hard before he became a monk, traveling for many years barefoot on pilgrimages. Through this terrible pain he accumulated the virtue of endurance, which is a wonderful virtue indeed! Here is a story. Just before one Rohatsu sesshin, Gempo Roshi, who was then a monk, decided that, despite a painful boil he had gotten, he would not move during the entire week! So for seven days he sat in Zazen, without moving, enduring great pain. During that Rohatsu, he says, he had a wonderful experience. *This* is what is meant by accumulating the virtue of endurance. Tomorrow, during the final Purification Ceremony, along with the names of the other Buddhas, we will chant "Namu Endurance Butsu" ("Salutations to the Buddha of Endurance"). You have all accumulated the virtue of endurance during this sesshin. Anger, greed, jealousy, and irritation of all kinds—all of these we must pass over through the power of endurance.

Today we will look at Rinzai's twelfth pilgrimage:

> Rinzai arrived at San-feng. P'ing Ho-shang asked him: "Where did you come from?" "I came from Obaku," replied Rinzai. "What does Obaku have to say?" Rinzai said: "The golden ox met with fire last night/And left not even one trace."

Obaku Zenji was Rinzai's teacher. Rinzai, as you can see, was a great poet too; he and P'ing responded to each other with beautiful poetry.

> P'ing said: "The autumn wind blows a flute of jade;/Who is he who knows the tune?"

The autumn wind is *kimpu*—"golden wind"; "jade" is merely an adjective—a bamboo flute is all right. The golden wind blows a beautiful flute—makes a wonderful tune. Who knows this true tune?

Rinzai said: "He goes right through the myriad-fold barrier, / And stays not even within the clear sky." "Your question is much too lofty," said P'ing. Rinzai said: "The dragon's given birth to a golden phoenix / Who breaks through the azure dome of heaven."

The baby dragon breaks through to paradise, without remaining or lingering even in heaven. This is the meaning. At present there are thirty-four sesshin attendants here at Dai Bosatsu. The dragon has given birth to thirty-four golden phoenixes or Bodhisattvas at Dai Bosatsu. And they linger not even in paradise! This is the true meaning of Ascension. On Mount Olive, very near our Zen hut, there is Ascension Stone, where Christ is said to have ascended into heaven. Whether this is true or not, I don't know. I do know that snow ascends into heaven—beautiful ascension—and falls down again, becoming pure water to nourish the earth. Water, snow, water—wonderful circulation, wonderful incarnation of Buddha.

Kuni guni no	Snow of all countries
Yuki tokete Namu	Melting into
Dai Bosa	Namu Dai Bosa

And spring has come to Dai Bosatsu Mountain.

"Do sit down and have some tea," said P'ing. Then he asked—

If they had simply taken tea together and then departed, that would have been all right, but—

Then he asked, "Where have you been recently?" "At Lung-kuang," said Rinzai.

So far so good.

"How is Lung-kuang these days?" asked P'ing.

No good. So—

At once Lin-chi went off.

All right? Do you understand? If not, you may think about it later.

Don't become confused about the relation between "meditation" and "thinking." Although it is true that Zen is not meditation and Zen is not thinking, this does not mean that thinking or meditating is no good. This sort of misconception is the result of a confusion in our means of expression. Thinking is important; meditation is important. All right? When we meditate, we meditate; when we think, we think. But meditation itself is not Zen. Zen is meditation, but it is also thinking, eating, drinking, sitting, standing, shitting, peeing—all of these are nothing else but Zen. There is *Za-zen* and there is *the*-Zen. Zazen is sitting Zen. But this is not *the* Zen. Don't be mistaken about this point.

Although I sometimes say that Zen is not to be found in a posture like that of Rodin's *Thinker*, on the other hand, one of the most beautiful Bodhisattva statues, that of the Bodhisattva Miroku—the Bodhisattva of the future—which is found in Nara, shows Miroku precisely in the posture of the thinker. He is probably thinking about how to save all sentient beings. This Bodhisattva, then, meditates in the posture of the thinker.

Meditation is all right; thinking is all right. Some of you come to my room during dokusan and say, "I guess I have to give up one of my greatest pleasures, thinking." This is a great mistake! When we must think about something, we must think about something; when we do Zazen, we do Zazen. Often during Zazen, while meditating, some wonderful inspiration comes to us, which helps us in our thinking about something. This is perfectly all right.

Let us pass over to the eighteenth pilgrimage of Rinzai. Here we find a wonderful old woman—but be careful! Rinzai was almost beaten by her!

> When Rinzai was going to Feng-lin, he met an old woman on the road, who asked: "Where are you going?" "I am going to Feng-lin," replied Rinzai. "Feng-lin happens to be away just now," said the old woman. "Where did he go?" asked Rinzai. At that the old woman walked away.

Had the old woman gotten away—walked more quickly—Rinzai might have been beaten. All right? But—

> Rinzai called to her. The old woman turned her head. Rinzai hit her.

All right? Wonderful battle. Just such an old woman, a Japanese, already eighty-two years old, donated the new Buddha which is now in the New York Zendo, but will eventually come to Dai Bosatsu Zendo. She wanted to take me to the Gobi Desert, but this is no longer possible this summer. This *Namu Dai Bosa* has spread to the desert of Judea, to Mount Olive, and almost to the Gobi Desert! It is still spreading, spreading. Please deliver this *Namu Dai Bosa* mind to your intimate friends (when you return home after this sesshin). No need for you to chant *Namu Dai Bosa*, or for you to ask them to do so. When your mind becomes that of a Bodhisattva, *that* is the true transmission of *Namu Dai Bosa* spirit. The true spreading. After sesshin, when you have returned home, you will find that even without your saying anything, your life will have changed somewhat. Your husband, who used to be so jealous, will have become more mild and cheerful. This is the true transmission of *Namu Dai Bosa*. If you are a nurse, you may help some miserable patient by chanting *Namu Dai Bosa*. Each of you is an apostle of *Namu Dai Bosa*, of *this mind*. "May we extend *this mind* over all beings, so that we and the world together, may attain…" true peace for all human beings.

Now on to the twentieth pilgrimage.

"Rinzai arrived at Chin-niu." Now this wonderful Zen master's name means "Golden Ox." He would have been very old at this time; he was one of the successors of Baso, a Dharma grandfather of Rinzai. Golden Ox. And here [pointing to a student] is Tetsugyu, Iron Ox. Dharma names are communal property; they do not belong to any one individual, really. Golden Ox. Golden Gate in San Francisco. Watergate in Washington. And the Gateless Gate. All right? Golden Gate, Watergate, Gateless Gate—we must pass over all of these. Even the Gateless Gate we must pass over.

Chin-niu's monastery was very small; there were only about twenty or thirty members. Just our size; just like us. The Roshi himself was at the same time tenzo. He always cooked for his students, for all of his disciples. Not only for one sesshin or one year—but for twenty years, mind you, Chin-niu cooked for his students. For him, each student was a Bodhisattva. So when the rice had boiled and the warm fragrance had begun to rise into the room, he put the rice into a big bowl and served his student-Bodhisattvas, embracing the big rice bowl and dancing a wonderful dance. To be tenzo is such a wonderful thing!

At this sesshin we did some *Namu Dai Bosa* dancing for the first time. This kind of dancing should be full of Dharma delight; we should feel so full of gratitude that we cannot sit still, that we naturally start dancing. To do this in a dance hall is all right, but our *Namu Dai Bosa* dancing should be like our Zazen. All right? Both are universal, dancing and sitting. During this dance, however, don't take each other's hand, don't embrace each other. Just dance by yourself. *That* kind of solitary dancing is a universal dance. Just as when we do sitting Zazen we don't take hold of each other's hand, the same is true for *Namu Dai Bosa* dancing.

To return to Golden Ox embracing his rice bowl. He used to cry out, upon entering the Zendo with his big bowl, "All Bodhisattvas, come on! Come one, come all! Get your rice now. Please come!" And he would dance and laugh. He didn't ring a meal gong. Just entered dancing and laughing—this is the way things were in his monastery. Indeed wonderful!

> Chin-niu saw Rinzai coming and, holding a stick crosswise, sat down at the gate. Rinzai struck the stick three times with his hand, then entered the Zendo and seated himself in the first seat. Chin-niu came in, saw him, and said: "In an interview between host and guest, each should conform to the prescribed formalities. Where do you come from, Shang-tso, that you are so rude?" "What are you talking about, old Ho-shang?" replied Rinzai. Chin-niu started to open his mouth, and Rinzai hit him. Chin-niu gave the appearance of falling down—

This giving the appearance of falling down is a most important point. As Rinzai hit him, old Chin-niu must have made some expression like "Oh-oh-oh...," as if he had been beaten, just as we do when we are wrestling with our grandchildren and pretend to fall down all by ourselves. All right? Like that.

> Rinzai hit him. Chin-niu gave the appearance of falling down. Rinzai hit him again. Chin-niu said: "I'm not doing so well today." Kuei-shan asked Yang-shan: "In the case of these two venerable ones, was there a winner or a loser?" "The winner indeed won; the loser indeed lost."

Now this is not a good translation! It should read: "Both won. Both lost. One match—two wins." Or, as in our own case this sesshin, one match, thirty-four wins.

Now the last, the twenty-first pilgrimage.

> When the Master was about to pass away, he seated himself and said: "After I am extinguished, do not let my True Dharma be extinguished." San-sheng—his successor— came forward and said: "How could I let your True Dharma be extinguished?" "Later on, when somebody asks you about it, what will you say to him?" asked the Master. "*Kwaaatz!*" replied San-sheng. "Who would have thought that my True Dharma would be extinguished upon reaching this blind ass!" said the Master. Having spoken these words, sitting erect, the Master revealed his Nirvana.

Really to understand this, we must practice Zazen and, entering into deep samadhi, communicate with Rinzai himself. Not only with Rinzai— with all Patriarchs.

This "blind ass" expression is probably very difficult for you all to understand, so I will explain. But first—"When the Master was about to pass away..."

We too will someday pass away from this world. You will die and I will die. Of course, every day, every moment we are dying, dying, dying, dying! Living, living, living, living *is* dying, dying, dying, dying. But the last moment of our life is our last opportunity, and this moment is very important; for the last is the best. At least it should be the best. This opportunity is most important.

There are many ways to die, of course. One way is lying on a bed in a hospital somewhere, feeble-bodied and ill; another is to be struck by a car—I might be struck by a car today on my way back to New York. I cannot say that such a thing will not happen. At that moment—*Aaagghhhh*! All right. But the ideal way to die is in such a way that one can foresee his own death—at least, say, one week in advance. This should be how we die. And this was how the Patriarchs passed away, knowing in advance when it would happen. They could thus prepare themselves. Having kept the precepts, the body having become free and happy, full of delight, transparent—this is the way Rinzai and the other Patriarchs died. And this is how we should die.

Before every meal we say:

> "First, let us reflect on our own work; let us see whence this comes. Secondly, let us reflect how imperfect our virtue is—"

Indeed, the more transparent our mind becomes, the more we realize, when we reflect on our own virtue, how miserable we are.

> "Thirdly, what is most essential is to hold our minds in control, and be detached from the various faults, greed, etc."

All right? Such bad, dismal, miserable feelings must be purified! If, even after constant Zazen, sitting, sitting, sitting, such jealous, impure feelings remain, such a person is not a Zen student, not a Bodhisattva. So we must practice, practice; train, train!

Now, finally, to get back to the meaning of "blind ass."

During the Edo period in Japan, before Hakuin's time, there lived another great and wonderful Zen master named Bankei. At the same time there lived a blind man who, because of his blindness, possessed very keen and very deep intuitions. As you know, although a blind man's physical eye is blind, his spiritual eye is extremely clear. So this blind man once said:

"When I hear people talking to each other—hear someone praising his friend, saying, 'I am so happy for you'—I usually detect, in the deep corners of their minds, some trace of envy. Or when I hear someone consoling someone else, saying, 'I am so sorry for you,' I hear, mingled with this, the trace of a glad or happy feeling. When I hear people talking to each other, I hear that their expression is not transparent. Their words are all right, but the feeling behind them is impure, mixed with jealousy, bad will, etc. But when I listen to Bankei, I hear only pure, transparent feeling. Only with Bankei is this so."

This is why we must train, train, train—make our everyday life just like sesshin—in order to achieve this transparent condition in our everyday life; this precious, everyday life. Let us keep this condition of mind while eating, sleeping, throughout our changing lives. Let us keep *this mind*. The minute we become careless, it is spoiled and destroyed. Our present Bodhisattva mind is like a newborn baby; so we must be careful and mindful with it. Each of you, watch your step closely; always keep your head cool and your mind warm (as Nyogen Senzaki always said).

After our voyage across the Pacific Ocean, Eido Roshi and I landed in Seattle. I wanted—this is one of my greedy wishes—to have a beautiful, small, very lovely tea bowl. I could not find one in Japan, but I knew I could find one in Seattle! Although the price was somewhat high, I paid it. Black, very lovely. I loved this bowl too much, always carrying it with me—but not in the proper way, not the way a tea student would. I loved that bowl. But on the fifth day of this sesshin, I got up early in the morning—just after midnight—and took out my beautiful bowl, my baby Bosatsu. I wanted to save something in it. It was my own carelessness; it should have been used for tea only. I took it from my room to put something I wished to save in it—I am a very stingy monk! As we begin to occupy more and more the entire universe, we become stingy—we must become so. When the whole universe is our possession, we become very stingy indeed! Anyway I was rushing around—my mind was rushing—

and I took up this tea bowl carelessly, and it broke! At that instant—what? *Congratulations!* All right? *Congratulations!* Even your own lovely child will one day die. All is a beautiful phantasm. So we should have no regrets. When the time comes...I loved that baby bowl too much.... When it is put back together again, it will probably become an ugly bowl, with an ugly face. All right!

Tomorrow we will have our Purification Ceremony and hear the three fundamental precepts: Don't do bad acts; do as many good acts as you can; and always keep your mind warm and pure for all sentient beings. These are our three fundamental precepts—for us as human beings, not as Buddhists; for us as true men and true women. Just before meals we chant:

Ikku i dan issai aku	Cut-kill—cut off—all bad feelings
Niku i shu issai zen	Let us do as many good acts as we can
Sanku i do shoshujo	and avoid bad actions
Kaiku jo Butsu do.	Let us save all sentient beings.

These are the most fundamental precepts of all human life.

In our everyday life, there is no need to admire the Patriarchs. We are no different from Buddha Shakyamuni and the Patriarchs. We are breathing the same air they breathed. We don't need their help to breathe it! Each of us is a wonderful true man, true woman, true human being. To realize and actualize this fact in our everyday life—*this* is the transmission of Dharma.

I said I would explain "blind ass," but I still have not done so. This is a most important matter.

There are four or five kinds of blindness. There is physical blindness; and then there is mental blindness. Most people are mentally blind—blind, that is, in their thinking. For example, they believe that life and death are different; that self and other are different. When they realize the true oneness of this universe, this mental blindness will cease. Mental blindness is the most familiar and popular form of blindness. Then there is another kind of blindness, called in Japanese jakatsu. This is the blindness of religious teachers, ministers, monks, and priests who, though blind themselves, presume to lead other blind people. This is a most *cruel* blindness! Blind people preaching and leading other blind people astray—this is jakatsu.

I myself am blind in the sense that I know I don't know anything. For example: take this cup. We all think this *is* a cup. But *is* this a cup really? As human beings we name things—"cup," "book," "arm," etc. But to tell you the truth, what something really is, is Unthinkable, Untouchable, Ungraspable. This world is an Untouchable world. We think this three- or four-dimension world is the whole world; but it is really only a very little part of the whole. Reality is Unthinkable and Untouchable. OK? This world is so wonderful, so Unthinkable and Ungraspable. *What are we touching right here now?* Bodhidharma said, "I don't know." *This* is true blindness. Superblindness. And this is the meaning of "blind ass" as Rinzai applies it to his successor, San-sheng. In using this expression, Rinzai is bestowing the highest possible praise on his successor. And so, smiling, he passed away. Like "the golden ox" who "met with fire last night," Rinzai passed away, having become completely extinguished, having melted, melted away completely, without leaving a single trace, with nothing of himself remaining behind. This is an occasion for the highest celebration. Rinzai's True Dharma had been completely extinguished by his successor. All right?

On this Cut-kill mountain, nothing remains. This is the true Passover celebration. We celebrated Buddha's birthday here with the birth of our own Bodhisattvas at this sesshin. Let us congratulate each other. Congratulations! But let us continue this experience in our everyday life. Let us continue, continue, continue! Let us help each other!

I wrote a waka [a thirty-one-syllable Japanese poem] recently, which I will try to translate into English:

Waga Soshi to
Oboshiki Hito ga
Bosatsu-ko no
Koori o watari
Atokata mo nashi.

A man who looks like our Patriarchs—
Bodhidharma, Rinzai, or Hakuin—I don't know—

Passed over the ice of Dai Bosatsu Lake
Without leaving even the slightest trace.

This is complete extinction. This is the real meaning of Crucifixion. And so tomorrow let us welcome Easter Sunday. The true meaning of Easter Sunday is contained in these words; let us recite them together:

"Having spoken these words, sitting erect, the Master revealed his Nirvana."

Nansen (Nanquan) Kills a Cat

Zenkei Shibayama

Gateless Gate, Case 14

Koan

ONCE THE MONKS of the Eastern Hall and the Western Hall were disputing about a cat. Nansen, holding up the cat, said, "Monks, if you can say a word of Zen, I will spare the cat. If you cannot, I will kill it!" No monk could answer. Nansen finally killed the cat. In the evening, when Joshu came back, Nansen told him of the incident. Joshu took off his sandal, put it on his head, and walked off. Nansen said, "If you had been there, I could have saved the cat!"

Mumon's Commentary

You tell me, what is the real meaning of Joshu's putting his sandal on his head? If you can give the turning words on this point, you will see that Nansen's action was not in vain. If you cannot, beware!

Mumon's Poem

> Had Joshu only been there,
> He would have taken action.
> Had he snatched the sword away,
> Nansen would have begged for his life.

254 Sitting With Koans

Teisho on the Koan

This is a very famous koan in Zen circles, one that has been included in many Zen books because of the unusual story, which denies all rational or intellectual approaches. It is therefore extremely difficult for scholars, except those who themselves have gone through Zen training, to understand the koan correctly. In most cases they interpret it from the standpoint of ethics alone, or from a common-sense point of view, since they do not have the authentic Zen eye and experience to grasp the essence.

Once more I should like to point out that koan are Zen Masters' sayings and doings in which they have freely and directly expressed their Zen experiences. We have to realize that they are fundamentally different from instructions in ethics and common sense. If we are not aware that koan belong to quite another dimension than the ethical or the prudential and practical activities of men, we shall forever be unable even to glimpse their real significance.

Some may criticize this statement by saying it implies that Zen ignores ethics and common sense. This is an extreme misunderstanding. Zen, on the contrary, frees us from our suffering and restraints caused by ethics and common sense. This does not mean to ignore or defy ethics and common sense, but to be the master of them and to make free and lively use of them. Unless this point is clearly understood, Zen sayings and doings can never be correctly appreciated.

The main figures in this koan are Nansen Fugan and his disciple Joshu Junen, two great Zen Masters who played active leading roles toward the end of the T'ang dynasty when Zen flourished most notably. In *Hekiganroku* the same koan appears as two koan: "Nansen Kills a Cat," and "Joshu Puts a Sandal on His Head." In the *Mumonkan* it is introduced as a single koan.

"Once the monks of the Eastern Hall and the Western Hall were disputing about a cat. Nansen, holding up the cat, said, 'Monks, if you can say a word of Zen, I will spare the cat. If you cannot, I will kill it!' No monk could answer. Nansen finally killed the cat."

The first half of the koan quite simply states the incident. It is recorded that at the monastery where Master Nansen was the abbot, there were always hundreds of monks who had come to study under him. One day the monks staying at the Eastern Hall and the Western Hall were having a dispute about a cat. The koan does not tell us what the real issue of the dispute was, and there is no way for us to know it today. From the context it may be inferred that they were engaging in some speculative religious arguments referring to a cat.

Master Nansen happened to come across this dispute. His irresistible compassion as their teacher burst forth to smash up their vain theoretical arguments and open their spiritual eye to the Truth of Zen. He seized the cat in one hand, a big knife in the other, and cried out, "You monks, if you can speak a word of Zen, I will spare the cat. If you cannot, I will kill it right away!" He challenged the monks to a decisive fight.

Setting aside the monks at the Nansen Monastery, I ask you, "What is the word to save the cat in response to Nansen's demand?" The koan is asking for your answer which would stop Nansen from killing the cat. This is the key point in the first half of the koan. In actual training, the Master will press the monk: "How do you save the cat right now?" And if you hesitate even for a moment, the Master, in place of Nansen, will at once take decisive action.

Commenting on the koan, an old Buddhist said, "Even Nansen's knife can never kill the Fundamental Wisdom. It is ever alive even at this moment." Even though this statement is undoubtedly true, it still smells of religious philosophy, for the term "Fundamental Wisdom" is an extremely philosophical expression which means "the Fundamental Truth that transcends all dualism." Master Nansen is actually holding up a cat in front of you. He is not inviting you to philosophical discussion or religious argument. If you refer to the Fundamental Wisdom, he will demand, "Show me that cat of the Fundamental Wisdom right here!" He insists on seeing your Zen presentation.

Be no-self; be thoroughly no-self. When you are really no-self, is there a distinction between you and the world? You and the cat? You and Nansen? Is there a distinction between the cat killed and Nansen the killer? At any cost, first you have to be actually no-self; this is the first and the absolute requisite in Zen. The word to save the cat will then naturally come out of you like lightning. Actual training and experience are definitely needed in Zen.

There are seldom truly capable men, either in the past or today. Many disciples were there with Nansen, but none of them could speak out to meet their teacher's request. "No monk could answer," the koan says. Keeping back his tears, probably, Nansen "finally killed the cat." We can read from the word "finally" with what a bleeding heart he killed it.

Be that as it may, "Nansen finally killed the cat" is a precipitous barrier in this koan which has to be broken through in actual training and discipline. The Zen Master will certainly grill the student, "What is the real meaning of Nansen's killing the cat?" If you are unable to give a concrete and satisfactory answer to him, your Zen eye is not opened. Only those who grasp the real meaning of killing the cat are the ones who can save the cat.

Master Toin said, "What Nansen killed was not only the cat concerned, but cats called Buddhas, cats called Patriarchs, are all cut away. Even the arayashiki, which is their abode, is completely cut away, and a refreshing wind is blowing throughout." Though rightly stated, it still sounds very much like an argumentative pretext not based on actual training and experience.

Master Seccho of *Hekigan-roku* commented on Nansen's killing the cat quite severely, "Fortunately Nansen took a correct action. A sword straightaway cuts it in two! Criticize it as you like." However, referring to the comment, "A sword straightaway cuts in two!" Dogen said, "A sword straightaway cuts it—no cut!" and pointed out quite a different standpoint. In other words, he is asking us to see "it," which no sword can ever cut, in Nansen's work of Zen.

In my training days I took sanzen with my teacher who suddenly asked, "Setting aside Nansen's killing the cat, where is the dead cat cut by Nansen right now?" A moment's hesitation in replying to his severe demand would immediately result in thirty blows of his stick, for it would clearly show that neither Nansen's killing the cat nor Dogen's "A sword straightaway cuts it—no-cut!" is really understood. Sanzen in Zen training is not so easy as outsiders may generally think.

A Zen man should be able to freely express and live his Zen in his killing, if he kills the cat. If the cat is killed, the whole universe is killed, and his Zen is at work in the dead cat. Otherwise he has not got even a glimpse of the real significance of this koan. Traditionally, he can never study Zen apart from his actual self—here, now. Intellectual and common-sense interpretations of koan may be possible, but they are all by-products.

The scene of the koan changes here. In the evening Joshu, well known as an outstanding monk under Nansen, came back to the monastery. Nansen told him what had happened while he was away. Hearing it, Joshu took off his sandal, put it on his head, and walked out of the room without a word. Nansen, seeing this, praised Joshu, saying, "If you had been with us there on that occasion, I could have saved the cat!" "The father well understands his child, and the child his father." They are in complete accord in silence.

Now, what is the real meaning of Joshu's putting a sandal on his head? Further, how can it save the cat? This is the vital point in the latter half of the koan. Here again, unfortunately, there are hardly any books that show an authentic Zen point of view on what Joshu did, because these authors themselves have not actually broken through the barrier of Nansen's killing the cat.

Master Dogen very aptly said, "Death: just death all through—complete manifestation!" When you die, just die. When you just die thoroughly and completely, you will have transcended life and death. Then, for the first time, free and creative Zen life and work will be developed. There, cats and dogs, mountains and rivers, sandals and hats, will all transcend their old names and forms and be given new birth in the new world. This is the wonder of revival. In this new world the old provisional names all lose their significance. Listen to an old Master who says,

> A man passes over the bridge.
> Lo! The bridge is flowing and the waters are unmoving.

It is said that Jesus Christ rose from death after his crucifixion. As I am not a Christian, I do not know the orthodox interpretation of the resurrection in Christianity. I myself believe, however, that Jesus' resurrection means to die in human flesh, and to revive as the Son of God transcending life and death. His resurrection means the advent of the Kingdom of God. It is the mysterious work of God to create the new and true world. There everybody, everything, lives in God, and all the provisional names and defilements of this earth are never found in the least.

Joshu availed himself of Nansen's killing the cat (i.e., the Great Death) as the opportunity for resurrection. Do not be deluded by old fixed names such as sandal or hat, a mountain or a river. A name is a temporary label given to Reality at one time at one place. Only when your attachments to such provisional given names are cast away will the Reality, the Truth, shine out. Joshu directly presented the Reality that can never be cut by anything. In this new world everything is revived with new significance. Why on earth do you have to cling to old provisional names? Joshu's action is the direct presentation of his Zen, which Master Nansen highly praised, saying, "If you had been there, I could have saved the cat!"

Master Shido Bunan illustrated the mystery of Zen working in his poem:

> Die while alive, and be completely dead,
> Then do whatever you will, all is good.

The first line, "Die while alive, and be completely dead," well describes Nansen's Zen at work, and the second line, "Then do whatever you will, all is good," refers to the working Zen of Joshu. Nansen's and Joshu's Zen are two yet one, one yet two. Master Mumon used this koan so that his disciples would grasp the mystery of Zen. Master Daito made the following poems on the koan. First, on "Nansen Kills a Cat":

> Nansen seizes the cat: lo! one, two, three!
> He kills it: behold, just solid iron!

Here all has been thoroughly cast away. The whole universe is just one finger. All has returned to One. Then, on "Joshu Puts a Sandal on His Head" Master Daito wrote:

> Joshu goes with a sandal on his head: lo! Three, two, one!
> Heaven is earth; earth is heaven!

Where Absolute Subjectivity works, the fixed ideas are of no avail. This is the world of Reality, or Truth, which transcends provisional names and labels, where everything is born anew with creative freedom.

Teisho on Mumon's Commentary

"You tell me, what is the real meaning of Joshu's putting his sandal on his head? If you can give the turning words on this point, you will see that Nansen's action was not in vain. If you cannot, beware!"

Master Mumon asks his disciples, "What is the real meaning of Joshu's putting his sandal on his head?" Master Daito, as I have quoted, admired the free working of Joshu in his poem, saying, "Heaven is earth; earth is heaven!" Where in the world is the source of this creative freedom? Cut, cut, cut! Cut everything away! When not only the cat, but Buddhist views and Dharma concepts are all cut away, leaving no trace behind, this creative freedom is yours. However, without actual hard searching and discipline you cannot expect to attain it. Mumon's address to his disciples is always from the standpoint of actual training. It is from this standpoint that he asks you to see the real significance of Nansen's action of Truth in Joshu's free presentation of Zen. In other words, he tells us to appreciate the wonder of resurrection in the fact of the Great Death. Then the killed cat will bloom in red as a flower; flow in blue as a stream. It is ever alive, not only with Master Joshu, but with you in your hand and in your foot today.

There is an old haiku poem in Japan:

A frog leaps into the water;
With that strength
It now floats.

It is interesting to read the poem in connection with this koan.

In the end Mumon admonishes his monks, "If you cannot, beware!" If you fail to grasp Nansen's and Joshu's Zen alive, and keep on chopping logic, you are in danger. You had better be killed once and for all by Nansen's sword.

Teisho on Mumon's Poem

Had Joshu only been there,
He would have taken action.

Had he snatched the sword away,
Nansen would have begged for his life.

Mumon says that if Joshu had been there when Master Nansen demanded, holding up the cat, "If you cannot say a word of Zen, I will kill the cat right away," it would have been Joshu who took the action of Truth of "One cut, all is cut!" Is it because they are both birds of the same feather? Only he who is capable of giving life is able to kill. Joshu was utterly free either to revive or to kill, to give or to take away. Such was the preeminent Zen ability of Joshu.

Placing wholehearted confidence in Joshu's Zen ability, Mumon says that if he had snatched the sword from Nansen even the great Master Nansen would have been unable to hold up his head before Joshu. Do not jump to the conclusion, however, that Joshu's work is good and Nansen's is not. When a Zen man wins, he just wins; that's all. When he loses, he just loses; that's all. No trace is left behind.

Master Mumon says, "If he had snatched the sword away." Let me ask you, "What kind of sword is this?" If it is the sword of the Fundamental Wisdom, not only Nansen but the cat, monks, mountains, and rivers all have to ask for their lives. Perhaps I have spoken too much.

Commentary on the Koan "Mu"

Hakuun Yasutani

TODAY I WILL TAKE UP the first case in *Mumonkan*, entitled "Joshu [on the inherent nature of a] dog." I will read the koan proper and then Mumon's comment:

> A monk in all seriousness asked Joshu: "Has a dog Buddha-nature or not?" Joshu retorted, "Mu!"

Mumon's Comment

In the practice of Zen you must pass through the barrier gate set up by the patriarchs. To realize this wondrous thing called enlightenment, you must cut off all [discriminating] thoughts. If you cannot pass through the barrier and exhaust the arising of thoughts, you are like a ghost clinging to the trees and grass.

What, then, is this barrier set by the patriarchs? It is Mu, the one barrier of the supreme teaching. Ultimately it is a barrier that is no barrier. One who has passed through it cannot only see Joshu face to face, but can walk hand in hand with the whole line of patriarchs. Indeed, he can, standing eyebrow to eyebrow, hear with the same ears and see with the same eyes.

How marvelous! Who would not want to pass through this barrier? For this you must concentrate day and night, questioning yourself through every one of your 360 bones and 84,000 pores. Do not construe Mu as nothingness and do not conceive it in terms of existence or non-existence. [You must reach the point where you feel] as though you had swallowed a red-hot iron ball that you cannot disgorge despite your every effort. When you have cast away all illusory thoughts and discriminations, and inside and outside are as one, you will be like a mute who has had a dream [but is unable to talk about it]. Once you burst into enlightenment you will astound the heavens and shake the earth. As though having captured the great sword of General Kuan, you will be able to slay the Buddha should you meet him [and he obstruct you] and dispatch all patriarchs you encounter [should they hinder you]. Facing life and death, you are utterly free; in the Six Realms of Existence and the Four Modes of Birth you move about in a samadhi of innocent delight.

How then, do you achieve this? Devote yourself to Mu energetically and wholeheartedly. If you continue this way without intermission, your mind will, like a light flashed on in the dark, suddenly become bright. Wonderful indeed!

Mumon's Verse

> A dog, Buddha-nature!
> This is the presentation of the whole,
>   the absolute imperative!
> Once you begin to think "has" or "has not"
> You are as good as dead.

The protagonist of this koan is Joshu, a renowned Chinese Zen master. I think it would be better to refer to him as the Patriarch Joshu. Inasmuch as my commentary on today's koan will be quite long, I shall omit telling you the facts of Joshu's life. Suffice it to say he was, as you all know, a great patriarch of Zen. While there are numerous koans centering around him, without a doubt this is one of the best known. Master Mumon worked zealously on it for six years and finally came to Self-realization. Evidently it made a deep impression on him, for he placed it first in the collection of his forty-eight koans. Actually there is no particular reason why this koan should be first—any of the others could have been placed at the head just as well—but Mumon's feeling for it was so intimate that he naturally put it at the very beginning.

The first line reads: "A monk *in all seriousness* asked Joshu..." That is, his question was neither frivolous nor casual but deeply considered.

The next portion, "Has a dog Buddha-nature or not?" raises the question: What is Buddha-nature? A well-known passage in the *Nirvana Sutra* states that every sentient being has Buddha-nature. The expression "every sentient being" means all existence. Not alone human beings, but animals, even plants, are sentient beings. Accordingly, a dog, a monkey, a dragonfly, a worm equally have Buddha-nature according to the *Nirvana Sutra*. In the context of this koan, however, you may consider the term as referring only to animals.

What then is Buddha-nature? Briefly, the nature of everything is such that it can become Buddha. Now, some of you, thinking there is something called *the* Buddha-nature hidden within us, may inquire as to the whereabouts of this Buddha-nature. You may tend to equate it with conscience, which everyone, even the wicked, is presumed to possess. You will never understand the truth of Buddha-nature so long as you harbor such a specious view. The Patriarch Dogen interpreted this expression in the *Nirvana Sutra* to mean that what is intrinsic to all sentient beings is Buddha-nature, and not that all sentient beings have something called *the* Buddha-nature. Thus in Dogen's view there is only Buddha-nature, nothing else.

In Buddhism, "Buddha-nature" is an intimate expression and "Dharma-nature" an impersonal one. But whether we say Buddha-nature or Dharma-nature, the substance is the same. One who has become enlightened to the Dharma is a Buddha; hence Buddha arises from Dharma. The *Diamond Sutra* says that all Buddhas and their enlightenment issue from this Dharma. Dharma, it follows, is the mother of Buddhahood. Actually there is neither mother nor son, for as I have said, it is the same whether you say Buddha or Dharma.

What is the Dharma of Dharma-nature? Dharma means phenomena. What we ordinarily term phenomena—that is, what is evident to the senses—in Buddhism is called Dharma. The word "phenomena," since it relates only to the observable features without implying what causes them to appear, has a limited connotation. These phenomena are termed Dharma (or Law) simply because they appear neither by accident nor through the will of some special agency superintending the universe. All phenomena are the result of the operation of the law of cause and effect. They arise when causes and conditions governing them mature. When one of these causes or conditions becomes altered, these phenomena change correspondingly. When the combination of causes and conditions completely disintegrates, the form itself disappears. All existence being the expression of the law of cause and effect, all phenomena are equally this Law, this Dharma. Now, as there are multiple modes of existence, so there are multiple dharmas corresponding to these existences. The substance of these manifold dharmas we call Dharma-nature. Whether we say Dharma-nature or use the more personal term Buddha-nature, these expressions refer to one reality. Stated differently, all phenomena are transformations of Buddha- or Dharma-nature. Everything by its very nature is subject to the process of infinite transformation—this is its Buddha- or Dharma-nature.

What is the substance of this Buddha- or Dharma-nature? In Buddhism it is called *ku [shunyata]*. Now, ku is not mere emptiness. It is that which is living, dynamic, devoid of mass, unfixed, beyond individuality or personality—the matrix of all phenomena. Here we have the fundamental principle or doctrine or philosophy of Buddhism.

For the Buddha Shakyamuni this was not mere theory but truth which he directly realized. With the experience of enlightenment, which is the source of all Buddhist doctrine, you grasp the world of ku. This world—unfixed, devoid of mass, beyond individuality or personality—is outside the realm of imagination. Accordingly, the true substance of things, that is, their Buddha- or Dharma-nature, is inconceivable and inscrutable. Since everything imaginable partakes of form or color, whatever one imagines to be Buddha-nature must of necessity be unreal. Indeed, that which can be conceived is but a picture of Buddha-nature, not Buddha-nature itself. But while Buddha-nature is beyond all conception and imagination, because we ourselves are intrinsically Buddhanature, it is possible for us to awaken to it. Only through the experience of enlightenment, however, can we affirm it in the Heart. Enlightenment therefore is all.

Once you realize the world of ku you will readily comprehend the nature of the phenomenal world and cease clinging to it. What we see is illusory, without substance, like the antics of puppets in a film. Are you afraid to die? You need not be. For whether you are killed or die naturally, death has no more substantiality than the movements of these puppets. Or to put it another way, it is no more real than the cutting of air with a knife, or the bursting of bubbles, which reappear no matter how often they are broken.

Having once perceived the world of Buddha-nature, we are indifferent to death since we know we will be reborn through affinity with a father and a mother. We are reborn when our karmic relations impel us to be reborn. We die when our karmic relations decree that we die. And we are killed when our karmic relations lead us to be killed. We are the manifestation of our karmic relations at any given moment, and upon their modification we change accordingly. What we call life is no more than a procession of transformations. If we do not change, we are lifeless. We grow and age because we are alive. The evidence of our having lived is the fact that we die. We die because we are alive. Living means birth and death. Creation and destruction signify life.

When you truly understand this fundamental principle you will not be anxious about your life or your death. You will then attain a steadfast mind and be happy in your daily life. Even though heaven and earth were turned upside down, you would have no fear. And if an atomic or hydrogen bomb were exploded, you would not quake in terror. So long as you become one with the bomb, what would there be to fear? "Impossible!" you say. But whether you wanted to or not, you would perforce become one with it, would you not? By the same token, if you were caught in a holocaust, inevitably you would be burnt. Therefore become one with fire when there is no escaping it! If you fall into poverty, live that way without grumbling—then your poverty will not be a burden to you. Likewise, if you are rich, live with your riches. All this is the functioning of Buddha-nature. In short, Buddha-nature has the quality of infinite adaptability.

Coming back to the koan, we must approach the question, "Has a dog Buddha-nature or not?" with caution, since we do not know whether the monk is ignorant or is feigning ignorance in order to test Joshu. Should Joshu answer either "It has" or "It has not," he would be cut down. Do you see why? Because what is involved is not a matter of "has" or "has not." Everything being Buddha-nature, either answer would be absurd. But this is "Dharma dueling." Joshu must parry the thrust. He does so by sharply retorting, "Mu!" Here the dialogue ends.

In other versions of the dialogue between Joshu and the monk the latter continues by inquiring: "Why hasn't a dog Buddha-nature when the *Nirvana Sutra* says all sentient beings do have it?" Joshu countered with: "Because it has ignorance and attachment." What this means is that the dog's Buddha-nature is not other than karma. Acts performed with a delusive mind produce painful results. This is karma. In plainer words, a dog is a dog as a result of its past karma's conditioning it to become a dog. This is the functioning of Buddha-nature. So do not talk as though there were a particular thing called "Buddha-nature." This is the implication of Joshu's Mu. It is clear, then, that Mu has nothing to do with the existence or non-existence of Buddha-nature but is itself Buddha-nature. The retort "Mu!" exposes and at the same time fully thrusts Buddha-nature before us. Now while you may be unable to fully understand what I am saying, you will not go astray if you construe Buddha-nature in this manner.

Buddha-nature cannot be grasped by the intellect. To experience it directly you must search your mind with the utmost devotion until you are absolutely convinced of its existence, for, after all, you yourself are this Buddha-nature. When I told you earlier that Buddha-nature was ku—impersonal, devoid of mass, unfixed, and capable of endless transformation—I merely offered you a portrait of it. It is possible to *think* of Buddha-nature in these terms, but you must understand that whatever you can conceive or imagine must necessarily be unreal. Hence there is no other way than to experience the truth in your own mind. This way has been shown, with the greatest kindness, by Mumon.

Let us now consider Mumon's comment. He begins by saying: "In the practice of Zen..." Zazen, receiving dokusan [that is, private instructions], hearing teisho—these are all Zen practice. Being attentive in the details of your daily life is also training in Zen. When your life and Zen are one you are truly living Zen. Unless it accords with your everyday activities Zen is merely an embellishment. You must be careful not to flaunt Zen but to blend it unpretentiously into your life. To give a concrete example of attentiveness: when you step out of the clogs at the porch or the kitchen or out of the slippers of the toilet room, you must be careful to arrange them neatly so that the next person can use them readily even in the dark. Such mindfulness is a practical demonstration of Zen. If you put your clogs or shoes on absent-mindedly you are not attentive. When you walk you must step watchfully so that you do not stumble or fall. Do not become remiss!

But I am digressing. To continue: "...you must pass through the barrier gate set up by the patriarchs." Mu is just such a barrier. I have already indicated to you that, from the first, there is no barrier. Everything being Buddha-nature, there is no gate through which to go in or out. But in order to awaken us to the truth that everything is Buddha-nature, the patriarchs reluctantly set up barriers and goad us into passing through them. They condemn our faulty practice and reject our incomplete answers. As you steadily grow in sincerity you will one day suddenly come to Self-realization. When this happens you will be able to pass through the barrier gate easily. The *Mumonkan* is a book containing forty-eight such barriers.

The next line begins: "To realize this wondrous thing called enlightenment..." Observe the word "wondrous." Because enlightenment is unexplainable and inconceivable it is described as wondrous. "...you must cut off all [discriminating] thoughts." This means that it is useless to approach Zen from the standpoint of supposition or logic. You can never come to enlightenment through inference, cognition, or conceptualization. Cease clinging to all thought-forms! I stress this, because it is the central point of Zen practice. And particularly do not make the mistake of thinking enlightenment must be this or that.

"If you cannot pass through the barrier and exhaust the arising of thoughts, you are like a ghost clinging to the trees and grass." Ghosts do not appear openly in the daytime, but come out furtively after dark, it is said, hugging the earth or clinging to willow trees. They are dependent upon these supports for their very existence. In a sense human beings are also ghostlike, since most of us cannot function independent of money, social standing, honor, companionship, authority; or else we feel the need to identify ourselves with an organization or an ideology. If you would be a man of true worth and not a phantom, you must be able to walk upright by yourself, dependent on nothing. When you harbor philosophical concepts or religious beliefs or ideas or theories of one kind or another, you too are a phantom, for inevitably you become bound to them. Only when your mind is empty of such abstractions are you truly free and independent.

The next two sentences read: "What, then, is this barrier set by the patriarchs? It is Mu, the one barrier of the supreme teaching." The supreme teaching is not a system of morality but that which lies at the root of all such systems, namely, Zen. Only that which is of unalloyed purity, free from the superstitious or the supernatural, can be called the root of all teachings and therefore supreme. In Buddhism Zen is the only teaching which is not to one degree or another tainted with elements of the supernatural—thus Zen alone can truly be called the supreme teaching and Mu the one barrier of this supreme teaching. You can understand "one barrier" to mean the sole barrier or one out of many. Ultimately there is no barrier.

"One who has passed through it cannot only see Joshu face to face…." Since we are living in another age, of course we cannot actually see the physical Joshu. To "see Joshu face to face" means to understand his Mind. "…can walk hand in hand with the whole line of patriarchs." The line of patriarchs begins with Maha Kashyapa, who succeeded the Buddha, it goes on to Bodhidharma, the twentieth-eighth, and continues right up to the present. "…eyebrow to eyebrow…" is a figure of speech implying great intimacy. "…hear with the same ears and see with the same eyes" connotes the ability to look at things from the same viewpoint as the Buddha and Bodhidharma. It implies, of course, that we have clearly grasped the world of enlightenment.

"How marvelous!" Marvelous indeed! Only those who recognize the preciousness of the Buddha, the Dharma, and the patriarchs can appreciate such an exclamation. Yes, how truly marvelous! Those who do not care for the Buddha and the Dharma may feel anything but marvel, but that cannot be helped.

"Who would not want to pass through this barrier?"—this phrase aims at enticing you to search for the truth within yourself. "For this you must concentrate day and night, questioning yourself [about Mu] through every one of your 360 bones and 84,000 pores." These figures reflect the thinking of the ancients, who believed that the body was constructed in this fashion. In any case, what this refers to is your entire being. Let all of you become one mass of doubt and questioning. Concentrate on and penetrate fully into Mu. To penetrate into Mu means to achieve absolute unity with it. How can you achieve this unity? By holding to Mu tenaciously day and night! Do not separate yourself from it under any circumstances! Focus your mind on it constantly. "Do not construe Mu as nothingness and do not conceive it in terms of existence or non-existence." You must not, in other words, think of Mu as a problem involving the existence or non-existence of Buddha-nature. Then what do you do? You stop speculating and concentrate wholly on Mu—just Mu!

Do not dawdle, practice with every ounce of energy. "[You must reach the point where you feel] as though you had swallowed a red-hot iron ball..." It is hyperbole, of course, to speak of swallowing a red-hot iron ball. However, we often carelessly swallow a hot rice-cake which, lodging in the throat, causes considerable discomfort. Once you swallow Mu up you will likewise feel intensely uncomfortable and try desperately to dislodge it. "...that you cannot disgorge despite your every effort"— this describes the state of those who work on this koan. Because Self-realization is so tantalizing a prospect they cannot quit; neither can they grasp Mu's significance readily. So there is no other way for them but to concentrate on Mu until they "turn blue in the face."

The comparison with a red-hot iron ball is apt. You must melt down your illusions with the red-hot iron ball of Mu stuck in your throat. The opinions you hold and your worldly knowledge are your illusions. Included also are philosophical and moral concepts, no matter how lofty, as well as religious beliefs and dogmas, not to mention innocent, commonplace thoughts. In short, all conceivable ideas are embraced within the term "illusions" and as such are a hindrance to the realization of your Essential-nature. So dissolve them with the fireball of Mu!

You must not practice fitfully. You will never succeed if you do zazen only when you have the whim to, and give up easily. You must carry on steadfastly for one, two, three, or even five years without remissions, constantly vigilant. Thus you will gradually gain in purity. At first you will not be able to pour yourself wholeheartedly into Mu. It will escape you quickly because your mind will start to wander. You will have to concentrate harder—just "Mu! Mu! Mu!" Again it will elude you. Once more you attempt to focus on it and again you fail. This is the usual pattern in the early stages of practice. Even when Mu does not slip away, your concentration becomes disrupted because of various mind defilements. These defilements disappear in time, yet since you have not achieved oneness with Mu you are still far from ripe. Absolute unity with Mu, unthinking absorption in Mu—this is ripeness. Upon your attainment to this stage of purity, both inside and outside naturally fuse. "Inside and outside" has various shades of meaning. It may be understood as meaning subjectivity and objectivity or mind and body. When you fully absorb yourself in Mu, the eternal and internal merge into a single unity. But, unable to speak about it, you will be like "a mute who has had a dream." One who is dumb is unable to talk about his dream of the night before. In the same way, you will relish the taste of samadhi yourself but be unable to tell others about it.

At this stage Self-realization will abruptly take place. Instantaneously! "Bursting into enlightenment" requires but an instant. It is as though an explosion had occurred. When this happens you will experience so much! "You will astound the heavens and shake the earth." Everything will appear so changed that you will think heaven and earth have been overturned. Of course there is not literal toppling over. With enlightenment you see the world as Buddha-nature, but this does not mean that all becomes as radiant as a halo. Rather, each thing *just as it is* takes on an entirely new significance or worth. Miraculously, everything is radically transformed though remaining as it is.

This is how Mumon describes it: "As though having captured the great sword of General Kuan..." General Kuan was a courageous general who was invincible in combat with his "blue-dragon" sword. So Mumon says you will become as powerful as he who captures the "blue-dragon" sword of General Kuan. Which is to say that nothing untoward can happen to you. Through Self-realization one acquires self-confidence and an imposing bearing. When one comes before the roshi his manner implies, "Test me in any way you wish," and such is his assurance that he could even thrash the master.

"...you will be able to slay the Buddha should you meet him and dispatch all the patriarchs you encounter." The timid will be flabbergasted when they hear this and denounce Zen as an instrument of the devil. Others, less squeamish yet equally unable to understand the spirit of these words, will feel uneasy. To be sure, Buddhism inspires in us the utmost respect for all Buddhas. But at the same time it admonishes us that eventually we must free ourselves from that attachment to them.

When we have experienced the Mind of Shakyamuni Buddha and cultivated his incomparable virtues, we have realized the highest aim of
Buddhism. Then we bid him farewell, shouldering the task of propagat-
ing his teachings. I have never heard of such an attitude in religions teaching belief in God. While the aim of the Buddhist is to become a Buddha,
nevertheless, to put it bluntly, you can slay the Buddha and all the patriarchs. You who realize enlightenment will be able to say: "Were the honored Shakyamuni and the great Bodhidharma to appear, I would cut them
down instantly, demanding: 'Why do you totter forth? You are no longer
needed!'" Such will be your resoluteness.

"Facing life and death, you are utterly free; in the Six Realms of Existence and the Four Modes of Birth you move about in a samadhi of innocent delight." You will be able to face death and rebirth without anxiety.
The Six Realms are the realms of maya, namely, hell, the worlds of pretas
[hungry ghosts], beasts, asuras [fighting demons], human beings, and
devas [heavenly beings]. The Four Modes of Birth are birth through the
womb, birth through eggs hatched outside the body, birth through moisture, and birth through metamorphosis. To be born in heaven and hell,
since it requires no physical progenitors, is birth through metamorphosis.
Who ever heard of a heavenly being that had to undergo the trauma of
being born? There are neither midwives nor obstetricians in heaven or hell.

Wherever you may be born, and by whatever means, you will be able
to live with the spontaneity and joy of children at play—this is what is
meant by a "samadhi of innocent delight." Samadhi is complete absorption. Once you are enlightened you can descend to the deepest hell or rise
to the highest heaven with freedom and rapture.

"How, then, do you achieve this?" Through zazen. "Devote yourself
to Mu energetically and wholeheartedly." Persevere with all the force of
your body and spirit. "If you continue this way without intermission..."
You must not start and then quit. You must carry on to the very end, like
a hen sitting on an egg until she hatches it. You must concentrate on Mu
unflinchingly, determined not to give up until you attain kensho.
"...your mind will, like a lamp flashed on in the dark, suddenly become
bright. Wonderful indeed!" With enlightenment the mind, released from
the darkness of its infinite past, will brighten immediately. "Wonderful
indeed!" is added since nothing could be more wonderful.

The first line of Mumon's verse reads: "A dog, Buddha-nature"—there is no need for "nature. "A dog *is* Buddha—"is" is superfluous. "A dog, Buddha"—still redundant. "Dog!"—that's enough! Or just "Buddha!" You have said too much when you say "A dog *is* Buddha." "Dog!"—that is all. It is completely Buddha.

"This is the...whole, the absolute imperative!" That is to say, it is the authentic decree of Shakyamuni Buddha—it is the correct Dharma. You are this Dharma to perfection! It is not being begrudged—it is fully revealed!

"Once you begin to think 'has' or 'has not' you are as good as dead." What does "you are as good as dead" mean? Simply that your precious Buddha life [of Oneness] will vanish.

Roso (Luzu) Faces the Wall

Taizan Maezumi

Book of Equanimity, Case 23

Preface to the Assembly

Bodhidharma's nine years are known as "wall-gazing." Shinko's three prostrations are outflowings of heavenly activity. How can the traces be swept away, the footprints be eliminated?

Main Case

Attention! Whenever Roso saw a monk coming, he would face the wall. Hearing of this, Nansen remarked. "I always tell others to receive directly even before the empty kalpa, and to realize even before the Buddha came into the world—but still I haven't found half a man, let alone a man. If he is thus, he will be stuck in the Year of the Donkey."

Appreciatory Verse

> Plain water has flavor, subtly transcending the senses.
> It precedes forms, though seeming endlessly to exist.
> The Way is precious, though seeming massively to be foolish.
> Inscribe designs on a jewel and its glory is lost.
> A pearl even from an abyss naturally beckons.
> Plenty of bracing air purely burnishes off autumn's swelter;
> Far away a single tranquil cloud divides sky and water.

Preface to the Assembly

Today is already the third day of sesshin. When you sit well, from around the third day, you can sit better and go deeper into samadhi. Before I begin to interpret these lines, I want to say that I don't know how much you can get out of them. But regardless of where each of us stands, or how long we have practiced, I appreciate each one of us equally, including myself.

In the preface, "Bodhidharma's nine years" of wall-gazing are mentioned. How much do we understand Bodhidharma? How much do we appreciate Bodhidharma? Indeed, it's really amazing how much just one person can do. The second line says "Shinko." Shinko was the successor of Bodhidharma. He was Chinese. Probably without Shinko we couldn't have had such a prosperous Zen heritage; nor would such a heritage have been possible without Bodhidharma.

These days, communication has been so well-developed that being in this country, you can get practically anything from anywhere in the world in a few days if you really want to. But fifteen hundred years ago, how was it? This country became independent only two hundred years ago. Even five hundred years ago, it's hard to imagine how this country was—just deserts, coastlines, the plains, the forests, and very few Indians living with lots of animals. One hundred years ago, how was Los Angeles? When we think of this historical development, it fascinates us. Fifteen hundred years ago, what happened?

Bodhidharma spent three years just to come from India to China. These three years...it strains our imagination to conceive of the difficulties he must have had, and you may not even believe how old he was— over one hundred years old. It is said he was close to one hundred twenty. Almost unbelievable! Prior to coming to China, he expounded the teaching in India for over sixty years. And before those sixty years of work in India, he served his teacher Hannyatara for forty years. Hannyatara was the favorite priest for the king who was Bodhidharma's father. Bodhidharma was the third son, and even as a child he was a brilliant person. Around the age of ten he was already fairly well enlightened. Anyway, it's altogether an unbelievable story. Then his teacher, Venerable Hannyatara died. He told Bodhidharma, "After sixty or seventy years, go to China. Then expound this teaching in the land of China." So Bodhidharma took his teacher's last will, last advice.

In this country people often ask me, "Bodhidharma was sitting nine years facing the wall—did he want to have enlightenment?" Nine years of just wall-gazing. Of course, that refers to Roso facing the wall in the main case—just wall contemplation, nothing else. Then what is the wall? Those of you doing shikan taza: it's supposed to be wall contemplation. What is the wall? Where is the wall? Some of you are working on muji. Those who are, better memorize all the words that Mumon uses in the comment on the first chapter in the *Gateless Gate*. In that comment he uses the phrase "silver mountain, iron wall." If you contemplate muji, you can't think about it. That's what Mumon says in the beginning, you can't think about it. If you think, that's okay, you think. Sooner or later, you get stuck. When you really get stuck, that's the place, the silver mountain, the iron wall. So, how do you remove it? How do you take care of it? How do you release yourself from such an obstacle? In shikan taza you have to face something else. So, what is it? How do you take care of it?

"Bodhidharma's nine years are known as 'wall-gazing'." Bodhidharma said something like this: "Externally, you eliminate relations between yourself and objects. And internally, don't be grasping." *Aegu* literally means (Roshi breathes deeply). That's physically, see. But mentally—the mental condition is more important—or the psychological, or emotional condition, whatever you call it. Don't be graspy, be peaceful, quiet. Make your mind like a wall. Then enter into the Way. The key is this *shin shoheki*. Make your mind like the wall. Wall-gazing, that's what it is. The wall stands for immovability, solidity. If you're really solid, unmovable, nothing will disturb you. It's not like a piece of stone or rock, even in the first stage, when you stop making contact with external objects. It doesn't mean to be like a dead man. "Perceiving everything, yet undisturbed," that's what it means.

A number of you are working on muji. One of you in dokusan expressed, "I really wish to climb up the silver mountain, the iron wall." How do you climb up? How do you crash through? The silver mountain and iron wall themselves are nothing but muji. So it's a very simple principle. Just be so. That's the way to take care of it.

Bodhidharma's wall-gazing is the same thing. Make your mind as the wall, be the wall. Then get into that. That's shikan taza. It is the immovable state, and yet in that state all activity is taking place. That's what Roso is doing here—expressing himself totally in that state. What he has been expressing can't be described by words. But that's what Nansen is trying to do. They are practically talking about the same thing.

"Shinko's three prostrations are outflowings of heavenly activity." "Shinko's three prostrations" has its origin in a story which I think you have heard. Bodhidharma had four Dharma successors. Maybe on one of the very last days of his life, Bodhidharma asked these four, "Tell me, what is your understanding, realization?" Then the four of them expressed their understanding.

The first one was Dofuku. What he said is something like this: "My understanding, realization, is not to be apart from words, and not to stick to words. And I freely use words."

The second person was the nun Soji, the daughter of Emperor Wu in the Yang Dynasty. What she said is something like this: "My realization is something like Ananda's when he saw the Buddhaland. He just glanced at it and never looked back again."

The third person, Doiku, said: "The four elements—earth, water, fire, wind—not only make up the world, but also the human body, and are originally empty."

Bodhidharma said to the first, "You have gained my skin." To the second: "You have gained my flesh." To the third: "You have gained my bones."

The last was Shinko, the Second Patriarch, Eka Daishi. He made three bows, and then just stood beside him without saying anything. Bodhidharma then said: "You have gained my marrow."

Dogen Zenji writes someplace in the *Shobogenzo*, "Do not think that skin, flesh, bone, and marrow are different depths of their understanding. Their understanding is equal." So that's where "Shinko's three prostrations are outflowings of heavenly activity" comes from. In his silence, and in his three prostrations, the very best activity is expressed effectively. His three prostrations are nothing but the expression of the dharma itself. That's what Bansho means by outflowings of heavenly activity.

"How can the traces be swept away, the footprints be eliminated?" Even though he did all right, isn't there kind of a trace or footprint still left? It is true whether he prostrated himself three times or not. Dharma is all over, anytime, everywhere. That finishes the Preface to the Assembly and brings up the Main Case.

Tomorrow is already the middle of the sesshin. As you know, the last half goes much faster than the first. In this country, as long as you sit as you have been doing, in one way or another this Way will grow. You are responsible, regardless of male or female, monk, nun, or layperson. So please, really take it seriously. That's the reason I talked about Bodhidharma and the others in such a way. It might encourage you to practice harder and better. Regardless of how hard we try, we can hardly pay our debts to them.

Teisho on the Main Case

Today is already the middle day of this sesshin. I think each of you might have been realizing that the atmosphere in the zendo while you are sitting is getting much more subtle; it is settling down. I noticed those who are in charge of the zendo are encouraging your sitting. Especially for those who are working on muji, please don't be hasty. That's no good. Ideally speaking, just sit well. Let it ripen.

This morning while holding dokusan, I had a flash of thought about the difference between koan study and shikan taza. As I mention from time to time, they are the same thing. Of course they are different, different and yet the same. Along with the lines we appreciate today, we will consider this matter, too. At any rate, since we are already in the last part of this sesshin, please—every bit of a second—take good care of it.

"Whenever Roso saw a monk coming, he would face the wall." What was he doing? A case such as this is really good for us to appreciate in as minute detail as possible. Whenever the monk came after him, he did so without even saying a single word. Regardless of what kind of questions the monk asked him, he just turned around and faced the wall. What is he showing? What is he expressing? What do you hear? He is expressing more than words can express. He is expounding the Dharma which cannot be expressed in words. That's shikan taza.

Maybe you have heard or read about various kinds of zazen. In one way or another, every religion has some kind of meditation. Even in Christianity you have meditation. Prayer itself, in a way, is almost like meditation. Hindus meditate, and so do Taoists, and maybe even Confucianists from time to time. They call it quiet thinking. In Yasutani Roshi's book you see *bompu* Zen, *gedo* Zen, *shojo* Zen, *daijo* Zen and *saijojo* Zen. The purposes of meditation can be different, such as for health. Health is not an insulting word. Non-Buddhists have meditation, but their purposes are different. Some practice in order to acquire occult powers. That's *gedo* Zen. They practice in order to improve the physical condition, in order to acquire stronger concentration or in order to center themselves and make themselves stronger. I'm not sure if it's appropriate or not, but these could be called Hinayana Zen. They're just concerned about their own salvation or liberation. All these meditations or Zen are in one way or another leaky. We say *urojo*. *Jo* is "samadhi." *Uro* means "there is a leak," "there is delusion."

Then we say *murojo*, "no leak in the samadhi." That's the Zen we have been transmitting. That's what Bodhidharma carried from India to China. Then what makes no leak? Wisdom. So, in one way or another we should become aware of that wisdom. Roso and Nansen are brother monks under Master Baso. Here they are expounding the wisdom from two different perspectives, like from the front and the back. Actually, they are doing the same thing.

Roso's facing the wall: It's an outflowing of heavenly activity. He's just showing the visiting monk the very first principle of life. Everything is just as it is—however, whatever, you see.

And Bansho puts *jakugo* on this: "I have met him already." In Japan an important procedure the first time you meet the roshi is to prepare your own incense, then burn it, show your respect and have your first meeting. That's called *shoken*, and we are not doing it here. Bansho says, "Shokenryo" (I have met him already). Who is Roso? He is manifesting himself as muji, or whatever you name it. So where do you meet Master Roso? Where and how? As a matter of fact, that's what all of us are doing here. Also, who is he? To realize each one of us without exception is Roso himself—to realize what is called kensho. You have been constantly meeting him, yet somehow there is something in between. That's what Nansen is trying to clarify. Being brother monks, they know each other quite well.

I want to mention another thing. You may have heard it said, "In the Rinzai school they use koans and in the Soto school we don't use koans." This Roso belongs to the same lineage as Rinzai. Actually, he lived prior to Rinzai, but their common lineage stems from Nangaku Ejo, a Dharma successor of the Sixth Patriarch. One of Nangaku Ejo's Dharma successors was Master Baso. And Baso was the teacher of Nansen and Roso. Then see what it says. Whenever whoever comes, he just turns around without even saying a single word, and sits. That was his way to free the students, the monks. I one hundred percent guarantee no Soto school teacher nowadays does what he did! So it's all up to the individual teacher, and also his training background, and also his wisdom and his awareness as to how to expound the truth. So in general, regarding our practice, we'd better not be partial.

"Hearing of this, Nansen remarked, 'I always tell others to receive directly even before the empty kalpa.'" A kalpa is a measurement of time. [There are different definitions, but one is: Take a rock that's ten cubic miles, and once every century an angel flies down and her wings brush against the rock. When the rock wears out, that's one kalpa.]

Anyway, we can't even imagine how long a kalpa is. There are four kalpas: the kalpa of growth, the kalpa of dwelling, the kalpa of decay, and the empty kalpa. Even before the empty kalpa, you receive. What does that mean? Here the empty kalpa stands for the time before your conscious mind arises. Receive directly. How much is the distance between the empty kalpa and right now?

> I always tell others to receive directly even before the empty
> kalpa, and to realize even before the Buddha came into the
> world.

After Buddha appeared, people started to worry about delusion and enlightenment. We are deluded. He's enlightened. What's that? Prior to such a dualistic way of dealing with life, immediately grasp what life is.

"—but still I haven't found half a man, let alone a man." These are a kind of figure of speech. It's very difficult to find the person. That is to say, only few can really appreciate.

"If he is thus," and Roso is just doing like that, "He will be stuck in the Year of the Donkey." There is no such year as the Year of the Donkey! In the Chinese calendar, which we also use in Japan, there is a cycle of twelve different years. First comes the mouse, then ox, tiger, rabbit, dragon, snake, horse, sheep, monkey, cock, dog, and bull. Unfortunately, we don't have the donkey. He is stuck in the Year of the Donkey. So, in other words, regardless of how many years you spend, you'll never come to an end.

So, all those working on breathing, please don't think that breathing as such is an exercise for beginners. Not at all so, not at all. We can say koan study was in existence since the time of the Buddha. But structured koan study as we know it is a very recent thing. Years ago, all they did was contemplate breathing as perhaps the most common practice. Then they attained awakening through that. But in almost twenty-five hundred years since the Buddha and the thousands of years before that in India, they developed effective means of practice. Each practice has its own unique advantages and disadvantages. But the point is this immovability, as Bodhidharma mentioned. It's not a sticky thing. Make your mind like a huge wall. Nothing, no one, can break through. Then your life becomes undistracted. So please have really good conviction and faith and trust in yourself, in your practice. And with deep devotion and aspiration, just keep on going.

Teisho on the Appreciatory Verse

Today is already the fifth day, tomorrow is the sixth day, and the next day sesshin will be over. Some of you must have fairly bad pain in your legs. It depends on the individual's bone and muscle structure—mostly the muscle structure and tight tendons. Some have more trouble or pain than others. Regardless of how much pain you have, I want you to sit well. If the pain is too bad, sitting on a chair is quite all right. Our practice is not asceticism. As Dogen Zenji said, zazen is supposed to be very comfortable and peaceful. So I want you to sit comfortably. But just being comfortable is not enough.

Before getting in too far, I want to review briefly what zazen is. We say *shikan taza*. In that phrase or word, we find "just sitting." *Shikan* is "just" or "only." *Ta* means "just me," practically nothing emphasized. And *za* means "sitting," "just sitting." But the point is to see the content of sitting. It should be sitting. Just physically sitting on the cushion is not sitting. Let the body sit, and also breathing sits, and your mind sits. In a sense, body and mind are not two but one. If you really make your body sit, mind is supposed to sit, too. So when you really make yourself sit, then that's zazen. Just sitting on the cushion, the mind wanders around. That's not zazen.

For convenience, we can sort of think in this way. First we have to physically sit. It's almost like catching a wild horse, tying it to a post. Then, gradually tame it. But it's running around, trying to get out. The first stage, to catch the horse and tie it, is almost like *za*, the sitting part. At the beginning, it's really painful, especially during sesshin. We have to get up early in the morning, sit until nine o'clock or so, all day long. Many of you have been struggling with it, just to sit. So then tame it down. That's the part of *zen*.

We try to calm our busy mind down, and soothe the painful body, get used to it and let the body take it. Originally, the word *zen*, as you know, derived from the Sanskrit term *dhyana*, which means "quiet thinking." Instead of letting our conscious mind go wild, think quietly. Let the body calm down first. Then try to let the mind calm down, too. Then in order to do so, as one of the effective means, we use techniques such as breathing. We concentrate on breathing by counting breaths or following breaths. Then try to calm it down.

The next process is to get into samadhi, really focus upon one single thing. Then become one with the object. So if you work on muji, become one with it. If you are counting the breath, become one with the counting. If you do shikan taza, become zazen yourself. By doing so, you get into samadhi. Then, when you really get into samadhi, eventually you forget yourself—dichotomy in one way or another is transcended.

First, what happens is you forget yourself; and technically, that stage is called, "man is forgotten, man empty." And yet there is the object on which you're concentrating. So you go farther into samadhi, then that object is also eliminated. That is called "dharma is empty." Then when that samadhi really ripens, we say, "both man and dharma are empty," and that state is called *Great Death*. That state is sort of the ideal condition of samadhi. But it's static. So remaining in that is no good. You forget about everything, but it's very static, no activity, no function. So it must function. That functioning of samadhi is wisdom. Once you really reach to that Great Death, then *Great Rebirth* will be in realization. So this is the fundamental principle, or process.

Then, the first opening-up or first breaking-through experience takes place along with emptying yourself. Even not completely emptying yourself in the ideal way, it happens. But when it's not complete, what you see is also rather limited and partial. That's what happens in many cases. In other words, before samadhi really ripens, you can have that experience. These days, we call that experience kensho. Strictly speaking, until you really come to the point where you eliminate subjects and objects altogether, you can't really say that you attain enlightenment as such. When you realize that, that's what great enlightenment means. So even for those who have had that breaking-through experience, in that sphere of emptying, practically each individual differs one from the other. The clarity is different. Maybe no two persons are exactly the same, because it is still partial.

What I want to emphasize is sitting itself. In order to get into that samadhi your sitting is supposed to be right. Otherwise, your mind just gets busy and you can't really get into the deep concentration.

When I look at it, some of your postures are much too weak. My posture isn't so good, especially when I talk and hold dokusan. My back is bent, almost like a cat. But it's supposed to be a very well-balanced posture. Again, just making your back straight is not quite enough.

Place the weight of the body in the proper place. The center of gravity of the body is supposed to fall in the center of the triangle formed by the two knees and the base of the spine. In order to do so, shift the gravity of your upper body slightly forward. Try to move altogether, almost like pushing in between your two hip joints. By doing so, the point of that gravity of the upper body is shifted.

When I look at your posture, some of you look rounded in your lower back. It's a very weak position and you can't really have that strength in your lower abdomen. So just making it straight is not enough. Shift it forward. Then don't make too much arch in your lower back. If you do too much, you start having pain. So, having that kind of disposition of the upper body, the center of gravity falls down into the center of the triangle. This is the base for sitting. Sensei has a crooked back, but even so he can do that. When I hold dokusan, I sit somewhat bent but still try to let the center of gravity fall down. When you sit, when you do zazen, please remember this and try to let your body really sit well.

When you sit like this, you will naturally start feeling slight tension in your lower abdomen, even without putting any artificial effort or strain on it. I want to remind you not to strain. That's what some of you do. Especially those who are working on muji have that tendency. Those concentrating on breathing become too conscious about it and unconsciously tighten up that stomach area trying to breathe deeply. That's very bad. Tightening the muscles around the stomach, the stomach can't function. So avoid that. And if you can't have any strength in the lower abdomen, I would rather advise you don't try pushing hard. Just wait until that strength comes naturally and try to have proper sitting. That's very important.

Another thing is to concentrate in the lower abdomen, the area known as the hara. It's like a centripetal force. Then, when you sit, you can imagine all of the energy of all parts of the body flowing back into that area, and at the same time that energy permeates into all parts of your body, too, so that going to the center and going out from the center, these two energies are balanced. That balanced condition is almost like zero. There is no conflict of any power or energy within the body. Physically, you can balance. Having that center of gravity placed in the lower portion of the abdomen, you are sitting in a very solid state. Then it starts creating, starts generating the energy by itself. That's what we call *joriki*, "power of stability." It's almost physical power. That's what I want you to acquire first.

Sometimes I say when you do sit well, this smoggy, dirty air of Los Angeles becomes tasty. That's true. I'm sure you don't believe it, but anyway, that's what it says in the appreciatory verse. The first line says, "Plain water has flavor."

Very plain but in that plainness, there is terrific taste. Water in a way is tasteless, but nobody really says that it's totally tasteless, not at all. Especially when we drink fresh spring water, especially during summer. Climb up the mountain and find the fountain or find the very chill spring. Drink it. What kind of taste does it have? Almost incredible taste. That's what Tendo says here, plain water has flavor.

Of course, this plain state—that's the state of zazen. It is Roso's wall-gazing, Bodhidharma's wall-gazing, and it also refers to your zazen, too.

It's plain. Who believes that we sit eight, nine, ten hours a day just doing nothing but sit? People say you're crazy. Right? They like beer or soda or Coca-Cola. It's more tasty for them. Like going to the beach or a picnic, it's more tasty. But in this zazen, when you really do it, there is terrific taste.

"Subtly transcending the senses." We translated *joi* as senses. But *joi* is more than that. *Jo* means "feeling" or "mind" or "emotion," and *i* means "words" or "verbal expression." That is what is transcended. In other words, that very subtle taste in zazen; it's indescribable. These lines refer to Roso's zazen.

"It precedes forms, though seeming endlessly to exist." What exists is that subtle taste, subtle zazen. The word we translated as form actually means our conscious mind, our discriminative mind. It says "seeming." By saying so, it gives more of a nuance than if it were just stated. Purposely, Master Tendo expresses it in that way. Thus it expresses the more subtle content of zazen. That's before your discriminative mind functions. That is to say, as long as you are being conscious of your discriminative mind, you can't appreciate this subtlety in zazen. You are just involved with your own talk or ideas. You can't go beyond that. Then you are bound by limited ideas. This subtle flavor precedes form, thought, and ideas. Then it endlessly exists.

"The Way is precious, though seeming massively to be foolish." It's a nice statement. Actually, that "massively" is a description of a high, solid mountain. In *Fukanzazengi* Dogen Zenji said, "Just like a mountain, sit and get into samadhi, sitting samadhi." Your zazen is supposed to be like a huge immovable mountain, just like a fool. Again, it refers to Master Roso. Whoever comes, he turns around and just sits, just like a fool. Seems like an idiot, like a fool, but he's not, and he's not a holy man either. He doesn't fall into enlightenment or delusion, good, bad, right or wrong. He transcends all these dichotomies, and expresses the Dharma as is. That's what it says, "the Way is precious." No way is better than that.

"Inscribe designs on a jewel and its glory is lost." The jewel again—you do zazen. Here it particularly refers to Roso's wall-gazing. And what is the inscription? It's Nansen's remark. In a way, it is true. When you really get into deep samadhi, then open up the eye of wisdom and just sit. What else besides that is necessary to describe? Everything is there—but Nansen telling the people you have to receive it directly even prior to the empty kalpa is almost a joke. We don't need that kind of comment. Koans are similar to that. Not studying koans would be one hundred percent okay. By doing that kind of thing, in a way we defile the genuineness of our life, of our being. "Inscribe designs on a jewel and its glory is lost." It's very best part is somewhat missed.

"A pearl even from an abyss naturally beckons." Again, he is praising Roso's genuine zazen. Even though he doesn't say a word, that jewel, pearl, shines as is.

"Plenty of bracing air purely burnishes off autumn's swelter; Far away a single tranquil cloud divides sky and water." Again, these two lines refer to Roso's wall-gazing. It's like bracing air in early autumn, so refreshing. That genuine zazen cools off our hot heads. "Far away a single tranquil cloud divides sky and water." It almost refers to Nansen's position, commenting on his words. It's almost as if he's dividing something else, like air from earth, sky from water. And yet what he is himself is like a single piece of cloud crossing the sky, according to the wind. It doesn't matter where it flies. With nothing sticking to it, and leaving no trace, no footprint, it just goes wherever it's supposed to. "Plenty of bracing air purely burnishes off autumn's swelter. Far away a single tranquil cloud divides sky and water."

So sesshin is almost over. All the last part goes fast. That means we can sit better. Please try to have a good sesshin.

THE BOOK OF MASTER RINZAI (LINJI)

Eido Shimano

RECORD OF PILGRIMAGES, CHAPTER 1

THE MASTER'S first training was under the guidance of Obaku. His attitude was sincere and direct. The head monk said with a sigh, "Even though he's a relatively new monk, he's quite different from the others." The head monk then asked the Master, "How long have you been here?" The Master replied, "Three years." The head monk asked, "Have you ever questioned the teacher?" The Master said, "No, I don't know what to ask." The head monk said, "I urge you to see the Abbot and ask him, 'What is the quintessence of Buddhadharma?'"

The Master went to Obaku and asked his question. Before he had finished, Obaku hit him. The Master withdrew. The head monk said, "How did your question go?" The Master said, "Before my question was over the Abbot hit me. I don't understand." The head monk said, "Just go and ask him again." The Master went again and asked. Obaku hit him again. Thus three times he asked the question and three times he was hit.

The Master humbly returned to the head monk and said, "I was lucky to receive your compassionate guidance. You forced me to ask the question three times, and three times I was hit. I deplore deeply that my accumulated evil karma is preventing me from getting the profound meaning of the Abbot's intention. I have decided to take my leave." The head monk said, "Before leaving, be sure to bid the Abbot farewell." The Master bowed and withdrew.

The head monk went ahead to the Abbot and said, "That young monk who has been questioning you is a vessel of Dharma. When he comes to take his leave, kindly give him some advice. I am positive that in the future, with much training, he will become like a great tree, providing cool shade for the people of the world."

The Master went to take his leave. Obaku said, "You must not go to any other place but to Daigu by the river of Ko-an. I am sure he will guide you." The Master arrived at Daigu. Daigu asked, "Where are you from?" The Master said, "I have come from Obaku." Daigu asked, "What did Obaku say to you?" The Master said, "Three times I asked him 'what is the quintessence of Buddhadharma,' and three times I was hit. I have no idea where is my fault?" Daigu said, "Obaku is indeed such a grandma, he completely exhausted himself for your sake. Nevertheless, you came here and said, 'I have no idea, where is my fault?'"

Upon hearing these words, the Master was greatly awakened and said, "Ah! From the beginning Obaku's Buddhadharma is nothing special." Daigu grabbed and lifted up the Master saying, "You little bed-wetting devil! A moment ago you said, 'I have no idea where is my fault?' now you are saying, 'Obaku's Buddhadharma is nothing special.' What did you SEE? SAY!" The Master punched Daigu in the ribs three times and pushed him off. Daigu pushed the Master away too, saying, "Your teacher is Obaku. It is none of my business."

The Master took his leave from Daigu and returned to Obaku. Obaku saw him coming and said, "Look at this fellow coming and going, coming and going. Will it ever end?" The Master said, "It's all because of your grandmotherly kindness." Then he stood next to Obaku. Obaku asked, "Where have you been?" The Master said, "Upholding your compassionate advice, I went to Daigu's place." Obaku said, "What did Daigu say?" The Master told him all that had happened. Obaku said, "I can't wait to give him a good dose of my stick." The Master said, "Why do you have to wait? Take it right away." He then slapped him. "*You Lunatic!*" screamed Obaku, "coming back here, pulling the tiger's whiskers." The Master shouted. Obaku said, "Attendant, drag this lunatic fellow out of here and take him to the Zendo."

Later Issan mentioned this story to Kyozan and asked, "On that occasion, did Rinzai get his power from Daigu or from Obaku?" Kyozan said, "He not only rode on the tiger's head, but he also understood how to take hold of its tail."

Over the past few years whenever I have found time, I have been translating the *Rinzai Roku*, the recorded sayings of Master Rinzai. It seems that at last the readiness of time has come, so either by the end of this year or the beginning of next year this book of Rinzai will be published. As you know there are many Zen centers in the United States. Perhaps Dai Bosatsu Zendo though is the only place where Teisho on the Rinzai Roku is being given. In fact, the last day of the Rohatsu Sesshin, which ended a little over a month ago, "Jishu," the section that means teaching, was completed. Today's Teisho is on Chapter One of Critical Examinations. Since many of you are here for the first time and may not know of the extremely important event in Chapter One, I thought it appropriate for you to learn how Master Rinzai came to his great enlightenment. Those of you who are relatively older, senior students, have heard this many times, but today I would like to approach it in a slightly different way.

"The Master's first training was under the guidance of Obaku." Here, "Master" refers to Rinzai, even though at the time he was still a monk. Obaku is well known in the West as Huang-po. "His attitude was sincere and direct." The opposite of devious. Not deceiving himself, not deceiving others. "The head monk said with a sigh, 'Even though he's a relatively new monk, he's quite different from the others.'" Evidently the head monk was watching monk Rinzai. So one day he asked, "'How long have you been here?' The Master replied, 'Three years.' The head monk asked, 'Have you ever questioned the teacher?'" Teacher, naturally, implies Obaku. The Master replied, "No, I don't know what to ask." For three years, he was living in Obaku's mountain and doing zazen patiently, and until the head monk asked him, he never went for dokusan. The reason he never went is simply that he didn't know what to ask. This too shows the honesty of Rinzai's personality. "The head monk said, 'I urge you to see the Abbot,'"—that is Obaku—"and ask him, 'What is the quintessence of Buddhadharma?'"

Many of you have a theistic religious background. What is the quintessence of Judaism? What is the quintessence of Christianity? What is the quintessence of Islam? What is the quintessence of Agnosticism? The Master went to Obaku's place and asked, "'What is the quintessence of Buddhadharma?' ...Before he had finished [his question], Obaku hit him." Once, twice, three times. We don't know. But we do know that it was painful. And when our body feels pain, our mind questions, Why?

What? I'm sure you know the story of Gutei. He cut off a boy's finger, far more than hitting! And because of that action, great enlightenment came. Pain. You may complain, but complaining doesn't produce anything. In this case, Master Rinzai was hit and was full of pain. He must have thought, "WHAT IS IT? WHAT DID I DO? WHY?"

The Master withdrew. The head monk was waiting and asked, "How did your question go?" This is a very kind thing to do. The Master said, "Before my question was over, the Abbot hit me. I don't understand." Maybe he is confused? The head monk pushed him and said, "Just go and ask him again." The Master went again and asked. "Hai!" [Yes!] sincere and direct. Hai. Hai. And again he asked, "What is the quintessence of Buddhadharma?" Obaku hit him again. Thus three times he asked the question and three times he was hit. The Master humbly returned to the head monk and said, "I was lucky to receive your compassionate guidance. You forced me to ask the question." Forced me. Otherwise, for four years, five years, six years, he might have stayed at Obaku's monastery without ever going to dokusan. "You forced me to ask the question three times, and three times I was hit. I deplore deeply that my accumulated evil karma is preventing me from getting the profound meaning of the Abbot's intention." I am sure that when Rinzai was telling this to the head monk he must have been crying. Even though his evil karma has been accumulated up from the past, it cannot do anything for him right now. At this, Rinzai felt deep remorse, and profound regret.

Speaking of tears, someone came to the dokusan room crying, not just ordinary crying, sincerely crying. I've never seen that student crying. So I asked, "What's the matter?" "I can't get what is preventing me from understanding. I have suffered enough," she said. "Not enough!" I said, "Suffer more!" Many of you, myself included, prefer comfort rather than pain. We prefer tranquillity rather than struggle. But this is a sort of gate, which everyone has to pass through. In order to pass through this gate, pain, struggle, tears, frustration, anger, self-pity—all these must occur.

"'I have decided to take my leave.' The head monk said, 'Before leaving, be sure to bid the Abbot farewell.'" Don't just disappear, say goodbye. "The Master bowed and withdrew. The head monk went ahead to the Abbot and said, 'That young monk who has been questioning you is a vessel of Dharma.'" This head monk had discerning eyes. "When he comes to take his leave, kindly give him some advice. I am positive that in the future, with much training, he will become like a great tree, providing cool shade for the people of the world." He was right. If this suggestion was not made, Rinzai Zen Buddhism might not have been born, Hakuin Zenji could not have taught Rinzai Zen. Certainly Rinzai became the great tree, providing cool shade for the dharma travelers of the world. "The Master went to take his leave. Obaku said, 'You must not go to any other place but to Daigu by the river of Ko-an. I am sure he will guide you.'"

So Master Rinzai, with a dark state of mind, walked, walked, walked, to Master Daigu's place. Daigu is the dharma cousin of Obaku. "Daigu asked, 'Where are you from?'" I have often wondered, why did Obaku send him to Daigu's place? One possibility is that, as a dharma cousin living at the same time, somehow Obaku knew Daigu's style of teaching. The other is that he realized "the readiness of time," with regard to Rinzai's awakening, had not yet come. It was best then to change the environment and see how things would go. This is my guess. "The Master said, 'I have come from Obaku.' Daigu asked, 'What did Obaku say to you?' The Master said, 'Three times I asked him, 'what is the essence of Buddhadharma,' and three times I was hit. I have no idea where is my fault?'" This must be an honest statement; I have no idea what is wrong with me? I just asked the most important question, three times, and three times he just hit me without saying anything. I have no idea where is my fault? Sincere, direct, honest. Honesty.

"Daigu said, 'Obaku is indeed such a grandma, he completely exhausted himself for your sake.'" Spiritually Obaku became naked and did as much as he could possibly do for a young monk known as Rinzai. "Obaku is indeed such a grandma, he completely exhausted himself for your sake. Nevertheless, you came here and said, 'I have no idea, where is my fault?'" Maybe this should be read in a slightly different way. Daigu said more harshly, "Obaku is indeed a grandma, he completely exhausted himself for your sake! Nevertheless, you came here and said, 'I have no idea where is my fault!'" Scolding Rinzai, stimulation by words. Hamlet's "words, words, words" then is not always necessarily bad. When "words" are said at the appropriate time, by the appropriate person, in the appropriate way, words have magnificent power.

"Upon hearing these words, the Master was greatly awakened…" Greatly awakened. Not "had insight." Greatly awakened! "…and said, 'Ah! From the beginning Obaku's Buddhadharma is nothing special.'" Not Obaku's Buddhadharma, Buddhadharma is nothing special. Rinzai, too, had been searching for something extremely special. And this, nothing special, is quite often misunderstood. Again, it becomes "words, words, words," but something extremely special can only be said of "nothing special." Mountain is mountain, nothing special! Snowflakes are snowflakes, nothing special! You may say, "I know that." But what we know and what Rinzai said in "nothing special" is a different level of understanding. As the famous saying goes, "At First Mountain is mountain, river is river." And this is what most of you see. And then, when we go into deep zazen, mountain is not mountain; river is not river. And then, returning, we can say, "Ah! From the beginning, mountain is mountain, river is river." Nothing special, but very special. "Daigu grabbed and lifted up the Master saying, 'You little bed-wetting devil! A moment ago you said, 'I have no idea, where is my fault,' now you are saying, 'Obaku's Buddhadharma is nothing special.' What did you SEE? SAY!'"

Even to Daigu this was not expected, since Rinzai's enlightenment was so splendid. He just wanted to make sure that he understood this "nothing special" reality. "SAY!" "The Master punched Daigu in the ribs three times and pushed him off." Daigu asked him "SAY," but Rinzai did not say. Instead he punched Daigu's ribs three times. Pow, pow, pow, and pushed him off. That's enough. This is the quintessence of Buddhadharma. No question. "Daigu pushed the Master away too, saying, 'Your teacher is Obaku. It is none of my business.'"

"The Master took his leave from Daigu and returned to Obaku." On the way from Daigu back to Obaku he must be happier than happy. His step was lighter than light. "Obaku saw him coming and said, 'Look at this fellow coming and going, coming and going. Will it ever end?'" Obaku too did not expect that the young monk who questioned, "what is the quintessence of Buddhadharma" had such a great awakening. "The Master said, 'It's all because of your grandmotherly kindness.'" He most likely put his palms together, and made a deep bow, and stood next to him. "Obaku asked, 'Where have you been?'" He was suspicious perhaps. Rinzai may have been some other place. "The Master said, 'Upholding your compassionate advice, I went to Daigu's place.' Obaku said, 'What did Daigu say?'" This is a rather important question to ask. What did he say? "The Master told him all that had happened. Obaku said, 'I can't wait to give him a good dose of my stick.'"

Obaku was so happy! This may be a difference between East and West. In the West perhaps, you say, "Oh, congratulations! Let's open a bottle of champagne!" And nothing is wrong with that. In the East we have a tendency to suppress, don't show that happiness. And in this case particularly, Obaku wanted to test Rinzai. So he could not say, "Let's have champagne." "'I can't wait to give him a good dose of my stick!' The Master said, 'Why do you have to wait? Take it right away.'" This is dharma *hataraki*—the spontaneous activity of wisdom. "Take it right away!" And "he then slapped him." So Obaku said, I can't wait to hit Daigu, so Rinzai said, "Why do you have to wait? Take it right away," and Rinzai slapped Obaku. Three became one, and yet three are three. And all occurs spontaneously.

"'*You Lunatic!*' screamed Obaku, 'coming back here, pulling the tiger's whiskers,' The Master shouted." This is Rinzai's first, *kkkwwwatzzzzz!* No longer an Unsui, no longer a training monk. With great confidence and great dignity, he gave a first shout to his Master, *kkkwwwatzzzzz!* Obaku did not say, "Good!" Rather he said, "Attendant, drag this lunatic fellow out of here and take him to the Zendo." Now this is another way to say, "I forgive your coming and going," and new permission was granted to reactivate his training at Obaku's monastery. Again this is another difference between East and West.

"Later Issan mentioned this story to Kyozan and asked, 'On that occasion did Rinzai get his power from Daigu or from Obaku?' Kyozan said, 'He not only rode on the tiger's head,'" which is another way to say he not only hit Daigu's ribs three times "pow," "pow," "pow," "but he also understood how to take hold of his tail." This may be difficult for you to understand, but "he understood how to take hold of his tail" means hitting Obaku. In other words, he has no specific teacher. We are all Buddhists, we can all say, "I am a student of Shakyamuni Buddha." But, at the same time each one of us is independent, no teacher, teacher-less, no student, student-less. This was the comment of Kyozan.

In conclusion this is the story of how the young, honest, sincere, direct, training monk Rinzai received the help of many teachers. However it was more than mere individual teachers, there must have been some kind of dharma energy as well, which forced him to go there. There must have been something to make him stay for three years, to meet the head monk, to ask Obaku questions, all of this occurred in an uncanny way. The reason why you are here, too, in the midst of January, on this cold Dai Bosatsu Mountain must be some kind of dharma energy. Yes, it is partially your decision to come, but also it is the dharma's decision for you to be here. I always thought that forty-three is the most ideal number to do sesshin, forty people in the Zendo, and three tenzos in the foyer. Just that way. At Ryutaku-ji, and at Shogen-ji, even as I speak, they are in the midst of Rohatsu sesshin. Although we held our Rohatsu sesshin already in December, they are doing Rohatsu now. Keep this in your mind. Let us march on with the same Rohatsu spirit! Hai!

Bodhidharma's Emptiness

Robert Aitken

Blue Cliff Record, Case 1

The Story

EMPEROR WU OF LIANG asked the great master Bodhidharma, "What is the first principle of the holy teaching?"

Bodhidharma said, "Vast emptiness, nothing holy."

The Emperor asked, "Who stands before me?"

Bodhidharma said, "I don't know." The Emperor did not understand. Bodhidharma then crossed the Yangtze River and went on to the kingdom of Wei.

Later, the Emperor took up this matter with Duke Chih. Chih said, "Your Majesty, do you know who that was?"

The Emperor said, "I don't know."

Chih said, "That was the Great Personage Kuan-yin, conveying the mind-seal of the Buddha." The Emperor felt regretful, and wanted to send an emissary to invite Bodhidharma to return.

Chih said, "Your Majesty, don't say you will send someone to bring him back. Even if everyone in the whole country were to go after him, he would not return."

Personae

Emperor Wu, Liang Wu-ti (Ryu Butei), ruled 502–549 in the Southern Sector of the Six Dynasties (428–588).

Bodhidharma, d. 532, is traditionally considered to be the 28th Dharma successor of the Buddha Shakyamuni, and is venerated as the founder of Ch'an (Zen) Buddhism in China.

Duke Chih (Shi), the priest Pao-chih (Hoshi), (417/421–514), was Wu's
  religious advisor.

Comment

At the time of this audience, Buddhism had been established in China for
five hundred years. The Emperor Wu of Liang was an especially devout
and learned follower. He wrote commentaries on *Prajñaparamita* literature and on the *Nirvana Sutra*. During his reign of forty-seven years,
he convened a total of sixteen Dharma assemblies, at which he would
sometimes don a monk's robe and explicate a sutra. These were great
gatherings, it is said, with as many as fifty thousand people taking part.
Era names were changed in honor of these occasions. General amnesty
was given to criminals. During the conventions, the Emperor would work
as a menial for a while at a Buddhist temple. He gave of his own treasure
to Buddhist establishments, and also set up a system of dana, whereby
wealthy patrons of Buddhism could deposit their money as endowments
for temples and monasteries. He was, we can understand, known as the
Imperial Bodhisattva.

Bodhidharma appeared in Southern China after a long career in India
as a master of the Buddha Way. His distinguished reputation preceded
him, and the Emperor invited him to an audience. It did not go well.

> The Emperor asked, "I have endowed hundreds of temples
> and monasteries, and endorsed the ordination of thousands
> of monks and nuns; what is my merit?"
> Bodhidharma replied, "No merit."

Merit, here, is the compound word *kung-te.* Both elements of this
term mean "merit"; *kung* refers to an act of benevolence, while *te* is the
authority one accumulates with selfless conduct that is appropriate for
the world. It is the *te* of the *Tao-te ching,* translated by Arthur Waley as
"The Way and Its Power." With each act of rectitude, your acknowledgment by others and your inner assurance builds a little, like incense-ash
building in its receptacle. Among traditional peoples, *te* by whatever
name is the path to the status of elder, and in all cultures the nobility of

a Gough Whitlam, a Vaclav Havel, or a Dag Hammarskjold, is widely acknowledged.

The denial of *kung-te* in the face of universal, timeless experience is, of course, a denial of karma itself, a denial that action leads to consequence. Bodhidharma was making a point beyond points, and the Emperor was astute enough to sense this much. He had the flexibility of an experienced interlocutor. It wasn't the first time that he had fallen back in a religious encounter.

If there is no merit in saving the many beings, he might be saying, if indeed I have no merit in establishing a dana system of accumulating large donations and dispersing them for the advancement of the Dharma, then let's look deeper.

He knew from his discussions with Fu Ta-shih and other wise Buddhist teachers of his time that appearance is the conventional and the real is its vacancy. Yet the two, he knew, are one. Form and emptiness are the same. As Yüan-wu implies, this is surely what the Emperor had in mind when he asked, "What is the first principle of the holy teaching?"

Bodhidharma was ready with a response every bit as uncompromising as his first reply. "Vast emptiness," he said, "nothing holy." How many people have bowed in reverence at such a holy teaching!—without a speck of irony! Yüan-wu quotes his teacher, Wu-tsu, saying, "If you can just see into 'Vast emptiness, nothing holy,' then you can return home and sit in peace."

Can you do that? It is at this point that you are vulnerable to the scrutiny of the ancients. You are vulnerable to the scrutiny of your spouse and children, your colleagues and superiors, and the lady at the bank. How do you show Bodhidharma's position?

The Emperor then asked, "Who stands before me?" Some say this was the defense of a veteran colloquist who had reached the end of his seasoned patience. He felt his back was to the wall. He used the imperial "me," a pronoun reserved for the Son of Heaven. Was he getting on his high horse a little?

No, it seems that the Emperor was not a defensive kind of person. Reading his brief biography in Kenneth Ch'en's *Buddhism in China*, I find a man who took his role as emperor seriously, but did not let it master him. I think he was simply making a final effort to grasp Bodhidharma's meaning. I don't understand, he was saying. If you say there is no such thing as essential truth, then who are you? Aren't you a distinguished priest of truth? Who are you to say that the first principle of the holy teaching is empty and not holy?

Bodhidharma loosed his final shaft. "I don't know." It was his ultimate endeavor to convey the fundamental fact of facts to the Emperor Wu— the cap to his earlier responses. Patiently, compassionately he had made the same point, first this way, then that. There is no merit, there is no first principle, and there is nothing holy. There is nothing at all. Finally, I can't say anything even about myself.

"Why did Bodhidharma come from the West?"—this was a stock question in T'ang period dialogues. Lin-chi said, "If he had any reason, he could not have saved even himself." Shih-t'ou Hsi-ch'ien said, "Ask the post standing there." When the monk said he didn't understand, Shih-t'ou said, "My ignorance is worse than yours."

I take a leaf from Wu-tzu. Unless you can acknowledge, "I don't know" to the very bottom, you can never return home and sit in peace, but you will live your life to the very end in meaningless chatter.

If, however, you come before a true teacher and, with a show of consequence, chant "I don't know," you still might be sent away. The words themselves, however emphasized, are not necessarily the message of the old founder. How do you see Bodhidharma here, confronting his Imperial Majesty with the inexpressible verity?

Just as form and emptiness are the basic complementarity of Mahayana Buddhism in its metaphysics, so intimacy with the other and with the unequivocal void are the basic complementarity of Mahayana experience. We perceive forms in our earliest childhood, and experience intimacy with the other in puberty, not only sexually, but also in nature and in the arts. Emptiness is still hidden, however. Bodhidharma and his great successors take students in hand to show how all perceptions are totally vacant. We evolve from what John Keats called the "sole self" to the universal, and from there with rigorous practice to realize vast and fathomless nothingness. Just as the sole self does not work in a relationship, so the universal self must drop off both the universe and the one who perceives. Then the self and forms of the world can be seen as they are, in their colors and sounds and textures, in their beauty and ugliness, but essentially without any substance whatever.

Moreover, it is not that I see that all things are void, but I myself am unknown and unknowable. This is by no means merely an experience of undifferentiated vacuum. It is liberation at last. In the *Cheng-tao ke* we read:

> The mind-mirror shines brilliantly, without obstruction;
> its light reaching worlds as countless as sands of the Ganges.
> The ten-thousand things are all reflected here,
> illumined perfectly, neither inside nor outside.

Teachers worth their salt will nod patiently while students rhapsodize upon oneness, and will wait until those students can truly show "I don't know" with a radiant smile and flashing eyes. Then it is prudent to go on to the ten thousand things.

There is, of course, the phenomenon called the "Den of Mara," the cave of Satan, where one is stuck in emptiness, and nothing matters. There is no distinction between old and young, male and female, virtue and vice. Nothing happens and everyone is paralyzed. Over and over the literature of Zen Buddhism renews the archetype of the Buddha Shakya-muni, arising from his samādhi beneath the Bodhi Tree to seek out his five disciples in Benares. His liberation and ours brings weighty responsibility. You can't stay under the Bodhi Tree. You can't go on babbling "Nothing special."

Nonetheless, it is under that Bodhi Tree that realization arises. Even the interbeing of the plenum as the self remains an incomplete perception, unless it is clear in peak experience that everything is void, empty, vacant. Even the marvelous panorama of the Hua-yen, with its model of the universe as a multidimensional net with each point containing all other points, is just a romantic notion, unless it is realized by the one with no skull and no skin.

But Bodhidharma could not get his message of essential emptiness across. "Your Majesty," asked the Duke, "Do you know who that was?" "I don't know," the Emperor replied. Yüan-wu asks, "Is this 'I don't know' the same as Bodhidharma's 'I don't know?'" Honored friends, what is your opinion?

Bodhidharma put away any thought that he might convert the Emperor from devotion and scholarship to the freedom of a great laugh, and any thought that such enlightenment might trickle down to the masses of the Chinese people. He crossed the Yangtze River and journeyed to the kingdom of Wei in Northwestern China. There he found a ruined temple and took up residence in a cave behind it, facing a wall in zazen, it is said, for the last nine years of his life. Four disciples gathered, three men and one woman, including the monk we venerate as Hui-k'o (Eka), through whom the Dharma line descended, ultimately in another seven generations to blossom in the efflorescence of Ch'an during the T'ang period.

Several masters in our great tradition became advisors to the emperors of their time—in China, then in Korea, Vietnam, and Japan—but the ideal of Zen Buddhism as a rigorous teaching for the few has never been completely lost. Duke Chih, about whom we know very little except that he was a priest the Emperor held in highest regard, intuitively understood Bodhidharma. "He is the Great Personage Kuan-yin," the Duke said. He is the incarnation of mercy and compassion, conveying the transmission of the Buddha that has been passed from mind to mind for twenty-eight generations. And he won't come back, ever, ever, ever.

The Emperor felt remorseful at the time, and indeed for the rest of his life. When Bodhidharma died, the Emperor mourned him, and personally wrote an inscription for his monument. It read:

> Alas! I saw him without seeing him; I met him without meeting him; I encountered him without encountering him. Now as before, I regret this deeply.

"He wrings his hands and beats his breast, addressing a plea to the sky," as Yüan-wu says. But the Emperor further eulogized Bodhidharma by saying, "If your mind exists, you are stuck in the mundane for eternity. If it does not exist, you experience wondrous enlightenment instantly." He gained some insight at last, it seems, but he could not meet again with the old foreigner to have it examined.

Many of us have had the experience of missing the truth on the first round. When I was sixteen or so, my Sunday-evening class at Central Union Church in Honolulu took up non-Christian faiths. We visited the Honpa Hongwanji Mission, the local headquarters of the Jodo Shinshu school of Buddhism, and heard a talk by the Venerable Ernest Hunt, a Theosophist turned Buddhist, who was a priest of that temple. He held forth on the Four Noble Truths and the Eightfold Path, and I thought it was the driest, more boring lecture I had ever heard in my whole life. Yet thirty years later Dr. Hunt and I were fast friends, and we exchanged insights with delight.

If Bodhidharma would not return to the palace, why didn't the Emperor hitch up his robes and chase after him? He couldn't. Maybe he could scrub toilets in a monastery for a day or so, but everybody knew this was part of his function as the Imperial Bodhisattva. As Emperor, however, he couldn't go haring off into somebody else's kingdom, even in disguise. He probably didn't even consider it. He was imprisoned by his position.

If, as Wu-men says, the truth is like a racehorse that dashes by your window, and you miss it because you blink, then it is important to place yourself where it can dash by again, and again, until you finally get a glimpse of it.

Do you have a glimpse? How do you see Bodhidharma as he makes his three responses? Please don't begin your reply with, "Well, I think he is…" That puts the old boy back in Asia in the sixth century. This is not a story about far away and long ago. It is my story and yours—our way to mature humanity.

THINK NEITHER GOOD NOR EVIL

Philip Kapleau

GATELESS GATE, CASE 23

The Case

THE SIXTH PATRIARCH was pursued by a monk into the mountains. The Patriarch, seeing him coming, laid the robe and the bowl on a rock and said, "The robe and bowl symbolize the faith; are they to be fought for? I allow you to take them away." The monk tried to lift them, but they were as immovable as a mountain. Hesitating and trembling, he said, "I have come for the dharma, not for the robe. I beg you to teach your servant!" The Sixth Patriarch said, "When you were pursuing me and not thinking of good or evil but only of obtaining the treasure, where was your Original-self?" Hearing this, the monk at once became enlightened. His whole body was dripping with sweat. With tears flowing he made obeisance and asked, "Besides the secret words and meanings, is there anything deeper still?" The Patriarch replied, "What I have just told you is not secret. You have realized your Original-self, and what is secret is in you yourself." The monk said, "When I was training under the Fifth Patriarch with the other monks, I did not awaken to my Original-self. Thanks to your instruction, which is to the point, I am like one who has drunk water and actually experienced himself whether it is cold or warm. You are my master!" The Sixth Patriarch said, "We both have the same teacher; hold fast to what you have learned from him."

304 *Sitting With Koans*

Mumon's Comment

Of the Sixth Patriarch it has to be said that in an emergency he did something extraordinary. He has a grandmotherly kindness; it is as if he had peeled a fresh litchi, removed its seed, and then put it into your mouth so that you need only swallow it.

Mumon's Verse

> You describe it in vain, you picture it to no avail;
> you can never praise it fully.
> Stop all your groping and maneuvering.
> There is nowhere to hide your True-self.
> When the universe is annihilated, "it" remains, indestructible.

The Sixth Patriarch is one of the most distinguished masters in the history of Zen. Almost single-handedly he stripped from Buddhism its Indian cloak of otherworldliness and emphasis on sutra reading and doctrinal study that had previously characterized it in China. In doing so, he laid the foundation for what we now know as Zen Buddhism. The episode of this koan is found in the Platform Sutra, which is a record of his life and teachings and one of only two sutras that do not revolve around the life and words of the Buddha.

The Sixth Patriarch was born in the year 638 and was thus a product of the T'ang era, the golden age of Zen. It is recorded that his father died when the master was young and that the boy was brought up by his mother in extreme poverty. Since he went to work at an early age in order to support his mother, he did not attend school and so never learned to read or write. Many would consider such poverty and struggle tragic in a young life, but the introspection and self-reliance they fostered in the child undoubtedly hastened his enlightenment, which came under circumstances unique in the history of Zen.

One day a merchant bought some firewood from the youth and asked him to carry it to his shop. When he had delivered the wood and was about to leave the shop, he heard a monk reciting a sutra outside the door. Upon hearing the words spoken by the monk, the youth, who was now seventeen or eighteen and, as far as is known, had never sat in zazen, was suddenly awakened. He asked the monk what he had recited and was told it was the *Diamond Sutra*.

At this point some of you may wonder, "If it is possible to gain enlightenment without strong exertion, why should I endure the discomforts of sesshin?" If this is what you are thinking, I can sympathize with you. Many years ago when I was feeling the pressure of Japanese friends in Kyoto to quit the austere rigors of the Zen monastery I put this same question to my teacher. And this is how he replied: "Rare indeed are those whose minds are so unstained that they can gain genuine enlightenment without zazen. The Sixth Patriarch was such a one. Undoubtedly he had so ardently disciplined himself in a previous lifetime that his mind, when he came into this existence, was uncommonly pure. This circumstance, and the fact that he had lost his father at an early age and had to struggle to support his mother, must have led him to question intensely the meaning of birth and death and brought about his awakening in such a manner. Most people, though, lacking his purity of mind and intense self-questioning, need to do zazen tirelessly to fully open their Mind's eye."

To continue with the Sixth Patriarch's life story: From the monk who had recited the sutra he learned about the Fifth Patriarch, who was teaching on a remote mountain. After thirty days of hard travel the youth reached the mountain temple of the Fifth Patriarch, who when he saw him asked, "Where do you come from and what do you seek?" Asking this question is like putting a stick in water to determine its depth. The future Sixth Patriarch replied, "I, one of the common people from the South, have come from far away to pay my respects to the venerable master in order to become a buddha." To this the master retorted, "How can you, a bumpkin from the South, possibly become a buddha?" Savor the young man's outspoken reply: "Although there are Northerners and Southerners, the Buddha-nature knows of no South or North. The appearance of a bumpkin may be different from that of a monk, but from the standpoint of Buddha-nature can there be a difference?"

In other words, Buddha-nature is our common birthright. Confirmation of this comes from the highest source, the Buddha himself. On the occasion of his supreme enlightenment he exclaimed, "Wonder of wonders! All living beings are inherently buddhas, endowed with wisdom and virtue."

Let me ask each of you: Do you truly believe the Buddha was not mistaken when he said this? Do you have the firm conviction that regardless of whether you are physically strong or weak, mentally keen or dull, well-educated or illiterate, you have the all-embracing, nothing-lacking Buddha-nature and can, with pure aspiration and strong determination, awaken to it at this very sesshin? Have you struggled to resolve the "doubt-sensation"—the seeming contradiction between the Buddha's pronouncement that all are innately flawless and the evidence of your senses that there is only imperfection, in yourself and others?

Unless your responses to these questions are in the affirmative, you won't open your Mind's eye no matter how often you do zazen or how many sesshins you attend. All you will gain is a certain calmness of body and clarity of mind, and while these qualities are not inconsequential, they are as different from enlightenment as chalk is from cheese. The ultimate aim of Zen training is full awakening, not serenity or high-energy states, which are only by-products of zazen. To awaken, what is most essential is a questioning mind growing out of a fundamental perplexity, or "ball of doubt." Zen masters have repeatedly said, "Where there is great questioning there is great enlightenment; where there is little questioning there is little enlightenment; no questioning, no enlightenment."

There is more to the Fifth Patriarch's response: "For a bumpkin you're very clever with words," said the master. "Say no more now but go to work with the other monks." The novice was then assigned to pound rice in the granary for eight months.

How many of you could go to a Zen center for training, be put down by the master in your first encounter, then be ignored by him and not even allowed into the zendo for eight months? If the master had not thought highly of the brilliant novice, you can be sure he would not have treated him this way. That the latter remained in spite of this treatment shows his strong faith in both his teacher and his own Buddha-nature.

When the Fifth Patriarch felt the time had come to transmit the dharma, he summoned all his disciples and asked that each compose a verse expressing his own understanding. He told them that the one who revealed the deepest truth would inherit the robe and become the Sixth Patriarch. The head monk submitted the following:

> Body is the tree of bodhi,
> the mind is the stand of a mirror bright.
> Wipe it constantly, and with ever watchful diligence
> keep it uncontaminated by worldly dust.

When the rice-pounder heard these words repeated by a young monk in the granary area, he realized that the author had not yet perceived his Self-nature, so later he composed his own verse and asked this same monk to write it down for him:

> Fundamentally no bodhi tree exists
> nor the stand of a mirror bright.
> Since all is voidness from the beginning,
> where can the dust alight?

The Fifth Patriarch, upon reading this verse and learning who had composed it, went to the granary and told the young granary worker to come to his quarters at night so that he would not be seen by the others. That night the Fifth Patriarch transmitted to him the robe and bowl, saying, "Now you are the Sixth Patriarch." The Fifth Patriarch knew that the monks would never tolerate this novice as the master's successor, so he urged the Sixth Patriarch to return to his native place in secrecy, telling him to live incognito while maturing his enlightenment and only after doing so to begin his formal teaching. He also told him that because the transmission of the robe might easily become a source of contention in the future, there were to be no further transmissions of the robe after him and that hereafter it was to be a transmission strictly from mind to mind. Then the Fifth Patriarch ferried with the new patriarch to the other shore of the river, where they parted, never again to see each other.

The present koan revolves around the incident of the Sixth Patriarch's departure from the monastery carrying with him the robe and bowl. Now even though the old patriarch had made the transmission in great secrecy, it soon became known that his heir was departing with the robe and bowl as the Sixth Patriarch. The succeeding events are related in the koan:

"The Sixth Patriarch was pursued by a monk into the mountains." This monk, it seems, was a rough and impulsive man who had been a general before he became a monk. But it would be a mistake to think of him as a villainous person. He should rather be looked upon as a zealous defender of the dharma, to which he was overly attached. To this middle-aged, simple-minded monk, and the others as well, it was inconceivable that the precious dharma, symbolized by the robe and bowl, be entrusted to the care of a young layman with practically no formal training. Such concern, misguided though it was, shows in itself that this general-turned-monk was a sincere and ardent follower of the Buddha's Way.

"The Patriarch, seeing him coming, laid the robe and the bowl on a rock and said, 'The robe and bowl symbolize the faith; are they to be fought for? I allow you to take them away.'" To get a handle on this koan you must first see why this statement by the Sixth Patriarch was not simply an attempt to avoid violence but was made as a challenge. Why the challenge? This is the first barrier of the koan.

"The monk tried to lift them, but they were as immovable as a mountain." If you believe that the reason for his inability to move them is that, suddenly realizing the enormity of the act he was about to perpetrate, he was paralyzed by feelings of remorse, then you are underrating the power of the dharma and that of the Sixth Patriarch who embodied it! If faith can move mountains, why can't it immobilize a robe and bowl?

"Hesitating and trembling, he said, 'I have come for the dharma, not for the robe. I beg you to teach your servant!'" Unless you sense his desperate mind state behind these words, the koan may seem to you no more than a charming fable about the would-be larceny of some insignificant religious objects, and the circumstances of the monk's enlightenment may appear a great mystery. The key to understanding his mind state is the supplication, "I beg you to teach your servant!" for it reveals his complete and sudden change of heart. Without the egolessness expressed by this cry for help, the monk's awakening could not have taken place. "All religion," said William James, "begins with the cry 'Help!'" One of the enlightenment accounts in *The Three Pillars of Zen* contains this passage: "'I am dying,' I sobbed. 'I have killed all my gods. I have no key to resurrection. I am totally alone.' Stark fear and utter despair possessed me and I lay on the floor for I don't know how long until from the pit of my abdomen a cry came forth, 'If there is any being in the entire earth who cares whether I live or die, *help* me, oh *help* me!'" This mind state is the precondition of awakening.

The koan resumes: "The Sixth Patriarch said, 'When you were pursuing me and not thinking of good or evil but only of obtaining the treasure, where was your Original-self?'" Here we come to the core of the koan. If you are to *demonstrate* in dokusan your understanding of this passage and not simply verbalize about it, you must put yourself into the mind and being of the agonized monk.

"Not thinking of good and evil" means not making the kind of gratuitous evaluations and judgments that erect a wall between you and others and divide the world into the familiar "here with me" and the alien "out there with you." Zen teaches that things are not good *or* bad but good *and* bad, or rather, *beyond* good and evil. "Original-self" is your fundamental aspect before your mother gave birth to you. In the words of an ancient Zen master, "It is the True-nature of all sentient beings, that which existed before our own birth, and which presently exists, unchangeable and eternal...When we are born it is not newly created and when we die it does not pass away. It has no disctinction of male or female nor has it any coloration of good or bad..."

Young though he was, the Sixth Patriarch must have perceived that his pursuer was a desperate man, driven by frustration and anxiety as well as by a deep hunger for Self-realization. Why otherwise would this general-turned-monk have persevered in a chase of, according to some accounts, one hundred miles? Picture him during the chase, arms and legs pumping vigorously, eyes staring intently, panting and sweating as he pursues the Patriarch, first excitedly, then doggedly, and finally nomindedly until he catches up with him. Unless you have yourself experienced that "dark night of the soul" in which you passionately struggle with a koan or other spiritual problem as the sweat and tears flow, you won't be able to enter deeply into the heart of the tormented monk. This heart-mind, purged now of greed and self-seeking, had become a clean slate. Unhesitatingly the master delivered the *coup de grâce* with his timely words, which must have struck like a bolt of lightning.

Now tell me: Where was the monk's Original-self at that moment?

"Hearing this, the monk at once became enlightened. His whole body was dripping with sweat. With tears flowing he made obeisance and asked, 'Besides the secret words and meanings, is there anything deeper still?'" These tears were tears of relief and gratitude, and the spontaneous prostration before the master a gesture of profound thanksgiving. Genuine though the enlightenment was, it fell short of total liberation, and so the monk asked, "Is there anything further still?" This question is understandable. Awakening, and the realization that one does not acquire anything one did not already have, is so simple and obvious that it is only natural to feel there must be something further still. "Secret words and meanings" here connote an intimate understanding. Enlightenment evokes the strongest feelings of intimacy. If you have ever been estranged from your spouse or child, from a family member or old friend, you know the joy of reunion. Realization of Buddha-nature is realization of the kinship of all forms of life. These feelings are beyond words. If there is a secret involved it is an open secret, known by everyone in his heart of hearts but forgotten or lost sight of in the hurly-burly of ego-dominated thinking and feeling.

"Thanks to your instruction...I am like one who has drunk water and actually experienced himself whether it is cold or warm." Zen emphasizes experience, tasting. If one picture is worth a thousand words, one taste is better than a thousand pictures. To know how honey tastes one must eat some; to know what enlightenment is one must awaken.

Observe the master's loyalty to the Fifth Patriarch: "We both have the same teacher; hold fast to what you have learned from him." He is really saying, "Be grateful for his having taught you that there is nothing to learn—wisdom is inherently yours—and therefore there is nothing to strive for."

Now Mumon's comment: "Of the Sixth Patriarch it has to be said that in an emergency he did something extraordinary." This seems to imply that the Patriarch, confronted suddenly with his pursuer's threatening presence and then with his quick change of heart, was at a loss and struck out blindly with the words, "When you were pursuing me and not thinking of good or evil...where was your Original-self?" Mumon appears to be criticizing the Patriarch, but actually he is praising him, although he does so in his usual tongue-in-cheek manner.

In the Platform Sutra, previously quoted, there is a somewhat different version of the events of this koan: "The Sixth Patriarch said to his pursuer, 'Allow no thoughts to arise in your mind and I will instruct you.' So the monk did zazen for a long time, after which the Patriarch began, 'Do not think this is good,'" etc. Note the words "After the monk had done zazen for a long time…" Whether his predisposing mind state was induced by sitting zazen, as in the second version, or brought about by running zazen, as implied in the koan proper, the precondition of awakening, a "clean slate" mind, was present.

To continue: "He has a grandmotherly kindness; it is as if he had peeled a fresh litchi, removed its seed, and then put it into your mouth so that you need only swallow it." "Grandmotherly kindness" is unnecessary or excessive kindness. Mumon appears to be putting down the Sixth Patriarch for his gentle manner and for doing more than needed to be done. Actually he is praising by condemning. After all, the monk did come to enlightenment through the Patriarch's words and actions. At the same time Mumon is admonishing us, "The Sixth Patriarch's words and manner were effective in this instance, true, but don't assume that full awakening is attained easily; it demands years of dedicated zazen, of sustained effort." Mumon's own enlightenment with the koan Mu came after six years of persistent zazen.

Finally Mumon's verse: "You describe it in vain, you picture it to no avail." While it is true that when the spoken word comes directly from the gut it has the power to move us in a way impossible for the devitalized written word, still all words, concepts, and imaginings are at best only sketches of the infinitely extensible "it." Makyo—that is, hallucinations and fantasies—are also only pictures, so don't cling to them even though they afford you relief from the tedium of concentrated, objectless zazen. And don't attach yourself to names and forms. "Original-self," "Buddha-nature," "Mind"—these are but tentative designations for what cannot be named or measured, for what is formless yet informs everything.

"You can never praise it fully: Stop all your groping and maneuvering." Mumon is saying that nothing equals this formless self, so why look for anything else? Stop flirting with the seductress Astrology or sorcerer I Ching, stop chasing after other vain pleasures. This fumbling and searching will never bring you to realization of your True-self.

"There is nowhere to hide your True-self." It stands revealed everywhere, right under your nose—no, it *is* your nose. To hide, your True-self would have to stand outside every conceivable universe, would it not?

"When the universe is annihilated, 'it' remains, indestructible." Your True-self cannot be destroyed for the very reason that it is destruction itself. Never having been born, it can never die. Yet it is the creative force behind every single thing.

A Buffalo Passes Through a Window

Dennis Genpo Merzel

Gateless Gate, Case 38

Main Case

Goso said, "To give an example, it is like a buffalo passing through a window. Its head, horns, and four legs have all passed through. Why is it that its tail cannot?"

A koan is basically either a dialogue, what we call a "mondo," between a teacher and student, or possibly just a story. You cannot resolve a koan with your intellectual, conceptual, rational mind; you have to move beyond that into more of a transcendental experience, an experience of oneness, of unity. You can't do it just with your head, it has to be a whole-body experience. I'd like to share with you a very famous koan, one of my all-time favorites, and talk about our practice, Zen training, in connection with this particular koan. I'll probably throw in a few others, too.

The koan is about a buffalo whose horns and four legs pass through a window, a lattice window with very narrow openings. The buffalo is able to get his huge body through this narrow window, but somehow his tiny tail gets stuck. The question is, how come? Why does his tail get stuck when his broad shoulders and whole body can pass through? This koan is considered one of the most difficult koans. In Zen a difficult koan doesn't have to be complicated. Instead, it's usually simple and obvious but we're so complex and sophisticated in our minds that we can't see it. To really see this koan we must simplify the way we perceive reality or our life—the koan of everyday life, or *genjo-koan*. Passing through with the head, horns, and four legs involves practice. We have to go through a process involving our dualistic way of understanding life.

Shakyamuni Buddha was sitting under the bodhi tree when he had a great realization, a great enlightenment. He realized that the way we perceive reality is delusion. We live in delusion and take it to be reality. We see everything from the point of view of the self, and so everything else appears separate or apart. I see you "out there," apart and separate from me, distinctly different from me. In one sense this is not untrue. You and I are different and separate. Just as a series of waves on the surface of the ocean appear to be separate, we too, appear to be distinctly different and separate. But under the surface of the waves, it is one ocean. In our ignorance, our delusion, we don't see that we are one body and mind. We don't see the deeper level of reality.

The horns of the buffalo represent our dualistic mind. For the horns to pass through, one must give up or drop the dualistic way of perceiving. If you think about it, you can see that the dualistic mind is the cause of our suffering: if I see you and me as separate, if I see the world as separate, then everything becomes a threat to me and my survival. When I draw a circle around "me," everything outside can threaten this bubble. And just as millions of bubbles can form on the surface of the ocean, millions of individual selves with unique identities are born in this world. The illusion is that these bubbles, these individual selves, are separate from the ocean.

When a bubble pops, where does it go? It returns to the Source. But to the bubble, its whole identity, its whole reason for being appears to be gone. A bubble definitely wants to hold on to its separate identity, yet it is also driven to search for its true identity. Do you see the conflict? We crave more than anything to know why we're here. But simply, we can't know why we're here until the bubble pops.

The horns going through the window is the bubble popping. In other words, we see reality—not duality, but reality. When the bubble is popped we see that we are all one, all interconnected. We see that the illusion of a separate self is just that. People often ask, is forming an individual identity a necessary part of our development as human beings? Can we help our children avoid that duality? No. We all have to develop the notion of self; otherwise, we would never develop a strong and healthy ego. But that doesn't mean we need to lose sight of reality forever. Inwardly we know that something is amiss, and we hunger to get back to the Source. This force drives us to want to know and become intimate with reality.

Our individual identity causes us to see everything "out there" as a potential threat. Therefore, we live in fear and anxiety that something could hurt us either physically or psychologically. Buddha saw that our fear is rooted in basic ignorance, our sense of a separate identity. As we grow up, we collect all sorts of ideas, concepts, opinions, and beliefs. We create our belief systems from everything that we have learned and experienced. Our view of reality is made up of all these concepts beginning with the basic one: "I am a separate individual entity." The four legs of the buffalo stand for all of our ideas and understandings. In order for the buffalo to get his whole body and four legs through the window, our concepts and beliefs have to somehow drop off. This is a very difficult part of practice because we're very attached to our notions and ideas of reality and truth. We love our opinions about right and wrong, good and bad, and society reinforces us for having these ideas. In fact, we're scared to death to let go because we fear that then we will not know what to do. We don't trust ourselves; that's the bottom line.

There's good reason for this lack of trust because the self is just an illusion and ultimately we know that. Psychologists know that although it occurs at a very young age, the concept of self is *developed*. Now, a concept is not reality. I may have a map of a territory, but it is just a map, not the territory. The problem is, we forget that the self is a concept and then go about living our lives accordingly, in a constant state of anxiety. A basic fear which we hardly think about because it's just too scary is that we're flying through space on a blue marble with no one at the helm. Anything could happen. All sorts of stuff is flying around out there; so far, we've been lucky nothing has hit us. That could change at any time. We might get a few days warning or even a few months, but there may be nothing we can do to save ourselves. We can try to delude ourselves into believing that someone is flying this planet, but nobody's there. Earth is just a rock flying through space; and our lives, our future, and everything that we love and cherish are in jeopardy. So of course we feel anxiety. We know that life is impermanent and that the world as we know it is temporary.

There's a big difference between the way Buddhism looks at our predicament and the way that Western religion and philosophy do. Buddhism starts with realization, with enlightenment. It's sort of like this: imagine you have a jigsaw puzzle. Western thinking starts with the pieces thrown all over and then tries to put the pieces together. But since there's no picture, you don't have a clue where to begin or where you're going. Now imagine seeing the puzzle as a whole and then cutting it up into pieces. Buddhism starts with the whole and then looks at the differences. Once you see the reality it's easier to see all the parts and how they come together. If you don't see the wholeness, it's really difficult.

The Western approach is to figure it all out. We want to understand, we want to know. As long as we cling to ideas and beliefs, the head, horns, and four legs simply can't pass through. When the body and mind drop off, the truth is revealed. What do you realize when you throw out your concepts of right and wrong, good and bad, self and others, me and you? You realize that from the beginning there hasn't been anything wrong, that everything is just perfect and fine. In fact, there wasn't ever anything to pass through. For there to be something to pass through means that one thing has to go through something else. This is just more dualistic thinking. When we look from duality at ourselves, we see how imperfect, how inadequate, how insufficient we are. Something is lacking and I must make it right. In reality, nothing is lacking and there is nothing wrong. Sure, we need right and wrong to guide our lives, to be moral, ethical, and so forth. But in reality there's no right or wrong.

When body and mind drop off and Truth is revealed, this is still not complete enlightenment; we've only realized the absolute. We've flipped the coin from seeing the relative view to seeing the absolute perspective. This is the head, horns, and four legs going through but the tail getting stuck. When we see that there is nothing to attain, no place to go, nothing to pass through, we're liberated. And just as with every insight and realization, particularly those which really transform our way of perceiving, we grab hold of that liberation. It's very human to grasp, yet what the Buddha said is true: this tendency to want, crave, grasp, and cling is the cause of our suffering. Sooner or later we will want something more. We will want our realization to be clearer; we will want to be more enlightened. All this wanting, wanting, wanting keeps us from being at peace with ourselves.

Realizing the absolute means that now we're seeing the ocean but ignoring the waves. We've put our head under the water, that's all. This is great for moving out of the superficial to the deeper reality, but we don't want to stay here long because we don't want to ignore or deny either aspect of reality. We may experience Big Mind, but we can't experience Big Heart; that's the tail getting stuck. In Big Mind everything is me. Nothing is separate, it's all One. But complete realization doesn't ignore or deny the relative reality. To let go of the absolute is scary: we go from enlightenment back into delusion. After working very hard to drop off body and mind so that the head, horns, and four legs can go through, we don't want to return to delusion. So we cling with all our might to the view of the absolute and end up ignoring causation. We can stay stuck here for years because the absolute is such a relief. Who wants to go back into the relative world with its worry and fear? Not anybody in his or her right mind!

And that's the point: with enlightenment, you're in your right mind, but it's still right versus left. It's still partial, not the whole view. When we're willing to leave Big Mind and experience the other side of reality with what we call Big Heart, boundless heart, we realize, "Yes, it's all me, and yet there are others." And with Big Heart we can see that those other beings, creatures and inanimate objects, are suffering. When we allow our hearts to be wide open, it's natural to want to do something to alleviate that suffering.

Now, let me digress a bit. The illusion that there is something to pass through or another shore to reach also causes suffering in our practice. When I believe there is somewhere to get to, I am suddenly locked into time and distance: I must try to go somewhere other than here. But in reality there is no time or space; it's all right here, right now. Zen is considered to be the "sudden school" because it knows there is no time or space. At any moment, body and mind can drop off. All we need to do is let go, yet we won't let go until clinging becomes too painful. So traditionally we've used beatings with the kyosaku, we've harassed and pushed, we've made retreats physically and mentally exhausting, in order to come up against our own pain and suffering; all methods to exhaust the self and help it let go.

But there are other ways. Maezumi Roshi would remind me of this because I was one of the pushiest and I would beat the hardest. I was notorious, dumb, and stupid. Roshi said, "There are many ways to bring one to realization." Joshu is a good example: he was one of the greatest masters of all time, yet he never said a harsh word and he never hit a student. He brought his students to realization with words, which were pithy and to the point—Mu, shitstick, oak tree in the garden. Then there's the story

of a young monk visiting Joshu. At the time, Joshu was very old, probably about 115 since he lived to 124. The monk comes in and says, "Joshu's
reputation is so great that I thought I was coming to meet a beautiful stone
bridge; all I see is an old beaten-down wooden bridge." Joshu replied, "All
you see is a broken-down wooden bridge. You don't see the stone bridge
of Joshu. This bridge is for any and all asses and donkeys to pass over."

When we let go of the absolute reality and return to the relative world,
what comes up is the great vow to liberate all sentient beings. When we're
stuck in the absolute, there is no self and no other, and there is no one to
suffer and no one suffering. Everything is perfect as it is. That's the reality. But the other side of the coin isn't less real just because it's the apparent reality. The coin has two sides; and yet, it's one coin. Big Mind and
Big Heart are together *daishin*: Big Mind-Heart, Great Heart-Mind.
First, we think there is another shore, that there's something to pass
through. This is delusion. Then we see there is nothing to pass through,
no suffering, no liberation. That, too, is delusion. Dogen Zenji said,
"Delusion is enlightenment and enlightenment is delusion."

And, they're different. Our delusion is no other than enlightenment.
Everything as it is, even our deluded perspective, is still enlightenment.
Everything manifesting is Big Mind. To put it in Christian terms, everything is God. God is all things; I wouldn't say "within." God *is* just as It
manifests. But to see that and to ignore the apparent, including causation
or karma, is delusion. The enlightened person is not completely free of
karma; the enlightened person *is* completely free of karma. There is no
karma. However, because we live in this both absolute and apparent reality, we cannot escape it.

So the enlightened person does not ignore causation. There are no
secrets and nothing goes unnoticed. The Christians say: God knows
everything. Well, of course. One Mind is always present—even if it's not
being revealed. Pure awareness, Buddha mind, Big Mind, whatever you
want to call it, is always right here and completely aware. We may choose
to ignore or deny it, but it is all One Mind, one ocean, one body. To see
the one reality and ignore the other is still ignorance. We must be able to
move freely back and forth; so freely that we live One reality.

The tail is endless because there are infinite sentient beings to be
saved. To liberate them is to help them see the reality of this life. That's

going to the root of the tree. In Western culture it's popular to focus on the leaves and branches; to try to fix things on the surface by trimming this and cutting out that. In Buddhism we go to the root of the problem: our ignorance, our delusion, not seeing reality.

Enough! I've talked much longer than I wanted to.

Student 1: I've heard you talk about this before so I knew there was compassion there, some heart. But I never understood that you should be on both sides of the coin, able to live freely between the two of them. Before I thought that somehow I needed to get rid of my anger and just get into one good mind.

Genpo Roshi: Good! Good insight.

Student 2: When you were talking about Big Mind being always present, I remembered something. Carl Jung, the psychoanalyst, had a sign over his door that said something like, "Whether or not invited, God is present." It seemed to say that whether or not we give the invitation, the reality is One.

Genpo Roshi: Yeah. Reality doesn't change whether we are aware of it or not. Reality is reality. Being aware of it is being aware of it. Even Dogen Zenji said, "some will realize it and some will not," and that's OK. It's still there, it's still reality.

Student 3: What about seeing the tail, the awareness of others, when you are still very busy finding out about the horns. I understand that realization is not in time, but can you elaborate on that?

Genpo Roshi: If I understand you, you see that there are sentient beings to liberate but you are still busy with your dualistic mind. Well, the first thing is to realize that the dualistic mind is no other than the One Mind manifesting as a dualistic mind. There's nothing wrong with it. Look at it this way: if I think that non-dual is superior to dual, that's a very dualistic notion. If I then grasp the non-dual and say, "Ahh, the non-dual is superior to the dual!" that's also a very dualistic notion. The non-dualistic understanding is: the dual and the non-dual are one. Delusion and enlightenment are one; samsara and nirvana are one; they are not different.

As soon as we create a difference we make one better than the other, and then we get stuck. It's very common. People attain enlightenment and then they make the enlightened understanding superior to the dualistic understanding. Haughtiness and arrogance come along with that stage because we know that my understanding is enlightened and yours is deluded. You see things in terms of good and bad, right and wrong, self and others. Why don't you see correctly with a Zen view, a Dharma view? It's frightening to relinquish our perspective and go back into delusion. But delusion is OK, it's perfect. In fact, except when we are stuck, we are always moving back and forth. Freely, we hope; yet even the idea "freely" is another dualistic idea. Ordinary mind is the way.

Student 4: Could you give an example of how that actually works in a situation?

Genpo Roshi: Yeah. We are doing it right now: you're talking, I'm listening. You're listening, I'm talking. It's working.

Student 4: That's too easy. What about something that's a problem, like a relationship in which you find yourself flipping back and forth? Maybe someone's got bad energy and you're trying to be "oh so good" about it.

Genpo Roshi: Why are you trying to be so good?

Student 4: Because the other person is so icky, you try to put a spin on it.

Genpo Roshi: Why are you adding a spin?

Student 4: Just accept it?

Genpo Roshi: Just be with it; I don't know if you have to accept it. To "accept it" sounds a bit like resigning yourself to a bad situation. No. Face the reality of the situation and do what you need to do. If you are in a bad relationship, you might need to get out of it. But first you need to see reality for what it is.

It's all a matter of appropriateness. If staying in the relationship is based on wisdom and compassion, then that's what you do. If it isn't, then you don't. How do you know what is appropriate? You have to follow the intuition that comes from your own wisdom. There are no rules because every situation is different. We also can't simply follow our cultural biases, like the belief that it is always best to be tolerant of bad situations. Our cultural biases can be so strong that we try to make Zen like our culture rather than shifting our perspective to be clear. For example, Zen has been in this country for forty or fifty years now and many people are trying to lay Judeo-Christian ethics and morality on Zen. They are trying to homogenize Zen with our culture rather than seeing how Zen can transform our culture and understanding. The ideal would be that we learn to live with more wisdom and compassion.

MOSHAN'S NATURE OF THE SUMMIT MOUNTAIN

John Daido Loori

KOANS OF THE WAY OF REALITY

Main Case

ZEN MASTER MOSHAN was a student of Gaoan Dayu. Once, the monastic Guanzhi arrived at Mount Mo and said, "If there is someone here who is worthy, I'll stay here; if not I'll overturn the meditation platform."[1] He then entered the hall. Moshan sent her attendant to query the visitor, saying, "Reverend, are you here sightseeing, or have you come seeking the Buddhadharma?" Guanzhi said, "I seek the dharma."

So Moshan sat upon the dharma seat in the abbess' room and Guanzhi entered for dokusan. Moshan said, "Reverend, where have you come from today?"[2] Guanzhi said, "From the intersection on the main road." Moshan said, "Why don't you remove your sunhat?" Guanzhi didn't answer for some time. Finally, he removed his hat and bowed, saying, "What is the nature of Mount Mo?" Moshan said, "The summit is not revealed." Guanzhi said, "Who is the master of Mount Mo?" Moshan said, "It does not have the form of female or male." Guanzhi shouted, "Ho!" and then he said, "Why doesn't it transform itself?"[3] Moshan said, "It is not a god or a demon, so what would it change itself into?"

Guanzhi then became Moshan's disciple and worked as her head gardener for three years.

Later he said to his assembly, "I received half a ladle full at Papa Linji's place and half a ladle full at Mama Moshan's. Since I took that drink, I've never been thirsty."

Commentary

When Guanzhi arrived at Master Moshan's place, he was carrying a belly-full of Linji's Zen. Moshan was an adept. She knew how to free what is stuck and loosen what is bound. She asked, "Are you sightseeing, or have you come seeking the Buddhadharma?" When Guanzhi said he was seeking the dharma, she lost no time in taking the high seat in the abbess' room. Her first question and the monastic's answer clearly established host and guest. Tell me, how were host and guest established?

Master Moshan then walked right into his belly, saying, "Why don't you take off your sunhat?" Guanzhi was silent for some time. Later, Fushan said of this, "The battle began right here." Do you understand Fushan's meaning? Finally Guanzhi removed his hat and bowed, saying, "What is the nature of Mount Mo?" The master answered, "The summit is not revealed." What is the meaning of "the summit is not revealed"? If you can say a word here, you're halfway to understanding Master Moshan's teaching.

Guanzhi then said, "Who is the master of Mount Mo?" Moshan said, "It does not have the form of female or male." In actual fact, it can also be said that neither does it have the form of both female and male. Or neither female nor male. This being the case, what is the master of Mount Mo? Say a word. Guanzhi shouted, "Ho!" and then said, "Why doesn't it transform itself?" Although Guanzhi's shout showed some life, he nevertheless sank up to his nostrils in a bog when he said, "Why doesn't it transform itself?" At this point Moshan should have run his smart ass out of there with her staff and let him go on his deluded way. Moshan, however, was compassionate and said, "It's not a god or a demon, so what would it change itself into?" That is, how could it change itself? Guanzhi got it, and then became Moshan's disciple and worked hard as her head gardener for three years.

Later, when he was teaching, he said to his own assembly, "I received half a ladle full at Papa Linji's place and half a ladle full at Mama Moshan's place. Since I took that drink, I've never been thirsty." I say, Bah! Still, it all comes down to only half a ladle full. Do you understand?

Capping Verse

> The summit is not revealed, not even a shadow.
> Neither female nor male; how can you approach it?
> Dropping off the skin bag, casting off the mask of red flesh
>   directly,
> The nose is vertical, the eyes horizontal.

Moshan lived around 800 A.D., the Golden Age of Zen in China. She was a contemporary of another famous woman teacher of those times, Iron Grindstone Liu, successor of Master Yangshan. Other significant Zen figures of that era were Guishan, Linji, Dongshan, Deshan, and Zhaozhou, a worthy company of sages.

In her name, "mo" means "summit" and "shan" means "mountain." Moshan literally translates into English as "Summit Mountain." She was a disciple of Dayu and the first woman dharma heir to be noted in the official Zen transmission records. Miriam Levering, who has translated Moshan's records and teachings, writes that Moshan was the first nun to be portrayed in Zen texts as taking up formal training activities traditionally reserved for male teachers. She was an abbess of a monastery and had a group of loyal students. She was a challenging and demanding teacher. There is a chapter dedicated to Moshan in the Record of the Transmission of the Lamp, a compilation of stories about Chinese Zen masters, written in 1004 A.D.

Moshan was not the first woman to receive the Zen mind-to-mind transmission, though. That distinction is attributed to Nun Zongchi, one of Bodhidharma's four disciples and successors. But there's not much written about Zongchi, and there is quite a bit known about Moshan.

Moshan's teacher Dayu received the mind-to-mind seal from Guishan, who in turn was a student of Master Mazu, the seminal Zen figure of that period. Dayu, who lived most of his life as a mountain hermit, was also the teacher directly responsible for bringing Master Linji to his enlightenment. Linji, a young monastic, was in the congregation of Master Huangbo. He studied there for three years but was reluctant to engage Huangbo face-to-face. One day, the head monastic, noticing his reserve, said, "You've been here a while already and you haven't been to dokusan.

Why don't you go?" Linji responded, "I don't know what to ask." The head monastic advised, "Just ask him 'What is the truth?'" Linji, being a good student, went in and before he even finished asking the question, Huangbo slugged him. He went back to the meditation hall. Later, the head monastic queried Linji, "What happened?" and Linji reported, "Well, he hit me." The head monastic said, "Then go back and ask him again. Be persistent." Linji went back and got hit a second time; then a third time. Finally, a bit flustered, he exclaimed, "I'm not going to stay here, I'm leaving." As he was about to depart, Huangbo advised him, "Why don't you go see hermit Dayu. Maybe he will be able to clarify this matter for you." On finding Dayu, Linji immediately told him what happened with Huangbo, "Three times I asked him what is the essential meaning of the Buddha's teaching, and three times he hit me. I don't know whether I was at fault or not." Dayu listened carefully, then exclaimed, "Old Huangbo is such a grandmother that he has utterly exhausted himself with your trouble. And now you've come here asking whether you're at fault or not." At these words, Linji attained great enlightenment. After this encounter with Dayu, Linji returned to Huangbo's monastery and continued his training there, eventually receiving transmission from Huangbo.

The monastic Guanzhi, the other person appearing in this koan, had already studied with Linji. At their first encounter, when Linji saw him coming, he grabbed Guanzhi by his vestments. Guanzhi yelled, "I understand, I understand." Linji released him and said, "I'll spare you a blow." Guanzhi stayed and became Linji's disciple.

This meeting with Moshan took place after Guanzhi left Linji and was doing his pilgrimage, which was a traditional aspect of Zen at the time. At one point in his travels, he came upon Moshan's place. When he arrived at Mount Mo, he proclaimed, *If there is someone here who is worthy, I'll stay here; if not I'll overturn the meditation platform.*

I added footnotes to this koan. The footnote to Guanzhi's challenge says, "The stink of Linji is all over him." The beginning of the commentary makes a similar point. It declares, *When Guanzhi arrived at Master Moshan's place, he was carrying a belly-full of Linji's Zen.* Linji's Zen is the shout, the thrusting of the staff or the fist, the hit. It is Zen teaching filled with the dynamics of confrontation, smashing, turning things over.

This style was actually initiated by Mazu. He passed it on to Huangbo and Huangbo transmitted it on to Linji, who perfected it. It continued in the Linji school down to the present time. Linji practitioners are very fond of shouts and blows, and a stout posture.

The commentary continues, *Moshan was an adept. She knew how to free what is stuck and loosen what is bound.* What was stuck and what was bound with Guanzhi? Essentially, she was asking Guanzhi, "What are your provisions? What have you got to offer?" Forget about imitating Linji; forget about imitating your teacher; forget about quoting the scriptures. How do you understand the dharma? How do you manifest the dharma? If we can't realize and actualize the dharma for ourselves, we'd all become clones of the Buddha, and that's not what the teaching is about. Moshan asked, *Are you sightseeing or have you come seeking the Buddhadharma?* Good question. Zen is not a spectator sport. You can't just watch. You can't remain on the sidelines. You have to either do it or leave it—one or the other. *When Guanzhi said that he was seeking the dharma, she took no time in taking the high seat in the abbess' room.* "I seek the dharma" is a powerful statement for a teacher to hear. It calls up in a genuine teacher a life of vow and commitment. It's like a hound dog picking up a scent. It's an all-encompassing imperative, not some decision. But it should be understood that just to hear that declaration, "I've come for the dharma," does not mean that the teaching can yet take place, or that a teacher-student relationship exists. It just means that the student is asking and the teacher is prepared to respond.

[Moshan's] first question and the monastic's answer clearly established host and guest. Her first question, *Reverend, where have you come from today?* His answer, *From the intersection on the main road.* This sets up "host and guest." "Host and guest" is Linji's teaching on the relationship that exists between two people. Linji expounded this as "the fourfold host and guest." The host seeing the host; the host seeing the guest; the guest seeing the host; the guest seeing the guest. So tell me, in what way were host and guest established? If you want to understand this koan, you must have some insight into this. Moshan said, *Reverend, where have you come from today?* The footnote says, "Don't mistake this for casual conversation." It's not. The question she was asking was a profound question. She was probing. Who are you? What's

your understanding? Where are you coming from in your view of reality? What is your Dharma?

Master Moshan then walked right into his belly. Once she saw where he was coming from, she saw where the gaps were and proceeded to close them. The gaps are the separation, the distancing we create with our minds. She said, *Why don't you take off your sunhat?* What does this have to do with anything? What kind of question is that? There is a protocol of entering and leaving a monastery, of approaching and departing from a teacher. Breaking that protocol can be an expression of the dharma. It can also be stupidity or just plain rudeness.

If you were to concentrate on the key point of this koan using the *huato* method, it would be very easy to miss the subtleties. It is easy to focus on the pivotal exchange: *What's the nature of Mount Mo? The summit's not revealed.* But there is much more depth to be explored. The whole encounter is essential to understanding what's happening here. There are other teachings to appreciate when you're thorough and go deeper.

Guanzhi was sassing Moshan. He was toying with her right from the beginning, *If there's someone worthy I'll stay; if not I'll turn over the meditation seat.* She challenged it. *Are you sightseeing or have you come seeking the Buddhadharma?* He said, *The dharma.* So she took him seriously and immediately went to the dokusan room. She wanted to see what he was made of. And she found out—not much. There were gaps. He was stuck. She kept up her probing, *Why don't you take off your sunhat?* If you are authentic in your asking for the teachings, take off that hat, open up your bowing mat, and prostrate yourself properly to the teacher. That shows that you're ready, that you're a student who comes for the dharma. When she said, *Why don't you take off your sunhat? Guanzhi was silent for some time.* What was that moment about—a hesitation, doubt, reflection, confusion? *Later, Fushan said of this, "The battle began right here."* Do you understand Fushan's meaning? The battle is the dharma encounter. Why is it that it began at this juncture? This is where the firm lines were established. Guanzhi hesitated and then finally removed his hat and bowed. The teaching could begin.

Guanzhi's bow is a critical point. His ears now can hear; the eyes can see. The heart can feel; the mind is open. A student is born. If that didn't happen, all she could have said was, "Go away. I'm not your teacher." He bowed and asked, *What is the nature of Mount Mo?* What is the nature of Moshan? What is the nature of Daido? He was asking, "What is the truth? Who are you? What is life? What is death? What is the ultimate nature of reality?" These are all religious questions. They can only be answered through practice and realization. Practice and realization are not about knowledge, information, or belief. They are about practice and realization, about making something real. *What is the nature of Mount Mo?* Moshan answered, *The summit is not revealed.* The summit of the mystic peak is never revealed.

What is the summit of the Heavenly Light Mountain, the dharma name for Mount Tremper? Have you seen it? The way to the top is steep and strewn with boulders. Those who get there are few. When you finally arrive, when you get to the peak of this mountain, you go deaf, dumb, and blind. Do you understand? That's why it's not revealed. *What is the meaning of "the summit is not revealed"?* If you can say a word here you're halfway to understanding Master Moshan's teaching. Though not revealed, throughout all time the summit is right before your eyes.

Guanzhi continued, *Who is the master of Mount Mo?* Moshan replied, *It does not have the form of female or male.* It's not what you think it is. He was falling back to the position of "Should I remove my hat? Is anybody worthy?" Having come this far, he was still being dragged down by his old habits, not being able to see the Buddha right in front of his eyes because of her gender. Or because she didn't act the way Linji acted. Guanzhi thought the dharma had to have a particular quality. Consciously or unconsciously, we all hold onto a similar notion. It's called expectation. It's called preconceived ideas. It's another kind of blindness, the blindness of delusion.

Moshan answered, *It does not have the form of female or male.* It's not what you think it is. In actual fact, it can be said further that neither does it have the form of both female and male or of neither female nor male. Not female, not male, not both, not neither—then what is it? If you work on this koan, you have to present something at this point. You have to show something that's alive and true. *This being the case, what is the master of Mount Mo?* Don't describe, show me! Forget rationalizations and explanations and go directly to the truth of the matter. Express the inexpressible. How do you express the inexpressible? *Guanzhi shouted*

"Ho!" Bah! Get that stink of Linji out of here and show me some of your own provisions.

Following his shout, Guanzhi asked, *Why doesn't it transform itself?* This added stupidity to clarity. For a moment, it seemed as though he was seeing something. That shout could have indicated an opening. The footnote to this says, "He deserves thirty blows of the staff. Why is she being so kind to him?" Having reached this point, having received four direct and clear responses, he still came up with this stupid question, *Why doesn't it transform itself?* It echoes the exchange between Shariputra and the goddess from the "Vimalakirti Sutra." The goddess appeared in Vimalakirti's house, joining all the bodhisattvas who gathered there. She performed all sorts of fantastic and magical feats. Witnessing her powers, Shariputra said to her, "What prevents you from transforming yourself out of your female state?" The goddess answered, "Although I have sought my female state for these past twelve years, I have still not found it. If a magician were to incarnate a woman by magic, would you ask her, 'What prevents you from transforming yourself out of your female state?'" Shariputra responded, "No, such a woman would not really exist, so what would there be to transform?" The goddess said, "Just so, venerable Shariputra, all things do not really exist." The goddess then exchanged form with Shariputra, so he found himself in a woman's body and she was in his body. Then she said, "Now, what prevents you from transforming out of your female state?" Shariputra said, "I don't know what to transform." The goddess said, "In all things there is neither male nor female, nor is there an end to male and female. Where do you find yourself?" This happened at the time of the Buddha. And here it is in this koan, thirteen hundred years later, and the same confusion creeps into this encounter. It needs to be restated again and again, over and over. The non-dual dharma needs to be reaffirmed by each generation, constantly. It needs to be practiced by each generation. It needs to be realized and actualized, again and again and again and again.

Although Guanzhi's shout showed some life, he nevertheless sank to his nostrils in a bog when he said, "Why doesn't it transform itself?" *At this point Moshan should have run his smart ass out of there with her staff and let him go on his deluded way.* She should have given him a little bit of Linji's food that he seemed to love so much. Hit him. But that wasn't her style. *Moshan, however, was compassionate and said, "It's not a god or a demon, so what would it change itself into?" That is, how could it change itself? Guanzhi [finally] got it.* Got what? What did he get? What do you get? *He then became Moshan's disciple and worked hard as her head gardener for three years. Later, when he was teaching, he said to his own assembly, "I received half a ladle full at Papa Linji's place and half a ladle full at Mama Moshan's place. Since I took that drink, I've never been thirsty."* But, for all his efforts, this still comes down to only half a ladle full. Do you understand? If he got half from Linji and half from Moshan, why is it still only a half?

The capping verse: *The summit is not revealed, not even a shadow. Neither female nor male, how can you approach it?* What is that which is neither male nor female? Where is the truth of the summit of the mountain not revealed? How do you approach it? The next line tells you. *Dropping off the skin bag, casting away the mask of red flesh directly, the nose is vertical, the eyes horizontal.* The nose is vertical, the eyes horizontal is one of Master Dogen's famous phrases. When he came back from China, after studying there with Jujing and receiving the transmission, someone asked him, "What did you learn? What did you bring back?" He said, "I have nothing. I only know that my nose is vertical and my eyes are horizontal." Does his response mean that there is nothing or does it mean that there is something, and if it means that there is something, what is that something? What is that fact of life that the nose is vertical and the eyes horizontal? This is called the dharma of thusness. The dharma of thusness is not to be found in form nor is it to be found in emptiness. The truth is not to be found in one side or the other side. It's not to be found in both and it's not to be found in neither. Then where is it to be found? What is the truth? What is that place that is not one side and not the other side? We refer to it as "two arrows meeting in mid-air," or as "the foot before and the foot behind in walking." We speak of it in terms of light within darkness, darkness within light—the merging of opposites. What does that all come down to? What has it got to do with your life? How can it free us of pain and suffering? It's all contained in that truth. We should not take it lightly.

A Song dynasty poet wrote a stanza in praise of Moshan. It's recorded in a classic Zen text called "The Venerable Ancient Teachers." It says:

Moshan does not reveal its pure summit,
but throughout all time the peak is before the eyes.
It's said it has no male or female form,
but does distinguish the lotus amidst the fire.
Without form, without mind, without intention,
becoming male or female just accords with conditions.
These times are replete with monastics and lay practitioners,
each one shines with flawless radiance.

NOTES

1. The stink of Linji is all over him.
2. Don't mistake this for casual conversation.
3. He deserves thirty blows of the staff. Why is she being so kind to him?

Everybody's Light

Roko Sherry Chayat

Blue Cliff Record, Case 86

Introduction

CONTROLLING THE WORLD, he allows not the least speck of dust to escape. He cuts off the deluded stream of thought, leaving not a drop behind. If you open your mouth, you are mistaken. If you doubt for a moment, you have missed the way. Tell me, what is the eye that has pierced the barriers? See the following.

Main Case

Ummon spoke to his assembly and said, "Everybody has his or her own light. If one tries to see it, everything is darkness. What is everybody's light?" Later, in place of the disciples, he said, "The halls and the gate." And again he said, "Blessing things cannot be better than nothing."

Setcho's Verse

> It illuminates itself,
> Absolutely bright.
> He gives a clue to the secret.
> Flowers have fallen, trees give no shade;
> Who does not see, if she looks?
> Seeing is non-seeing, non-seeing is seeing.
> Facing backward on the ox,
> She rides into the buddha hall.

332 Sitting With Koans

It's amazing, this practice. Amazing and impossible to explain to any-one who isn't doing it and even to ourselves, before Rohatsu, when we may feel anxiety or dread along with excitement and anticipation; all of which, of course, we have to just throw away the minute we sit down. The sitting does it all by itself, but as we've heard repeatedly each night from Hakuin Zenji in his Exhortations, we have to have a strong intention, a strong vow, and a strong willingness to push past all the delusory thoughts—not only thoughts, but all of our habitual ways of regarding what we think works for our lives. All of it has to be thrown away, the sooner the better.

In the Introduction to this Case, Engo says, "Controlling the world, he allows not the least speck of dust to escape." In this translation, Sekida uses the word controlling, but this has some pejorative conno-tation. We often say, "So-and-so is very controlling." And we also think, in a kind of vain attempt to make sense of our lives, "I've got to be in control."

This kind of control is not what is meant here. A better word would be "master" of the world. Master. When my son was a young boy, he used to play with little figures called Masters of the Universe. Masters of the Universe, we allow not the least speck of dust to escape. But as we have experienced, almost every time we sit down, with our good intentions, somehow some insidious thing happens, and before we know it, some of our wonderful Ki is escaping, leaking out. We are gone, elsewhere. Each thought that takes us elsewhere is this speck of dust. But as the days go on, we become more and more attuned to this, and we are able to recognize it right away. Hakuin Zenji calls this speck of dust the deity of disturbance. We can recognize these deities before they get anywhere close: ah, I see you, demon; out! Out, out! Thus we "cut off the deluded stream of thought," as Engo puts it. What is this deluded stream of thought? What was it most recently, in the last moment? These deluded streams of thought are generated by a very strong force: the self-protecting strategies, the preoccupations of the ego—Me, Me, Me. It's so hard to be free of this, but the more we sit here together, the more quickly we recognize Ah, that's what this is all about. That's why I'm sitting here in terrible pain, because my mind has wandered off thinking about what IS? It doesn't matter! Cut it off, leaving not a drop behind. No leakage. Not the least speck of dust. The moment there is this Me diversion, it's very easy for this leakage to occur. So cut it off.

"If you open your mouth, you are mistaken." What does this mean? All the time, in our zazen, we are opening our mouths—having some wonderful insight and then thinking, "Oh, that's great, I must tell Roshi about it in dokusan," conceptualizing, killing it. Opening our mouths, immediately mistaken.

"If you doubt for a moment, you have missed the way." Doubt. What is this doubt? Ummon Zenji says, "Everybody has his or her own light." You have your own light, right? Welllll.... There might be a slight trace of doubt, right? This doubt in what we chant each morning, *Atta dipa....* If you doubt for a moment, you have missed It. *Viharatta:* Do not doubt! This is not the doubt of "Great Doubt;" rather, this doubt is completely ego-ridden. It's all wrapped up in I Me Mine. Our lack of self-esteem is ego-based.

"Tell me, what is the eye that has pierced the barriers?" What are the barriers? Doubt in our own light, deluded streams of thought, all the veils or blankets that we use to improve the ways others perceive us, so they won't see what we're really like, when all along what we're really like is *Atta dipa!* To see this, to pierce the barriers! Then Engo says, "See the following," and we go into the Main Subject, which is Ummon Zenji speaking to his assembly.

Ummon is so well-known that I don't think I need to say too much about him. There are many exchanges between Ummon Zenji and his monks that were compiled in *The Ummon Roku,* several of which have been translated into English in a book called *The Roaring Stream.* Here's one that's particularly relevant to Rohatsu sesshin:

> Having entered the Dharma Hall for formal instruction, Ummon said, "The Buddha attained the way when the morning star appeared." A monk asked, "What is it like when one attains the way at the appearance of the morning star?" Master Ummon said, "Come here, come here!" The monk went closer. Master Ummon hit him with his staff and chased him out of the Dharma Hall.

What is it like? What was Shakyamuni's realization like? We all want someone to tell us what it's like. But as you know, Zen is not a simulacrum. It's not like anything!

Here's another exchange:

> Someone asked Ummon, "I request your instruction, Master." The master said, "A-B-C-D-E-F." "I don't understand." The Master: "G-H-I-J-K-L." So that's cleared up!

Someone asked, "I heard a teaching that speaks of the purity of all-encompassing wisdom. What is that purity like?" Oh, yeah, all-encompassing wisdom, that sounds like a good idea. Ummon spat on him. The questioner continued. "How about the teaching method of the old masters?" There must be something you can give me, besides your spit, right? The master said, "Come here. Cut off your feet, replace your skull, and take away the spoon and chopsticks from your bowl. Now pick up your nose." The monk asked, "Where would one find such teaching methods?" The master said, "You windbag," and struck him.

So today, Ummon says to us, "You have your own light. But if you try to see it, everything is darkness. What is your own light?"

I read that he continued to speak this way to his students, "You have your own light—what is your own light?" for twenty years. Here, in this translation, it says, "Later, in place of his disciples...." Later. We think, oh, maybe they were still in the room together, and a few minutes went by. No, twenty years of saying, "You are the light, but you don't understand...everything seems so dark and dim." Does this sound familiar? Lost in the darkness of ignorance! This darkness. When we are chanting *Atta dipa*, we think, it just can't be! It may be that YOU are the light, but it can't be that I am the light! As Roshi once put it, we totally believe in *Atta DUKKHA*. No question. Of course, the Buddha's first sermon after his profound realization was what? The Four Noble Truths, about *dukkha*, right? Dukkha there is, and the origin of *dukkha*, and the end of *dukkha*, and the path of ending *dukkha*. But when Shakyamuni looked at the dawn sky and saw that star, he knew: *Atta dipa!* Everything—all beings and I together—are nothing but this light.

Eido Roshi was speaking the other day about the deep meaning of the word *cool*, about coolness. One of my favorite haiku by Soen Roshi, in English, goes:

> At last
> I have found
> My own cool star.

How do we discover this for ourselves? We have to go through *atta dukkha*, completely, thoroughly. As we heard the other day, the Buddha didn't sit down for one sitting or for one sesshin; he sat down, period. He was at the end of his tether. He had tried everything. He had been in such deep awareness of suffering, and of the need to end suffering. I was thinking the other day about this, and remembering when I was a child enveloped in an intense awareness of the darkness of suffering.

I had strong early Zen training, with a head monk for a stepfather. A very angry head monk. Some of you who have trained at a monastery may remember when something had gone wrong, and everybody was pointing at you. Everybody seemed to know it was your fault. You knew it was your fault, too, but you didn't have a clue about what was wrong or why you were at fault. This kind of condition—we hate it. It really is horrible to endure, especially if it goes on for a long time; but something really important can happen along the way: a building of resolve, determination, backbone. Or we become mass murderers! Probably the reason I didn't was my grandmother. We had a seasonal rhythm to our lives. Nine months or so of darkness, feeling I was to blame but not knowing why; and two or three months at my grandmother's summer house at Kiamesha Lake, which is down the road from Dai Bosatsu Zendo, near Monticello. She had a great old house, and it was a really amazing respite each year, filled with light. She herself was so loving, so staunch an ally. With her I began doing takuhatsu. She and I would carry the little blue charity box to collect money for Hadassah, the organization for helping others. We would take the long, stony dirt road from her house up high on the hill overlooking the lake down toward the village of Kiamesha, where there were about five stores and a bar. My grandmother was full of confidence and had a jovial nature; she would talk to everybody. It didn't matter whether or not they were Jewish or whether they knew about Hadassah; she would have her blue box and we would collect money. We even went into the bar, and they would give her money, too.

Those summers were when I started to sit, informally, alone on the banks of Kiamesha Lake. Some years later, when my grandmother became ill, the nurses told us, "You know, all the other cancer patients want her near them. She's so full of light, even in pain; she just has something that makes other people feel better."

Everybody has her own, his own light. But if we try to see it, what happens? What happens when we look for the light? Everything is darkness. Looking for the light elsewhere, we're lost in the darkness of ignorance. Ummon said, "You come and go by daylight. You distinguish people by daylight. Suddenly it's midnight, and there's no sun, moon, or lamplight. Now what?" We try to distinguish and discriminate, asking, "What is the light?" But how can we see it when we're in the midst of it? There's no light! The moment we think, "Oh, I have to get something," the truth is so far away. What about this darkness at midnight? That indeed is the darkness by which we can realize our own light. No distinguishing—then, what is everybody's light?

So, some twenty years later, the monks finally prevailed upon him to say something about this. And he answered, "The halls and the gate."

The halls and the gate. In our morning service, we chant the Bodhisattva's Vow, "In any event, in any moment, and in any place, none can be other than the marvelous revelation of its glorious light." When we first start chanting this verse, it may sound so flowery, too much. But then—just recently, maybe this morning, I chanted, "None can be other than the marvelous revelation of its glorious light," and I thought, "That's just pure fact, that's not flowery at all!" It's just the way things are—just pure description, just like "the halls and the gate." Of course when we hear, "the halls and the gate," we may think that it's not very poetic. Ummon Zenji's poetry is so spare, so bare, that we almost miss it. But that's the point, isn't it? Nothing added. Just this: the halls and the gate. The floors we're walking on. The halls we walk through each day. Do we think, "Oh, the light!" No, because it's dark. Our minds naturally go this rational way. We can turn on the baseboard nightlights to get light. But the halls and the gate: already, could not be brighter. We are always looking outside of what is, or looking to make something more than it is, and therefore cannot get it.

Suddenly it's midnight, and there's no sun, no moon, no lamplight. Now what? Now our discriminating mind is not able to function. At this point in Rohatsu sesshin, we're less and less able to be caught up by the discriminating consciousness that we call reality. No eyes, no ears, no nose, no tongue, no body, no mind. Cutting off knowing, cutting off seeing, then what? The halls and the gate. To experience this: Halls! Gate! Of course hearing this, we may think there's something mystical that we should be getting from the halls and the gate. What are we not seeing? Ummon Zenji then says, "Blessing things cannot be better than nothing." Take it away! Blessing things. Saying anything about it, we lose it. There is nothing to say. If we really feel this, then anything we say is ok. Any answer is right. Ummon Zenji said, "Every day is a good day." Every answer is a good answer.

To have it all stripped bare, just experienced directly, naked: this is sesshin. Sitting after sitting, the blankets and veils and barriers fall away. Old habits die hard—we try to enshroud ourselves again, again, and again. There is a subversive longing for the familiar, even though the familiar is what causes our suffering. It's the project of our lives, continuing to tread in those well-worn grooves. But here, at Rohatsu sesshin at Dai Bosatsu Zendo, we just don't have to do that anymore! We can believe this, we can have faith in this. We don't have to do those things to ourselves any more. It's something we have to keep reminding ourselves about, because it's so easy to forget and fall back into what's familiar.

Setcho's Verse: "It illuminates itself." Your light is not dependent upon anything, is it? Certainly not upon teachers. No matter how wonderful Eido Roshi is, your light is not dependent upon his teaching. You don't need batteries, you don't need extension cords, you don't even need an outlet. Just plug in. Sit down on the cushion and plug in to the universe. I'm back! Over and over, plug in. Some of us are old enough to remember Timothy Leary, in the good old days of "Turn on, Tune in, and Drop out!" Yeah. Turn on. This is what we're doing, right? We don't need any substance. Here we are in our own light, just turning it on! Come to sesshin, turn it on, what are you waiting for? Turn it on!

Tune in! This light. The universe. Everything we could possibly need is right here. The halls, the gate, the floorboards. Everything. Tune in! You know the tune. "This tune, another tune…" It's your tune.

Drop out, Timothy Leary said. At that time, it was taken to be, "Well I'm not going to work for IBM anymore." But to drop out—of all the stuff that we've been heaping upon ourselves—just drop out of all our accumulated layers. Remember Dogen went to China, and while sitting he heard his teacher say, "Mind and body dropped. Dropped off, dropped away."

"It illuminates itself, absolutely bright. He gives a clue to the secret." As R. H. Blythe puts it, "It's an open secret." It's right here. "Flowers have fallen, trees give no shade." Bare naked, no embellishment, nowhere to hide or to cling. "Who does not see, if she looks?" That's an interesting sentence. Who does not see? We can understand this one way: who does not see if he looks, that is, if you look, you will see. Or we can understand it the other way, Who does not-see if he looks? If we seek it, it's far away. If we look, with some idea of what we're looking for, we can't see it. "Seeing is non-seeing." When we're looking around, trying to figure it out, turning on the light of rational thinking, grabbing at somebody else's light, the one that needs the extension cord—we don't see a thing. Just lost in the darkness of ignorance. The more we think we know, the deeper into that darkness of ignorance we go. So the light of the discriminating mind results in confusion, darkness.

As we have found sitting here together these five days, the more we let go of that addiction to knowing what's going on—a terrible addiction—the more we can be free of that, the more we can enter into non-seeing, the seeing of non-seeing. Eido Roshi was speaking the other day about Gempo Roshi, who was almost completely blind. And it was the brightness of his extraordinary acuity, his power of true seeing, that heads of state and students came from all over to receive.

"Facing backward on the ox, she rides into the buddha hall." Facing backwards, here we sit, no direction, learning how to trust in our own freedom, no looking ahead, no flashlight, no map, just carried, carried along by our faith in Mind. Whenever a thought comes about progress, what's up next, what's going to happen next, just jettison it—throw it away. Ride backwards, in this crazy freedom. The ox knows where it's going. Our zazen is carrying us. No need to direct traffic—forget about it. We are being carried. And we find that the Buddha Hall is right here. Really here!

Roshi was talking the other day about a man who had come back from Iraq, who felt that he didn't know at any moment whether he was in so-called life or so-called death. Actually this is true for us all. It is so easy to succumb to the great deception that we are not going to die. And even though we know we will, it doesn't seem real until we're in that kind of extremity. As some of you know, at Hoen-ji, we just lost a little being of light. One of our residents had a baby, not quite two months old, who was killed in a car accident. This resident came here for Thanksgiving, and in Roshi's teisho that day, and then afterward in meeting with her, he spoke about giving, the true giving that completely rights our upside-down views. We chant every day, "*Buddham saranam gachami.*" And the usual translation is, I go to the Buddha for refuge, or I take refuge in the Buddha. The genius of Eido Roshi's teaching is to translate this the way it really is: I give my life to the Buddha. There is no refuge unless we give our life. *Atta dipa, viharatta. Atta sarana.* This refuge, *sarana,* can only be experienced when we give our life. And what Roshi said about this tragedy is that this baby, Morgan, truly gave: *Buddham saranam gachami, Dhammam saranam gachami, sangham saranam gachami.* The power of that one being, that two-month old life, resonates on and on, in our sangha togetherness, in her mother's great vow, among and for all of us. Each one of us sitting here: we don't know how much time we have, so let's give completely, let's burn ourselves up completely!

Robert Aitken studied with Soen Nakagawa and Hakuun Yasutani. In 1959, he and his wife, Anne, established the Diamond Sangha in Hawaii. Aitken Roshi was authorized to teach by Koun Yamada in 1974.

William M. Bodiford teaches in the department of East Asian Languages and Cultures at the University of California, Los Angeles. He is the author of *Soto Zen in Medieval Japan,* and has contributed to many publications on Zen.

Robert E. Buswell, Jr. is assistant professor of oriental languages at the University of California, Los Angeles. He is the author of *The Korean Approach to Zen: The Collected Works of Chinul,* and is the editor of, and contributor to, *Buddhist Apocryphal Literature.*

Roko Sherry Chayat studied with Eido Shimano, Hakuun Yasutani, and Soen Nakagawa. Roko was installed as abbot of the Zen Center of Syracuse in 1996 by Eido Shimano. Two years later she received inka (dharma transmission) in the Hakuin/Torei lineage, becoming the first American woman to receive official Rinzai transmission.

Francis Dojun Cook is a longtime student of Zen and the translator of many Buddhist texts, including *How to Raise an Ox: Zen Practice as Taught in Master Dogen's* Shobogenzo.

Eihei Dogen (1200–1253) was the founder of the Japanese Soto School of Zen; Dogen established Eihei-ji, one of the two main Soto training monasteries in Japan; he is the author of the *Shobogenzo,* an important collection of Dharma essays that uses as seeds many koans from the *Chinese Shobogenzo* and other sources.

HEINRICH DUMOULIN, S. J. was professor of philosophy and the history of religions at Sophia University in Tokyo. He is the author of many books and articles on Asian religions—especially Buddhism.

HAKUIN EKAKU (1685–1768) is known both as an astounding poet and calligrapher, and a unique Zen master. He is credited with almost single-handedly revitalizing Rinzai Zen, and his systematization of the koan system—including his signature koan, "What is the sound of one hand clapping?"—is still used in Zen monasteries to this day.

VICTOR SOGEN HORI is associate professor in Japanese religions at McGill University. After receiving his Ph.D. in Western philosophy, he was ordained as a Rinzai monastic and trained for thirteen years at Daitokuji. He is the author of *Zen Sand: The Book of Capping Phrases for Koan Practice*.

KEIZAN JOKIN (1268–1325) was the founder of Soji-ji, one of the two main Soto training monasteries in Japan; he is known as the Great Patriarch of Japanese Zen.

PHILIP KAPLEAU (1912–2004) became ordained in 1965 under Hakuun Yasutani and received his permission to teach. He is the author of *The Three Pillars of Zen*, the first book in English to introduce Zen to Westerners, and the founder of the Rochester Zen Center.

THOMAS YUHO KIRCHNER is an ordained Zen Buddhist monastic living at Rinsen-ji in Kyoto, associate researcher at the Institute for Zen Studies and the Hanazono University International Research Institute, as well as translator of the Rinzai koan collection *Kattoshu (Entangling Vines)*.

CHUNG-FEN MING-PEN (1263–1323) lived in a hut on the Middle Peak of Mount Tianmu and was the dharma successor of Gaofeng Yuanmiao. He was greatly respected by Emperors Renzong, Yinzong, and Wenzong, and was given the title of Great Master, among others.

JOHN DAIDO LOORI is abbot of Zen Mountain Monastery, as well as founder and director of the Mountains and Rivers Order. A successor to Hakuyu Taizan Maezumi, Daido Loori trained in rigorous koan Zen and in the subtle teachings of Master Dogen, and is a lineage holder in the Soto and Rinzai schools of Zen.

TAIZAN MAEZUMI (1931–1995) was one of the few teachers to receive inka (seal of approval) from both the Inzan and Takuju Rinzai lineages, as well as dharma transmission in the Soto school of Zen. He founded the Zen Center of Los Angeles and the Kuroda Institute for the Study of Buddhism and Human Values.

DENNIS GENPO MERZEL is the founder of Kanzeon Sangha International and abbot of Kanzeon Zen Center in Utah. He received dharma transmission in the Soto and Rinzai traditions from Hakuyu Taizan Maezumi and is now president of the White Plum Lineage.

SOEN NAKAGAWA was born in 1907 near Hiroshima, Japan. He studied Japanese literature at Tokyo Imperial University, and after graduating in 1930 was ordained as a monk. He became abbot of Rutakuji in 1950, and later traveled with Nyogen Senzaki to the United States, where he founded Dai Bosatsu Monastery. Because of his artistic genius, Soen is considered in Japan to be the Basho of the twentieth century.

RUTH FULLER SASAKI was the author of *Zen: A Religion; Zen: A Method for Religious Awakening;* and, with Heinrich Dumoulin, of *The Development of Chinese Zen.* Mrs. Sasaki was married to Sokei-an Sasaki, founder of the First Zen Institute of America.

SOKEI-AN SASAKI (1882–1945) first came to the United States in 1906, then began his career as Zen master in 1930 in New York City, where he founded the First Zen Institute of America.

NYOGEN SENZAKI, abandoned as a baby in Siberia in 1876, was then adopted by a Japanese Buddhist scholar-monk under whom he read the scriptures until he was eighteen. He traveled to America in 1909, and in 1929 moved to Los Angeles, where he spent most of his life teaching Zen.

ZENKEI SHIBAYAMA (1894–1974) was Zen Master of Nanzenji Zen Monastery for twenty-five years, as well as head abbot of the Nanzenji Organization of over five hundred Japanese Rinzai temples. Shibayama Roshi also taught at Hanazono and Otani Universities.

EIDO SHIMANO trained in Japan under Soen Nakagawa, and came to the United States in the 1960s. He opened New York Zendo Shoboji in 1968, and four years later he received dharma transmission from Soen. Dai Bosatsu Zendo Kongoji, a Japanese-style training monastery where Eido lives and teaches, was dedicated on July 4, 1976.

PHILIP B. YAMPOLSKY was professor of East Asian languages and cultures at Columbia University until his death in 1996.

HAKUUN YASUTANI (1885–1973) was a successor of Sogaku Harada Roshi and one of the first authentic Japanese Zen masters who taught in the West. He became known through an introduction to Zen practice edited by his student, Phillip Kapleau, titled *The Three Pillars of Zen*.

WAYNE YOKOYAMA is an ordained Zen monastic, independent researcher, Buddhist translator, and member of the editorial board of the Shin Buddhism Translation Series (Nishi Hongwanji International Center), as well as special foreign instructor in English at Hanazono University, Kyoto.

KATSUHIRO YOSHIZAWA is a leading Hakuin researcher, as well as professor and Associate Director at the International Research Institute for Zen Buddhism, Hanazono University, Kyoto. He is also the editor of *Hakuin Zenji Hogo Zenshu* 1999–2003, Institute of Zen Studies, Kyoto.

PERMISSION CREDITS

"The Definition of a Koan." Ming-pen, Chung-fen. Excerpted from *The Zen Koan: Its History and Use in Rinzai Zen.* © 1965 by Ruth F. Sasaki and renewed 1993 by Michael Gamer, Ann Watts, and Joan Watts Tabernik, reprinted by permission of Harcourt, Inc.

"The Song Period: A Time of Maturation." Dumoulin, Heinrich. From *PPK2 Zen Buddhism: A History. India and China.* © 1988, Macmillan. Reprinted by permission of The Gale Group.

"Five Houses of Zen." Dumoulin, Heinrich. Ibid.

"The 'Short-cut' Approach of *K'an-hua* Meditation." Buswell, Jr., Robert E. reprinted from *Sudden and Gradual: Approaches to Enlightenment in Chinese Thought,* Peter Gregory, ed. © 1987 Kuroda Institute, University of Hawai'i Press, Honolulu. Reprinted by permission of the Kuroda Institute.

"Koan Practice." Bodiford, William M. Reprinted from *Soto Zen in Medieval Japan.* © 1993 Kuroda Institute. University of Hawai'i Press, Honolulu.

"The Nature of the Rinzai (Linji) Koan Practice." Hori, Victor Sogen. Reprinted from *Zen Sand.* © 2003 University of Hawai'i Press.

"The Steps of Koan Practice." Hori, Victor Sogen. Ibid.

"Dogen and Koans." Loori, John Daido. Unpublished. Reprinted by permission of Dharma Communications, Inc.

"Keizan, Koans, and Succession in the Soto School" and "Ancestor Dajian Huineng" taken from *The Record of Transmitting the Light.* Jokin, Keizan. Introduction by Francis Dojun Cook. © Zen Center of Los Angeles 2003. Wisdom Publications, Boston.

"Hakuin Ekaku and the Modern Koan System." Ekaku, Hakuin. Reprinted from *The Zen Master Hakuin* by Philip B. Yampolsky. © 1971 Columbia University Press. Reprinted with permission of the publisher.

"The Voice of the Sound of One Hand." Adapted by Yoshizawa, Katsuhiro and translated by Yokoyama, Wayne. Japanese reprinted from *Sekishu onjo, Sankyo itchi no ben, Hokyo kutsu no ki, Tosen shiko,* vol. 12 of the series *Hakuin Zenji Hogo Zenshu* with permission of Katsuhiro Yoshizawa, chief researcher at the International Research Institute for Zen Buddhism. Translation reprinted by permission of Wayne Yokoyama.

"Ninth Koan." Sasaki, Sokei-an. Unpublished. Reprinted by permission of the First Zen Institute of America.

"Prajnatara Recites His Sutra." Senzaki, Ven. Nyogen. Reprinted from *Namu Dai Bosa: A Transmission of Zen Buddhism to America.* © 1976 by The Zen Studies Society, Inc.

"Passover Teisho." Nakagawa, Soen. Reprinted from *Namu Dai Bosa: A Transmission of Zen Buddhism to America.* Ibid.

"Nansen (Nanquan) Kills a Cat." Shibayama, Zenkei. Reprinted from *Zen Comments on the Mumonkan* by Zenkei Shibayama. English language translation © 1974 by Zenkei Shibayama. Reprinted by permission of HarperCollins Publishers, Inc.

"Commentary on the Koan 'Mu.'" Yasutani, Hakuun. Reprinted from *The Three Pillars of Zen* by Philip Kapleau. © 1989 by Roshi Philip Kapleau. Afterword (c) 2000 by Bodhin Kjolhede. Used by permission of Anchor Books, a division of Random House, Inc.

Keizan Jokin, 101
  life of, 171–174
  Record of Transmitting the Light,
    163–183
kensho, 119–120, 122, 132
  See also enlightenment
Kikan (Dynamic Action) koan, 137
killing-sword koans, 4
koan collections, 75–77
  early, 17–19
  during Song period, 17–26
  used in medieval Soto school,
    109–110
  See also koan literature; *specific
    collections*
koan-gazing Zen, 33, 37–39
koan literature
  beginnings of Soto, 99–101
  initiation documents (*kirikami*),
    106–109
  koan manuals (*monsan*), 98, 102–106
  medieval Soto, 101–115
  transcription commentaries (*kiki-
    gakisho*), 109–114
koan manuals (*monsan*), 98, 102–106
koan practice
  aspects of, 26–32
  in early Japanese Zen, 92–98
  importance of, 27
  vs. mediation, 191–210
  origins of, 17–18
  psychological structure of, 29–30
  as religious practice, 117–120
  in Rinzai school, 117–129
  role of, 91
  in Soto school, 91–115
  steps in, 131–147
  Ta-hui and, 34–37
koans
  categorization of, 95–96
  as contemplative tools, 77–90,
    120–121
  definition of, 13–15, 17
  functions of, 27–28
  initial, 132–133, 136–137
  intellectual interpretation of,
    127–129
  Last Barrier koans, 144
  meditation and, 131–132
  "Moshan's Nature of the Summit
    Mountain," 321–330
  realization model of, 121
  sassho (checking questions),
    132–133

understanding, 1–5
koan system
  Goi (Five Ranks) koan, 140–142
  Gonsen (Explication of Words)
    koan, 138
  Hakuin's, 134–144, 185–189
  Hosshin (dharmakaya) koan,
    136–137
  Juju kinkai (Ten Grave Precepts),
    142–143
  Kikan (Dynamic Action) koan, 137
  Kojo (Directed Upwards) koan,
    143–144
  progression through, 3–4
Kojo (Directed Upwards) koan,
  143–144
Kokai Ryotatsu, 110–111
ku, 264–265
Kuei-shan Ling-yu, 43–48
Kuei-yang
  House of, 42, 43–48
kung-an. *See* koans
kung (ko), 13, 14
kung-te, 296–297
Kyoo Unryo, 100–101

L
Last Barrier koans, 144
Lin-chi (Rinzai) *See also* Record of
    Pilgrimages
  House of, 42, 48–54
Lin-chi Ch'an, 18, 84
Lin-chi school (Rinzai), 75–90 *See
  also* Rinzai School
Li Tsun-hsü, 19
live words, 79, 81
long nurturing of the sacred fetus,
  145–146

M
Mahakashyapa, 4–5
Mahayana Buddhism, 30, 48
Mana Shobogenzo (Dogen), 151–153,
  155, 157, 159–162
master-disciple relationship. *See*
  teacher-student relationship
meditation. *See* Zen meditation
merit, 296–297
mind-to-mind transmission, 4–5
  See also teacher-student relation-
    ship
moon, 47
"Moshan's Nature of the Summit
  Mountain," 321–330

WISDOM PUBLICATIONS

WISDOM PUBLICATIONS, a nonprofit publisher, is dedicated to making available authentic Buddhist works for the benefit of all. We publish translations of the sutras and tantras, commentaries and teachings of past and contemporary Buddhist masters, and original works by the world's leading Buddhist scholars. We publish our titles with the appreciation of Buddhism as a living philosophy and with the special commitment to preserve and transmit important works from all the major Buddhist traditions.

To learn more about Wisdom, or to browse books online, visit our website at wisdompubs.org.

You may request a copy of our mail-order catalog online or by writing to this address:

Wisdom Publications
199 Elm Street, Somerville, Massachusetts 02144 USA
Telephone: (617) 776-7416 • Fax: (617) 776-7841
Email: info@wisdompubs.org
www.wisdompubs.org

THE WISDOM TRUST

As a not-for-profit publisher, Wisdom is dedicated to the publication of fine Dharma books for the benefit of all sentient beings and dependent upon the kindness and generosity of sponsors in order to do so. If you would like to make a donation to Wisdom, please do so through our Somerville office. If you would like to sponsor the publication of a book, please write or email us at the address above.

Thank you.

Wisdom is a nonprofit, charitable 501(c)(3) organization affiliated with the Foundation for the Preservation of the Mahayana Tradition (FPMT).